Book

1

SEVENTH EDITION

The Humanistic Tradition

The First Civilizations and the Classical Legacy

Book

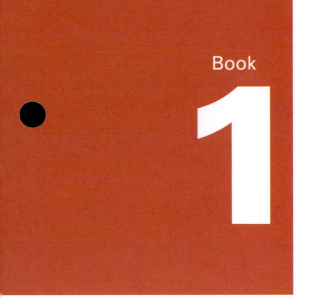

1

SEVENTH EDITION

The Humanistic Tradition

The First Civilizations and the Classical Legacy

Gloria K. Fiero

Mc
Graw
Hill
Education

Boston   Burr Ridge, IL   Dubuque, IA   New York   San Francisco   St. Louis
Bangkok   Bogotá   Caracas   Kuala Lumpur   Lisbon   London   Madrid   Mexico City
Milan   Montreal   New Delhi   Santiago   Seoul   Singapore   Sydney   Taipei   Toronto

THE HUMANISTIC TRADITION, BOOK 1
THE FIRST CIVILIZATIONS AND THE CLASSICAL LEGACY
SEVENTH EDITION

Published by McGraw-Hill Education, 2 Penn Plaza, New York, NY 10121. Copyright 2015 by McGraw-Hill Education. All rights reserved. Printed in the United States of America. Previous edition © 2011, 2006, 2002, 1998, 1995, 1992. No part of this publication may be reproduced or distributed in any form or by any means, or stored in a database or retrieval system, without the prior consent of McGraw-Hill Education, including, but not limited to, in any network or other electronic storage or transmission, or broadcast for distance learning.

Some ancillaries, including electronic and print components, may not be available to customers outside the United States.

This book is printed on acid-free paper.

1 2 3 4 5 6 7 8 9 0 DOW/DOW 1 0 9 8 7 6 5

ISBN 978-0-07-337666-0
MHID 0-07-337666-3

Senior Vice President, Products & Markets: *Kurt L. Strand*
Vice President, General Manager, Products & Markets: *Michael Ryan*
Vice President, Content Design & Delivery: *Kimberly Meriwether David*
Managing Director: *William Glass*
Brand Manager: *Sarah Remington*
Director, Product Development: *Meghan Campbell*
Marketing Manager: *Kelly Odom*
Director of Development: *Dawn Groundwater*
Digital Product Developer: *Betty Chen*
Director, Content Design & Delivery: *Terri Schiesl*
Program Manager: *Debra Hash*
Content Program Manager: *Sheila Frank*
Buyer: *Susan K. Culbertson*
Printer: *R. R. Donnelley*

Permissions Acknowledgments appear on page 181, and on this page by reference.

 Library of Congress Cataloging-in-Publication Data

Fiero, Gloria K.
 The humanistic tradition / Gloria K. Fiero. – Seventh edition.
    volumes cm
 Includes bibliographical references and index.

  Contents: BOOK 1. The First Civilizations and the Classical Legacy – BOOK 2. Medieval Europe and the World Beyond – BOOK 3. The European Renaissance, the Reformation, and Global Encounter – BOOK 4. Faith, Reason, and Power in the Early Modern World – BOOK 5. Romanticism, Realism, and the Nineteenth-Century World – BOOK 6. Modernism, Postmodernism, and the Global Perspective – VOLUME I. Prehistory to the Early Modern World – VOLUME II. The Early Modern World to the Present.

  ISBN 978-1-259-36066-4 (volume 1 : acid-free paper) – ISBN 1-259-36066-0 (volume 1 : acid-free paper) – ISBN 978-1-259-35168-6 (volume 2 : acid-free paper)) – ISBN 1-259-35168-8 (volume 2 : acid-free paper) – ISBN 978-0-07-337666-0 (looseleaf : book 1 : acid-free paper) – ISBN 0-07-337666-3 (looseleaf : book 1 : acid-free paper) – ISBN 978-1-259-35209-6 (looseleaf : book 2 : acid-free paper) – ISBN 1-259-35209-9 (looseleaf : book 2 : acid-free paper) – ISBN 978-1-259-35210-2 (looseleaf : book 3 : acid-free paper) – ISBN 1-259-35210-2 (looseleaf : book 3 : acid-free paper) – ISBN 978-1-259-35539-4 (looseleaf : book 4 : acid-free paper) – ISBN 1-259-35539-X (looseleaf : book 4 : acid-free paper) – ISBN 978-1-259-35540-0 (looseleaf : book 5 : acid-free paper) – ISBN 1-259-35540-3 (looseleaf : book 5 : acid-free paper) – ISBN 978-1-259-35211-9 (looseleaf : book 6 : acid-free paper)

 1. Civilization, Western–History–Textbooks. 2. Humanism–History–Textbooks. I. Title.
  CB245.F47 2015
  909'.09821–dc23

                    2014037553

This book was designed and produced by Laurence King Publishing Ltd., London
www.laurenceking.com

Commissioning Editor: *Kara Hattersley-Smith*
Production: *Simon Walsh*
Designer: *Ian Hunt*
Picture Researcher: *Louise Thomas*
Text Permissions: *Rachel Thorne*
Copy-editor: *Rosanna Lewis*

Front cover
Cover of the coffin of Tutankhamen (ca. 1345–1325 B.C.E.) (detail), from the Valley of the Kings. Gold with inlay of enamel, carnelian, lapis lazuli, and turquoise, height 6 ft.

Frontispiece and page x
Stonehenge trilitons (lintel-topped pairs of stones at center), ca. 3000–1800 B.C.E, Tallest upright 22 ft. (including lintel).

Series Contents

Book 1 Contents

Letter from the Author

The Humanistic Tradition originated more than two decades ago. As a long-time humanities instructor, I recognized that the Western-only perspective was no longer adequate to understanding the cultural foundations of our global world. However, none of the existing humanities textbooks served my needs. The challenge was daunting—covering the history of Western literature, philosophy, art, music, and dance was already an ambitious undertaking for a humanities survey; how could I broaden the scope to include Asia, Africa, and the Americas without over-loading the course?

I found the solution in my classroom: Instead of assuming a strictly historical approach to the past, (as I did in my history classes), I would organize my humanities lectures topically, focusing on universal themes, major styles, and significant movements—gods and rulers, classicism, imperialism, the Romantic hero, racial and sexual equality, globalism—as they reflected or shaped the culture of a given time or place. What evolved was *The Humanistic Tradition*, a thematic, yet global and chronological approach to humanities, one that provokes thought and discussion without burying students under mountains of encyclopedic information.

Now in its seventh edition, *The Humanistic Tradition* continues to celebrate the creative mind by focusing on how the arts and ideas relate to each other, what they tell us about our own human nature and that of others on our planet. Its mission remains relevant to the present, and essential (I would hope) to enriching the future of each student who reads its pages.

The Seventh Edition of *The Humanistic Tradition*

To the seventh edition of *The Humanistic Tradition* I have added a new feature: **Looking Into** is a diagrammatic analysis of key works, such as Neolithic stone circles (including the latest archeological discoveries in Southeast Turkey), the Parthenon, the sonnets of Petrarch and Donne, *Shiva: Lord of the Dance*, Jan van Eyck's *Arnolfini Double Portrait*, and Judy Chicago's *Dinner Party*.

The new edition expands two popular features that promote critical thinking: **Exploring Issues**, which focuses on controversial ideas and current debates (such as the battle over the ownership of antiquities, and creationism versus evolution); and **Making Connections**, which brings attention to contrasts and continuities between past and present. To **Exploring Issues**, I have added the debate over the origins of India's Vedic culture (chapter 3). To **Making Connections** I offer a novel illustration of the contemporary affection for Chinese landscape painting (chapter 14).

The chapter-by-chapter integration of literary, visual, and aural primary sources remains a hallmark of *The Humanistic Tradition*. In an effort to provide the most engaging and accessible literary works, some selected readings in this edition appear in alternate translations. **Marginal logos** have been added to direct students to additional literary resources that are discussed but not included in the text itself.

Additions to the art program include the Nebra Sky Disk, Hellenistic mosaics, Delacroix's *Women of Algiers*, Oceania's art of tattoo, Japan's Amida Buddha, Charles Willson Peale's *Portrait of Yarrow Mamout* (the earliest known portrait of a Muslim in America), Ai Wei Wei's *Forever Bicycle*, Ernesto Neto's *Anthropodino*, and Zaha Hadid's Heydar Aliyev Center. Chapters 37 and 38, which treat the Information Age and Globalism, have been updated to present a cogent overview of contemporary issues, including terrorism, ecological concerns, ethnic conflict, and the digital arts.

The Humanistic Tradition pioneered a flexible six-book format in recognition of the varying chronological range of humanities courses. Each slim volume was also convenient for students to bring to classes, the library, and other study areas. The seventh edition continues to be available in this six-book format, as well as in a two-volume set for the most common two-term course configuration.

In preparing the seventh edition, I have depended on the excellent editorial and production team led by Donald Dinwiddie at Laurence King Publishing. Special thanks also go to Kara Hattersley-Smith at LKP and Sarah Remington at McGraw-Hill Higher Education.

Gloria K. Fiero

The Humanistic Tradition—a personalized learning

Each generation leaves a creative legacy, the sum of its ideas and achievements. This legacy represents the response to our effort to ensure our individual and collective survival, our need to establish ways of living in harmony with others, and our desire to understand our place in the universe. Meeting the challenges of *survival, communality,* and *self-knowledge,* we have created and transmitted the tools of science and technology, social and political institutions, religious and philosophic systems, and various forms of personal expression—the totality of which we call **culture**. Handed down from generation to generation, this legacy constitutes the humanistic tradition, the study of which is called *humanities.*

Understanding that a global humanities course is taught in varying ways, Gloria Fiero redefines the discipline for greater flexibility via a variety of innovative digital tools. Enhanced by McGraw-Hill Education's LearnSmart and SmartBook, Fiero delivers a learning experience tailored to the needs of each institution, instructor, and student. With the ability to incorporate new extended readings, streaming music, and artwork, *The Humanistic Tradition* renews the understanding of the relationship between world cultures and humankind's creative legacy.

Personalized Learning Experience

McGraw Hill Education connect®
|HUMANITIES

In **Connect Humanities**, you can access all of the art and music from *The Humanistic Tradition* on your computer or mobile device. Music logos (right) that appear in the margins of the text refer to listening selections available for streaming.

As part of McGraw-Hill Education's Connect Humanities, LearnSmart is an adaptive learning program designed to personalize the learning experience. LearnSmart helps students learn faster, study smarter, and retain more knowledge for greater success. Distinguishing what students know from what they don't, and touching on concepts they are most likely to forget, LearnSmart continuously adapts to each students' needs by building a personalized learning path. LearnSmart is proven to strengthen memory recall, keep students in class, and boost grades. By helping students master core concepts ahead of time, LearnSmart enables instructors to spend more meaningful time in the classroom.

McGraw Hill Education |SMARTBOOK™

Enhanced by LearnSmart, SmartBook is the first and only adaptive reading experience currently available.

- **Making It Effective** SmartBook creates a personalized reading experience by highlighting the most impactful concepts a student needs to learn at that moment in time. This ensures that every minute spent with SmartBook is returned to the student as the most valuable minute possible.
- **Make It Informed** Real-time reports quickly identify the concepts that require more attention from individual students—or the entire class.

and teaching experience in global humanities

Personalized Teaching Experience

Personalize and tailor your teaching experience to the needs of your humanities course with Create, Insight, and instructor resources.

Create What You've Only Imagined

No two humanities courses are the same. That is why Gloria Fiero has personally hand-picked additional readings that can be added easily to a customized edition of *The Humanistic Tradition*. Marginal icons (right) that appear throughout this new edition indicate additional readings, a list of which is found at the end of the Table of Contents.

To customize your book using McGraw-Hill Create™, follow these steps:
1. Go to http://create.mheducation.com and sign in or register for an instructor account.
2. Click Collections (top, right) and select the "Traditions: Humanities Readings Through the Ages" Collection to preview and select readings. You can also make use of McGraw-Hill's comprehensive, cross-disciplinary content as well as other third-party resources.
3. Choose the readings that are most relevant to your students, your curriculum, and your own areas of interest.
4. Arrange the content in a way that makes the most sense for your course.
5. Personalize your book with your course information and choose the best format for your students—color, black-and-white, or ebook. When you are done, you will receive a free PDF review copy in just minutes.

Or contact your McGraw-Hill Education representative, who can help you build your unique version of *The Humanisitic Tradition*.

Powerful Reporting on the Go

The first and only analytics tool of its kind, Connect Insight is a series of visual data displays—each framed by an intuitive question—that provide at-a-glance information regarding how your class is doing.
- **Intuitive** You receive an instant, at-a-glance view of student performance matched with student activity.
- **Dynamic** Connect Insight puts real-time analytics in your hands so you can take action early and keep struggling students from falling behind.
- **Mobile** Connect Insight travels from office to classroom, available on demand wherever and whenever it's needed.

Instructor Resources

Connect Image Bank is an instructor database of images from select McGraw-Hill Education art and humanities titles, including *The Humanistic Tradition*. It includes all images for which McGraw-Hill has secured electronic permissions. With Connect Image Bank, instructors can access a text's images by browsing its chapters, style/period, medium, and culture, or by searching with key terms. Images can be easily downloaded for use in presentations and in PowerPoints. The download includes a text file with image captions and information. You can access Connect Image Bank on the library tab in Connect Humanities (http://connect.mheducation.com).

Various instructor resources are available for *The Humanistic Tradition*. These include an instructor's manual with discussion suggestions and study questions, music listening guides, lecture PowerPoints, and a test bank. Contact your McGraw-Hill sales representative for access to these materials.

Studying humanities engages us in a dialogue with primary sources: works original to the age in which they were produced. Whether literary, visual, or aural, a primary source is a text; the time, place, and circumstances in which it was created constitute the context; and its various underlying meanings provide the subtext. Studying humanities from the perspective of text, context, and subtext helps us understand our cultural legacy and our place in the larger world.

Text

The *text* of a primary source refers to its medium (that is, what it is made of), its form (its outward shape), and its content (the subject it describes).

Literature: Literary form varies according to the manner in which words are arranged. So, *poetry*, which shares rhythmic organization with music and dance, is distinguished from *prose*, which normally lacks regular rhythmic patterns. Poetry, by its freedom from conventional grammar, provides unique opportunities for the expression of intense emotions. Prose usually functions to convey information, to narrate, and to describe.

Philosophy (the search for truth through reasoned analysis) and *history* (the record of the past) make use of prose to analyze and communicate ideas and information.

In literature, as in most forms of expression, content and form are usually interrelated. The subject matter or form of a literary work determines its *genre*. For instance, a long narrative poem recounting the adventures of a hero constitutes an *epic*, while a formal, dignified speech in praise of a person or thing constitutes a *eulogy*.

The Visual Arts: The visual arts employ a wide variety of media, ranging from the traditional colored pigments used in painting, to wood, clay, marble, and (more recently) plastic and neon used in sculpture, to a wide variety of digital media, including photography and film. The form or outward shape of a work of art depends on the manner in which the artist manipulates the elements of color, line, texture, and space. Unlike words, these formal elements lack denotative meaning.

The visual arts are dominantly spatial, that is, they operate and are apprehended in space. Artists manipulate form to describe or interpret the visible world (as in the genres of portraiture and landscape), or to create worlds of fantasy and imagination. They may also fabricate texts that are nonrepresentational, that is, without identifiable subject matter.

Music and Dance: The medium of music is sound. Like literature, music is durational: it unfolds over the period of time in which it occurs. The major elements of music are melody, rhythm, harmony, and tone color—formal elements that also characterize the oral life of literature. However, while literary and visual texts are usually descriptive, music is almost always nonrepresentational: it rarely has meaning beyond sound itself. For that reason, music is the most difficult of the arts to describe in words.

Dance, the artform that makes the human body itself the medium of expression, resembles music in that it is temporal and performance-oriented. Like music, dance exploits rhythm as a formal tool, and like painting and sculpture, it unfolds in space as well as in time.

Studying the text, we discover the ways in which the artist manipulates medium and form to achieve a characteristic manner of execution or expression that we call *style*. Comparing the styles of various texts from a single era, we discover that they usually share certain defining features and characteristics. Similarities between, for instance, ancient Greek temples and Greek tragedies, or between Chinese lyric poems and landscape paintings, reveal the unifying moral and aesthetic values of their respective cultures.

Context

The *context* describes the historical and cultural environment of a text. Understanding the relationship between text and context is one of the principal concerns of any inquiry into the humanistic tradition. To determine the context, we ask: In what time and place did our primary source originate? How did it function within the society in which it was created? Was it primarily decorative, didactic, magical, or propagandistic? Did it serve the religious or political needs of the community? Sometimes our answers to these questions are mere guesses. For instance, the paintings on the walls of Paleolithic caves were probably not "artworks" in the modern sense of the term, but, rather, magical signs associated with religious rituals performed in the interest of communal survival.

Determining the function of the text often serves to clarify the nature of its form, and vice-versa. For instance, in that the Hebrew Bible, the *Song of Roland*, and many other early literary works were spoken or sung, rather than read, such literature tends to feature repetition and rhyme, devices that facilitate memorization and oral delivery.

Subtext

The *subtext* of a primary source refers to its secondary or implied meanings. The subtext discloses conceptual messages embedded in or implied by the text. The epic poems of the ancient Greeks, for instance, which glorify prowess and physical courage, suggest an exclusively male perception of virtue. The state portraits of the seventeenth-century French king Louis XIV bear the subtext of unassailable and absolute power. In our own time, Andy Warhol's serial adaptations of Coca-Cola bottles offer wry commentary on the commercial mentality of American society. Examining the implicit message of the text helps us determine the values of the age in which it was produced, and offers insights into our own.

Introduction

Prehistory and the Birth of Civilization

ca. 7 million B.C.E.–1500 B.C.E.

*"But, after all, who knows, and who can say
whence it all came, and how creation happened?"*
Rig Veda

Figure 0.1 Spotted horses and negative hand prints, Pech-Merle caves, Lot, France, ca. 15,000–10,000 B.C.E. Length 11 ft. 2 in.

The first chapters in the history of human life are often regarded as the most challenging. They present us with a gigantic puzzle that requires scientists and historians to piece together various fragments of information, most of which, like buried treasure, have been dug out of the earth. Reassembled, they reveal the progress of humankind from its earliest beginnings; they track a record of the genetic and behavioral adaptation of human beings to their natural (and often hostile) surroundings. The story of modern humans is the last chapter in a long history that begins with the simplest forms of life that thrived in the primeval seas hundreds of millions of years ago. To understand that story, we must turn to the evidence provided by prehistory.

Prehistory

The study of history before the appearance of written records, an enterprise that originated in France around 1860, is called **prehistory**. In the absence of written records, prehistorians depend on information about the past provided by the disciplines of geology, paleontology, anthropology, archeology, and ethnography. For instance, using instruments that measure the radioactive atoms remaining in the organic elements of the earth's strata, geologists have determined that our planet is approximately 4.5 billion years old. Paleontologists record the history of fossil remains and that of the earth's earliest living creatures. Anthropologists study human biology, society, and cultural practices, while archeologists uncover, analyze, and interpret the material remains of past societies. Finally, a special group of cultural anthropologists known as ethnographers study surviving preliterate societies. All of these specialists contribute to producing a detailed picture of humankind's earliest environment and the prehistoric past.

The earliest organic remains in the earth's strata are almost four billion years old. From one-celled organisms that inhabited the watery terrain of our planet, higher forms of life very gradually evolved. Some hundred million years ago, dinosaurs stalked the earth, eventually becoming extinct—possibly because they failed to adapt to climatic change. Eighty million years ago, mammals roamed the earth's surface. Although even the most approximate dates are much disputed, it is generally agreed that between ten and five million years ago ancestral humans first appeared on earth, probably in eastern and southern Africa. The exact genealogy of humankind is still a matter of intense debate. However, in the last fifty years, anthropologists have clarified some aspects of the relationship between human beings and earlier primates—the group of mammals that today includes monkeys, apes, and human beings. Fossil evidence reveals structural similarities between human beings and chimpanzees (and other apes). More recent research in molecular biology indicates that the DNA of chimpanzees is approximately 99 percent identical to human DNA, suggesting that humans are more closely related to chimpanzees than domestic cats are to lions.

Paleolithic ("Old Stone") Culture*
(ca. 7 million–10,000 B.C.E.)**

Early in the twentieth century, anthropologists discovered the first fossil remains of the near-human or proto-human creature known as **hominid**, who lived some five or more million years ago. Hominids lived in packs; they gathered seeds, berries, wild fruits, and vegetables, and possibly even hunted the beasts of the African savannas. Hominid footprints found in South Africa in the mid-1990s and fossil remains uncovered since 2002 in Central Africa and near the Black Sea suggest that hominids may have walked upright as early as six million years ago. What is the relationship between modern humans and their now-extinct relatives? Molecular biologists have analyzed fossil DNA and determined that the human family tree has numerous branches. Diverse groups of the genus *Homo* left Africa at different times, some co-existing before dying out. The branch that represents our ancestors, that is, modern humans (*Homo sapiens*) departed from Africa some 66,000 years ago. However, many human species preceded us.

About three million years ago, a South African variety of hominid known as *Australopithecus* was using sharp-edged pebbles for skinning animals and for chopping. Creating the first stone and bone tools and weapons, *Homo habilis* ("tool-making human") met the challenge of survival with problem-solving ingenuity. Stone-tipped spears were in use some 500,000 years ago. Anthropologists have long considered tool-making the distinguishing feature of modern humans. Tool-making represents the beginnings of **culture**, which, in its most basic sense, proceeds from the manipulation of nature; and the appearance of tools and weapons—humankind's earliest technology—constitutes the initial act of extending control over nature. Co-existing with *Homo habilis* for half a million years in parts of Africa and East Asia, hunter-gatherers known as *Homo erectus* ("upright human") made tools that were more varied and efficient than those of their predecessors. These tools included hand-axes, cleavers, chisels, and a wide variety of choppers. The hand-ax became the standard tool for chopping, digging, cutting, and scraping. Fire, too, became an important part of the early culture of humankind, providing safety, warmth, and a means of cooking food. Although it is still not certain how long ago fire was first

---

*The terms Paleolithic and Neolithic do not describe uniform time periods, but, rather, cultures that appeared at different times in different parts of the world.

**Dates are signified as B.C.E., "Before the Christian (or common) era," or C.E., "Christian (or common) era."

used, archeologists confirm that fire was a regular feature in the hearths of most *Homo erectus* dwellings.

Some 100,000 years ago, a group of humanoids with anatomical features and brain size similar to our own appeared in the Neander Valley near Düsseldorf, Germany. The burial of human dead (their bodies dyed with red ocher) among Neanderthals and the practice of including tools, weapons, food, and flowers in Neanderthal graves are evidence of the self-conscious, symbol-making human known as *Homo sapiens*. Characterized by memory and foresight, these now-extinct cousins of modern-day humans were the first to demonstrate—by their ritual preparation and disposal of the deceased—a self-conscious concern with human mortality. That concern may have involved respect for, or fear of, the dead and the anticipation of life after death.

The development of the primate brain in both size and complexity was integral to the evolution of *Homo sapiens*: over millions of years, the average brain size of the human being grew to roughly three times the size of the gorilla's brain. Equally critical was the growth of more complex motor capacities. Gradually, verbal methods of communication complemented the nonverbal ones shared by animals and proto-humans. Over time, modern humans came to use spoken language as a medium for transmitting information. Communication by means of spoken language distinguished *Homo sapiens* from other primates. Chimpanzees have been known to bind two poles together in order to reach a bunch of bananas hanging from the top of a tree, but, short of immediate physical demonstration, they have developed no means of passing on this technique to subsequent generations of chimpanzees. *Homo sapiens*, on the other hand, have produced symbol systems that enable them to transmit their ideas and inventions. Thus, in the fullest sense, culture requires both the manipulation of nature and the formulation of a symbolic language for its transmission.

Paleolithic culture evolved during a period of climatic fluctuation called the Ice Age. Between roughly three million and 10,000 years ago, at least four large glacial advances covered the area north of the equator. As hunters and gatherers, Paleolithic people were forced either to migrate or to adapt to changing climatic conditions. It is likely that more than fifteen species of human co-existed with one another, and all but *Homo sapiens* became extinct. Ultimately, the ingenuity and imagination of *Homo sapiens* were responsible for the fact that they fared better than many other creatures.

Early modern humans devised an extensive technology of stone and bone tools and weapons that increased their comfort and safety, and almost certainly their confidence. A 7-foot stone-tipped spear enabled a hunter to attack an animal at a distance of 6 or more yards. Other devices increased the leverage of the arm and thus doubled that range. Spears and harpoons, and—toward the end of the Ice Age—bows and arrows, extended the efficacy and safety of Paleolithic people, just as axes and knives facilitated their food-preparing abilities.

Figure 0.2 Hall of Bulls, left wall, Lascaux caves, Dordogne, France, ca. 15,000–10,000 B.C.E. Paint on limestone rock, length of individual bulls 13–16 ft.

Science and Technology

2,500,000 B.C.E.	first stone tools are utilized in East Africa[†]
500,000 B.C.E.	in China, *Homo erectus* uses fire for domestic purposes
24,000 B.C.E.	fish hooks and lines are utilized in Europe
20,000 B.C.E.	bows and arrows are in use in North Africa and Spain; oil lamps, fueled by animal fat, come into use
13,000 B.C.E.	devices to hurl harpoons and spears are in use

†All dates in this introduction are approximate.

Cave Art

Since 1875 archeologists have found painted, drawn, and engraved images on cave walls in Europe, Africa, Australia, and North America. The most recent of these discoveries was made at the El Castillo cave in northwestern Spain, where painted disks, clublike symbols, and hundreds of handprints, at least 37,000 years old, appear to be the world's oldest known wall-paintings. Handprints, probably made by blowing or splattering earth pigments through a hollow reed as the hand rested against the wall, are commonly found in most prehistoric caves (Figure **0.1**). The hand, an essential ally in the creation of tools and weapons, as well as in the depiction of imagery, held an obviously prized place in Paleolithic culture.

At Lascaux, a site discovered in southern France in 1940, a magnificent array of animals and symbols is now tragically disappearing under the ruinous attack of algae, bacteria, and fungi (the caves have been closed to the public since 1963). While Lascaux features a variety of commonly hunted species—bison, reindeer, elk, mammoths, and zebras—caves at Cosquer and Chauvet on the southern coast of France, found in the early 1990s, depict an even wider variety of Paleolithic creatures: rhinoceros, horses, bears, lions, panthers, hyenas, and sea birds. Executed between 30,000 and 10,000 years ago, the images at these various sites were skillfully painted with **polychrome** mineral pigments. The animals, shown standing or running, often wounded by spears or arrows, are strongly **naturalistic**: shaded with bitumen and burnt coal, and sometimes protruding from the uneven rock surface, they appear three-dimensionally lifelike (Figure **0.2**).

What was the purpose or function of so-called cave art? Scholars have long debated this question. Some hold that it served as part of a hunting ritual. Others contend that the creatures pictured on cave walls were **clan totems** (heraldic tribal emblems) or symbols of male and female forces. Still others read certain abstract markings on cave walls as lunar calendars, notational devices used to predict seasonal change or the seasonal migration of animals. Long associated with the procreative womb and cosmic underworld, the cave itself may have served as a ceremonial chamber, shrine, or council room in which rituals were orchestrated by **shamans**, that is, mediators between the natural and the spiritual worlds. In the preliterate societies of Native America, Africa, and Polynesia, shamans have traditionally made use of animals as message-bearers, clan totems, and spirit guides; the animals painted on prehistoric cave walls may have served in similar ways.

Located in the most inaccessible regions of the caves, and usually drawn one over the other with no apparent regard for clarity, it is unlikely that cave paintings served as formal decoration or as records of actual hunts. Nevertheless, the association between cave art and hunting remains convincing. It is supported by ethnographic evidence of hunting rituals practiced in the African Congo as recently as the early twentieth century. At such rituals, leaders of the hunt make sand drawings of the animals they are about to hunt, then fire arrows into the drawings. If the hunt is successful, they smear the images with the blood and fur of their prey. Such rituals constitute a form of *sympathetic magic* whereby power is gained over a person, animal, or object by capturing it visually (in the painted mark), orally (in the proper combination of words, chanted or sung), or by way of prescribed gestures and body movements (dance).

It has been argued that some of the animals depicted in the Chauvet cave were never or rarely hunted; however, archeologists confirm that extinct species of panther, jaguar, and lion were indeed hunted by early humans, not exclusively for food, but because such animals were predators—Paleolithic people were as much preyed upon as they were themselves predators—and competitors for smaller game. Some animals, such as the wooly mammoth, were hunted for their bones, which were used for weapons, musical instruments, and the construction of Ice Age huts, at least seventy of which have been found in Ukraine and parts of Russia (Figure **0.3**). Sympathetic magic has characterized religious ritual throughout the history of humankind, but it was especially important in the prehistoric world, where mastery of nature was crucial to physical survival. While we may never know its exact function, cave art, like tools and weapons, surely served the communal well-being of a hunting-gathering culture.

Mother Earth

It is likely that shared responsibility characterized humankind's earliest societies. Women probably secured food by gathering fruits and berries; they also acted as healers and nurturers. Since the female (in her role as child-bearer) assured the continuity of the tribe, she assumed a special importance. As life-giver, she was identified with the mysterious powers of procreation and exalted as Mother Earth. Her importance in the prehistoric community is confirmed by the great number of female statuettes uncovered by archeologists throughout the world. A good many of these objects show the female nude with pendulous breasts, large buttocks, and a swollen abdomen, indicating pregnancy (Figure **0.4**).

Figure 0.3 Reconstruction of a mammoth-bone house, Mezhirich, Ukraine, ca. 16,000–10,000 B.C.E.

Figure 0.4 "Venus" of Willendorf, from Lower Austria, ca. 25,000–20,000 B.C.E. Limestone, height 4⅜ in.

Neolithic ("New Stone") Culture (ca. 10,000–4000 B.C.E.)

Paleolithic people lived at the mercy of nature. However, toward the end of the Ice Age, between 10,000 and 8,000 B.C.E., as the glaciers covering the Northern hemisphere melted, and grassy plains and forests replaced regions once covered with ice and snow, there occurred a transition from nomadic, hunting-gathering culture to a sedentary one marked by settled, food-producing communities. The domestication of wild animals, the production of polished stone tools and weapons, the construction of mud or brick and timber dwellings and huge stone ceremonial centers, and the development of more sophisticated forms of social organization were some of the main features of this transition. But the defining event of the Neolithic culture was the development of agriculture: the discovery that wild grains and fruits might be planted to grow food. The transition to Neolithic culture occurred gradually and at different stages in different regions.

Science and Technology

12,000 B.C.E.	domesticated dogs (descended from Asian wolves) appear
10,000 B.C.E.	goats are domesticated; herding begins in Asia and Africa
8000 B.C.E.	clay tokens are used in Mesopotamia to tally goods
7000 B.C.E.	cloth is woven in Anatolia (now Turkey)
5000 B.C.E.	crop irrigation is first employed in Mesopotamia

Figure 0.5 Saharan rock-painting, Tassili, Algeria, ca. 8000–4000 B.C.E. Copy of the original. Men and women are shown herding domestic cattle.

The rock art paintings discovered at Tassili in Africa's Sahara Desert—once fertile grasslands—tell the story of a transition from hunting to herding and the domestication of cattle and camels (Figure 0.5). Gradually, over a period of centuries, as hunters, gatherers, and herdsmen became farmers and food producers, the dynamic Neolithic culture emerged. Food production freed people from a nomadic way of life. They gradually settled permanent farm communities, raising high-protein crops such as wheat and barley in Asia, rice in China, and maize in the Americas. They raised goats, pigs, cattle, and sheep that provided regular sources of food and valuable by-products, such as wool and leather. The transition from the hunting-gathering phase of human subsistence to the agricultural-herding phase was a revolutionary development in human social organization, because it marked the shift from a nomadic to a sedentary way of life.

Neolithic sites excavated in Southwest Asia (especially Israel, Jordan, Turkey, Iran, and Iraq), East Asia (China and Japan), and (as late as 1000 B.C.E.) in Meso-America center on villages consisting of a number of mud- and limestone-faced huts—humankind's earliest architecture (Figure 0.6). At Jericho, in present-day Israel, massive defense walls surrounded the town, while tombs held the ornamented remains of local villagers. At Jarmo, in northern Iraq, a community of more than 150 people harvested wheat with stone sickles. Polished stone tools, some designed especially for farming, replaced the cruder tools of Paleolithic people. Ten thousand years before plant cultivation and agriculture came to China, communities in the southern part of the country were producing pottery in the form of simple concave ceramic vessels. But it is in Southwest Asia that some of the finest examples of painted pottery have come to light. Clay vessels, decorated with abstract motifs such as the long-necked birds that march around the rim of a beaker from Susa (Figure 0.7), held surplus foods for the lean months of winter, and woven rugs and textiles provided comfort against the wind, rain, and cold. Homemakers, artisans, and shepherds played significant roles in Neolithic society.

Agricultural life stimulated a new awareness of seasonal change and a profound respect for those life-giving powers, such as sun and rain, that were essential to the success of the harvest. The earth's fertility and the seasonal cycle were the principal concerns of the farming culture. The overwhelming number of female statuettes found

Figure 0.6 Isometric reconstruction of a Neolithic house at Hassuna, Mesopotamia (level 4). Originally mud and limestone.

in Neolithic graves suggests that Mother Earth may have become increasingly important in the transition from food gathering to food production, when fertility and agricultural abundance were vital to the life of the community. Nevertheless, as with cave art, the exact meaning and function of the so-called mother goddesses remain a matter of speculation: they may have played a role in the performance of rites celebrating seasonal regeneration, or they may have been associated with fertility cults that ensured successful childbirth. The symbolic association between the womb and Mother Earth played an important part in almost all ancient societies. In contrast with the Paleolithic "Venus" of Willendorf (see Figure 0.4), whose sexual characteristics are boldly exaggerated, the marble statuettes produced in the Cyclades, the Greek islands of the Aegean Sea, are as streamlined and highly stylized as some modern sculptures (Figure **0.8**). Although lacking the pronounced sexual characteristics of the "Venus," the Cycladic figure probably played a similar role in rituals that sought the blessings of Mother Earth.

Figure 0.8 Female figure, early Cycladic II, Late Spedos type, ca. 2600–2400 B.C.E. Marble, height 24¾ in.

Figure 0.7 Beaker painted with goats, dogs, and long-necked birds, from Susa, southwest Iran, ca. 5000–4000 B.C.E. Baked clay, height 11¼ in.

Neolithic Earthworks

Almost all early cultures regarded the dead as messengers between the material world and the spirit world, hence the need for careful burial. Neolithic peoples marked graves with **megaliths** (literally, "great stones"), upright stone slabs roofed by a capstone to form a stone tomb or **dolmen** (Figure **0.9**). At some sites, the tomb was covered over with dirt and rubble to form a mound (Figure **0.10**), symbolic of the sacred mountain (the abode of the gods) and the procreative womb (the source of regenerative life). The shape prevails in sacred architecture ranging from the Meso-American temple (see Figure 3.11) to the Buddhist shrine (see chapter 9). The dolmen tomb made use of the simplest type of architectural construction: the **post-and-lintel** principle.

At ceremonial centers and burial sites, megaliths might be placed upright in circles or multiple rows and capped by horizontal slabs. The oldest of such Neolithic earthworks are those found recently in southeastern Turkey (see LOOKING INTO, Figures 0.11 and 0.12). At a site known as Göbekli Tepe ("Potbelly Hill"), located between the Tigris and Euphrates rivers at the northwestern rim of the Fertile Crescent (see Map 0.1), archeologists have uncovered a series of at least four stone circles dating from ca. 9000 B.C.E.

The best-known Neolithic earthwork, however, is the sanctuary at Stonehenge in southern England, where a group of concentric stone circles, constructed in stages over a period of 2000 years, forms one of the most mysterious and impressive ritual spaces of the prehistoric world (see LOOKING INTO, Figures 0.13 and 0.14). It is probable that Stonehenge, a hub for neighboring Neolithic towns such as Amesbury, served as a celestial calendar, predicting the movements of the sun and moon, clocking the seasonal cycle, and thus providing information that would have been essential to an agricultural society. However, since excavations of the fifty-six pits that circle the rim of the henge have revealed numerous cremated human remains, it is likely that Stonehenge served as a major burial site.

Recent excavations at nearby Durrington Walls confirm that Stonehenge probably functioned as the site of funerary rituals for the cremated dead. Dated at around 2600 B.C.E., the huge settlement at Durrington consists

Figure 0.10 Burial site. Dolmen (upright stones supporting a horizontal slab), Crucuno, north of Carnac, France, Neolithic period.

of hundreds of houses, as well as a ceremonial complex featuring concentric timber rings. Buildings thought by archeologists to have housed religious shrines stand along a wide avenue built on the "solstice axis" that may have served as a processional highway connecting Durrington and Stonehenge.

Some scholars speculate that the model for Stonehenge may be found at yet another recently uncovered Neolithic earthwork: the settlement on the Scottish islands of Orkney. This waterside site, known as the Ness of Brodgar ("Brodgar Promontory"), includes ceremonial stone circles and earthwork walls dating from 3500 B.C.E. Excavations in 2011 brought to light polished stone tools, clay pottery, and the first evidence of building surfaces covered with red and yellow painted designs. Ongoing excavation will no doubt unlock more of the mysteries of this and other monumental Neolithic landmarks.

The Birth of Civilization

Around 4000 B.C.E., a new chapter in the history of humankind began: Neolithic villages grew in population and size. They produced surplus food and goods that might be traded with neighboring villages. The demands of increased production and trade went hand in hand with changes in division and specialization of labor, which rapidly enhanced economic efficiency. Advances in technology, such as the invention of the wheel, the plow, and the solar calendar, occurred in the earliest known civilizations of Sumer and Egypt. Wheeled carts transported people, food, and goods overland, and sailboats used the natural resource of wind for travel by water. Large-scale farming required artificial systems of irrigation, which, in turn, required cooperative effort and a high degree of communal organization. Neolithic villages grew in complexity to become the bustling cities of a new era. The birth of civilization (the word derives from the Latin *civitas*, or "city") marks the shift from rural/pastoral to urban/commercial

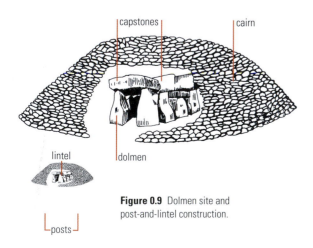

Figure 0.9 Dolmen site and post-and-lintel construction.

Map 0.1 Ancient River Valley Civilizations In the four great river valleys shown on the map, agriculture flourished to support the rise of cities and the beginnings of civilization. The Nile valley regions are the site of modern-day Egypt and the Sudan. The area designating Mesopotamia and the Fertile Crescent is shared by modern-day Iraq, Iran, Syria, Israel, Lebanon, Kuwait, Bahrain, and Saudi Arabia. The Indus valley civilization was located primarily in modern-day Pakistan, northwestern India, and parts of Iran and Afghanistan.

culture; or, more specifically, the transition from simple village life to the more complex forms of social, economic, and political organization associated with urban existence.

The first civilization of the ancient world emerged in Mesopotamia, a fertile area that lay between the Tigris and Euphrates rivers of the Southwest Asian landmass (Map **0.1**). Mesopotamia formed the eastern arc of the Fertile Crescent, which stretched westward to the Nile delta. At the southeastern perimeter of the Fertile Crescent, about a dozen cities collectively constituted Sumer, the earliest civilization known to history. Shortly after the rise of Sumer, around 3500 B.C.E., Egyptian civilization emerged along the Nile River in Northeast Africa. In India, the earliest urban centers appeared in the valley of the Indus River that runs through the northwest portion of the Indian subcontinent. Chinese civilization was born in the northern part of China's vast central plain, watered by the Yellow River. The appearance of these four civilizations was not simultaneous. Fully a thousand years separate the birth of civilization in Sumer from the rise of cities in China. Two newly discovered sites, dating from ca. 3000 B.C.E., in Lima on the west coast of Peru, may be added to those of the river valley civilizations. While no evidence of writing has been found in these early American cultures, other hallmarks of civilization are evident (see chapter 3).

By comparison with the self-sustaining Neolithic village, the early city reached outward. Specialization and the division of labor stimulated productivity and encouraged trade, which, in turn, enhanced the growth of the urban economy. Activities related to the production and distribution of goods could not be committed entirely to memory; rather, they required an efficient system of accounting and record keeping.

Science and Technology

4500 B.C.E.	sailboats are used in Mesopotamia
4200 B.C.E.	the first known calendar (365 days) is devised in Egypt
4000 B.C.E.	copper ores are mined and smelted by Egyptians; bricks are fired in Mesopotamian kilns
3600 B.C.E.	bronze comes into use in Mesopotamia
3500 B.C.E.	the plow, wheeled cart, potter's wheel, tokens with pictographic impressions, and fermentation processes for wine and beer are all introduced in Sumer

The Evolution of Writing

Writing made it possible to preserve and transmit information. More a process than an invention, writing evolved from counting. As early as 7500 B.C.E., people used tokens—pieces of clay molded into shapes to represent specific commodities: a cone for a unit of grain, an egg shape for a unit of oil, and so on. Tokens were placed in hollow clay balls that accompanied shipments of goods. Upon arrival at their destination, the balls were broken open and the tokens—the "record" of the shipment—were counted. Eventually, traders began to stamp the tokens into wet clay to identify the content and quantity of the traded goods. By 3100 B.C.E. these pictorial symbols, or **pictographs**, had replaced the tokens, and other graphic

Neolithic Stone Circles

The circles at Göbekli Tepe, consisting of 10- to 16-ton limestone megaliths adorned with low-relief sculptures of lions, foxes, snakes, scorpions, wild boars, spiders, carrion birds, and human body parts (Figure **0.11**), belong to a larger complex (Figure **0.12**) that probably served as a religious sanctuary. Since only 5 percent of the site has been excavated, its significance for unraveling the history of our human origins is still to be determined. But the presence of such a ceremonial center in an area lacking evidence of farm-based villages suggests that open-air shrines may have preceded the more complex agricultural communities historically associated with Neolithic culture.

It is likely that Stonehenge also served as a ceremonial center. To this windswept site, 20-foot-high megaliths, some weighing 25–50 tons each, were dragged from a quarry 20 miles away, then shaped and assembled without metal tools to form a huge outer circle and an inner horseshoe of post-and-lintel stones. In the center, arranged in two additional circles, were eighty 4–6-ton bluestones transported from southwest Wales, 170 miles away (Figures **0.13** and **0.14**, and p. ii). A 35-ton **stele** (known as the Heel Stone) stands apart from the complex, marking the point—visible from the exact center of the inner circle—at which the sun rises at the summer solstice (the longest day of the year).

Figure 0.11 Göbekli Tepe pillar with low-relief animal. The T-shaped stones (ranging from 9 to 19 ft. in height) resemble stylized human beings, while the animals are visibly male, and may have served as totems.

Figure 0.12 Reconstruction of Göbekli Tepe. No burial remains have been uncovered yet; however, evidence indicates that every few decades, an earlier circle was buried, and a new one constructed. This building program seems to have terminated around 8200 B.C.E.

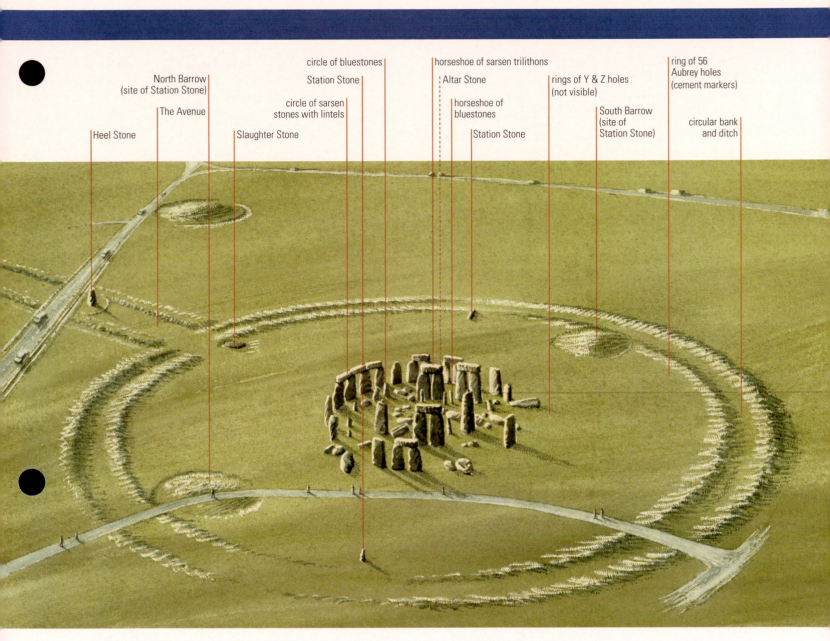

Heel Stone

The Avenue

North Barrow
(site of Station Stone)

Slaughter Stone

circle of sarsen
stones with lintels

circle of bluestones

Station Stone

horseshoe of sarsen trilithons

Altar Stone

horseshoe of
bluestones

Station Stone

rings of Y & Z holes
(not visible)

South Barrow
(site of
Station Stone)

ring of 56
Aubrey holes
(cement markers)

circular bank
and ditch

Figure 0.13 Stonehenge, Salisbury Plain, Wiltshire, England, ca. 3000–1800 B.C.E. Stone, diameter of circle 97 ft., tallest height 22 ft.

Figure 0.14 Hypthetical construction of Stonehenge. Above: raising the megaliths into an upright position by way of levers, ropes, and piled logs. Below: raising a lintel to the top of two sarsens by way of a working platform of stacked timbers.

Earliest pictographs (3000 B.C.E.)	Denotation of pictographs	Pictographs in rotated position	Cuneiform signs ca. 1900 B.C.E.	Basic logographic values	
				Reading	Meaning
	head and body of a man			lú	man
	head with mouth indicated			ka	mouth
	bowl of food			ninda	food, bread
	mouth + food			kú	to eat
	stream of water			a	water
	mouth + water			nag	to drink
	fish			kua	fish
	bird			mušen	bird
	head of an ass			anše	ass
	ear of barley			še	barley

Figure 0.15 The development of Sumerian writing from a pictographic script to cuneiform script to a phonetic system.

Figure 0.16 Reverse side of a pictographic tablet from Jamdat Nasr, near Kish, Iraq, ca. 3000 B.C.E. Clay, 2⅕ × 2½ × 1½ in . The tablet lists accounts involving animals and various commodities, including bread and beer.

Science and Technology

3100 B.C.E. cuneiform, the earliest known form of script, appears in Sumer; an early form of hieroglyphics appears in Egypt

3000 B.C.E. candles are manufactured in Egypt; cotton fabric is woven in India; Sumerian math evolves based on units of 60 (60 becomes the basic unit for measuring time)

2600 B.C.E. Imhotep (Egyptian) produces the first known medical treatise

2600 B.C.E. a lost-wax method of bronze casting is used in east Mesopotamia

2500 B.C.E. the beginning of systematic standards in weights and measurement emerges in Sumer

1600 B.C.E. Nebra Sky Disk configures the heavens

symbols (for people and places) were added to produce a total of some 1500 early pictographs. Pictographs were often combined to express an idea. For instance, the signs for "mouth" and for "food" were combined to form an **ideogram** (a sign that represents an idea or thing) meaning "to eat" (Figure **0.15**). Inscribed on tablets of wet clay, pictographs assumed a more angular and wedged shape. **Cuneiform** (from *cuneus*, the Latin word for "wedge"), a form of writing used throughout the Near East for well over 3000 years, ushered in the world's first Information Age (Figure **0.16**). Thousands of clay tablets have survived. The earliest of them come from Sumer in Mesopotamia. Most bear notations concerning production and trade, while others are inventories and business accounts, historical records, myths, prayers, and genealogies of local rulers.

In Egypt, a set of "sacred signs" known as **hieroglyphs** answered similar needs (see Figure 2.4). Ancient Egyptian writing remained a mystery to the world until 1822, when the Rosetta Stone (a black basalt slab discovered in 1799 in the Egyptian town of Rashid, or "Rosetta") was deciphered (Figure **0.17**). The stone's inscription, written in two different types of Egyptian script and one Greek script, arranged in tiers, was understood only after a number of scholars, and ultimately Jean-François Champollion (1790–1832), matched the hieroglyphs for certain Egyptian rulers (such as Cleopatra) with their names in Greek. As Champollion showed, hieroglyphic writing combined ideograms and **phonograms** (signs that represent sounds).

The development of a written language is often cited as the defining feature of a "civilized" society, but, in fact, some complex urban cultures (such as those of the pueblo communities and Andean peoples in the ancient Americas) have existed without writing systems. Writing was only one of many inventions mothered by necessity

Hieroglyphic script | Demotic script

Greek

Figure 0.17 Rosetta Stone, 196 B.C.E. Basalt, height 3 ft. 9 in. The same information is inscribed in hieroglyphic (a pictographic script), demotic script (a simplified form of hieroglyphic), and Greek.

Hence, bronze weapons were costly and available only to a small and well-to-do minority of the population. This minority formed a military elite who wielded power by virtue of superior arms. As the victory monument pictured in Figure **0.18** indicates, Sumerian warriors were outfitted with bronze shields, helmets, and lances.

The technology of bronze casting spread throughout the ancient world. Mesopotamians of the third millennium B.C.E. were among the first to use the **lost-wax** method of casting (Figure **0.19**). Spreading eastward into the Indus valley, the lost-wax technique became popular for the manufacture of jewelry, musical instruments, horse fittings, and toys (Figure **0.20**). The ancient Chinese cast the separate parts of bronze vessels in sectional clay molds, and then soldered the parts together. Master metallurgists, the Chinese transformed the techniques of bronze casting into one of the great artforms of the ancient world (see chapter 3).

The European Bronze Age, evolving during the second millennium B.C.E., left tangible evidence of ancient astronomy in the form of the Nebra Sky Disk, humankind's oldest known representation of the heavens (Figure **0.21**). This extraordinary artifact, one that until recently was thought to be a forgery, is a 5-pound, twelve-and-a-half-inch bronze disk inlaid with gold symbols representing the sun, a crescent moon, and stars. Found in the Saxon-Anhalt region of Germany and dated to ca. 1600 B.C.E., it may have functioned as a portable calendar or navigational tool.

on the threshold of the urban revolution. Technology itself would undergo dramatic transformation.

Metallurgy

At about the same time that systems of writing emerged in Mesopotamia, metal began to replace stone and bone tools. Metallurgy, which was first practiced around Asia Minor in about 4000 B.C.E., afforded humans a significant extension of control over nature by providing them with harder and more durable tools and weapons. At first, copper ore was extracted from surface deposits, but eventually metalsmiths devised sophisticated methods of mining and smelting ores. The result was bronze, an alloy of copper and tin that proved far superior to stone or bone in strength and durability. Since copper and tin were often located far apart, travel and trade were essential to Bronze Age cultures. (The discovery in 1995 of Caucasian mummies in graves found in East Asia's Gobi Desert argues for the existence of long-distance trade and cross-cultural contact.) Metallurgy was a time-consuming process that required specialized training and the division of labor.

Figure 0.18 The king of Lagash leads his phalanx into battle. Detail of Eannatum's Stele of Victory, Tello, formerly Girsu, ca. 2450 B.C.E. Limestone, 5 ft. 10⅞ in. × 4 ft. 3⅝ in.

Figure 0.19 (above) The lost-wax process of bronze casting developed in Mesopotamia, third millennium B.C.E. A positive model (1) is used to make a negative mold (2), which is then coated with wax. Cool fireclay is poured into the wax shell; the mold is then removed (3). Metal rods are added to hold the layers in place, as are wax vents for the even flow of bronze (4). The whole structure is immersed in sand; the wax is burned out. Investment ready for molten bronze (5). Bronze head, ready for removal of gates and metal rods (6).

Figure 0.20 (left) Chariot from Daimabad, Maharashtra, ca. 1500 B.C.E. Bronze, 8⅝ × 20½ × 6⅞ in. Similar models of carts and chariots are found in shrines and tombs in Syria and elsewhere in West Asia, dating from the third millennium B.C.E., an era in which domesticated animals were used to transport goods on land. Along with bronze technology, wheeled vehicles gave urban communities a leading edge at the beginning of civilization.

People and Nature

Like their prehistoric ancestors, the inhabitants of the earliest civilizations lived in intimate association with nature. They looked upon the forces of nature—sun, wind, and rain—as vital and alive, indeed, as inhabited by living spirits—a belief known as **animism**. Just as they devised tools to manipulate the natural environment, so they devised strategies by which to understand and control that environment. In ancient belief systems, the living spirits of nature assumed human qualities and characteristics. They might be vengeful or conciliatory, ugly or beautiful, fickle or reliable. They might become a family of superhumans—gods and goddesses who very much resembled humans in their physical features and personalities, but whose superior strength and intelligence far exceeded that of human beings. The gods were also immortal, which made them the envy of ordinary humans. The enactment of rituals honoring one or more of the gods accompanied seasonal celebrations, and almost every other significant communal event. In the early history of civilization, goddesses seem to have outnumbered gods, and local deities reigned supreme within their own districts. By means of specially appointed priests and priestesses, who mediated between human and divine realms, ancient people forged contractual relationships with their gods: in return for divine benefits, they lived as they believed the gods would wish.

Myth and the Quest for Beginnings

Today, no less than thousands of years ago, humans are driven to explain the origins of the universe and define their place in it. While modern speculation on

the origins of life usually draws on science, ancient societies formulated their answers in the shape of myth. In everyday speech, the word "myth" describes a popular fiction accepted as truth or half-truth. Historically, however, myths constitute a body of speculation that reflects the collective beliefs of a society. Myths of creation are stories that rationalize and explain the unknown. Often fantastic, they are usually grounded in the evidence of the senses, and are thus rich in visual imagery. They are closely linked to the moral values and religious systems of a given culture, since what is considered true is also often held sacred.

Figure 0.21 Nebra Sky Disk, bronze, diameter 12½ in. The golden arcs along the side and bottom were probably added later and are variously interpreted.

Almost every culture has produced a creation myth. Such myths were probably associated with rituals of seasonal renewal. The creation myths of various cultures show remarkable similarities, the most notable of which is the primacy of water as the medium for the genesis of life—a notion that modern science now supports as fact. The following four creation myths represent only a small sample of those generated over thousands of years.

The first, a hymn from the *Rig Veda*—the oldest religious literature of India—locates our beginnings in a watery darkness (see chapter 3). The second is but one example drawn from the huge fund of creation stories told by African tribal people and transmitted orally for centuries. It situates the origins of life in the slender grasses that grow in wet, marshy soil. The third, an account of creation from the *Popol Vuh* ("Sacred Book") of Central America's Maya Indians, links creation to light, thought, and language itself. Finally, from the Native American Iroquois Federation, a Mohawk tale recounts how the Good Spirit fashioned humankind in its diversity (see chapter 18).

— READING 0.1 Creation Tales

"The Song of Creation" from the *Rig Veda*

Then even nothingness was not, nor existence.   1
  There was no air then, nor the heavens beyond it
  What covered it? Where was it? In whose keeping?
  Was there then cosmic water, in depths unfathomed?
Then there were neither death nor immortality,   5
  nor was there then the torch of night and day.
  The One breathed windlessly and self-sustaining.
  There was that One then, and there was no other.
At first there was only darkness wrapped in darkness.
  All this was only unillumined water.   10
  That One which came to be, enclosed in nothing,
  arose at last, born of the power of heat.
In the beginning desire descended on it—
  that was the primal seed, born of the mind.
  The sages who have searched their hearts with wisdom   15
  know that which is, is kin to that which is not.
And they have stretched their cord across the void,
  and know what was above, and what below.
  Seminal powers made fertile mighty forces
Below was strength, and over it was impulse.   20
But, after all, who knows, and who can say
  whence it all came, and how creation happened?
  The gods themselves are later than creation,
  so who knows truly whence it has arisen?
Whence all creation had its origin,   25
  he, whether he fashioned it or whether he did not,
  he, who surveys it all from highest heaven,
  he knows—or maybe even he does not know.

(India)

An African Creation Tale

. . . It is said all men sprang from Unkulunkulu, who sprang   1
up first. The earth was in existence before Unkulunkulu. He
had his origin from the earth in a bed of reeds.

All things as well as Unkulunkulu sprang from a bed of reeds—everything, both animals and corn, everything came into being with Unkulunkulu.

He looked at the sun when it was finished (worked into form as a potter works clay) and said: "There is a torch which will give you light, that you may see." He looked down on the cattle and said: 10
"These are cattle. Be ye broken off, and see the cattle and let them be your food; eat their flesh and their milk." He looked on wild animals and said: "That is such an animal. That is an elephant. That is a buffalo." He looked on the fire and said: "Kindle it, and cook, and warm yourself; and eat meat when it has been dressed by the fire." He looked on all things and said: "So and so is the name of everything."

Unkulunkulu said: "Let there be marriage among men, that there may be those who can intermarry, that children may be born and men increase on earth." He said, "Let there be black   20
chiefs; and the chief be known by his people, and it be said, 'That is the chief: assemble all of you and go to your chief.'"

(Amazulu)

From the *Popol Vuh*

This is the account of how all was in suspense, all calm, in   1
silence; all motionless, still, and the expanse of the sky was empty.

This is the first account, the first narrative. There was neither man, nor animal, birds, fishes, crabs, trees, stones, caves, ravines, grasses, nor forests; there was only the sky.

The surface of the earth had not appeared. There was only the calm sea and the great expanse of the sky.

There was nothing brought together, nothing which could make a noise, nor anything which might move, or tremble, or   10
could make noise in the sky.

There was nothing standing; only the calm water, the placid sea, alone and tranquil. Nothing existed.

There was only immobility and silence in the darkness in the night. Only the Creator, the Maker, Tepeu, Gucumatz, the Forefathers, were in the water surrounded with light. They were hidden under green and blue feathers, and were therefore called Gucumatz [the Feathered Serpent: Aztec Quetzalcoatl; Maya Kukulkan]. By nature they were great sages and great thinkers. In this manner the sky existed and also the   20
Heart of Heaven, which is the name of God and thus He is called.

Then came the word. Tepeu and Gucumatz came together in the darkness, in the night, and Tepeu and Gucumatz talked together. They talked then, discussing and deliberating; they agreed, they united their words and their thoughts.

Then while they meditated, it became clear to them that when dawn would break, man must appear. Then they planned the creation, and the growth of the trees and the thickets and the birth of life and the creation of man. Thus it was arranged   30
in the darkness and in the night by the Heart of Heaven who is called Huracán.

Then Tepeu and Gucumatz came together; then they conferred about life and light, what they would do so that there would be light and dawn, who it would be who would provide food and sustenance.

Thus let it be done! Let the emptiness be filled! Let the water recede and make a void, let the earth appear and

become solid; let it be done. Thus they spoke. Let there be
light, let there be dawn in the sky and on the earth! There shall **40**
be neither glory nor grandeur in our creation and formation
until the human being is made, man is formed. So they spoke.

Then the earth was created by them. So it was, in truth,
that they created the earth. Earth! . . . they said, and instantly
it was made. . . .

(Maya)

A Native American Creation Tale, "How Man Was Created"

After Sat-kon-se-ri-io, the Good Spirit, had made the **1**
animals, birds, and other creatures and had placed them to
live and multiply upon the earth, he rested. As he gazed
around at his various creations, it seemed to him that there
was something lacking. For a long time the Good Spirit
pondered over this thought. Finally he decided to make a
creature that would resemble himself.

Going to the bank of a river he took a piece of clay, and out
of it he fashioned a little clay man. After he had modeled it, he
built a fire and, setting the little clay man in the fire, waited **10**
for it to bake. The day was beautiful. The songs of the birds
filled the air. The river sang a song and, as the Good Spirit
listened to this song, he became very sleepy. He soon fell
asleep beside the fire. When he finally awoke, he rushed to
the fire and removed the clay man. He had slept too long.
His little man was burnt black. According to the Mohawks,
this little man was the first Negro. His skin was black. He had
been overbaked.

The Good Spirit was not satisfied. Taking a fresh piece of
clay, he fashioned another man and, placing him in the fire, **20**
waited for him to bake, determined this time to stay awake

and watch his little man to see that he would not be
overbaked. But the river sang its usual sleepy song. The Good
Spirit, in spite of all he could do, fell asleep. But this time he
slept only a little while. Awakening at last, he ran to the fire
and removed his little man. Behold, it was half baked.
This, say the Mohawks, was the first white man. He was
half baked!

The Good Spirit was still unsatisfied. Searching along the
riverbank he hunted until he found a bed of perfect red clay. **30**
This time he took great care and modeled a very fine clay man.
Taking the clay man to the fire, he allowed it to bake.
Determined to stay awake, the Good Spirit stood beside the
fire, after a while Sat-kon-se-ri-io removed the clay man.
Behold, it was just right—a man the red color of the sunset sky.
It was the first Mohawk Indian.

(Mohawk)

Q. **What do all the creation myths in this reading have in common? How do they differ?**

Civilization emerged not as a fleeting moment of change, but as a slow process of urban growth. By the operation of an increasingly refined abstract intelligence, and by means of ingenuity, imagination, and cooperation, the earliest human beings took the first steps in perpetuating their own survival and the security of their communities. Technology provided the tools for manipulating nature, while mythology and the arts lent meaning and purpose to nature's mysteries. By such cultural achievements, the earliest human beings laid the foundations for the humanistic tradition.

Glossary

animism the belief that the forces of nature are inhabited by spirits

clan a group that traces its descent from a common ancestor

culture the sum total of those things (including traditions, techniques, material goods, and symbol systems) that people have invented, developed, and transmitted

cuneiform ("wedge-shaped") one of humankind's earliest writing systems, consisting of wedge-shaped marks impressed into clay by means of a reed stylus

dolmen a stone tomb formed by two posts capped by a lintel

hieroglyph (Greek, "sacred sign") the pictographic script of ancient Egypt

hominid any of a family of bipedal primate mammals, including modern humans and

their ancestors, the earliest of which is *Australopithecus*

ideogram a sign that represents an idea or thing

lost wax (also French, *cire-perdu*) a method of metal casting in which a figure is modeled in wax, then enclosed in a clay mold that is fired; the wax melts, and molten metal is poured in to replace it; finally, the clay mold is removed and the solid metal form is polished (see Figure 0.19)

megalith a large, roughly shaped stone, often used in ancient architectural construction

naturalism a descriptive approach to the visual world that seeks to imitate natural appearance

phonogram a sign that represents a sound

pictograph a pictorial symbol used in humankind's earliest systems of writing

polychrome having many or various colors

post-and-lintel the simplest form of architectural construction, consisting of vertical members (posts) and supporting horizontals (lintels) (see Figure 0.9)

prehistory the study of history before written records

shaman a priestly leader or healer who mediates between the natural and the spiritual worlds

stele an upright stone slab or pillar

totem a heraldic emblem of a tribe, family, or clan

Mesopotamia: Gods, Rulers, and the Social Order

ca. 3500–330 B.C.E.

"From the days of old there is no permanence.
The sleeping and the dead, how alike they are, they are like a painted death."
The Epic of Gilgamesh

Figure 1.1 Winged human-headed bull from Khorsabad, Iraq, ca. 720 B.C.E. Limestone, height 13 ft. 10 in. (approx.). Hybrid creatures bearing the features of the monarch guarded the gateways of the Assyrian palace at Khorsabad in present-day Iraq.

Mesopotamia, literally "the land between the two rivers," was the stage upon which many civilizations rose and fell. Rather than tell the story of each, we will explore their cultural legacies by way of three principal themes: gods, rulers, and social organization. The first deals with the belief systems that linked the secular and spiritual realms; the second focuses on the establishment of leadership within the earliest urban communities; and the third examines the nature of the social order as revealed in law and other forms of cultural expression. These three themes, which dominate the visual and literary works of humankind's earliest civilizations, reflect universal concerns that remain with us today. Religious beliefs and political and social practices differ from culture to culture, but all belief systems and social practices reflect the human effort to come to terms with the unknown, to master the perils of the environment, to achieve communal cooperation, and to understand the destiny and purpose of humankind.

The Land Between the Two Rivers

The land between the Tigris and Euphrates rivers formed part of a fertile crescent that occupied the western end of Asia (Map **1.1**). Sumer, the first of Mesopotamia's many civilizations, arose some time around 3500 B.C.E., at the point at which the Tigris and Euphrates empty into the Persian Gulf. Watered by the rivers, the rich soil at the southeastern tip of the Fertile Crescent promoted agricultural activity and supported the growth of humankind's first cities: Uruk, Ur, Kish, Nippur, and Lagash. However, the rivers upon which life depended overflowed unpredictably, often devastating whole villages and cities. Mesopotamians also suffered fierce changes in weather, ranging from violent rainstorms, wind, and hail, to long periods of drought.

Compounding these conditions of insecurity, the region experienced repeated attacks by tribal nomads, who, attracted by the fertile lands along the rivers, descended from the mountainous areas to the north, bringing an end to the history of one civilization, and establishing a new civilization that often absorbed the culture of the previous one.

Sumer consisted of small groups of self-ruling city-states. Other civilizations, such as the Assyrian, founded great empires, while the people of still another, the Hebrews, remained nomadic for centuries before forming a political state. No one language or single, continuous form of government united these various Mesopotamian peoples; yet they shared a common world-view and, with the exception of the Hebrews, a common belief system based in **polytheism**, the worship of many gods.

Map 1.1 Mesopotamia, 3500–2000 B.C.E. This area of Southwest Asia is often referred to as the "Near East" or "Middle East," the latter a Eurocentric term coined by the British ca. 1900. The region of the Hittite Empire is modern-day Turkey. For the other modern-day countries in these territories, see the legend to Map 0.1.

The Gods of Mesopotamia

Mesopotamia's gods and goddesses were associated with the forces of nature. Like its climate, its divinities were fierce and capricious, its mythology filled with physical and spiritual woe, and its cosmology based on the themes of chaos and conflict. *The Babylonian Creation*, humankind's earliest cosmological myth, illustrates all these conditions. A Sumerian poem recorded early in the second millennium B.C.E., and recited during the festival of the New Year, it celebrates the birth of the gods and the order of creation. It describes a universe that originated by means of spontaneous generation: at a moment when there was neither heaven nor earth, the sweet and bitter waters "mingled" to produce the first family of gods.

As the story unfolds, chaos and discord prevail amid the reign of Tiamat, the Great Mother of the primeval waters, until Marduk, hero-god and offspring of Wisdom, takes matters in hand: he destroys the Great Mother and proceeds to establish a new order. Marduk founds the holy city of Babylon (literally, "home of the gods") and creates human beings, whose purpose it is to serve heaven's squabbling divinities.

READING 1.1 From *The Babylonian Creation*

When there was no heaven,   1
no earth, no height, no depth, no name,
   when Apsu[1] was alone,
the sweet water, the first begetter; and Tiamat[2]
   the bitter water, and that   5
return to the womb, her Mummu,[3]
   when there were no gods—

   When sweet and bitter
mingled together, no reed was plaited, no rushes
   muddied the water,   10
the gods were nameless, natureless, futureless, then
   from Apsu and Tiamat
in the waters gods were created, in the waters
   silt precipitated,

Lahmu and Lahamu,[4]   15
were named; they were not yet old,
   not yet grown tall
when Anshar and Kishar[5] overtook them both,
   the lines of sky and earth
stretched where horizons meet to separate   20
   cloud from silt.

   Days on days, years

---

[1] The primeval sweet waters.
[2] The primeval bitter waters.
[3] One of the primordial beings of the universe.
[4] Male and female primordial beings.
[5] The horizon of the sky (male) and the horizon of the earth (female).

on years passed till Anu,[6] the empty heaven,
   heir and supplanter,
first-born of his father, in his own nature   25
   begot of Nudimmud-Ea[7]
intellect, wisdom, wider than heaven's horizon,
   the strongest of all the kindred.

   Discord broke out among the gods although they were
brothers, warring and jarring in the belly of Tiamat,   30
heaven shook, it reeled with the surge of the dance.
Apsu could not silence the clamor. Their behavior was
bad, overbearing, and proud. . . .

[Ea kills Apsu; Marduk is born, and Tiamat spawns serpents and monsters to make war on the gods.]

When her labor of creation was ended, against her children   1
Tiamat began preparations of war. This was the evil she did to
requite Apsu, this was the evil news that came to Ea.

When he had learned how matters lay he was stunned, he sat in
black silence till rage had worked itself out; then he remembered
the gods before him. He went to Anshar, his father's father, and
told him how Tiamat plotted,

   "She loathes us, father, our mother Tiamat has raised up
that Company, she rages in turbulence and all have joined her,
all those gods whom you begot,   10

   "Together they jostle the ranks to march with Tiamat, day
and night furiously they plot, the growling roaring rout, ready
for battle, while the Old Hag, the first mother, mothers a new
brood. . . ."

[The gods make Marduk Supreme Commander of the wars; he leads the attack on Tiamat.]

Then Marduk made a bow and strung it to be his own weapon,   1
he set the arrow against the bow-string, in his right hand he
grasped the mace and lifted it up, bow and quiver hung at his
side, lightnings played in front of him, he was altogether an
incandescence.

He netted a net, a snare for Tiamat; the winds from their
quarters held it, south wind, north, east wind, west, and no
part of Tiamat could escape. . . .

He turned back to where Tiamat lay bound, he straddled the
legs and smashed her skull (for the mace was merciless), he   10
severed the arteries and the blood streamed down the north
wind to the unknown ends of the world.

When the gods saw all this they laughed out loud, and they
sent him presents. They sent him their thankful tributes.

The lord rested; he gazed at the huge body, pondering how to

---

[6] God of the sky (the offspring of Anshar and Kishar).
[7] Another name for Ea, god of wisdom (the offspring of Anu).

use it, what to create from the dead carcass. He split it apart like a cockle-shell; with the upper half he constructed the arc of sky, he pulled down the bar and set a watch on the waters, so they should never escape. . . .

[Marduk makes Babylon "the home of the gods" and proceeds to create Man.]

Now that Marduk has heard what it is the gods are saying, he   1
is moved with desire to create a work of consummate art. He
told Ea the deep thought in his heart.

> Blood to blood
> I join,
> blood to bone
> I form
> an original thing,
> its name is MAN,
> aboriginal man   10
> is mine in making.
> All his occupations
> are faithful service,
> the gods that fell
> have rest,
> I will subtly alter
> their operations,
> divided companies
> equally blest.

Ea answered with carefully chosen words, completing the   20
plan for the gods' comfort. He said to Marduk,
   "Let one of the kindred be taken; only one need die for the
new creation. Bring the gods together in the Great Assembly;
there let the guilty die, so the rest may live."

Q How does this creation myth compare with those in Reading 0.1?

From Matriarchy to Patriarchy

Marduk's destruction of the Great Mother Tiamat reflects the shift from matriarchy to patriarchy in the polytheistic history of the ancient world. Whereas many early cultures venerated female divinities, ancient civilizations gradually came to give primacy to male deities. Some of the earliest literature from Sumer celebrates the colorful "Queen of Heaven" known as Inanna (or Ishtar), goddess of chaos and love, associated with fertility, the moon, and the planet Venus (Figure **1.2**). She seems to have held priestly authority in the ancient city of Uruk. The most famous of the myths surrounding Inanna recounts her descent to the underworld, where she consigns her mate (her husband or brother) Dumuzi to the shadowy realm of darkness. The descent myth, which appears in the literature of a great many ancient agricultural societies, including those of Egypt and Greece, was probably associated with seasonal celebrations involving the cycles of vegetation: the "birth" of the crops in spring and their "death" in winter, when vegetation disappears from the earth.

Principal Mesopotamian Gods

Name	Role
Adad	storm and rain god
Anu	father of the gods, god of heaven
Apsu	god of the primeval sweet waters
Dumuzi (Tammuz)	god of vegetation, fertility, and the underworld; husband of Ishtar
Ea	god of wisdom and patron of the arts
Enlil	god of earth, wind, and air
Ishtar (Inanna)	goddess of love, fertility, and war; Queen of Heaven
Ninhursag	mother goddess, creator of vegetation; wife of Enlil
Nisaba	goddess of grain
Shamash	god of the sun; judge and law-giver; god of wisdom
Sin (Nanna)	goddess of the moon

The Search for Immortality

The theme of human vulnerability and the search for everlasting life are the central motifs in the *Epic of Gilgamesh*, the world's first epic. An **epic**, that is, a long narrative poem that recounts the deeds of a hero in quest of meaning and identity, embodies the ideals and values of the culture from which it comes. The *Epic of Gilgamesh* was recited orally for centuries before it was recorded at Sumer in the late third millennium B.C.E. It may have been chanted or sung to the accompaniment of a harp, such as those found in the royal graves at Ur (Figures **1.3** and **1.4**). As literature, it precedes the Hebrew Bible and all the other major writings of antiquity. Its hero is a semihistorical figure who probably ruled the ancient Sumerian city of Uruk around 2800 B.C.E. Described as two-thirds god and one-third man, Gilgamesh is blessed by the gods with beauty and courage. But when he spurns the affections of the Queen of Heaven, Ishtar, he is punished with the loss of his dearest companion, Enkidu. Despairing over Enkidu's death, Gilgamesh undertakes a long and hazardous quest in search of everlasting life. He meets Utnapishtim, a mortal who (like Noah of the Hebrew Bible) has saved humankind from a devastating flood. As a reward he (unlike Noah) has received the secret Gilgamesh seeks: eternal life. Utnapishtim warns Gilgamesh that all classes of people—the master and the slave—are equal in death. Nevertheless, he guides Gilgamesh to the plant that miraculously restores lost youth. Although Gilgamesh retrieves the plant, he guards it carelessly: while he sleeps, it is snatched by a serpent (whose ability to shed its skin made it an ancient symbol of rebirth).

Figure 1.2 The "Queen of Heaven," Babylonian goddess, southern Iraq, 1800–1750 B.C.E. Painted terracotta plaque, height 19½ in (approx.). Scholars identify this winged figure as Inanna (or Ishtar). She wears a horned headdress and holds the rod and ring of authority in each hand. She stands on a pair of lions, symbols of power, and is flanked by owls, symbols of wisdom. The plaque has lost most of its brightly painted colors.

Figure 1.3 Gilgamesh between two human-headed bulls (top portion). Soundbox of a harp, from Ur, Iraq, ca. 2600 B.C.E. Wood with inlaid gold, lapis lazuli, and shell, height 12 in (approx.). Some of the other images that figure in the epic, such as the Man-Scorpion, appear in the other registers of the soundbox of the harp. The meaning of these figures is obscure; they may illustrate nonsurviving portions of the epic, or they may refer to popular fables.

Figure 1.4 Harp (reconstructed) from Ur, ca. 2600 B.C.E. Wood and inlays of gold, lapis lazuli, and shell, height 3 ft. 6 in.

READING 1.2 From the *Epic of Gilgamesh*

O Gilgamesh, Lord of Kullab,[1] great is thy praise. This was **1**
the man to whom all things were known; this was the king
who knew the countries of the world. He was wise, he saw
mysteries and knew secret things, he brought us a tale of the
days before the flood. He went on a long journey, was weary,
worn-out with labor, and returning engraved on a stone the
whole story.

When the Gods created Gilgamesh they gave him a perfect
body. Shamash the glorious sun endowed him with beauty,
Adad the god of the storm endowed him with courage, the **10**
great gods made his beauty perfect, surpassing all others.
Two thirds they made him god and one third man.

In Uruk[2] he built walls, a great rampart, and the temple of
blessed Eanna for the god of the firmament Anu, and for Ishtar
the goddess of love [see Figure 1.2].

*[Gilgamesh and his bosom companion, Enkidu, destroy Humbaba,
the guardian of the cedar forest, and perform other heroic deeds.
But Gilgamesh spurns the affections of Ishtar, and in revenge, she
takes Enkidu's life.]*

Bitterly Gilgamesh wept for his friend Enkidu; he wandered
over the wilderness as a hunter, he roamed over the plains;
in his bitterness he cried, "How can I rest, how can I be at
peace? Despair is in my heart. What my brother is now, that
shall I be when I am dead. Because I am afraid of death I will **20**
go as best I can to find Utnapishtim whom they call the
Faraway, for he has entered the assembly of the gods." So
Gilgamesh traveled over the wilderness, he wandered over the
grasslands, a long journey, in search of Utnapishtim, whom the
gods took after the deluge; and they set him to live in the land
of Dilmun,[3] in the garden of the sun; and to him alone of men
they gave everlasting life.

At night when he came to the mountain passes Gilgamesh
prayed: "In these mountain passes long ago I saw lions, I was
afraid and I lifted my eyes to the moon; I prayed and my **30**
prayers went up to the gods, so now, O moon god Sin, protect
me." When he had prayed he lay down to sleep, until he was
woken from out of a dream. He saw the lions round him
glorying in life; then he took his ax in his hand, he drew
his sword from his belt, and struck and destroyed and
scattered them.

So at length Gilgamesh came to that great mountain whose
name is Mashu, the mountain which guards the rising and the
setting sun. Its twin peaks are as high as the wall of heaven
and its paps reach down to the underworld. At its gate the **40**
Scorpions stand guard, half man and half dragon; their glory is
terrifying, their stare strikes death into men, their shimmering
halo sweeps the mountains that guard the rising sun. When
Gilgamesh saw them he shielded his eyes for the length of a
moment only; then he took courage and approached. When
they saw him so undismayed the Man-Scorpion called to his
mate, "This one who comes to us now is flesh of the gods."
The mate of the Man-Scorpion answered, "Two thirds is god
but one third is man."

Then he called to the man Gilgamesh, he called to the child **50**
of the gods: "Why have you come so great a journey; for what
have you traveled so far, crossing the dangerous waters; tell

me the reason for your coming?" Gilgamesh answered, "For
Enkidu; I loved him dearly, together we endured all kinds of
hardships; on his account I have come, for the common lot of
man has taken him. I have wept for him day and night, I would
not give up his body for burial, I thought my friend would come
back because of my weeping. Since he went, my life is
nothing; that is why I have traveled here in search of
Utnapishtim my father; for men say he has entered the **60**
assembly of the gods, and has found everlasting life. I have
a desire to question him concerning the living and the dead."
The Man-Scorpion opened his mouth and said, speaking to
Gilgamesh, "No man born of woman has done what you have
asked, no mortal man has gone into the mountain; the length
of it is twelve leagues[4] of darkness; in it there is no light, but
the heart is oppressed with darkness. From the rising of the
sun to the setting of the sun there is no light." Gilgamesh said,
"Although I should go in sorrow and in pain, with sighing and
with weeping, still I must go. Open the gate of the mountain." **70**
And the Man-Scorpion said, "Go, Gilgamesh, I permit you to
pass through the mountain of Mashu and through the high
ranges; may your feet carry you safely home. The gate of the
mountain is open."

When Gilgamesh heard this he did as the Man-Scorpion
had said, he followed the sun's road to his rising, through the
mountain. When he had gone one league the darkness
became thick around him, for there was no light, he could see
nothing ahead and nothing behind him. After two leagues the
darkness was thick and there was no light, he could see **80**
nothing ahead and nothing behind him. After three leagues
the darkness was thick, and there was no light, he could see
nothing ahead and nothing behind him. After four leagues
the darkness was thick and there was no light, he could see
nothing ahead and nothing behind him. At the end of five
leagues the darkness was thick and there was no light, he
could see nothing ahead and nothing behind him. At the end
of six leagues the darkness was thick and there was no light,
he could see nothing ahead and nothing behind him. When he
had gone seven leagues the darkness was thick and there was **90**
no light, he could see nothing ahead and nothing behind him.
When he had gone eight leagues Gilgamesh gave a great cry,
for the darkness was thick and he could see nothing ahead
and nothing behind him. After nine leagues he felt the north
wind on his face, but the darkness was thick and there was
no light, he could see nothing ahead and nothing behind him.
After ten leagues the end was near. After eleven leagues the
dawn light appeared. At the end of twelve leagues the sun
streamed out.

There was the garden of the gods; all round him stood **100**
bushes bearing gems. Seeing it he went down at once, for
there was fruit of carnelian with the vine hanging from it,
beautiful to look at; lapis lazuli leaves hung thick with fruit,
sweet to see. For thorns and thistles there were hematite and

---

[1] Part of Uruk, a city located in Sumer.
[2] Gilgamesh was the fifth ruler in the dynasty of Uruk after the flood.
[3] The Sumerian paradise, a mythical land resembling the Garden of
    Eden described in the Hebrew Bible.
[4] Approximately 36 miles.

rare stones, agate, and pearls from out of the sea. While Gilgamesh walked in the garden by the edge of the sea Shamash[5] saw him, and he saw that he was dressed in the skins of animals and ate their flesh. He was distressed, and he spoke and said, "No mortal man has gone this way before, nor will, as long as the winds drive over the sea." And to Gilgamesh he said, "You will never find the life for which you are searching." Gilgamesh said to glorious Shamash, "Now that I have toiled and strayed so far over the wilderness, am I to sleep, and let the earth cover my head forever? Let my eyes see the sun until they are dazzled with looking. Although I am no better than a dead man, still let me see the light of the sun."

[Gilgamesh meets Siduri, the maker of wine, who advises him to give up his search and value more highly the good things of the earth. Gilgamesh prepares to cross the Ocean and, with the help of the ferryman Urshanabi, finally reaches Dilmun, the home of Utnapishtim.]

"Oh, father Utnapishtim, you who have entered the assembly of the gods, I wish to question you concerning the living and the dead, how shall I find the life for which I am searching?"

Utnapishtim said, "There is no permanence. Do we build a house to stand for ever, do we seal a contract to hold for all time? Do brothers divide an inheritance to keep for ever, does the flood-time of rivers endure? It is only the nymph of the dragonfly who sheds her larva and sees the sun in his glory. From the days of old there is no permanence. The sleeping and the dead, how alike they are, they are like a painted death. What is there between the master and the servant when both have fulfilled their doom? When the Annunaki, the judges, come together, and Mammetun the mother of destinies, together they decree the fates of men. Life and death they allot but the day of death they do not disclose."

Then Gilgamesh said to Utnapishtim the Faraway, "I look at you now, Utnapishtim, and your appearance is no different from mine; there is nothing strange in your features. I thought I should find you like a hero prepared for battle, but you lie here taking your ease on your back. Tell me truly, how was it that you came to enter the company of the gods and to possess everlasting life?" Utnapishtim said to Gilgamesh, "I will reveal to you a mystery, I will tell you a secret of the gods."

[Utnapishtim relates the story of the flood.]

In those days the world teemed, the people multiplied, the world bellowed like a wild bull, and the great god was aroused by the clamor. Enlil heard the clamor and he said to the gods in council, "The uproar of mankind is intolerable and sleep is no longer possible by reason of the babel." So the gods in their hearts were moved to let loose the deluge; but my lord Ea warned me in a dream. He whispered their words to my house of reeds.... "Tear down your house, I say, and build a boat. These are the measurements of the barque as you shall build her: let her beam equal her length, let her deck be roofed like the vault that covers the abyss; then take up into the boat the seed of all living creatures...."

For six days and six nights the winds blew, torrent and tempest and flood overwhelmed the world, tempest and flood

raged together like warring hosts. When the seventh day dawned the storm from the south subsided, the sea grew calm, the flood was stilled; I looked at the face of the world and there was silence, all mankind was turned to clay. The surface of the sea stretched as flat as a roof-top; I opened a hatch and the light fell on my face. Then I bowed low, I sat down and I wept, the tears streamed down my face, for on every side was the waste of water.

[Utnapishtim leads Gilgamesh to Urshanabi the Ferryman.]

Then Gilgamesh and Urshanabi launched the boat onto the water and boarded it, and they made ready to sail away; but the wife of Utnapishtim the Faraway said to him, "Gilgamesh came here wearied out, he is worn out; what will you give him to carry him back to his own country?" So Utnapishtim spoke, and Gilgamesh took a pole and brought the boat in to the bank. "Gilgamesh, you came here a man wearied out, you have worn yourself out; what shall I give you to carry you back to your own country? Gilgamesh, I shall reveal a secret thing, it is a mystery of the gods that I am telling you. There is a plant that grows under the water, it has a prickle like a thorn, like a rose; it will wound your hands, but if you succeed in taking it, then your hands will hold that which restores his lost youth to a man."

When Gilgamesh heard this he opened the sluices so that a sweet-water current might carry him out to the deepest channel; he tied heavy stones to his feet and they dragged him down to the water-bed. There he saw the plant growing; although it pricked him he took it in his hands; then he cut the heavy stones from his feet, and the sea carried him and threw him on the shore. Gilgamesh said to Urshanabi the ferryman, "Come here, and see this marvelous plant. By its virtue a man may win back all his former strength. I will take it to Uruk of the strong walls; there I will give it to the old to eat. Its name shall be 'the Old Men are Young Again'; and at last I shall eat it myself and have back all my lost youth." So Gilgamesh returned by the gate through which he had come, Gilgamesh and Urshanabi went together. They traveled their twenty leagues and then they broke their fast; after thirty leagues they stopped for the night.

Gilgamesh saw a well of cool water and he went down and bathed; but deep in the pool there was lying a serpent,[6] and the serpent sensed the sweetness of the flower. It rose out of the water and snatched it away, and immediately it sloughed its skin and returned to the well. Then Gilgamesh sat down and wept, the tears ran down his face, and he took the hand of Urshanabi; "O Urshanabi, was it for this that I toiled with my hands, is it for this I have wrung out my heart's blood? For myself I have gained nothing; not I, but the beast of the earth has joy of it now. Already the stream has carried it twenty leagues back to the channels where I found it. I found a sign and now I have lost it. Let us leave the boat on the bank and go."

Q. What makes Gilgamesh an epic hero? Are there any comparable figures in contemporary literature or life?

---

[5] The Semitic sun god.
[6] More literally "earth lion" or "chameleon."

The *Epic of Gilgamesh* is important not only as the world's first epic poem, but also as the earliest known literary work that tries to come to terms with death, or nonbeing. Its subtext is the profound human need for an *immortality ideology**—a body of beliefs that anticipates the survival of some aspect of the self in a life hereafter. Typical of the mythic hero, Gilgamesh is driven to discover his human limits, to bring about change through human ingenuity, but his quest for personal immortality is frustrated and his goals remain unfulfilled.

The Rulers of Mesopotamia

The area collectively known as Sumer was a loosely knit group of city-states, that is, urban centers that governed the neighboring countryside. Here, men and women produced humankind's earliest Bronze Age technology and refined the cuneiform script that became the first written language. They began the use of a base-60 number system that is the origin of the seconds and minutes still used today in telling time. In each of the city-states of Sumer, individual priest-kings ruled as agents of one or another of the gods. The priest-king led the army, regulated the supply and distribution of food, and provided political and religious leadership. From the temple at his palace, he conducted the services that were designed to win the favor of the gods.

Disunited and rivalrous, the city-states of Sumer were vulnerable to invasion. Around 2350 B.C.E., a gifted Akkadian warlord named Sargon I (Figure **1.5**) conquered Sumer and united the city-states under his command. For fifty-six years, he reigned as **theocratic monarch** (sole ruler and representative of the gods). Consolidating various peoples and language groups, Sargon created the world's first multi-ethnic **empire**, extending his authority from Elam (see Map 1.1) to the Mediterranean Sea. By 2000 B.C.E., however, his dynasty collapsed under the attacks of nomadic tribespeople from the north. The invaders—establishing the pattern that dominated all of Mesopotamian history—built on the accomplishments of the very states they conquered. So, theocratic monarchy, religious polytheism, and established traditions of trade and barter would prevail from civilization to civilization. The myths and legends, indeed the *Epic of Gilgamesh* itself, would be transmitted from century to century to be transcribed in ever more refined versions of cuneiform script.

The Social Order

In the newly formed civilizations of the ancient world, community life demanded collective effort in matters of production and distribution, as well as in the irrigation of fields and the construction of roads, temples, palaces, and military defenses. Specialization of labor and the complexity of urban life encouraged the development of social classes with different kinds of training, different

---

* The phrase is from Ernest Becker. *The Denial of Death.* New York: The Free Press, 1973.

Figure 1.5 Head of the Akkadian ruler Sargon I, from Nineveh, Iraq, ca. 2350 B.C.E. Bronze, height 12 in. Iraq Museum, Baghdad.

The Standard of Ur

The Standard of Ur constitutes a visual text that sheds light on class divisions and royal authority in ancient Mesopotamian culture. On the side of the panel generally called "War," the lowest register records a battle in which four-wheeled chariots trample the enemy; in the middle register, prisoners are stripped of their clothes; and in the top register, they are paraded before the ruler and his officials. The top register of the panel known as "Peace" depicts a victory banquet: the ruler and six of his officials, entertained by a harpist, raise their goblets. The middle register shows a procession of servants herding animals that will probably serve as culinary fare or as sacrificial tribute; on the bottom register, foreigners (probably prisoners of war) carry bundles on their backs.

Figure 1.6 The Standard of Ur, ca. 2700 B.C.E. Double-sided panel inlaid with shell, lapis lazuli, and red limestone, 8 × 19 in. (approx.). Leonard Woolley, the early twentieth-century British archeologist who excavated Ur, imagined that the object was carried on a pole as a battle standard. More recently, scholars have suggested that the panels belong to the soundbox of a musical instrument.

infantry with axes | wheeled cart | draft animals | Sumerian ruler receiving prisoners

armored cloaks | war chariots carrying lances | enemies trampled in battle | victims of war stripped of clothes

animal procession | Sumerian ruler | high officials | musician with lyre

porters with bundles | donkeys | goat and two rams | female companion responsibilities, and different types of authority. In the first civilizations, the priest who prepared the wine in the ritual vessel, the soldier who protected the city, and the farmer who cultivated the field represented fairly distinct classes of people with unique duties and responsibilities to society as a whole.

The social order and division of labor that prevailed in Mesopotamia around 2700 B.C.E. are depicted in the "Standard of Ur," a double-sided wooden panel found in the royal tombs excavated at the city of Ur (see LOOKING INTO, Figure **1.6**). The panel, ornamented in **mosaic** consisting of mother-of-pearl, red limestone, and **lapis lazuli** (a semiprecious blue stone), appears to commemorate a Sumerian victory. Leonard Woolley, the early twentieth-century British archeologist who excavated Ur, imagined that the object was carried on a pole as a battle standard, but more recently scholars have suggested that the panels belong to the soundbox of a musical instrument.

Law and the Social Order in Babylon

Shortly after 2000 B.C.E., rulers of the city-state of Babylon unified the neighboring territories of Sumer to establish the First Babylonian Empire. In an effort to unite these regions politically and provide them with effective leadership, Babylon's sixth ruler, Hammurabi, called for a systematic codification of existing legal practices. He sent out envoys to collect the local statutes and had them consolidated into a single body of law. Hammurabi's Code—a collection of 282 clauses engraved on a 7-foot-high stele—is our most valuable index to life in ancient Mesopotamia (Figure **1.7**). The Code is not the first example of recorded law among the Babylonian kings; it is, however, the most extensive and comprehensive set of laws to survive from ancient times. Although Hammurabi's Code addressed primarily secular matters, it bore the force of divine decree. This fact is indicated in the prologue to the Code, where Hammurabi claims descent from the gods. It is also manifested visually in the low-relief carving that appears at the top of the stele: here, in a scene that calls to mind the story of the biblical Moses on Mount Sinai, Hammurabi is pictured receiving the law (symbolized by a staff) from the sun god Shamash.

Written law represented a landmark advance in the development of human rights in that it protected the individual from the capricious decisions of monarchs. Unwritten law was subject to the hazards of memory and

Figure 1.7 Stele of Hammurabi, first Babylonian dynasty, ca. 1750 B.C.E. Basalt, entire stele 7 ft. 4½ in. × 25½ in. (approx.). Wearing a conical crown topped with bull's horns, and discharging flames from his shoulders, the god Shamash sits enthroned atop a sacred mountain symbolized by triangular markings beneath his feet.

the eccentricities of the powerful. Written law, on the other hand, permitted a more impersonal (if more objective and impartial) kind of justice than did oral law. It replaced the flexibility of the spoken word with the rigidity of the written word. It did not usually recognize exceptions and was not easily or quickly changed. Ultimately, recorded law shifted the burden of judgment from the individual ruler to the legal establishment. Although written law necessarily restricted individual freedom, it safeguarded the basic values of the community.

Hammurabi's Code covers a broad spectrum of moral, social, and commercial obligations. Its civil and criminal statutes specify penalties for murder, theft, incest, adultery, kidnapping, assault and battery, and many other crimes. More importantly for our understanding of ancient culture, it is a storehouse of information concerning the nature of class divisions, family relations, and human rights. The Code informs us, for instance, on matters of inheritance (clauses 162 and 168), professional obligations (clauses 218, 219, 229, and 232), and the individual's responsibilities to the community (clauses 109 and 152). It also documents the fact that under Babylonian law, individuals were not regarded as equals. Human worth was defined in terms of a person's wealth and status in society. Violence committed by one free person upon another was punished reciprocally (clause 196), but the same violence committed upon a lower-class individual drew considerably lighter punishment (clause 198), and penalties were reduced even further if the victim was a slave (clause 199). Similarly, a principle of "pay according to status" was applied in punishing thieves (clause 8): the upper-class thief was more heavily penalized or fined than the lower-class one. A thief who could not pay at all fell into slavery or was put to death. Slaves, whether captives of war or victims of debt, had no civil rights under law and enjoyed only the protection of the household to which they belonged.

In Babylonian society, women were considered intellectually and physically inferior to men and—much like slaves—were regarded as the personal property of the male head of the household. A woman went from her father's house to that of her husband, where she was expected to bear children (clause 138). Nevertheless, as indicated by the Code, women enjoyed commercial freedom (clause 109) and considerable legal protection (clauses 134, 138, 209, and 210), their value as child-bearers and housekeepers clearly acknowledged. Clause 142 is an astonishingly early example of no-fault divorce: since a husband's neglect of his spouse was not punishable, neither party to the marriage was legally "at fault."

READING 1.3 From Hammurabi's Code (ca. 1750 B.C.E.)

. . . Hammurabi, the shepherd, named by Enlil am I, who increased plenty and abundance. The ancient seed of royalty, the powerful king, the sun of Babylon, who caused light to go forth over the lands of Sumer and Akkad . . . the favorite of Inanna [Ishtar] am I. When Marduk sent me to rule the people

and to bring help to the land, I established law and justice in the language of the land and promoted the welfare of the people.

Clause 8 If a man has stolen an ox, or sheep or an ass, or a pig or a goat, either from a god or a palace, he shall pay thirty-fold. If he is a plebeian,[1] he shall render ten-fold. If the thief has nothing to pay, he shall be slain.

14 If a man has stolen a man's son under age, he shall be slain.

109 If rebels meet in the house of a wine-seller and she does not seize them and take them to the palace, that wine-seller shall be slain.

129 If the wife of a man is found lying with another male, they shall be bound and thrown into the water; unless the husband lets his wife live, and the king lets his servant live.

134 If a man has been taken prisoner, and there is no food in his house, and his wife enters the house of another; then that woman bears no blame.

138 If a man divorces his spouse who has not borne him children, he shall give to her all the silver of the bride-price, and restore to her the dowry which she brought from the house of her father; and so he shall divorce her.

141 If a man's wife, dwelling in a man's house, has set her face to leave, has been guilty of dissipation, has wasted her house, and has neglected her husband; then she shall be prosecuted. If her husband says she is divorced, he shall let her go her way; he shall give her nothing for divorce. If her husband says she is not divorced, her husband may espouse another woman, and that woman shall remain a slave in the house of her husband.

142 If a woman hate her husband, and says "Thou shalt not possess me," the reason for her dislike shall be inquired into. If she is careful and has no fault, but her husband takes himself away and neglects her; then that woman is not to blame. She shall take her dowry and go back to her father's house.

143 If she has not been careful, but runs out, wastes her house, and neglects her husband; then that woman shall be thrown into the water.

152 If, after that woman has entered the man's house, they incur debt, both of them must satisfy the trader.

154 If a man has known his daughter, that man shall be banished from his city.

157 If a man after his father has lain in the breasts of his mother, both of them shall be burned.

162 If a man has married a wife, and she has borne children, and that woman has gone to her fate; then her father has no claim upon her dowry. The dowry is her children's.

168 If a man has set his face to disown his son, and has said to the judge, "I disown my son," then the judge shall look into his reasons. If the son has not borne a heavy crime which would justify his being disowned from filiation, then the father shall not disown his son from filiation.

195 If a son has struck his father, his hand shall be cut off.

196 If a man has destroyed the eye of a free man,[2] his own eye shall be destroyed.

198 If he has destroyed the eye of a plebeian, or broken the bone of a plebeian, he shall pay one mina[3] of silver.

199 If he has destroyed the eye of a man's slave, or broken the bone of a man's slave, he shall pay half his value.

209 If a man strike the daughter of a free man, and causes her fetus to fall; he shall pay ten shekels[4] of silver for her fetus.

210 If that woman die, his daughter shall be slain.

213 If he has struck the slave of a man, and made her fetus fall; he shall pay two shekels of silver.

214 If that slave die, he shall pay a third of a mina of silver.

218 If a doctor has treated a man with a metal knife for a severe wound, and has caused the man to die, or has opened a man's tumor with a metal knife, and destroyed the man's eye; his hands shall be cut off.

219 If a doctor has treated a slave of a plebeian with a metal knife for a severe wound, and caused him to die, he shall render slave for slave.

229 If a builder has built a house for a man, and his work is not strong, and if the house he has built falls in and kills the householder, that builder shall be slain.

232 If goods have been destroyed, he shall replace all that has been destroyed; and because the house that he built was not made strong, and it has fallen in, he shall restore the fallen house out of his own personal property.

282 If a slave shall say to his master, "Thou are not my master," he shall be prosecuted as a slave, and his owner shall cut off his ear.

Q   What does Hammurabi's Code tell us about women in ancient Babylon?

[1] A member of the lower class, probably a peasant who worked the land for the ruling class.

[2] Above the lower-class peasant, the free man who rented land owed only a percentage of the produce to the ruling class.

[3] A monetary unit equal to approximately 1 pound of silver.

[4] 60 shekels = 1 mina.

The Arts in Mesopotamia

The royal graves found at Ur and elsewhere in Mesopotamia have yielded artifacts of great beauty. Jewelry, weapons, household goods, and musical instruments testify to the wealth of Mesopotamia's princely rulers (see Figures 1.3 and 1.4). Rather than building elaborate homes for the dead, however, the inhabitants of Sumer and Babylon raised temple-towers that might bring them closer to heaven. The **ziggurat**—a massive terraced tower made of rubble and brick—was the spiritual center of the Mesopotamian city-state. Serving as both a shrine and a temple, and also possibly as a burial site, it symbolized the sacred mountain that linked the realms of heaven and earth (Figure **1.8**; see also Figure 3.12). At the top level of a series of platforms joined by a steep stairway stood a sanctuary dedicated to local deities. Tended by priests and priestesses, the shrine rooms of the sanctuary stored clay tablets inscribed with cuneiform records of the city's economic activities, its religious customs, and its rites. At Tell Asmar in Sumer the shrine room also housed a remarkable group of statues representing men and women of various sizes, with large, staring eyes and hands clasped across their chests (Figure **1.9**). Carved out of soft stone, alabaster, and marble, some of these cult images may represent the gods, but it is more likely that they are votive (devotional) figures that represent the townspeople of Tell Asmar in the act of worshiping their local deities. The larger figures may be priests, and the smaller figures, laypersons. Rigid and attentive, they stand as if in perpetual prayer. Their enlarged eyes, inlaid

Figure 1.8 Ziggurat at Ur (partially reconstructed), third dynasty of Ur, Iraq, ca. 2150–2050 B.C.E.

Figure 1.9 Statuettes from the Abu Temple, Tell Asmar, Iraq, ca. 2900–2600 B.C.E. Marble, tallest figure ca. 30 in.

with shell, lapis lazuli, and black limestone, convey the impression of dread and awe, visual testimony to the sense of human apprehension in the face of divine power. These images express the insecurity of a people whose vulnerability was an ever-present fact of life.

The Iron Age

During the course of the second millennium B.C.E., all of Mesopotamia felt the effects of a new technology: iron was introduced into Asia Minor (present-day Turkey) by the Hittites, tribal nomads who built an empire that lasted until ca. 1200 B.C.E. Cheaper to produce and more durable than bronze, iron represented new, superior technology. In addition to their iron weapons, the Hittites made active use of horse-drawn war chariots, which provided increased speed and mobility in battle. The combination of war chariots and iron weapons gave the Hittites clear military superiority over all of Mesopotamia.

As iron technology spread slowly throughout the Near East, it transformed the ancient world. Iron tools contributed to increased agricultural production, which in turn supported an increased population. In the wake of the Iron Age, numerous small states came to flower, bringing with them major cultural innovations. By 1500 B.C.E., for instance, the Phoenicians, an energetic seafaring people who lived on the Mediterranean Sea (see Map 1.1), had developed an alphabet of twenty-two signs. These signs eventually replaced earlier forms of script and became the basis of all Western

alphabets. In Asia Minor, the Lydians, successors to the Hittites, began the practice of minting coins. And along the arid coast of the eastern Mediterranean, a nomadic people known as the Hebrews founded a theocratic state based on a unique belief system that would become the wellspring of three great world religions: Judaism, Christianity, and Islam.

The Hebrews

Archeologists have traced the origins of the tribal people called by their neighbors *habiru* or "Hebrews" to the region of Sumer. While their history originates around 2000 B.C.E., the books from which we reconstruct that history (known collectively as the Bible, from the Greek word *biblia*, meaning "books") were written some 1000 years later. The beginnings of Hebrew history are associated with the name Abraham of Ur, the patriarch who is believed to have led the Hebrews westward across the Fertile Crescent to settle in Canaan (ancient Israel, see Map 1.1). In Canaan, according to the first book of the Bible (Genesis), a special bond or **covenant** was forged between God and Abraham ("I will be your God, you will be my people," Genesis 17:7). In return for their unswerving obedience and loyalty, God would protect Abraham's descendants, giving them "all the land of Canaan for an everlasting possession" in order that they might become "a great nation" (Genesis 17:8).

Some time after 1700 B.C.E., the Hebrews migrated into Egypt, there to prosper until, during a period of political and military instability, they were reduced to the status of state slaves. Their liberation occurred under the leadership of the patriarch Moses (ca. 1250 B.C.E.), who led the Hebrews across the Red Sea (then probably a reed swamp); the event became the basis for the second book of the Hebrew Bible, Exodus (literally, "going out"). Since the "promised land" of Canaan was occupied by local tribes with sizable military strength, the Hebrews settled in the Sinai desert near the Dead Sea. Here, during a forty-year period that archeologists place some time between 1300 and 1150 B.C.E., the Hebrews forged the fundamentals of their faith: **monotheism**, the belief in a single, all-powerful creator-god,* and the renewal of the covenant binding them to their god in exchange for divine protection. The terms of the covenant required obedience to a set of ethical and spiritual obligations, delivered by Moses, and known as the Ten Commandments (the Decalogue). These moral laws define the proper relationship between God and the faithful; they also define the ethical obligations between and among the members of the Hebrew community.

Hebrew Monotheism

Monotheism first appeared in the ancient world around 1350 B.C.E. In Egypt, the pharaoh Amenhotep IV (Akhenaten) advanced the worship of the sun god Aten as the country's sole deity, more powerful than all the other Egyptian gods (see chapter 2). But Hebrew monotheism differed from that of Egypt, for while Aten was elevated above the other gods of the Egyptian pantheon, the Hebrews perceived their god as the one and *only* god. Moreover, while Aten (like other ancient gods) was associated with a specific natural phenomenon, in his case the sun, the god of the Hebrews was said to transcend nature and all natural phenomena. Hebrew religious beliefs also stood apart from those of other Mesopotamian societies. As Supreme Creator, the Hebrew god did not descend from nature or from other gods, but preceded the physical universe. Unlike the Babylonian universe, described as spontaneously generated and perpetually chaotic, the Hebrew Creation (see Reading 1.4a) was divinely planned and invested with moral order by a benevolent, all-knowing Being. Finally, in contrast to the Babylonian world, where squabbling gods made human beings their servants, the Hebrew universe was the gift given by its Creator to his supreme creation: humankind.

The Hebrew belief system stands apart from other ancient concepts of divine power in yet another dimension: its ethical charge. *Ethical monotheism*, the veneration of a single god as moral monitor, was unique in the ancient world. Its practice dignified individual moral judgment and became the most lasting of the Hebrew contributions to world culture.

* In the Hebrew Bible, God's name is written with four consonants (the Latinized letters YHWH), pronounced "Yahweh." This ancient name was considered too sacred to speak or write; other names for God (such as *Elohim*) found in the Hebrew Bible probably reflect different aspects of God's divinity. Greek transcriptions of the Bible replaced the Hebrew YHWH with *Kyrios* ("Lord"), while medieval Latin bibles translated God's name as "Jehovah."

The Hebrew Bible

The excerpts that follow belong to the Hebrew Bible (often called the Old Testament to distinguish it from the Christian canon known as the New Testament). Like the *Epic of Gilgamesh*, the stories that make up the early history of the Hebrews were passed orally from generation to generation, and recorded in the centuries following the founding of the first Hebrew state in 1000 B.C.E. The first five books of the Bible, known as the **Torah** (literally "instruction"), were assembled from four main sources some time between the tenth and seventh centuries B.C.E. Parts of the text in the first book of the Torah, Genesis, belong to a common context: the world and lore of ancient Sumer. The story of the Flood, for instance, appears in both Genesis and the *Epic of Gilgamesh*, as well as in other Mesopotamian texts. Like the *Epic of Gilgamesh*, the Bible conflates centuries of fact and legend. Its significance as great literature is unquestionable, but its value as a historical document remains in question. It is held by many as the revealed word of God, and is regarded as sacred scripture by the adherents of Judaism, Christianity, and Islam.

— READING 1.4a From the Hebrew Bible (Genesis 1, 2)

Chapter 1
The Creation
[26]Then God said, "Let us make man in our image, according to our likeness; and let them rule over the fish of the sea and over the birds of the sky and over the cattle and over all the earth, and over every creeping thing that creeps on the earth."

[27]God created man in his own image, in the image of God he created him; male and female he created them.

[28]God blessed them; and God said to them, "Be fruitful and multiply, and fill the earth, and subdue it; and rule over the fish of the sea and over the birds of the sky and over every living thing that moves on the earth." [29]Then God said, "Behold, I have given you every plant yielding seed that is on the surface of all the earth, and every tree which has fruit yielding seed; it shall be food for you; [30]and to every beast of the earth and to every bird of the sky and to every thing that moves on the earth which has life, I have given every green plant for food"; and it was so. [31]God saw all that he had made, and behold, it was very good. And there was evening and there was morning, the sixth day.

Chapter 2
The Creation of man and woman
[1]Thus the heavens and the earth were completed, and all their hosts. [2]By the seventh day God completed his work which he had done, and he rested on the seventh day from all his work which he had done. [3]Then God blessed the seventh day and sanctified it, because in it he rested from all his work which God had created and made.

[4]This is the account of the heavens and the earth when they were created, in the day that the Lord God made earth and heaven.

[5]Now no shrub of the field was yet in the earth, and no plant of the field had yet sprouted, for the Lord God had not sent rain upon the earth, and there was no man to cultivate the ground. [6]But a mist used to rise from the earth and water the whole surface of the

Translating the Hebrew Bible

One's understanding and interpretation of the Hebrew Bible depends to a large extent on which translation one reads. Generated over a thousand-year period, the largest portion of the Bible was written in ancient Hebrew, while some of the later chapters were written in Aramaic. A Greek version of the Hebrew Bible did not appear until the second century B.C.E. (see chapter 8). The first Latin translation was made by Jerome, a fourth-century church father who was versed in Greek, Hebrew, and Aramaic. In the course of this and later translations, the Hebrew Bible was Christianized. For example, Jerome translated the Hebrew word *nefesh*, meaning "life breath" or "life," as the Latin word *anima*. Subsequent translations, such as the seventeenth-century authorized English translation known as the King James Bible, translated *anima* as "soul," suggesting a Christian body/soul dualism (with implications of an afterlife) that is absent from the early portions of the Hebrew Bible.

A second example: the King James Bible translates the Hebrew *Sheol* as the English word "Hell." *Sheol*, however, describes a shadowy underworld, the common grave of the good and bad alike (see the Book of Job, 14:13, Reading 1.4d). There is no explicit designation of Heaven and Hell as places or conditions of reward and punishment in the Hebrew Bible. The first reference to the "Kingdom of God," taken by some to suggest Heaven, occurs in the Book of Daniel, written in Aramaic in the second century B.C.E. While the accurate translation of the Bible may not be crucial to belief, it remains critical to scholarly debate concerning the meaning and interpretation of the West's primary scripture.

---

ground. [7]Then the Lord God formed man of dust from the ground, and breathed into his nostrils the breath of life; and man became a living being.

[8]The Lord God planted a garden toward the east, in Eden; and there he placed the man whom he had formed. [9]Out of the ground the Lord God caused to grow every tree that is pleasing to the sight and good for food; the tree of life also in the midst of the garden, and the tree of the knowledge of good and evil.

[10]Now a river flowed out of Eden to water the garden; and from there it divided and became four rivers. [11]The name of the first is Pishon; it flows around the whole land of Havilah, where there is gold. [12]The gold of that land is good; the bdellium* and the onyx** stone are there. [13]The name of the second river is Gihon; it flows around the whole land of Cush. [14]The name of the third river is Tigris; it flows east of Assyria. And the fourth river is the Euphrates.

[15]Then the Lord God took the man and put him into the garden of Eden to cultivate it and keep it. [16]The Lord God commanded the man, saying, "From any tree of the garden you may eat freely; [17]but from the tree of the knowledge of good and evil you shall not eat, for in the day that you eat from it you will surely die."

[18]Then the Lord God said, "It is not good for the man to be alone; I will make him a helper suitable for him." [19]Out of the ground the Lord God formed every beast of the field and every bird of the sky, and brought them to the man to see what he would call them; and whatever the man called a living creature, that was its name. [20]The man gave names to all the cattle, and to the birds of the sky, and to every beast of the field, but for Adam there was not found a helper suitable for him. [21]So the Lord God caused a deep sleep to fall upon the man, and he slept; then he took one of his ribs and closed up the flesh at that place. [22]The Lord God fashioned into a woman the rib which he had taken from the man, and brought her to the man. [23]The man said,

"This is now bone of my bones,
And flesh of my flesh;
She shall be called Woman,
Because she was taken out of Man."

[24]For this reason a man shall leave his father and his mother, and be joined to his wife; and they shall become one flesh.

[25]And the man and his wife were both naked and were not ashamed.

Q How does this creation story differ from those in Readings 0.1 and 1.1?

The Hebrew Laws

Two groups of laws are represented below. In the first group, which is framed in the negative, the consequences of violating the law are left unspecified. There is no promise of reward for obedience, no promise of heaven, no threat of hell; only the terrible warning that God will punish those who fail to keep the commandments to the third generation. That is, the fault of the parents will fall on their children, grandchildren, and great-grandchildren (Exodus 20:5).

The legal practices in the second excerpt, which belongs to a much larger body of Hebrew laws, resemble those of Hammurabi (Reading 1.3). These, which deal primarily with social obligations, prescribe specific penalties for their violation. Some so closely parallel the laws of the First Babylonian Empire that scholars believe both look back to a common source. It is worth noting, however, a major difference between the laws of the Hebrews and those of Babylon: among the Hebrews, punishment was not levied according to social class. This is not to say that class distinctions did not exist in Hebrew society, but rather that the law was meant

---

* Variously interpreted as a deep-red gem or a pearl.
** A semiprecious red stone (carnelian).

to apply equally to all classes, with the exception of slaves. The humanitarian bias of the Hebrew laws is best reflected in God's frequent reminder to the Hebrews that since they themselves were once aliens and slaves, they must treat even the lowest members of the social order as worthy human beings. If Babylonian law prized economic prosperity and political stability, it was the unity of religious and moral life that formed the core of the Hebrew message.

READING 1.4b From the Hebrew Bible (Exodus 20:1–21; 21:1–2, 18–27, 37; 23:1–9)

The Ten Commandments (The Decalogue)
[1]Then God spoke all these words, saying, [2]"I am the LORD your God, who brought you out of the land of Egypt, out of the house of slavery.

[3]"You shall have no other gods before me.

[4]"You shall not make for yourself an idol, or any likeness of what is in heaven above or on the earth beneath or in the water under the earth.

[5]You shall not worship them or serve them; for I, the LORD your God, am a jealous God, visiting the iniquity of the fathers on the children, on the third and the fourth generations of those who hate me, [6]but showing loving kindness to thousands, to those who love me and keep my commandments.

[7]"You shall not take the name of the LORD your God in vain, for the LORD will not leave him unpunished who takes his name in vain.

[8]"Remember the sabbath day, to keep it holy. [9]Six days you shall labor and do all your work, [10]but the seventh day is a sabbath of the LORD your God; in it you shall not do any work, you or your son or your daughter, your male or your female servant or your cattle or your sojourner who stays with you. [11]For in six days the LORD made the heavens and the earth, the sea and all that is in them, and rested on the seventh day; therefore the LORD blessed the sabbath day and made it holy.

[12]"Honor your father and your mother, that your days may be prolonged in the land which the LORD your God gives you.

[13]"You shall not murder.

[14]"You shall not commit adultery.

[15]"You shall not steal.

[16]"You shall not bear false witness against your neighbor.

[17]"You shall not covet your neighbor's house; you shall not covet your neighbor's wife or his male servant or his female servant or his ox or his donkey or anything that belongs to your neighbor."

[18]All the people perceived the thunder and the lightning flashes and the sound of the trumpet and the mountain smoking; and when the people saw it, they trembled and stood at a distance. [19]Then they said to Moses, "Speak to us yourself and we will listen; but let not God speak to us, or we will die." [20]Moses said to the people, "Do not be afraid; for God has come in order to test you, and in order that the fear of him may remain with you, so that you may not sin." [21]So the people stood at a distance, while Moses approached the thick cloud where God was.

Ordinances for the people
[1]"Now these are the ordinances which you are to set before them: [2]If you buy a Hebrew slave, he shall serve for six years; but on the seventh he shall go out as a free man without payment."

Personal injuries
[18]"If men have a quarrel and one strikes the other with a stone or with his fist, and he does not die but remains in bed, [19]if he gets up and walks around outside on his staff, then he who struck him shall go unpunished; he shall only pay for his loss of time, and shall take care of him until he is completely healed.

[20]"If a man strikes his male or female slave with a rod and he dies at his hand, he shall be punished. [21]If, however, he survives a day or two, no vengeance shall be taken; for he is his property.

[22]"If men struggle with each other and strike a woman with child so that she gives birth prematurely, yet there is no injury, he shall surely be fined as the woman's husband may demand of him, and he shall pay as the judges decide. [23]But if there is any further injury, then you shall appoint as a penalty life for life, [24]eye for eye, tooth for tooth, hand for hand, foot for foot, [25]burn for burn, wound for wound, bruise for bruise.

[26]"If a man strikes the eye of his male or female slave, and destroys it, he shall let him go free on account of his eye. [27]And if he knocks out a tooth of his male or female slave, he shall let him go free on account of his tooth."

. . . .

Theft of animals
[37]"When someone steals an ox or a sheep and slaughters or sells it, he shall restore five oxen for the one ox, and four sheep for the one sheep."

Sundry laws
[1]"You shall not bear a false report; do not join your hand with a wicked man to be a malicious witness. [2]You shall not follow the masses in doing evil, nor shall you testify in a dispute so as to turn aside after a multitude in order to pervert justice; [3]nor shall you be partial to a poor man in his dispute.

[4]"If you meet your enemy's ox or his donkey wandering away, you shall surely return it to him. [5]If you see the donkey of one who hates you lying helpless under its load, you shall refrain from leaving it to him, you shall surely release it with him.

[6]"You shall not pervert the justice due to your needy brother in his dispute.

[7]Keep far from a false charge, and do not kill the innocent or the righteous, for I will not acquit the guilty. [8]"You shall not take a bribe, for a bribe blinds the clear-sighted and subverts the cause of the just.

[9]"You shall not oppress a stranger, since you yourselves know the feelings of a stranger, for you also were strangers in the land of Egypt."

Q **Why are many of the Commandments framed in the negative?**

Q **How do these laws differ from those in Hammurabi's Code?**

The Hebrew State and the Social Order

Under the military leadership of the patriarch Joshua, the Hebrews returned to Canaan, gradually wresting control of the "promised land" from powerful tribes of Philistines ("People of the Sea"). The new Hebrew state consisted

Figure 1.10 Reconstruction of Solomon's Temple.

city of Jerusalem (see Map 1.1) by constructing a royal palace and a magnificent temple (Figure **1.10**) to enshrine the Ark of the Covenant. Lacking the raw materials for this enterprise, he established trade relations with the wealthy neighboring state of Phoenicia, which provided timber from nearby Lebanon. Ornamentation of the Temple was abstract or symbolic, owing to the biblical injunction against carved images (Exodus 20:4). Prohibiting the representation of three-dimensional form did not so much reflect a fear that the Hebrews might worship pagan idols; rather, it asserted that human efforts to create lifelike images disrespected God as Supreme Creator. Early **synagogues** (houses of worship) were embellished with symbols of the faith, such as the curtained enclosure that sheltered the Torah, the **menorah** (a seven-branched candelabrum), and a **shofar** (ram's horn used to call the faithful to prayer) (Figure **1.11**).

The social order of the Hebrews was shaped by biblical precepts. Between Hebrew kings and their people, there existed a covenant—protection in exchange for loyalty and obedience—similar to that which characterized the relationship between God and the Hebrews. This same patriarchal bond also prevailed between Jewish fathers and their families. Hebrew kings were considered the divinely appointed representatives of God; and Hebrew wives and children came under the direct control of the male head of the household and were listed among his possessions. In short, the covenant between God and the Hebrews, as

of twelve tribes, each descended from one of the sons of Jacob, whom God had named "Israel." Under the rule of the Hebrew kings Saul (ca. 1040–1000 B.C.E.), David (ca. 1000–960 B.C.E.), and Solomon (ca. 960–920 B.C.E.), Canaan became a powerful state defended by armies equipped with iron war chariots. As related in the Book of Kings, the scriptural history of the Hebrew rulers descended from David, Solomon embellished the capital

Figure 1.11 The Ark of the Covenant and sanctuary implements, Hammath, near Tiberias, fourth century. Mosaic, 6 ft. 7 in. × 16 ft. 5 in. The stone tablets bearing the Ten Commandments are said to have been carried back to Canaan in a secure container known as the Ark of the Covenant. In modern synagogues, the Ark houses the Torah.

expressed in the laws, established the model for both secular and familial authority.

The Hebrew Prophets

Toward the end of his reign, Solomon divided the Hebrew state into two administrative divisions: the northern portion, retaining the name Israel with its capital at Samaria, and the southern portion, called Judah (from which comes the name "Jews") with its capital at Jerusalem. While the commercial pursuits of the Hebrew nation brought them wealth and material comforts, the less rigorous cults of Canaanite fertility gods and goddesses lured Hebrews away from strict adherence to their moral obligations. By the eighth century B.C.E., the voices of reform grew loud. A group of religious zealots, known as **prophets** (literally "spokespersons") claimed to have heard words of divine disapproval, indeed, anger. Warning that the violations of the covenant would invite harsh punishment, the prophets Amos, Hosea, and Isaiah urged the Hebrews to return to the laws of the Torah. A century after the fall of Jerusalem to the Assyrians in 722 B.C.E., the prophet Jeremiah urged the Hebrews to reaffirm the covenant, citing the Assyrian assault on Judah as divine chastisement, an expression of God's wrath. Nowhere is the Hebrew concept of destiny as being divinely directed more clearly illustrated than in Jeremiah's message: God rewards and punishes not in a life hereafter, but here on earth.

READING 1.4c From the Hebrew Bible (Jeremiah 11: 1–14)

The broken covenant

[1]The word which came to Jeremiah from the Lord, saying, [2]"Hear the words of this covenant, and speak to the men of Judah and to the inhabitants of Jerusalem; [3]and say to them, Thus says the Lord, the God of Israel, Cursed is the man who does not heed the words of this covenant [4]which I commanded your forefathers in the day that I brought them out of the land of Egypt, from the iron furnace, saying, Listen to my voice, and do according to all which I command you; so you shall be my people, and I will be your God, [5]in order to confirm the oath which I swore to your forefathers, to give them a land flowing with milk and honey, as it is this day." Then I said, "Amen, O Lord." [6]And the Lord said to me, "Proclaim all these words in the cities of Judah and in the streets of Jerusalem, saying, 'Hear the words of this covenant and do them. [7]For I solemnly warned your fathers in the day that I brought them up from the land of Egypt, even to this day, warning persistently, saying, "Listen to my voice." [8]Yet they did not obey or incline their ear, but walked, each one, in the stubbornness of his evil heart; therefore I brought on them all the words of this covenant, which I commanded them to do, but they did not.'"

[9]Then the Lord said to me, "A conspiracy has been found among the men of Judah and among the inhabitants of Jerusalem. [10]They have turned back to the iniquities of their ancestors who refused to hear my words, and they have gone after other gods to serve them; the house of Israel and the house of Judah have broken my covenant which I made with their fathers." [11]Therefore thus says the Lord, "Behold I am bringing disaster on them which they will not be able to escape; though they will cry to me, yet I will not listen to them. [12]Then the cities of Judah and the inhabitants of Jerusalem will go and cry to the gods to whom they burn incense, but they surely will not save them in the time of their disaster.

[13]For your gods are as many as your cities, O Judah; and as many as the streets of Jerusalem are the altars you have set up to the shameful thing, altars to burn incense to Baal.

[14]"Therefore do not pray for this people, nor lift up a cry or prayer for them; for I will not listen when they call to me because of their disaster."

Q **For what failings does Jeremiah chastise the Hebrews?**

The Babylonian Captivity and the Book of Job

In 586 B.C.E., Judah fell to Chaldean armies led by the mighty King Nebuchadnezzar (ca. 630–562 B.C.E.). Nebuchadnezzar burned Jerusalem, raided the Temple, and took the inhabitants of the city into captivity. In the newly restored city of Babylon, with its glazed brick portals (Figure **1.12**), its resplendent "hanging" gardens, its towering ziggurat—the prototype for the Tower of Babel

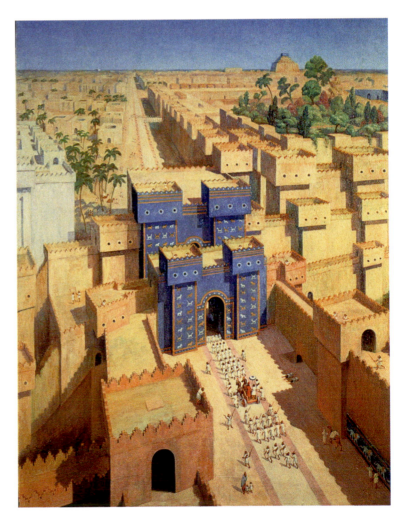

Figure 1.12 A drawing of Babylon as it might have looked in the sixth century B.C.E. The Ishtar Gate, one of Babylon's eight monumental portals, spanned the north entrance route into the city. Faced with deep blue glazed bricks, it is the earliest example of a round arch employed on a colossal scale. The palace of Nebuchadnezzar II and the Hanging Gardens lie behind and to its right. On the horizon and the east bank of the Euphrates looms the Marduk Ziggurat.

described in Genesis—the Hebrews experienced almost fifty years of exile (586–538 B.C.E.). Their despair and doubt in the absolute goodness of God are voiced in the Book of Job, probably written in the years after the Babylonian Captivity. The finest example of wisdom literature in the Hebrew Bible, the Book of Job raises the question of unjustified suffering in a universe governed by a merciful god. The "blameless and upright" Job has obeyed the Commandments and has been a devoted servant of God throughout his life. Yet he is tested unmercifully by the loss of his possessions, his family, and his health. His wife begs him to renounce God, and his friends encourage him to acknowledge his sinfulness. But Job defiantly protests that he has given God no cause for anger. Job asks a universal question: "If there is no heaven (and thus no justice after death), how can a good man's suffering be justified?" or simply phrased, "Why do bad things happen to good people?"

READING 1.4d From the Hebrew Bible (Job 1; 2; 3:1–5; 7:17–21; 14; 38:1–18; 42:1–6)

The Book of Job

Chapter 1: Job's character and wealth

[1]There was a man in the land of Uz whose name was Job; and that man was blameless, upright, fearing God and turning away from evil. [2]Seven sons and three daughters were born to him. [3]His possessions also were 7,000 sheep, 3,000 camels, 500 yoke of oxen, 500 female donkeys, and very many servants; and that man was the greatest of all the men of the east. [4]His sons used to go and hold a feast in the house of each one on his day, and they would send and invite their three sisters to eat and drink with them. [5]When the days of feasting had completed their cycle, Job would send and consecrate them, rising up early in the morning and offering burnt offerings according to the number of them all; for Job said, "Perhaps my sons have sinned and cursed God in their hearts." Thus Job did continually.

[6]Now there was a day when the sons of God came to present themselves before the Lord, and Satan also came among them. [7]The Lord said to Satan, "From where do you come?" Then Satan* answered the Lord and said, "From roaming about on the earth and walking around on it." [8]The Lord said to Satan, "Have you considered my servant Job? For there is no one like him on the earth, a blameless and upright man, fearing God and turning away from evil." [9]Then Satan answered the Lord, "Does Job fear God for nothing? [10]Have you not made a hedge about him and his house and all that he has, on every side? You have blessed the work of his hands, and his possessions have increased in the land. [11]But put forth your hand now and touch all that he has; he will surely curse you to your face." [12]Then the Lord said to Satan, "Behold, all that he has is in your power, only do not put forth your hand on him." So Satan departed from the presence of the Lord.

Satan allowed to test Job

[13]Now on the day when his sons and his daughters were eating

* Literally, "adversary."

and drinking wine in their oldest brother's house, [14]a messenger came to Job and said, "The oxen were plowing and the donkeys feeding beside them, [15]and the Sabeans attacked and took them. They also slew the servants with the edge of the sword, and I alone have escaped to tell you." [16]While he was still speaking, another also came and said, "The fire of God fell from heaven and burned up the sheep and the servants and consumed them, and I alone have escaped to tell you." [17]While he was still speaking, another also came and said, "The Chaldeans formed three bands and made a raid on the camels and took them and slew the servants with the edge of the sword, and I alone have escaped to tell you." [18]While he was still speaking, another also came and said, "Your sons and your daughters were eating and drinking wine in their oldest brother's house, [19]and behold, a great wind came from across the wilderness and struck the four corners of the house, and it fell on the young people and they died, and I alone have escaped to tell you."

[20]Then Job arose and tore his robe and shaved his head, and he fell to the ground and worshiped. [21]He said,

"Naked I came from my mother's womb,
And naked I shall return there.
The Lord gave and the Lord has taken away.
Blessed be the name of the Lord."

[22]Through all this Job did not sin nor did he blame God.

Chapter 2: Job loses his health

[1]Again there was a day when the sons of God came to present themselves before the Lord, and Satan also came among them to present himself before the Lord. [2]The Lord said to Satan, "Where have you come from?" Then Satan answered the Lord and said, "From roaming about on the earth and walking around on it." [3]The Lord said to Satan, "Have you considered my servant Job? For there is no one like him on the earth, a blameless and upright man fearing God and turning away from evil. And he still holds fast his integrity, although you incited me against him to ruin him without cause." [4]Satan answered the Lord and said, "Skin for skin! Yes, all that a man has he will give for his life. [5]However, put forth your hand now, and touch his bone and his flesh; he will curse you to your face." [6]So the Lord said to Satan, "Behold, he is in your power, only spare his life."

[7]Then Satan went out from the presence of the Lord and smote Job with sore boils from the sole of his foot to the crown of his head. [8]And he took a potsherd to scrape himself while he was sitting among the ashes. [9]Then his wife said to him, "Do you still hold fast your integrity? Curse God and die!" [10]But he said to her, "You speak as one of the foolish women speaks. Shall we indeed accept good from God and not accept adversity?" In all this Job did not sin with his lips.

[11]Now when Job's three friends heard of all this adversity that had come upon him, they came each one from his own place, Eliphaz the Temanite, Bildad the Shuhite and Zophar the Naamathite; and they made an appointment together to come to sympathize with him and comfort him. [12]When they lifted up their eyes at a distance and did not recognize him, they raised their voices and wept. And each of them tore his robe and they threw dust over their heads toward the sky. [13]Then they sat down on the ground with him for seven days and seven nights with no one speaking a word to him, for they saw that his pain was very great.

Chapter 3: Job's lament

[1]Afterward Job opened his mouth and cursed the day of his birth. [2]And Job said,

[3]"Let the day perish on which I was to be born,
And the night which said, 'A boy is conceived.'
[4]"May that day be darkness;
Let not God above care for it,
Nor light shine on it.
[5]"Let darkness and black gloom claim it;
Let a cloud settle on it;
Let the blackness of the day terrify it."

Chapter 7: Job's life seems futile

[17]"What is man that you magnify him,
And that you are concerned about him,
[18]That you examine him every morning
And try him every moment?
[19]"Will you never turn your gaze away from me,
Nor let me alone until I swallow my spittle?
[20]"Have I sinned? What have I done to you,
O watcher of men?
Why have you set me as your target,
So that I am a burden to myself?
[21]"Why then do you not pardon my transgression
And take away my iniquity?
For now I will lie down in the dust;
And you will seek me, but I will not be."

Chapter 14: Job speaks of the finality of death

[1]"Man, who is born of woman,
Is short-lived and full of turmoil.
[2]"Like a flower he comes forth and withers.
He also flees like a shadow and does not remain.
[3]"You also open your eyes on him
And bring him into judgment with yourself.
[4]"Who can make the clean out of the unclean?
No one!
[5]"Since his days are determined,
The number of his months is with you;
And his limits you have set so that he cannot pass.
[6]"Turn your gaze from him that he may rest,
Until he fulfills his day like a hired man.
[7]"For there is hope for a tree,
When it is cut down, that it will sprout again,
And its shoots will not fail.
[8]"Though its roots grow old in the ground
And its stump dies in the dry soil,
[9]At the scent of water it will flourish
And put forth sprigs like a plant.
[10]"But man dies and lies prostrate [cast face down].
Man expires, and where is he?
[11]"As water evaporates from the sea,
And a river becomes parched and dried up,
[12]So man lies down and does not rise.
Until the heavens are no longer,
He will not awake nor be aroused out of his sleep.
[13]"Oh that you would hide me in Sheol,**

**The shadowy underworld.

That you would conceal me until your wrath returns to you,
That you would set a limit for me and remember me!
[14]"If a man dies, will he live again?
All the days of my struggle I will wait
Until my change comes.
[15]"You will call, and I will answer you;
You will long for the work of your hands.
[16]"For now you number my steps,
You do not observe my sin.
[17]"My transgression is sealed up in a bag,
And you wrap up my iniquity.
[18]"But the falling mountain crumbles away,
And the rock moves from its place;
[19]Water wears away stones,
Its torrents wash away the dust of the earth;
So you destroy man's hope.
[20]"You forever overpower him and he departs;
You change his appearance and send him away.
[21]"His sons achieve honor, but he does not know it;
Or they become insignificant, but he does not perceive it.
[22]"But his body pains him,
And he mourns only for himself."

Chapter 38: God speaks now to Job

[1]Then the Lord answered Job out of the whirlwind and said,
[2]"Who is this that darkens counsel
By words without knowledge?
[3]"Now gird up your loins like a man,
And I will ask you, and you instruct me!
[4]"Where were you when I laid the foundation of the earth?
Tell me, if you have understanding,
[5]Who set its measurements? Since you know.
Or who stretched the line on it?
[6]"On what were its bases sunk?
Or who laid its cornerstone,
[7]When the morning stars sang together
And all the sons of God shouted for joy?
[8]"Or who enclosed the sea with doors
When, bursting forth, it went out from the womb;
[9]When I made a cloud its garment
And thick darkness its swaddling band,
[10]And I placed boundaries on it
And set a bolt and doors,
[11]And I said, 'Thus far you shall come, but no farther;
And here shall your proud waves stop'?"

God's mighty power

[12]"Have you ever in your life commanded the morning,
And caused the dawn to know its place,
[13]That it might take hold of the ends of the earth,
And the wicked be shaken out of it?
[14]"It is changed like clay under the seal;
And they stand forth like a garment [in splendor].
[15]"From the wicked their light is withheld,
And the uplifted arm is broken.
[16]"Have you entered into the springs of the sea
Or walked in the recesses of the deep?
[17]"Have the gates of death been revealed to you,
Or have you seen the gates of deep darkness?

¹⁸"Have you understood the expanse of the earth?
Tell me, if you know all this."

Chapter 42: Job's confession
¹Then Job answered the Lord and said,
²"I know that you can do all things,
And that no purpose of yours can be thwarted.
³'Who is this that hides counsel without knowledge?'
Therefore I have declared that which I did not understand,
Things too wonderful for me, which I did not know."
⁴"Hear, now, and I will speak;
I will ask you, and you instruct me."
⁵"I have heard of you by the hearing of the ear;
But now my eye sees you;
⁶Therefore I retract,
And I repent in dust and ashes."

— **Q Why is the Book of Job called "wisdom literature"?**

— **Q Why is this book essential to an understanding of the Hebrew covenant?**

God's answer to Job is an eloquent vindication of unquestioned faith: God's power is immense and human beings cannot expect rational explanations of the divine will. Proclaiming the magnitude of divine power and the fragility of humankind, the Book of Job confirms the pivotal role of faith (the belief and trust in God) that sustains the Hebrew covenant. The anxious sense of human vulnerability that pervades the Book of Job recalls the *Epic of Gilgamesh*. Job and Gilgamesh are tested by superhuman forces, and both come to realize that misfortune and suffering are typical of the human condition. Gilgamesh seeks but fails to secure personal immortality; Job solicits God's promise of heavenly reward but fails to secure assurance that once dead, he might return to life. Just as Utnapishtim tells Gilgamesh, "There is no permanence," so Job laments that man born of woman "Like a flower he comes forth and withers. He also flees like a shadow and does not remain" (Job 14.2). Such pessimism was not uncommon in Mesopotamia, the region in which both the *Epic of Gilgamesh* and the Hebrew Bible originated. The notion of life after death (so prominent in Egyptian religious thought; see chapter 2) is as elusive a concept in Hebraic literature as it is in Mesopotamian myth. Job anticipates a final departure to an underworld, an abode of the dead known among the Hebrews as *Sheol* or Shadowland. Yet, even without the promise of reward, Job remains stubbornly faithful to the covenant. His tragic vision involves the gradual but dignified acceptance of his place in a divinely governed universe.

The Book of Psalms

In 538 B.C.E., the Jewish remnant returned to Jerusalem to rebuild the Temple of Solomon. The post-exile age—the period following the Babylonian Captivity—was marked by apocalyptic hopes and the renewal of the covenant. This era also produced one of the best-loved books of the Hebrew Bible. The Book of Psalms (or "Psalter," from

The Hebrew Bible

The Torah	Genesis	Numbers
	Exodus	Deuteronomy
	Leviticus	
The Prophets	Joshua	Isaiah
	Judges	Jeremiah
	Samuel I & II	Ezekiel
	Kings I & II	Twelve Minor Prophets
The Writings	Psalms	Ecclesiastes
	Proverbs	Esther
	Job	Daniel
	Song of Songs	Ezra
	Ruth	Nehemiah
	Lamentations	Chronicles I & II

the Greek word *psalterion*, a stringed instrument) is a collection of 150 songs of praise, thanksgiving, confession, and supplication. Traditionally attributed to King David, whose name was associated with leadership in religious music, the psalms were transmitted orally for more than half a century. In Hebrew culture, music was closely tied to prayer and worship. **Cantors** chanted biblical passages as part of the Hebrew **liturgy** (the rituals for public worship), and members of the congregation participated in the singing of psalms. Both prayers and psalms might be performed in the **responsory** style, in which the congregation answered the voice of the cantor, or in the **antiphonal** manner, in which the cantor and the congregation sang alternate verses. Sung in public worship, the psalms forge a link between the individual and the Hebrew community, as reflected in the line: "O magnify the Lord with me, and let us exalt his name together!" (Ps. 34:3). Psalm 8, reproduced below, is one of the most eloquent songs of praise in the Hebrew Bible.

— **READING 1.4e** From the Hebrew Bible (Psalms 8: 1–9)

The Lord's glory and man's dignity
¹O Lord, our Lord,
How majestic is your name in all the earth,
Who have displayed your splendor above the heavens!

²From the mouth of infants and nursing babes you have established strength
Because of your adversaries,
To make the enemy and the revengeful cease.

³When I consider your heavens, the work of your fingers,
The moon and the stars, which you have ordained;
⁴What is man that you take thought of him,
And the son of man that you care for him?

⁵Yet you have made him a little lower than God,
And you crown him with glory and majesty!

⁶You make him to rule over the works of your hands;
You have put all things under his feet,

⁷All sheep and oxen,
And also the beasts of the field,
⁸The birds of the heavens and the fish of the sea,
Whatever passes through the paths of the seas.

⁹O Lord, our Lord,
How majestic is your name in all the earth!

Q How does this song of praise compare with "The Hymn to the Aten" (Reading 2.1)?

The Hebrew Bible played a major role in shaping the humanistic tradition in the West. It provided the religious and ethical foundations for Judaism, and, almost 2000 years after the death of Abraham, for Christianity and Islam. Biblical teachings, including the belief in a single, personal, caring god who intervenes on behalf of a faithful people, have become fundamental to Western thought. Bible stories—from Genesis to Job—have inspired some of humankind's greatest works of art, music, and literature. And the Book of Psalms, along with the later books of the Bible (see Box above), have had a profound influence on the religious history of the West.

Empires of the Iron Age

Iron technology encouraged the rise of large and powerful empires. Cheaper and stronger weapons meant larger,

more efficient armies: war was no longer the monopoly of the elite. Equipped with iron weapons, the Assyrians (ca. 750–600 B.C.E.), Chaldeans (ca. 600–540 B.C.E.), and Persians (ca. 550–330 B.C.E.) followed one another in conquering vast portions of Mesopotamia. Each of these empires grew in size and authority by imposing military control over territories outside their own natural boundaries—a practice known as *imperialism*.

The Assyrian Empire

The first of the Iron Age empire builders, the Assyrians earned a reputation as the most militant civilization of ancient Mesopotamia. Held together by a powerful army that systematically combined engineering and fighting techniques, the Assyrians turned their iron weapons against most of Mesopotamia. In 721 B.C.E., they conquered Israel and dispersed its population. By the middle of the seventh century B.C.E., they had swallowed up most of the land between the Persian Gulf and the Nile valley. Assyrian power is reflected in the imposing walled citadel of Khorsabad, located some 10 miles from Nineveh (see Map 1.1). Covering 25 acres, this walled complex featured a ziggurat and an elaborate palace with more than 200 rooms: a maze of courtyards, harem quarters, treasuries, and state apartments (Figure **1.13**). The palace walls were adorned with low-relief scenes of war and pillage and with cuneiform inscriptions celebrating Assyrian military victories. One seventh-century B.C.E. relief shows the imperial armies of King Ashurbanipal (668–627 B.C.E.) storming the battlements of an African city

Figure 1.13 Reconstruction of the walled citadel at Khorsabad, Assyria (Iraq), ca. 720 B.C.E.

Figure 1.15 King Ashurnasirpal II killing lions, from the Palace of King Ashurnasirpal II, Nimrud, ca. 883–859 B.C.E. Alabaster relief, 3 ft. 3 in. × 8 ft. 4 in. The most militant of the iron-wielding empires of Mesopotamia, the Assyrians carved low-relief depictions of royal hunts that pitted the courage of the king against the lion, a traditional symbol of power.

(Figure **1.14**). In the lower left, male captives (their chieftains still wearing the feathers of authority) are led away, followed in procession by women, children, and the spoils of war.

Flanking the scenes of military conquest on the palace walls at Nineveh and Nimrud are depictions of the royal lion hunt. Hunting and war, two closely related enterprises, were ideal vehicles by which to display the ruler's courage and physical might. In Assyrian reliefs, the lion, a traditional symbol of power throughout the ancient world, is depicted as the adversary of the king. Ceremonial lion hunts symbolized the invincibility of the monarch, who, in earlier times, might have proved his prowess by

Figure 1.14 Ashurbanipal besieging an Egyptian city, 667 B.C.E. Alabaster relief, 2 ft. 11 in. × 7 ft. 4¼ in.

combating wild animals in the field—in the manner of the legendary Gilgamesh (see Figure 1.3). One dramatic relief from Nimrud depicts a wounded lion fiercely pursuing the royal chariot as it speeds away, while another beast lies dying before the wheels of the king's chariot (Figure **1.15**). Spatial depth is indicated by superimposing the chariot wheels over the rear lion's legs. Yet the heads and legs of the horses are shown on a single plane, and clarity of design required that the second wounded lion, crouching in pain, fit precisely within the space between the front and rear legs of the prancing steeds. The balance between figures (positive shapes) and ground (negative or "empty" space) results in a brilliant formal composition. The Assyrian reliefs—housed in large numbers at the British Museum in London—are superb examples of the artist's ability to infuse violent subject matter with narrative grandeur. If the lion-hunt reliefs made implicit reference to the ruler's invincibility, colossal sculpture clearly manifested his superhuman status. Thirteen-foot-tall hybrid beasts guarded the gateways of Assyrian palaces (see Figure 1.1). Bearing the facial features of the monarch, these colossi united the physical attributes of the bull (virility), the lion (physical strength), and the eagle (predatory agility). The winged, human-headed bulls from the citadel at Khorsabad were power-symbols designed to inspire awe and fear among those who passed beneath their impassive gaze. Clearly, the art of Assyria was visual propaganda, designed not only to celebrate Assyrian rulership, but also to intimidate its enemies.

The Persian Empire

The Persian Empire, the last and the largest of the empires of Mesopotamia, was brought to its peak by Cyrus II (ca. 585–ca. 529 B.C.E.), called "the Great" for his conquests over territories ranging from the frontiers of India to the Mediterranean Sea. The linguistic and ethnic diversity of this empire made it the first multicultural civilization of the ancient world. At Persepolis, its capital and ceremonial center, the Persians built a huge stone palace ornamented with carved reliefs of the king's royal guard.

The powerful monarchs of Persia (modern-day Iran), aided by a large cadre of administrators, oversaw a vast network of roads connecting the major cities of the Empire. Across some 1600 miles of terrain, fresh horses (located at post stations 14 miles apart) carried couriers "unhindered by snow, or rain, or heat, or by the darkness of night," according to the Greek historian Herodotus, who (unwittingly) provided the motto for the United States Postal Service.

The Persians devised a religion based on the teachings of the prophet Zoroaster (ca. 628–ca. 551 B.C.E.). Denying the nature gods of earlier times, Zoroaster exalted the primal spirit Ahura-Mazda ("Wise Lord"), who, opposing the evil spirit Angra Mainyu, demanded good thoughts, good works, and good deeds. As described in hymns known as the Gathas, Zoroaster (also known as Zarathustra) taught that life was a battlefield on which the dual forces of light and darkness contended for supremacy. Human beings took part in this cosmic struggle by way of their freedom to

Figure 1.16 Achaemenid (Persian) gold vessel, fifth to third century B.C.E. 6¾ × 9 in.

choose between good and evil, the consequences of which would determine their fate at the end of time. According to Zoroaster, a Last Judgment would consign the wicked to everlasting darkness, while the good would live eternally in an abode of luxury and light: the Persian *pairidaeza*, from which the English word "paradise" derives. Zoroastrianism came to influence the moral teachings of three great world religions: Judaism, Christianity, and Islam (see chapters 8 and 10).

At Persepolis, artists perpetuated the architectural and sculptural traditions of Assyria. The Persians also brought to perfection the art of metalworking that had flourished in Mesopotamia since the beginning of the Bronze Age. Utensils, vessels, and jewelry produced by Persian crafts-people display some of the most intricate and sophisticated techniques of goldworking known to the history of that medium (Figure **1.16**). Many of these techniques would be practiced for centuries to come.

LOOKING BACK

The Land Between the Two Rivers

- The Tigris and Euphrates rivers formed part of a fertile crescent at the western end of Asia; here, agricultural activity encouraged the rise of Sumer, humankind's earliest civilization.
- Mesopotamia's geographic vulnerability contributed to invasion and instability. In the history of its rapid turnover of civilizations, language and government were as versatile and varied as the civilizations themselves.

The Gods of Mesopotamia

- The deities of Mesopotamia were associated with the forces of nature. According to *The Babylonian Creation*, Marduk, hero-god and offspring of Wisdom, destroyed the Great Mother, founded the city of Babylon, and created human beings.

- The *Epic of Gilgamesh*, the world's first heroic epic, follows the semihistorical ruler of Uruk on his quest for everlasting life. The epic reflects the sense of human vulnerability that prevailed in Mesopotamian culture.

The Rulers of Mesopotamia

- Individual priest-kings ruled Sumerian city-states as agents of the gods; they led the army, regulated the supply and distribution of food, provided political and religious leadership, and conducted services designed to win the favor of the gods.
- Around 2350 B.C.E., the Akkadian warlord Sargon I conquered the Sumerian city-states and ruled over them as a theocratic monarch.

The Social Order

- The social order and division of labor that prevailed in Mesopotamia around 2700 B.C.E. are depicted in the Standard of Ur; the ruler and his officials are shown in the top register, soldiers and servants below, and victims of war or slaves at the bottom.
- After 2000 B.C.E., rulers of the city-state of Babylon established the First Babylonian Empire. Its sixth king, Hammurabi, called for a written code of law covering a broad spectrum of moral, social, and commercial obligations.
- Mesopotamian women were considered intellectually and physically inferior to men and were regarded as personal property; however, as indicated by Hammurabi's Code, women enjoyed commercial freedom and gained considerable legal protection.

The Arts in Mesopotamia

- Artifacts from Mesopotamia, including jewelry, weapons, household goods, and musical instruments, testify to the wealth of its early civilizations.
- The ziggurat, the culture's most notable architectural symbol, was the spiritual center of the Mesopotamian city-states. Both a shrine and a temple, it symbolized the sacred mountain that linked heaven and earth.

The Iron Age

- During the second millennium B.C.E., iron was introduced into Asia Minor by the Hittites, tribal nomads who built an empire that lasted until ca. 1200 B.C.E.
- Cheaper and more durable than bronze, iron represented a new, superior technology. Iron tools contributed to increased agricultural production, facilitating the rise of small states, such as Phoenicia and Lydia, while iron weapons and chariots expedited the militant expansion of empires.

The Hebrews

- Archeologists trace the beginnings of Hebrew history to the region of Sumer around 2000 B.C.E. The Hebrew Bible cites Abraham of Ur as the patriarch who led the Hebrews westward across the Fertile Crescent into Canaan.
- The first book of the Hebrew Bible (Genesis) recounts the covenant by which the Hebrew god promised to protect Abraham's descendants in return for their unswerving obedience.
- Hebrew monotheism holds that there is only one god. Believed to transcend nature and all natural phenomena, this god differed from those of other ancient societies.
- The first five books of the Hebrew Bible, collectively known as the Torah, were written down between the tenth and seventh centuries B.C.E.
- The Decalogue, or Ten Commandments, is said to have been handed directly from God to Moses after the Hebrew exodus from Egypt. This set of moral and spiritual obligations is fundamental to ethical monotheism, the belief in God as the sole moral monitor.
- The first Hebrew state was forged under the theocratic rules of Saul, David, and Solomon; it came under successive attacks by Mesopotamia's aggressive empires.
- The writings of the prophets and the Book of Job reflect the Hebrew history of insecurity and exile. The Hebrew Bible provided the religious and ethical foundations for Judaism, Christianity, and Islam.

Empires of the Iron Age

- Equipped with iron weapons, the Assyrians, Chaldeans, and Persians followed one another in conquering large portions of Mesopotamia, creating vast empires.
- The Assyrians combined fighting techniques and engineering ingenuity to swallow up most of the land between the Persian Gulf and the Nile valley by 721 B.C.E.
- The Persian Empire, the last and largest of Mesopotamia's empires, was a multicultural civilization that reached its peak in the sixth century B.C.E. The Persian prophet Zoroaster imagined a cosmic struggle between the forces of good and evil, and warned of a Last Judgment that consigned souls to abodes of light or darkness.

Glossary

antiphonal a type of music in which two or more groups of voices or instruments alternate with one another

cantor the chief singer of the liturgy

covenant contract; the bond between the Hebrew people and their god

empire a state achieved militarily by the unification of territories under a single sovereign power

epic a long narrative poem that recounts the deeds of a legendary or historical hero in his quest for meaning or identity

lapis lazuli a semiprecious blue stone

liturgy the rituals for public worship

menorah a seven-branched candelabrum

monarch a single or sole ruler

monotheism the belief in one and only one god

mosaic a medium by which small pieces of glass or stone are used to ornament a flat surface

polytheism the belief in many gods

prophet (Greek, "one who speaks for another"), a divinely inspired teacher

responsory a type of music in which a single voice answers another voice or a chorus

shofar a trumpet made of a ram's horn, used to summon Jews to prayer

synagogue the Jewish house for worship and religious study

theocracy rule, by god or god's representative

Torah (Hebrew, "instruction," "law," or "teaching"), the first five books of the Hebrew Bible: Genesis, Exodus, Leviticus, Numbers, and Deuteronomy

ziggurat a terraced tower of rubble and brick that served ancient Mesopotamians as a temple-shrine

Africa: Gods, Rulers, and the Social Order

ca. 3100–330 B.C.E.

"The barges sail upstream and downstream too,
for every way is open at your rising."
The Hymn to the Aten

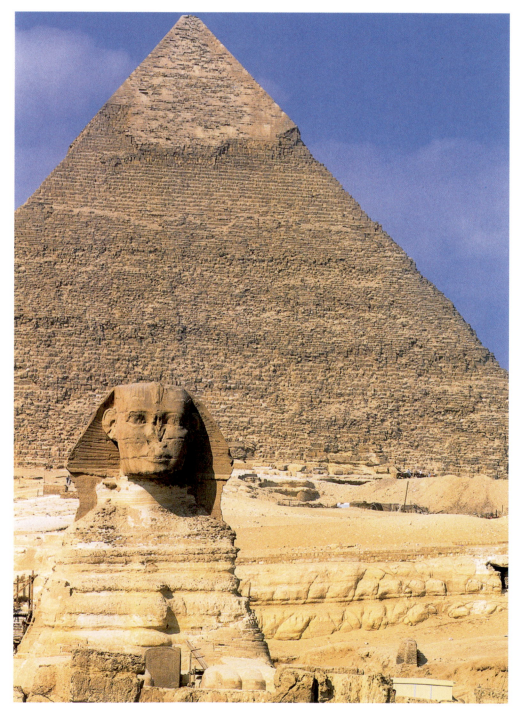

Figure 2.1 Sphinx at Gizeh, Egypt, ca. 2540–2514 B.C.E. Limestone, length 240 ft., height 65 ft. The Sphinx looks to the East: the place of revival and rebirth associated with the rising sun, a natural life force deified by the ancient Egyptians.

In Africa, as in Mesopotamia, the forces of nature challenged the rise of civilization. The sun that nourished a bountiful harvest, the winds that swept away whole villages, the rains that caused rivers to flood the land—all these affected daily life, even as they do in our own time. Among our ancestors, however, for whom survival was a day-to-day struggle, such forces and the gods that represented them assumed supreme importance. The success of ancient Africa's first civilization depended on a shared view of the earthly order as god-given and as immutably fixed in nature, on strong leadership, and on communal cooperation. As in Mesopotamia, the bonds between the divine and secular realms governed social and moral life. So, "gods, rulers, and the social order" remains the threefold focus of our survey.

Africa: Ancient Egypt

Ancient Egyptian civilization emerged along the banks of the Nile River in Northeast Africa. From the heart of Africa, the thin blue thread of the Nile flowed some 4000 miles to its fan-shaped delta at the Mediterranean Sea. Along this river, agricultural villages thrived, coming under the rule of a sole ruler around 3150 B.C.E. Surrounded by sea and desert, Egypt was relatively invulnerable to foreign invasion (Map **2.1**), a condition that lent stability to Egyptian history. Unlike Mesopotamia, home to many different civilizations, ancient Egypt enjoyed a fairly uniform religious, political, and cultural life that lasted for almost 3000 years. Its population shared a common language and a common perception of reality.

The Gods of Ancient Egypt

Geography, climate, and the distinctive features of the natural environment worked to shape the world-views and religious beliefs of all ancient peoples. In the hot, arid climate of Northeast Africa, where ample sunlight made possible the cultivation of crops, the sun god held the place of honor. Variously called Amon, Rē (Ra), or Aten, this god was considered greater than any other deity in the Egyptian pantheon. His cult dominated the polytheistic belief system of ancient Egypt for three millennia. Equally important to Egyptian life was the Nile, the world's longest river. Egypt, called by the Greek historian Herodotus "the gift of the Nile," depended on the annual overflow of the Nile, which left fertile layers of rich silt along its banks. The 365-day cycle of the river's inundation became the basis of the solar calendar and the primary source of Egypt's deep sense of order. In the regularity of the sun's daily cycle and the Nile's annual deluge, ancient Egyptians found security. From the natural elements—the sun, the Nile, and the largely flat topography of North Africa—they also constructed their **cosmology**, that is, their theory of

Map 2.1 Ancient Egypt. The Nile River begins in the mountains of modern-day Ethiopia and southern Sudan. It flows north for more than 4000 miles to the delta, where it empties into the Mediterranean Sea. Ancient Egypt flourished along the 750-mile stretch from Aswan to the Mediterranean. The terms "Upper Egypt" and "Lower Egypt" reflect the fact that the Nile flows from highlands in the south to the lowlands of the north.

the origin and structure of the universe. Egyptian myths of creation describe the earth as a flat platter floating on the waters of the underworld. At the beginning of time, the Nile's primordial waters brought forth a mound of silt, out of which emerged the self-generating sun god; and from that god, the rest of Egypt's gods were born.

Ancient Egyptians viewed the sun's daily ascent in the east as symbolic of the god's "rebirth"; his daily resurrection signified the victory of the forces of day, light, purity, goodness, and life over those of night, darkness, ignorance, evil, and death. In the cyclical regularity of nature evidenced by the daily rising and setting of the sun, the ancient Egyptians perceived both the inevitability of death and the promise of birth. The cult of the sun dominated the religious history of ancient Egypt. In the earliest hymns of the Old Kingdom, Rē (or Ra) was celebrated as the self-generating life force. Like other ancient deities, he was known by many names, each of which described a different aspect of his power: Amun or Amon (giver of the breath

Principal Egyptian Gods

Name	Role	Depicted As
Amon	sun god, creator of heaven and earth	falcon, sun rays
Anubis	patron of embalmers, god of cemeteries	jackal
Aten	god of the solar disk	solar disk
Bes	helper of women in childbirth, protector against snakes	lion-faced dwarf
Hapi	god of the Nile	bull
Hathor	mother, wife, and daughter of Ra, sky goddess	cow
Horus	son of Isis and Osiris, sky god	falcon
Isis	wife of Osiris, mother of Horus, fertility goddess	female
Maat	goddess of truth and universal order	head-feather
Osiris	god of the underworld	mummified king
Ptah	creator of humans, patron of craftspeople	mummified man
Set	brother of Osiris, god of storms and violence	pig, ass, hippopotamus
Thoth	inventor of writing, patron of scribes	ibis

of life), Atum (the setting sun), and Aten (the disk of the sun; see Reading 2.1). Hymns of praise were probably accompanied by rituals of renewal honoring the pharaoh, the divinely appointed representative of the sun:

> Praise to thee, O Rē, when thou settest, Atum . . .
> Divine divinity that came into being of himself,
> Primeval god, that existed at the beginning.

The transfer of power from the sun god to the pharaoh was frequently shown in Egyptian tombs and temples. In a carved relief from the White Chapel at Karnak, the pharaoh Sesostris, wearing the combined crowns of Upper and Lower Egypt, and holding the scepter and staff of authority, receives from Amon the symbol of life known as the *ankh* (Figure **2.2**).

Second only to the sun as the major natural force in Egyptian life was the Nile River. Ancient Egyptians identified the Nile with Osiris, ruler of the underworld and god of the dead. According to Egyptian myth, Osiris was slain by his evil brother, Set, who chopped his body into pieces and threw them into the Nile. But Osiris' loyal wife, Isis, Queen of Heaven, gathered the fragments and restored Osiris to life. The union of Isis and the resurrected Osiris produced a son, Horus, who ultimately avenged his father by overthrowing Set and becoming ruler of Egypt. The Osiris myth vividly describes the idea of resurrection that

Figure 2.2 Amon receives Sesostris (Senusret) I, pillar relief, White Chapel, Karnak, ca. 1925 B.C.E. The god Amon, on the right, grants everlasting life (in the form of the *ankh*) to the Middle Kingdom pharaoh Sesostris. Behind the pharaoh stands the protective falcon-headed god Horus.

was central to the ancient Egyptian belief system. Although the cult of the sun in his various aspects dominated the official religion of Egypt, local gods and goddesses—more than 2000 of them—made up the Egyptian pantheon. These deities, most of whom held multiple powers, played protective roles in the daily lives of the ancient Egyptians. However, the following invocation to Isis, found inscribed on a sculpture of the goddess, suggests her central role among the female deities of Egypt:

> Praise to you, Isis, the Great One
> God's Mother, Lady of Heaven,
> Mistress and Queen of the Gods.

The Rulers of Ancient Egypt

Local rulers governed the Neolithic villages along the Nile until roughly 3150 B.C.E., when they were united under the authority of Egypt's first pharaoh, Narmer (also known as Menes). This important political event—the union of Upper and Lower Egypt—is commemorated on a 2-foot-high slate object known as the Palette of King Narmer (see LOOKING INTO, Figure **2.4**, see page 48), and initiated Egypt's first **dynasty**. For some 2500 years to follow, ancient Egypt was ruled by a succession of dynasties, the history of which was divided into chronological periods by an Egyptian priest of the third century B.C.E.

Civil dissent marked the intermediate period between the Old and Middle kingdoms, while the era between the Middle and New kingdoms (the second intermediate period) withstood the invasion of the Hyksos, warlike tribes who introduced the horse and chariot into Egypt. Following the expulsion of the Hyksos, New Kingdom pharaohs (the word means "great house" in the sense of "first family") created Egypt's first empire, extending royal authority far into Syria, Palestine, and Nubia. The last eleven Egyptian dynasties (XXI–XXXI) struggled through centuries of political volatility. Foreign invasions, ending with the conquest of Egypt by Alexander the Great in 332 B.C.E., finally brought the 3000-year-old civilization to an end.

Throughout their long history, ancient Egyptians viewed the land as sacred. It was owned by the gods, ruled by the pharaohs, and farmed by the peasants with the assistance of slaves. The fruits of each harvest were shared according to the needs of the community. This divinely sanctioned way of life, known as *theocratic socialism*, provided Egypt with an abundance of food and a surplus that encouraged widespread trade. The land itself, however, passed from generation to generation not through the male but

through the female line, that is, from the king's daughter to the man she married. For the pharaoh's son to come to the throne, he would have to marry his own sister or half-sister (hence the numerous brother–sister marriages in Egyptian dynastic history). This tradition, probably related to the practice of tracing parentage to the child-bearer, lasted longer in Egypt than anywhere else in the ancient world. In the free-standing sculpture of the Old Kingdom pharaoh Mycerinus, the queen stands proudly at his side, one arm around his waist and the other gently touching his arm (Figure **2.3**). A sense of shared purpose is conveyed by

Figure 2.3 Pair statue of Mycerinus and Queen Kha-merer-nebty II, Gizeh, Mycerinus, fourth dynasty, ca. 2599–1571 B.C.E. Slate schist, height 4 ft. 6½ in. (complete statue).

Chronology

Early dynastic period	ca. 3100–2700 B.C.E.	(Dynasties I–II)
Old Kingdom	ca. 2700–2150 B.C.E.	(Dynasties III–VI)
Middle Kingdom	ca. 2050–1785 B.C.E.	(Dynasties XI–XII)
New Kingdom	ca. 1575–1085 B.C.E.	(Dynasties XVIII–XX)

The Palette of King Narmer

The back of the slate palette (right) shows the triumphant Narmer seizing a fallen enemy by the hair. Below his feet lie the bodies of the vanquished. To his left, a slave (represented smaller in size than Narmer) dutifully carries his master's sandals. At the upper right is the victorious falcon, symbol of the god Horus. Horus/Narmer holds by the leash the now-subdued lands of Lower Egypt, symbolized by a severed head and **papyrus**, the reedlike plants that grow along the Nile. On the front (left), the top register bears a victory procession flanked by rows of defeated soldiers, who stand with their decapitated heads between their legs.

Figure 2.4 The Palette of King Narmer (front and back), ca. 3100 B.C.E. Slate, height 25 in.

hieroglyph with Narmer's name | royal palace

Narmer wearing crown of Lower Egypt

royal symbols carried in procession

Narmer's vizier

sandal-bearer

the defeated with their decapitated heads

royal lion tamers

long-necked lions

bull symbolizing royal power

city walls

palace of the defeated city

Front

hieroglyph with Narmer's name | Hathor, the sky goddess

Hathor, the sky goddess

Horus, the sky god, holding the conquered by a leash

mace

white crown of Upper Egypt

Narmer

papyrus blossoms, symbols of Lower Egypt

sandal-bearer

hieroglyph identifying Narmer's victim

defeated enemies

Back

Science and Technology

2650 B.C.E.	Pharaoh Khufu (or Cheops) orders construction of the Great Pyramid of Gizeh [†]
1500 B.C.E.	Egyptians employ a simple form of the sundial
1450 B.C.E.	the water clock is devised in Egypt
1400 B.C.E.	glass is produced in Egypt and Mesopotamia

[†]*All dates in this chapter are approximate*

their lifted chins and confident demeanor. While Egypt's rulers were traditionally male, women came to the throne three times. The most notable of all female pharaohs, Hatshepsut (ca. 1500–1447 B.C.E.), governed Egypt for twenty-two years. She is often pictured in male attire, wearing the royal wig and false beard, and carrying the crook and the flail—traditional symbols of rulership.

Egyptian Theocracy

From earliest times, political power was linked with spiritual power and superhuman might. The Egyptians held that divine power flowed from the gods to their royal agents. In this theocracy, reigning monarchs represented heaven's will on earth. While the pharaoh ruled in the name of the immortal and generative sun god, he was also identified with the falcon-headed god Horus, the avenging son of Osiris and Isis (see Figure 2.2). So close was the association between rulers and the gods that Egyptian hymns honoring the pharaoh address him in terms identical with those that supplicate the gods.

In the visual arts, rulers and gods alike were depicted with the attributes and physical features of powerful animals. Such is the case with the Great Sphinx, the recumbent creature that guards the entrance to the ceremonial complex at Gizeh (see Figure **2.1**). This haunting figure, antiquity's largest and earliest surviving colossal statue, bears the portrait head of the Old Kingdom pharaoh Khafre and the body of a lion, king of the beasts. As such, it is a hybrid symbol of superhuman power and authority.

Law in Ancient Egypt

In ancient Egypt, long-standing customs and unwritten rules preceded the codification and transcription of civil and criminal law. Indeed, Egyptian law consisted of the unwritten decrees of the pharaoh (passed down orally until they were transcribed during the New Kingdom). An inscription on an Old Kingdom tomb wall sums up this phenomenon as follows: "The law of the land is the mouth of the pharaoh." In Egypt, no written laws have been preserved from any period before the fourth century B.C.E. When one considers that toward the end of the thirteenth century B.C.E. the pharaoh Rameses II ruled approximately three million people, it is clear that the oral tradition—the verbal transmission of rules, conventions, and customs—played a vital part in establishing political continuity.

The Cult of the Dead

Ancient Egyptians venerated the pharaoh as the living representative of the sun god. They believed that on his death, the pharaoh would join with the sun to govern Egypt eternally. His body was prepared for burial by means of a special ten-week embalming procedure that involved removing all his internal organs (with the exception of his heart) and filling his body cavity with preservatives. His intestines, stomach, lungs, and liver were all embalmed separately; the brain was removed and discarded. The king's corpse was then wrapped in fine linen and placed in an elaborately ornamented coffin (Figure **2.5**), which was floated down the Nile on a royal barge to a burial site at Gizeh, near the southern tip of the Nile delta (see Map 2.1). The earliest Egyptian tombs—homes for the dead— were probably modeled on Egypt's domestic dwellings. These rectangular single-story mud-brick tombs, called **mastabas**, consisted of an offering chamber, a room that held a statue of the dead, and a shaft that descended to the burial chamber some 100 feet below the ground. Stacking five mastabas of decreasing size one on top of another, the third-dynasty architect Imenhotep produced the impressive stepped pyramid for King Zoser, who ruled shortly before 2600 B.C.E. (Figure **2.6**). The pyramidal shape may have been inspired by the mythical mound of silt from which the primordial sun god was said to have risen. With the fourth-dynasty pharaohs of the Old Kingdom, the true geometric **pyramid** took shape.

Figure 2.5 Egyptian mummy and coffin, ca. 1000 B.C.E.

Figure 2.6 Stepped pyramid of King Zoser, Saqqara, ca. 2630 B.C.E.

Figure 2.7 Pyramid construction. Some historians speculate that the vast stone building-blocks were hauled into position using log sleds and inclined ramps made of packed sand.

log sled

mud and rubble ramp

Constructed between 2600 and 2500 B.C.E., the pyramids are technological wonders, as well as symbols of ancient Egypt's endurance through time. A workforce of some 50,000 men (divided into gangs of twenty-five) labored for almost thirty years to raise the Great Pyramid of Khufu. According to recent DNA analysis of the workers found buried at Gizeh, the pyramid builders were Egyptians, not foreign slaves as was previously assumed. This native workforce quarried, transported, and assembled thousands of mammoth stone blocks, most weighing between 2 and 50 tons. These they lifted from tier to tier by means of levers—although some historians speculate that they were slid into place on inclined ramps of sand and rubble (Figure 2.7). Finally, the laborers faced the surfaces of the great tombs with finely polished limestone. All these feats were achieved with copper saws and chisels, and without pulleys or mortar.

The Great Pyramid of Khufu, which stands as part of a large walled burial complex at Gizeh (Figures 2.8 and 2.9), consists of more than two million stone blocks rising to a height of approximately 480 feet and covering a base area of 13 acres. The royal burial vault, hidden within a

Figure 2.8 Great pyramids of Gizeh: from left to right, Menkure, ca. 2575 B.C.E., Khufu (Khefren), ca. 2650 B.C.E., Khafre, ca. 2600 B.C.E. Top height 480 ft. (approx.).

Figure 2.9 Reconstruction of the pyramids of Khufu and Khafre at Gizeh, ca. 2650–2600 B.C.E.

Figure 2.10 Burial chambers within a typical pyramid.

series of chambers connected to the exterior by tunnels (Figure **2.10**), was prepared as a home for eternity—a tribute to communal faith in the eternal benevolence of the pharaoh. Its chambers were filled with his most cherished possessions: priceless treasures of jewelry, weapons, and furniture, all of which he might require in the life to come. The walls of the chamber were painted with colored pigments, a technique known as **fresco secco** (dry fresco), or carved in **relief** with images visualizing sacred rituals and daily activities (see Figure 2.18). Hieroglyphs formed an essential component of pictorial illustration, narrating the achievements of Egypt's rulers, listing the grave goods, and offering perpetual prayers for the deceased (see also Figures 2.2, 2.4, and 2.13). Carved and painted figures representing important royal officials, such as administrators and scribes, accompanied the pharaoh to the afterlife (Figure **2.11**). Other figures representing servants carried provisions such as bread, fowl, beer, and linens.

The carved images may have served as surrogates for servants and slaves who, in earlier times, went to the grave with their masters. Death masks or "reserve" portrait heads of the pharaoh might be placed in the tomb to provide the king's *ka* (life force or divine essence) with safe and familiar dwelling places.

Intended primarily as homes for the dead, the pyramids were built to assure the ruler's comfort in the afterlife. However, in the centuries after their construction, grave robbers greedily despoiled them, and their contents were largely plundered and lost. Middle and Late Kingdom pharaohs turned to other methods of burial, including interment in the rock cliffs along the Nile and in unmarked graves in the Valley of the Kings, west of Thebes. In time, these too were pillaged. One of the few royal graves to have escaped vandalism was that of a minor fourteenth-century B.C.E. ruler named Tutankhamen (ca. 1345–1325 B.C.E.). Uncovered by the British archeologist Howard

Figure 2.11 Seated scribe, Saqqara. Fifth dynasty, ca. 2400 B.C.E. Painted limestone, height 21 in. The scribe was one of the highest officials in ancient Egypt. Trained in reading, writing, law, religion, and mathematics, scribes often ranked as scholars and priests. The eyes of this limestone figure were once inlaid with rock crystal, calcite, and magnesite mounted in copper.

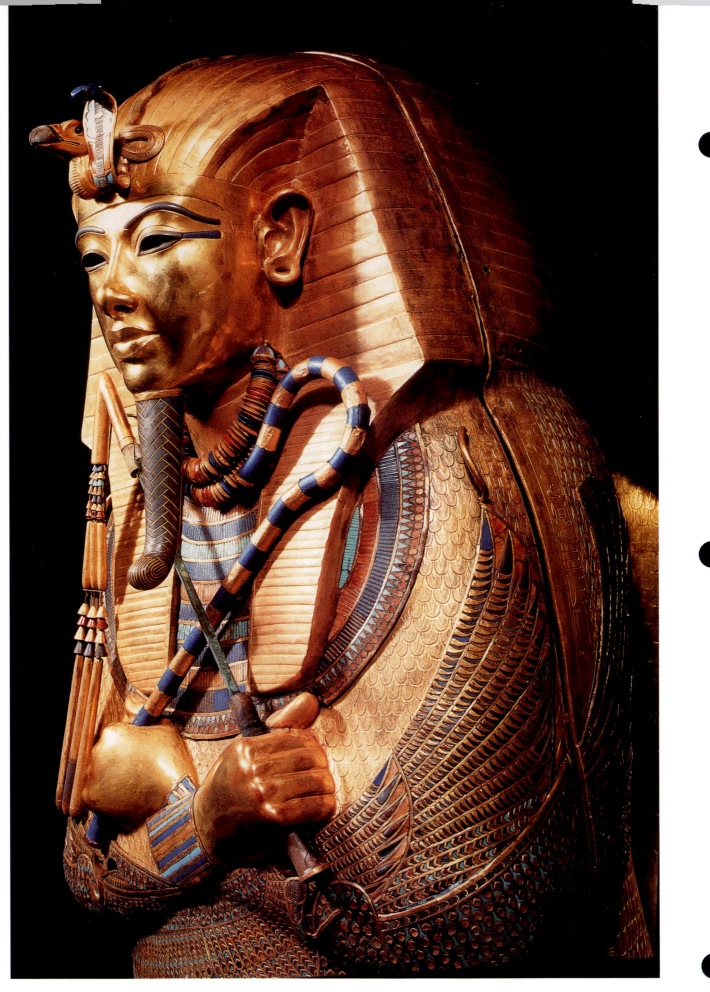

Figure 2.12 Cover of the coffin of Tutankhamen (ca. 1345–1325 B.C.E.) (detail), from the Valley of the Kings. Gold with inlay of enamel, carnelian, lapis lazuli, and turquoise, height 6 ft.

Figure 2.13 Throne with Tutankhamen (ca. 1345–1325 B.C.E.) and Queen (detail of the back), late Marana period, New Kingdom, eighteenth dynasty. Wood, plated with gold and silver, inlays of glass paste, 12 × 12 in. (approx.). The rays of the sun god shine down on Tutankhamen and his consort. Both wear lavish crowns that symbolize authority over Upper and Lower Egypt.

Carter in 1922, the tomb housed riches of astonishing variety, including the pharaoh's solid-gold coffin, inlaid with semiprecious carnelian and lapis lazuli (Figure **2.12**), and a lavish throne depicting Tutankhamen and his wife (Figure **2.13**). Standing below the shining disk of the sun god, the queen, in an ankle-length gown, tenderly straightens her consort's collar. Above them the sun disk's rays end in human hands, some of which carry the *ankh*.

The promise of life after death seems to have dominated at all levels of Egyptian culture. The most elaborate homes for the dead were reserved for royalty and members of the aristocracy, but recent excavations of the lower cemetery at Gizeh reveal at least 700 graves of workmen and artisans. In the coffins of ancient Egypt's dead are found papyrus scrolls inscribed with prayers and incantations to guide the soul in the afterlife. The *Book of the Dead,* a collection of funerary prayers originating as far back as 4000 B.C.E., prepared each individual for final judgment.

In the presence of the gods Osiris and Isis, the dead souls were expected to recite a lengthy confession attesting to their purity of heart, including:

I have not done iniquity.
I have not robbed with violence.
I have not done violence [to any man].
I have not committed theft.
I have not slain man or woman.
I have not made light the bushel.
I have not acted deceitfully.
I have not uttered falsehood.
I have not defiled the wife of a man.
I have not stirred up strife.
I have not cursed the god.
I have not behaved with insolence.
I have not increased my wealth, except with such things as are my own possessions.

Figure 2.14 Scene from a funerary papyrus, *Book of the Dead*, ca. 1285 B.C.E. Height 11¾ in. Princess Entiu-ny stands to the left of a set of scales on which Anubis, the jackal-headed god, weighs her heart against the figure of Truth, while Osiris, Lord of the Dead, judges from his throne. His wife, Isis, stands behind the princess.

A painted papyrus scroll from the *Book of the Dead* brings to life the Last Judgment itself: the enthroned Osiris, god of the underworld (far right), and his wife, Isis (far left), oversee the ceremony in which the heart of the deceased Princess Entiu-ny is weighed against the figure of Truth (Figure **2.14**). Having made her testimony, the princess watches as the jackal-headed god of death, Anubis, prepares her heart for the ordeal. "Grant thou," reads the prayer to Osiris, "that I may have my being among the living, and that I may sail up and down the river among those who are in thy following." If the heart is not "found true by trial of the Great Balance," it will be devoured by the monster Ament, thus meeting a second death. If pure, it might sail with the sun "up and down the river," or flourish in a realm where wheat grows high and the living souls of the dead enjoy feasting and singing. An image of this heavenly domain is depicted on the walls of the tomb of Sennudjem: the "fields of the blessed" are bordered by beneficent gods (top) and flourishing fruit trees (bottom) (Figure **2.15**). Here, death is a continuation of daily life in a realm that floats eternally on the primordial waters—indicated by the jagged blue lines that frame the registers.

Akhenaten's Reform

Throughout the dynastic history of Egypt, the central authority of the pharaoh was repeatedly contested by local temple priests, each of whom held religious and political sway in their own regions along the Nile. Perhaps in an effort to consolidate his authority against priestly encroachment, the New Kingdom pharaoh Amenhotep IV (ca. 1353–1336 B.C.E.) defied the tradition of polytheism by elevating Aten (god of the sun disk) to a position of supremacy over all other gods. "The Hymn to the Aten," which is based on earlier Egyptian songs of praise, dates from the reign of Amenhotep IV.

READING 2.1 From "The Hymn to the Aten"

(ca. 1352–1336 B.C.E.)

You rise in perfection on the horizon of the sky	1
living Aten,[1] who started life.	
Whenever you are risen upon the eastern horizon	
you fill every land with your perfection.	
You are appealing, great, sparkling, high over every land;	5
your rays hold together the lands as far as everything you have made.	
Since you are Rē,[2] you reach as far as they do,	
and you curb them for your beloved son.	
Although you are far away, your rays are upon the land;	
you are in their faces, yet your departure is not observed.	10
Whenever you set on the western horizon,	
the land is in darkness in the manner of death.	
They sleep in a bedroom with heads under the covers,	
and one eye does not see another.	
If all their possessions which are under their heads were stolen,	15
they would not know it.	

[1] The sun disk.
[2] Another name for the sun god, associated with his regenerative powers.

Figure 2.15 Illustration of Spell 110 from the *Book of the Dead* in the burial chamber of Sennudjem, ca. 1279 B.C.E. Frescoes like this one were preserved by Egypt's dry climate. The blue color (a compound of calcium copper tetrasilicate) used in frescoes like this one is believed to be the world's oldest artificial pigment.

Every lion who comes out of his cave
　　and all the serpents bite,
　　for darkness is a blanket.
The land is silent now, because he who made them　　**20**
　　is at rest on his horizon

But when day breaks you are risen upon the horizon,
　　and you shine as the Aten in the daytime.
When you dispel darkness and you give forth your rays
　　the two lands[3] are in festival,　　**25**
　　alert and standing on their feet,
　　now that you have raised them up.
Their bodies are clean,
　　and their clothes have been put on;
　　their arms are [lifted] in praise at your rising.　　**30**
The entire land performs its work:
　　all the cattle are content with their fodder,
　　trees and plants grow,
　　birds fly up to their nests,
　　their wings [extended] in praise for your Ka.[4]　　**35**
All the Kine[5] prance on their feet;
　　everything which flies up and alights,
　　they live when you
　　have risen for them.
The barges sail upstream and downstream too,　　**40**
　　for every way is open at your rising.
The fishes in the river leap before your face
　　when your rays are in the sea.

You who have placed seed in woman
　　and have made sperm into man,　　**45**
　　who feeds the son in the womb of his mother,
　　who quiets him with something to stop his crying;
　　you are the nurse in the womb,
　　giving breath to nourish all that has been begotten.

Q　**Which of Aten's powers are glorified
　　in this hymn?**

Changing his own name to Akhenaten ("Shining Spirit of Aten"), the pharaoh abandoned the political capital at Memphis and the religious center at Thebes to build a new palace midway between the two at a site called Akhetaten ("Place of the Sun Disk's Power") (see Map 2.1).

Akhenaten's chief wife, Queen Nefertiti, along with her mother-in-law, assisted in organizing the affairs of state. The mother of six daughters, Nefertiti is often pictured as Isis, the goddess from whom all Egyptian queens were said to have descended. Nefertiti's confident beauty inspired numerous sculpted likenesses, some of which are striking in their blend of realism and abstraction (Figure **2.16**). Akhenaten's monotheistic reform lasted only as long as his reign, and in the years following his death, Egypt's conservative priests and nobles returned to the polytheism of their forebears.

---

[3] Upper and Lower Egypt.
[4] The governing spirit or soul of a person or god.
[5] Cows.

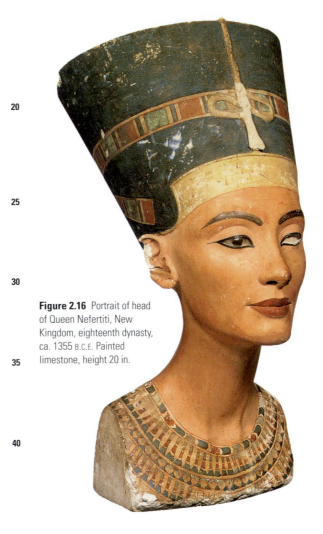

Figure 2.16 Portrait of head of Queen Nefertiti, New Kingdom, eighteenth dynasty, ca. 1355 B.C.E. Painted limestone, height 20 in.

The Social Order

Like all ancient civilizations, Egypt could not have existed without a high level of cooperation among those whose individual tasks—governing, trading, farming, fighting—contributed to communal survival. Powerful families, tribes, and clans, usually those that had proved victorious in battle, established long-standing territorial claims. Such families often claimed descent from, or association with, the gods. Once royal authority was entrenched, it was almost impossible to unseat. The ruling dynasty, in conjunction with a priestly caste that supervised the religious activities of the community, formed an elite group of men and women who regulated the lives of the lower classes: merchants, farmers, herders, artisans, soldiers, and servants. Nevertheless, the class structure in ancient Egypt seems to have been quite flexible. Ambitious individuals of any class were free to rise in status, usually by way of education.

For well over 2000 years, Egypt was administered by the pharaoh's vast bureaucracy, members of which collected taxes, regulated public works, and mobilized the army. In the social order, these individuals, along with large land-owners and priests, constituted the upper classes. As in all ancient societies, power was not uniformly distributed but descended from the top rung of the hierarchy in diminishing degrees of influence. Those closest to the pharaoh participated most fully in his authority and prestige. Other individuals might advance their positions and improve their status through service to the pharaoh.

At the top of the bureaucratic pyramid stood the vizier. Essential to the administration and the security of the state, the vizier was in charge of appointing members of the royal bureaucracy and dispatching the local officials. He oversaw the mobilization of troops, the irrigation of canals, and the taking of inventories, and, with the assistance of official scribes, he handled all litigation for the Egyptian state. Merchants, traders, builders, and scribes made up a prosperous middle class, who ranked in status just below the aristocracy. At the base of the social pyramid, the great masses of peasants constituted the agricultural backbone of ancient Egypt. Aided by slaves, peasant men and women worked side by side to farm the land. Even in the afterlife, husbands and wives shared the tasks of reaping and plowing (see Figure 2.15). Class status seems to have extended into the afterlife: in the cemeteries recently uncovered at Gizeh, artisans received separate and more elaborate burials than common laborers. Slaves constituted a class of unfree men and women. In the ancient world, slaves were victims of military conquest. Enslaving one's enemy captives was a humane alternative to executing them. Some people became slaves as punishment for criminal acts, and still others as a result of falling into debt. Slaves might be sold or traded like any other form of property, but in Egypt and elsewhere in the ancient world, it appears that some slaves were able to acquire sufficient wealth to buy their own or their children's freedom.

Egyptian Women

Possibly because all property was inherited through the female line, Egyptian women seem to have enjoyed a large degree of economic independence, as well as civil rights and privileges. Women who could write and calculate might go into business. Women of the pharaoh's harem oversaw textile production, while others found positions as shopkeepers, midwives, musicians, and dancers (Figure 2.17). Nevertheless, men were wary of powerful women, as is indicated in a Middle Kingdom manual of good conduct, which offers the husband this advice concerning his wife: "Make her happy while you are alive, for she is land profitable to her lord. Neither judge her nor raise her to a position of power . . . her eye is a stormwind when she sees."

The Arts in Ancient Egypt

Literature

Ancient Egypt did not produce any literary masterpieces. Nevertheless, from tomb and temple walls, and from papyrus rolls, come prayers and songs, royal decrees and letters, prose tales, and texts that served to educate the young. One school text, which reflects the fragile relationship between oral and written traditions, reads: "Man decays, his corpse is dust,/ All his kin have perished;

Figure 2.17 Procession of female musicians with instruments, including a harp, double pipes, and a lyre, Tomb of Djeserkarasneb, Thebes, ca. 1580–1314 B.C.E. Copy of the original.

/ But a book makes him remembered,/ Through the mouth of its reciter." The so-called wisdom literature of Egypt, which consists of words of advice and instruction, anticipates parts of the Hebrew Bible.

During the Middle Kingdom, as Egypt's government grew in size, increasing emphasis was placed on the importance of keeping written records. *The Satire on Trades*, a standard exercise for student scribes, argues that the life of a government clerk is preferable to that of a farmer, baker, soldier, metalworker, or priest. "Behold," it concludes, "there is no profession free of a boss—except for the scribe: he is the boss!"

From the New Kingdom came a very personal genre of poetry that would come to be called **lyric** (literally, accompanied by the **lyre** or harp, see Figure 2.17). In the following three poems, two in a male voice and one female (from a group of poems known as "songs of the Birdcatcher's Daughter"), images from nature are freely employed to evoke sentiments of love and desire. Lines 5 to 7 of the second poem illustrate the effective use of **simile**, while the third poem operates as an extended **metaphor**.

READING 2.2 Egyptian Poetry

I will lie down inside,	1
and there I will feign illness.	
Then my neighbours will enter to see,	
and then my sister[1] will come with them.	
She'll put the doctor to shame,	5
for she will understand	
my illness.	

———◆———

My sister has come,	1
my heart exults,	
My arms spread out	
to embrace her;	
My heart bounds	5
in its place,	
Like the red fish	
in its pond.	
O night, be mine forever,	
Now that my lady has come!	10

———◆———

The voice of the goose complains,	1
when it is caught by the bait.	
Your love takes me (to you),	
and I cannot loose it.	
I must abandon my nets.	5
What shall I say to my mother,	
to whom I go back every day,	
laden with my birds?	
'You have set no trap to-day?'	
I am the captive of your love.	10

Q **How do simile and metaphor operate to enrich these poems?**

[1] Meaning "mistress" or "lady."

The Visual Arts

Egyptian art comes almost exclusively from tombs and temples. Such art was not intended as decoration; rather, it was created to replicate the living world, to benefit or honor the dead. Perhaps for that reason, the Egyptians found a unique way to express the deep sense of order that dominated ancient Egyptian life. For 3000 years, Egypt followed a set of conventions that dictated the manner in which subjects should be depicted. In representations of everyday life, figures are usually sized according to a strict hierarchy, or graded order: upper-class individuals are shown larger than lower-class ones, and males usually outsize females and servants (Figure **2.18**). In monumental sculptures of royalty, however, the chief wife of the pharaoh is often shown the same size as her husband (see Figure 2.3). The same is true in frescoes illustrating the *Book of the Dead*, where men and women share the task of reaping wheat (see Figure 2.14).

Very early in Egyptian history, artists developed a **canon** (or set of rules) by which to represent the human form. The proportions of the human body were determined according to a **module** (or standard of measurement) represented by the width of the clenched fist (Figure **2.19**). More generally, Egyptian artists adhered to a set of guidelines by which they might "capture" the most characteristic and essential aspects of the subject matter: in depicting the human figure, the upper torso is shown from the front, while the lower is shown from the side; the head is depicted in profile, while the eye and eyebrow are frontal. This method of representation is *conceptual*—that is, based on ideas—rather than *perceptual*—that is, based on visual evidence.

The Egyptian artist's approach to space was also conceptual. Spatial depth is indicated by placing one figure above (rather than behind) the next, often in horizontal registers, or rows. Cast in timeless space, Egyptian figures share the symbolic presence of the hieroglyphs by which they are framed (see Figure 2.2). Nowhere else in the ancient world do we see such an intimate and intelligible conjunction of image and word—a union designed to immortalize ideas rather than imitate reality.

This is not to say that Egyptian artists ignored the world of the senses, nor that they were incapable of naturalistic representation. The painted limestone figure of the seated scribe (see Figure 2.11) assumes a lifelike presence. His fleshy torso contrasts with the more stylized physique of the pharaoh Mycerinus pictured in Figure 2.3. Realistic detail also enlivens many Egyptian frescoes. For instance, in the New Kingdom tomb of the scribe Neb-amon (himself depicted in a stylized and conventional pose), the figures are surrounded by marsh birds so accurately rendered that ornithologists have been able to identify them by species (see Figure 2.18). It is in the union of the particular and the general that Egyptian art achieves its timeless quality.

New Kingdom Temples

Temples were built by the Egyptians from earliest times, but most of those that have survived date from the

Figure 2.18 Scene of fowling, from the tomb of Neb-amon at Thebes, Egypt, ca. 1400 B.C.E. Fragment of a fresco secco, height 32¼ in. Neb-amon, an Egyptian scribe and grain-counter, stands on a light papyrus raft that floats on the shallow waters of a marsh. He holds three birds (possibly stuffed decoys) in his right hand and a throw-stick shaped like a snake in his left. (The stick acts like a boomerang to break the neck of his prey.) He is accompanied by his wife and by his daughter, who crouches between his legs, gently steadying his stance.

Figure 2.19 The Egyptian canon of proportion.

New Kingdom. The basic plan of the temple mirrored the central features of the Egyptian cosmos: the **pylons** (two truncated pyramids that made up the gateway) symbolized the mountains that rimmed the edge of the world, while the progress from the open courtyard through the **hypostyle** hall into the dark inner sanctuary housing the cult statue represented a voyage from light to darkness (and back) symbolic of the sun's cyclical journey (Figure **2.20**). Oriented on an east–west axis, the temple received the sun's morning rays, which reached through the sequence of hallways into the sanctuary. The Great Temple of Amon-Ra at Karnak was the heart of a 5-acre religious complex that included a sacred lake, a sphinx-lined causeway, and numerous **obelisks** (commemorative stone pillars). The temple's hypostyle hall is adorned with painted reliefs that cover the walls and the surfaces of its 134 massive columns shaped like budding and flowering papyrus—these plants were identified with the marsh of creation (Figure **2.21**). Decorated with stars and other celestial images, the ceiling of the hall symbolized the heavens. Such sacred precincts were not intended for communal assembly—in fact, commoners were forbidden to enter. Rather, Egyptian temples were sanctuaries in which priests performed daily rituals of cosmic renewal on behalf of the pharaoh and the people. Temple rituals were celebrations of the solar cycle, associated not only with the birth of the sun god but also with the regeneration of the ruler upon whom cosmic order depended.

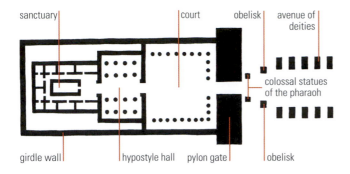

Figure 2.20 Plan of a typical pylon temple.

sanctuary — court — obelisk — avenue of deities

colossal statues of the pharaoh

girdle wall — hypostyle hall — pylon gate — obelisk

Music in Ancient Egypt

Tomb paintings reveal much about ancient Egyptian culture. They are, for example, our main source of information about ancient Egyptian music and dance (see Figure 2.17). It is clear that song and poetry were interchangeable (hymns like those praising the Aten were chanted, not spoken). Musical instruments, including harps, small stringed instruments, pipes, and sistrums (a type of rattle)—often found buried with the dead—accompanied song and dance. Greek sources indicate that Egyptian music was based in theory; nevertheless, we have no certain knowledge how that music actually sounded. Visual representations confirm, however, that music had a special place in religious rituals, in festive and funeral processions, and in many aspects of secular life.

Africa: The Sudan

Northern Sudan: Nubia

The ancient civilization of Nubia arose along the Nile in what is now known as northern Sudan (see Map 2.1). Located between the first and sixth cataracts of the Nile, this independent kingdom was the first literate urban civilization to appear in Africa south of the Sahara. It was probably populated by peoples from the south and southwest portions of Africa as early as the third millennium B.C.E., as the Sahara Desert became too arid to support human settlements. Famous for its large quantities of gold—the name "Nubia" may derive from the Egyptian word *nub*, meaning "gold"—the area became a trade corridor between the upper and lower regions of the Nile. Nubia provided its northern neighbors with cattle and a variety of luxury goods, including ivory, ebony, and incense. Royal officials of Old Kingdom Egypt made frequent expeditions to Nubia to report on political conditions there and to arrange for the importation of desirable tribute, such as elephant tusks, panther skins, and gold jewelry. While Nubia came under Egyptian jurisdiction during the Middle Kingdom, its rulers continued to oversee trade between Egypt and sub-Saharan Africa.

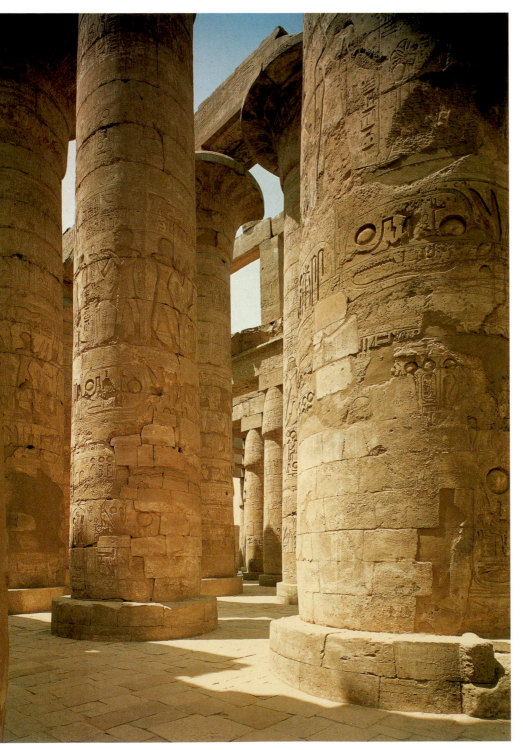

Figure 2.21 Hypostyle hall, Great Temple of Amon-Ra, Karnak, ca. 1220 B.C.E.

Figure 2.22 King Shabaqo, from the area of the ancient Kush, ca. eighth century B.C.E. Solid cast bronze, height 6 in. The Kushan king is shown kneeling, his palms facing each other, as if he is making an offering. He wears a crown of double serpents (unified Kush and Egypt), ornamented arm and wrist bands, and a necklace consisting of three ram's-head pendants (symbols of Amon) surmounted by a serpent crest and sun disk.

Figure 2.23 Head, Nok culture, ca. 500 B.C.E.–200 C.E. Terracotta, height 14 3/16 in.

Around 1550 B.C.E., the powerful state of Kush in Nubia defeated the Egyptian army. The conquerors adopted many aspects of Egyptian culture, including the practice of pyramid building. While New Kingdom Egypt reestablished its authority over the region, by the ninth century B.C.E. Kush came to govern all of southern (Upper) Egypt. For at least a century, Nubian artists crafted objects of great technical sophistication. This is especially visible in the area of metalworking, as reflected, for instance, in the bronze statue of the Kushan king Shabaqo (Figure **2.22**). In this small but forceful portrait, Nubia anticipated the birth of an African tradition in portraiture that began in western Sudan as early as 500 B.C.E. and continued to flourish for at least a thousand years.

Western Sudan: Nok Culture

While East Africa's ancient civilizations were known to the world as early as the eighteenth century, the western parts of the continent were not fully investigated by archeologists until the mid-twentieth century. In 1931, near a farming village called Nok, on the Niger River in western Sudan (see Map 2.1), tin miners accidentally uncovered a large group of terracotta sculptures (Figure **2.23**). Dating from the first millennium B.C.E., these hand-modeled figures, representing people and animals, are the earliest known three-dimensional artworks of sub-Saharan Africa. They are the first evidence of a long tradition of naturalistic portraiture in African art. The Nok heads, many of which display clearly individualized personalities, probably represent tribal rulers or revered ancestors.

LOOKING BACK

Africa: Ancient Egypt

- The Nile River, flowing from the heart of Africa to its fan-shaped delta at the Mediterranean Sea, provided the ideal setting for the rise of Egyptian civilization.
- Surrounded by sea and desert, and blessed with a stable climate, ancient Egypt flourished for almost 3000 years.

The Gods of Ancient Egypt

- The geography, climate, and topography of ancient Egypt played an important part in the shaping of the civilization's world-views and religious beliefs. Egyptian myth held that at the beginning of time, the Nile brought forth a mound of silt, out of which emerged the sun god called Amon or Rē (Ra), from whom the rest of Egypt's gods were born.
- The pharaohs of Egypt were the divinely appointed representatives of the sun god, a sharing of power depicted frequently in Egyptian tombs and temples.

The Rulers of Ancient Egypt

- Upper and Lower Egypt were united in ca. 3150 B.C.E. under the rule of Egypt's first pharaoh, Narmer.
- Egypt's theocratic monarchs required elaborate burials that ensured their well-being in the afterlife. Royal graves were filled with frescoes, relief carvings, and precious goods that reflect the Egyptian cult of the dead.
- A belief that the land was owned by the gods supported a way of life known as theocratic socialism, by which Egypt's population shared in the production and distribution of agricultural harvests.
- Egyptian rulers followed a matriarchal lineage by which land passed through the female line. For the pharaoh's son to come to the throne, he would have to marry his own sister or half-sister.
- In an effort to consolidate his power, the New Kingdom pharaoh Akhenaten denied all gods except Aten (god of the sun disk); his reforms did not outlast him.

The Social Order

- The class structure in ancient Egypt was flexible. Ambitious individuals of any class were free to rise in status, usually by way of education.
- A huge bureaucracy administered Egypt's affairs; its appointees collected taxes, regulated public works, and mobilized the army. Along with large landowners and priests, they constituted the upper classes.
- Merchants, traders, builders, and scribes made up a prosperous middle class. At the base of the social pyramid, peasants constituted Egypt's agricultural backbone.
- Egyptian women seem to have enjoyed a large degree of economic independence, as well as civil rights and privileges.

The Arts in Ancient Egypt

- Egyptian literature included manuals of instruction and advice, and lyric poetry, much of which appear in texts that served to educate the young.
- Egyptian art comes almost exclusively from tombs and temples. For 3000 years, Egypt followed a set of pictorial conventions that dictated the manner in which subjects should be depicted.
- The plan of the Egyptian temple mirrored the central features of the Egyptian cosmos and the daily "voyage" of the sun.
- Poems were sung or chanted at Egypt's religious and secular events. Musical instruments, including harps, pipes, and sistrums, accompanied song and dance.

Africa: The Sudan

- Nubia, an ancient civilization that arose along the Nile in what is now known as northern Sudan, was the first urban civilization to appear in Africa south of the Sahara.
- Around 1550 B.C.E., the powerful state of Kush in Nubia defeated the Egyptian army. The conquerors adopted many aspects of Egyptian culture, including the practice of pyramid building. During the ninth century B.C.E., Kush came to govern all of Upper Egypt.
- In 1931, archeologists found evidence of cultures in Africa's western Sudan near a farming village called Nok. Terracotta sculptures representing people and animals anticipate the long tradition of naturalistic portraiture in African art.

Glossary

canon a set of rules or standards used to establish proportions

cosmology the theory of the origins, evolution, and structure of the universe

dynasty a sequence of rulers from the same family

fresco secco (Italian, "fresh," "dry") a method of painting on walls or ceilings surfaced with moist lime plaster

hypostyle a hall whose roof is supported by columns

lyre any one of a group of plucked stringed instruments; usually made of tortoise shell or horn and therefore light in weight

lyric literally "accompanied by the lyre," hence, verse that is meant to be sung rather than spoken; usually characterized by individual and personal emotion

mastaba an early rectangular Egyptian tomb with sloping sides and a flat roof

metaphor a figure of speech in which two unlike things are compared without the use of the words "like" or "as"

module a unit of measurement used to determine proportion

obelisk a tall, four-sided pillar that tapers to a pyramidal apex

papyrus a reedlike plant from which the ancient Egyptians made paper

pylon a massive gateway in the form of a pair of truncated pyramids

pyramid a four-sided structure rising to a peak

relief a sculptural technique in which figures or forms are carved either to project from the background surface (raised relief) or cut away below the background level (sunk relief); the degree of relief is designated as high, low, or sunken

simile a figure of speech in which two unlike things are compared

Chapter 3

India, China, and the Americas

ca. 3500–500 B.C.E.

"He knows peace who has forgotten desire.
He lives without craving:
Free from ego, free from pride."
The Bhagavad-Gita

Figure 3.1 "Baby" Figure, Mexico, Olmec, twelfth to ninth century B.C.E. Ceramic, height 13⅜ in. Hundreds of pudgy, nearly life-sized human baby sculptures like this one have been found in Olmec graves.

The civilizations of India and China emerged somewhat later than those of Mesopotamia and ancient Egypt. Both are among the only continuous civilizations in world history: their language, belief systems, and many of their cultural practices flourish today in much the same form as they took in ancient times. Independent of the West, India and China produced works of literature, philosophy, art, and music that rank with those of their Western contemporaries. The Asian world-view differs somewhat from that of Western cultures. In India, for instance, religion is grounded in **pantheism**, the belief that an all-pervading divine spirit infuses all aspects of the universe. The identification of the divine with the unvarying rhythms of nature is also common to ancient Chinese culture. For the Chinese, the natural order dominated secular and spiritual life.

India and China shared a holistic view of the cosmos, one that perceived an organic and intimate interrelationship between gods, rulers, and the social order.

The ancient history of the Americas is not as well understood as that of the two Asian civilizations. This is partly because of the number and variety of cultures that flourished in the third to first millennia B.C.E., and partly because these cultures—lacking written records—are available to us only by way of artifacts, many of which remain the object of archeological analysis. Nevertheless, similarities between the cultures of the Americas and the civilizations of the ancient world invite our examination—if only to anticipate the wealth of information that still lies buried in unexcavated ruins.

Ancient India

Indus Valley Civilization (ca. 2700–1500 B.C.E.)

India's earliest known civilization was located in the lower Indus valley, in an area called Sind—from which the words "India" and "Hindu" derive (Map **3.1**). At Mohenjo-daro ("Mound of the Dead") and Harappa (in modern-day Pakistan), a sophisticated Bronze Age culture flourished before 2500 B.C.E. India's first cities were planned communities: Mohenjo-daro's wide streets, lined with fired-brick houses, were laid out in a grid pattern, and their covered drains, bathing facilities, and sewage systems were unmatched in other parts of the civilized world. Bronze Age India also claimed a form of written language, although the 400 pictographic signs that constitute the earliest script are still undeciphered. At Mohenjo-daro there is little evidence of temples or tombs; while first excavated in 1921, only 10 percent of the site has been uncovered. Nevertheless, there existed a vigorous sculptural tradition in both bronze and stone. The lively female dancer pictured in Figure **3.2** is one of many objects (see also Figure 0.20) that reflect India's mastery of the lost-wax method of working bronze. In the medium of stone, the powerful portrait of a bearded man (possibly a priest or ruler) distinguished by an introspective expression anticipates the meditative images of India's later religious art (Figure **3.3**).

The Vedic Era (ca. 1500–500 B.C.E.)

India's oldest devotional texts, the *Vedas* (literally, "sacred knowledge"), give their name to the thousand-year period after 1500 B.C.E. The *Vedas* are a collection of prayers, sacrificial formulae, and hymns, one example of which appears in Reading 0.1 in the Introduction. Transmitted orally for centuries, these sacred hymns reflect a blending of the native folk traditions of the Indus valley along with those of the Aryan populations. Among the chief Vedic deities were the sky gods Indra and Rudra (later known as Shiva), the fire god Agni, and the sun god Vishnu. The *Vedas* provide a wealth of information concerning astronomical phenomena. The study of the stars, along with the practice of surgery and dissection, mark the beginnings of scientific inquiry in India.

Map 3.1 Ancient India, ca. 2700–1500 B.C.E.

The Vedic Era also saw the institution of the **caste system**, a societal division based on differences in wealth, rank, occupation, and possibly skin color. While a hierarchical order marked the social systems of all ancient civilizations, India developed the most rigid kind of class stratification, one that prevailed until modern times. By 1000 B.C.E., four principal castes existed: priests and scholars; rulers and warriors; artisans and merchants; and unskilled workers. Slowly, these castes began to subdivide according to occupation. At the very bottom of the social order—or, more accurately, outside it—lay those who held the most menial and degrading occupations. They became known as Untouchables.

Some time around 1500 B.C.E., Sanskrit became the classic language of India. The bards of India recounted stories of the bitter tribal wars between rivalrous clans. These stories were the basis for India's two great epics—the *Mahabharata* (*Great Deeds of the Bharata Clan*) and the *Ramayana* (*Song of Prince Rama*)—which were transmitted orally for generations but not recorded until the eighth century B.C.E. The *Mahabharata*—the world's longest folk epic—recounts a ten-year struggle for control of the Ganges valley, occurring around the year 1000 B.C.E. Along with the *Ramayana*, this epic assumed a role in the cultural history of India not unlike that of the *Iliad* and the *Odyssey* in Hellenic history. Indeed, the two epics have been treasured resources for much of the poetry, drama, and art produced throughout India's long history.

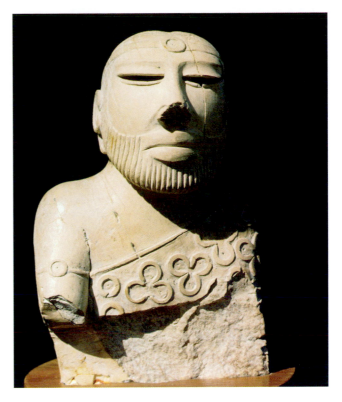

Figure 3.3 Bearded man, from Mohenjo-daro, Indus valley, ca. 2000 B.C.E. Limestone, height 7 in. The inward gaze of this figure suggests the practice of meditation that would come to characterize Hinduism in ancient India.

Hindu Pantheism

From the Indus valley civilization came the most ancient of today's world religions: Hinduism. Hinduism is markedly different from the religions of the West. It identifies the sacred not as a superhuman personality, but as an objective, all-pervading Cosmic Spirit called **Brahman**. Pantheism, the belief that divinity is inherent in all things, is basic to the Hindu view that the universe itself is sacred. While neither polytheistic nor monotheistic in the traditional sense, Hinduism venerates all forms and manifestations of the all-pervasive Brahman. Hence, Hindus embrace all the Vedic gods, a multitude of deities who are to this day perceived as emanations of the divine (see chapter 14). In the words of the *Rig Veda*, "Truth is one, but the wise call it by many names."

Hinduism is best understood by way of the religious texts known as the *Upanishads*, some 250 prose commentaries on the *Vedas*. Like the *Vedas* themselves, the *Upanishads* were orally transmitted and recorded in Sanskrit between the eighth and sixth centuries B.C.E. While the *Vedas* teach worship through prayer and sacrifice, the *Upanishads* teach enlightenment through meditation. They predicate the concept of the single, all-pervading Brahman. Unlike the nature deities of Mesopotamia and Egypt, Brahman is infinite, formless, and ultimately unknowable. Unlike the

Figure 3.2 Dancing girl, from Mohenjo-daro, Indus valley, ca. 2300–1750 B.C.E. Bronze, height 4¼ in.

The "Out of India" Debate

Two theories dominate the narrative of India's early history: The traditional one holds that warlike seminomadic foreigners speaking Indo-European languages and calling themselves Aryans ("nobles") invaded the Indus valley around 1500 B.C.E., enslaving or removing the native Dravidian population and initiating the unique cultural developments of Sanskrit (India's classic language) and the caste system. More recently, revisionist scholars have argued that the Aryans in fact migrated gradually from Central to South Asia during the second millennium B.C.E., blending with the native peoples of the Indus valley to form a single population that generated India's cultural traditions.

Supporters of the revisionist "Out of India" theory hold that a series of natural disasters and environmental changes (rather than military conquest) was responsible for the decline of Indus valley civilization between 1700 and 1500 B.C.E. They maintain that India's unique culture and its devotional texts, the *Vedas*, emerged before ca. 1500 B.C.E., when Sanskrit became the dominant language; that the caste system grew out of tribelike social and economic organization; and that India's great epics were the product of native tribal warfare. Traditionalists, however, point to the fact that the *Vedas* themselves refer frequently to military conflict between Aryans and native peoples. To date, the available evidence—archeological, linguistic, and genetic—is insufficient to resolve the question of India's origins. The subject remains hotly debated.

Hebrew god, Brahman assumes no personal and contractual relationship with humankind. Brahman is the Uncaused Cause and the Ultimate Reality.

In every human being, there resides the individual manifestation of Brahman: the Self, or **Atman**, which, according to the *Upanishads*, is "soundless, formless, intangible, undying, tasteless, odorless, without beginning, without end, eternal, immutable, [and] beyond nature." Although housed in the material prison of the human body, the Self (Atman) seeks to be one with the Absolute Spirit (Brahman). The spiritual (re)union of Brahman and Atman—a condition known as *nirvana*—is the goal of every Hindu. This blissful reabsorption of the Self into Absolute Spirit must be preceded by one's gradual rejection of the material world, that is, the world of illusion and ignorance, and by the mastery of the techniques of meditation and through a system of spiritual exercises known as **yoga**. Yoga (literally "to yoke") seeks the joining of one's Atman to Brahman through control of the mind and body. A complex combination of physical positions and breathing exercises, which was not codified until the second century B.C.E., yoga (and its manifold schools) developed as one of the many Hindu ascetic disciplines aimed at achieving liberation of the Self and union with the Supreme Spirit.

A literature of humility, the *Upanishads* offer no guidelines for worship, no moral laws, and no religious dogma. These texts neither exalt divine power, nor interpret it. They do, however, instruct the individual Hindu on the subject of death and rebirth. The Hindu anticipates a succession of lives: that is, the successive return of the Atman in various physical forms. The physical form, whether animal or human and of whatever species or class, is determined by the level of spiritual purity the Hindu has achieved by the time of his or her death. The Law of *Karma* holds that the collective spiritual energy gained from accumulated deeds determines one's physical state in the next

life. Reincarnation, or the Wheel of Rebirth, is the fate of Hindus until they achieve *nirvana*. In this ultimate state, the enlightened Atman is both liberated and absorbed—a process that may be likened to the dissolution of a grain of salt in the vast waters of the ocean.

The *Bhagavad-Gita*

The fundamental teachings of Hinduism are lyrically expressed in one of India's most popular religious poems: the *Bhagavad-Gita* (*Song of God*), which constitutes one episode from the *Mahabharata*. In this most famous part of the poem, a dialogue takes place between Arjuna, the warrior-hero, and Krishna, the incarnation of the god Vishnu and a divine manifestation of Brahman. Facing the prospect of shedding the blood of his own kinsmen in the battle to come, Arjuna seeks to reconcile his material obligations with his spiritual quest for selflessness. Krishna's answer to Arjuna—a classic statement of resignation—represents the essence of Hindu thought as distilled from the *Upanishads*. Although probably in existence earlier, the *Bhagavad-Gita* was not recorded until some time between the fifth and second centuries B.C.E.

READING 3.1 From the *Bhagavad-Gita*

He knows bliss in the Atman   1
And wants nothing else.
Cravings torment the heart:
He renounces cravings.
I call him illumined.   5
Not shaken by adversity,
Not hankering after happiness:
Free from fear, free from anger,
Free from the things of desire,
I call him a seer, and illumined.   10

The bonds of his flesh are broken.
He is lucky, and does not rejoice:
He is unlucky, and does not weep.
I call him illumined.

. . . .

Thinking about sense-objects
Will attach you to sense-objects; 15
Grow attached, and you become addicted;
Thwart your addiction, it turns to anger;
Be angry, and you confuse your mind;
Confuse your mind, you forget the lesson of experience; 20
Forget experience, you lose discrimination;
Lose discrimination, and you miss life's only purpose.
When he has no lust, no hatred,
A man walks safely among the things of lust and hatred.
To obey the Atman 25
Is his peaceful joy:
Sorrow melts
Into that clear peace;
His quiet mind
Is soon established in peace. 30
The uncontrolled mind
Does not guess that the Atman is present:
How can it meditate?
Without meditation, where is peace?
Without peace, where is happiness? 35
The wind turns a ship
From its course upon the waters:
The wandering winds of the senses
Cast man's mind adrift
And turn his better judgment from its course. 40
When a man can still the senses
I call him illumined.
The recollected mind is awake
In the knowledge of the Atman
Which is dark night to the ignorant: 45
The ignorant are awake in their sense-life
Which they think is daylight:
To the seer it is darkness.
Water flows continually into the ocean
But the ocean is never disturbed: 50
Desire flows into the mind of the seer
But he is never disturbed.
The seer knows peace:
The man who stirs up his own lusts
Can never know peace. 55
He knows peace who has forgotten desire.
He lives without craving:
Free from ego, free from pride.
This is the state of enlightenment in Brahman:
A man who does not fall back from it 60
Into delusion.
Even at the moment of death
He is alive in that enlightenment:
Brahman and he are one. . . .

Q **What are the obstacles to the state of enlightenment, according to Krishna?**

The Hindu view of the relationship between people and gods differs significantly from the religious views of the Mesopotamians and the ancient Egyptians. While these two cultures regarded human beings as separate from the gods, Hindus, guided by the *Upanishads* and the *Bhagavad-Gita*, asserted the oneness of matter and spirit. Where Western religions emphasize the imperishability of individual consciousness, Hinduism aspires to its sublimation, or rather, its reabsorption into the spiritual infinite. Although Hinduism still embraces the vast pantheon of Vedic gods and goddesses (see chapter 14), it has remained relatively unaffected by the religious precepts of Western Judaism and Christianity. Unlike the latter, Hinduism has no institutional forms of worship and no doctrinal laws. On the other hand, since the nineteenth century, Hinduism's holistic view of nature has increasingly influenced Western thought and belief. And since the last decades of the twentieth century, Hindu techniques of deep meditation have made a notable impact on the disciplines of religion, philosophy, and medical science.

Ancient China

Ancient Chinese civilization emerged in the fertile valleys of two great waterways: the Yellow and the Yangzi* rivers (Map **3.2**). As early as 3500 B.C.E., the Neolithic villages of China were producing silk, a commodity that would bring wealth and fame to Chinese culture.

Map 3.2 Ancient China.

* All transcriptions of Chinese names appear in the system known as Hanyu Pinyin.

It is likely that China's early dynasties flourished for some four centuries before the appearance of writing. The first dynasty described in ancient Chinese historical records, the Xia (originating ca. 2200 B.C.E.), has only recently been excavated. Near Luoyang (see Map 3.2), archeologists have uncovered a city with a large palace-type structure, pottery workshops, and a bronze foundry. Such evidence gives credibility to age-old legends honoring Xia's dynastic founder, King Yu, who is said to have reduced the flooding of the Yellow River by authorizing the construction of canals along its tributaries.

The Shang Dynasty (ca. 1766–1027 B.C.E.)

The warrior tribe known as the Shang initiated the first fully developed urban culture in Bronze Age China. Shang rulers were hereditary monarchs who ruled, like the pharaohs of Egypt, by divine right. They claimed their authority from the Lord on High (Shang-di). Royal authority was symbolized by the dragon, a hybrid beast that stood for strength, fertility, and life-giving water (Figure 3.4). Occupants of the "dragon throne," China's early monarchs defended their position by way of a powerful bureaucracy (the landholding nobility) and huge armies of archer-warriors recruited from the provinces. The king's soldiers consisted of peasants, who, in peacetime, farmed the land with the assistance of slaves captured in war.

The Chinese social order is clearly articulated in Shang royal tombs, where the king is surrounded by the men and women who served him in his lifetime. Royal graves also contain several hundred headless bodies, probably those of the slaves who built the tombs. As in Mesopotamia and Egypt, China's royal tombs were filled with treasures—a vast array of ritual and grave goods that include silk fabrics, ceramic sculptures, jade artifacts, bronze vessels (Figure 3.5), and objects of personal adornment. Unlike the tombs of ancient Egypt, China's graves were rarely plundered. Nevertheless, the early history of China is still largely hidden from us. Some of the richest discoveries have taken place in only the last few decades. For instance, in 1986, archeologists working in Sichuan province (an area beyond the rule of the Shang) uncovered graves that contained gold and silver objects, along with more than 200 bronze objects, including the earliest life-sized human figures in Chinese art (Figure 3.6).

Beginning in Neolithic times and continuing throughout ancient Chinese history, large numbers of jade objects—especially finely carved jade disks (see Figure 3.4)—were placed in royal graves. The meaning and function of these objects is a matter of some speculation. The Chinese used jade for tools, but also for carved insignias and talismans probably related to ceremonial ritual. Jade was prized by the Chinese for its durability, its musical qualities, its subtle, translucent colors, and its alleged protective powers—it was thought to prevent fatigue and delay the decomposition of the body. Jade disks were usually placed at the center of the body in the tomb. In the tombs of later rulers, the deceased were often encased in shrouds made up of thousands of carved jade plaques sewn with gold wire (see Figure 7.6).

Chinese pictograms, probably identifying individual clans, were incised on pottery as early as the second half of the third millennium B.C.E. But by 1750 B.C.E., the Chinese developed a pictographic writing system employing characters that stood for specific things or concepts. To a special group of priests fell the

Figure 3.4 Ritual disk, Zhou dynasty, fifth to third century B.C.E. Jade, diameter 6½ in. Jade disks such as this, placed on the body of the deceased, may have served as cosmic talismans that ensured protection from evil and decay.

responsibility for foretelling future events: whether the harvest would be bountiful, whether to declare or delay war, and so on. Shang diviners etched such questions with sharp tools on turtle shells and animal bones (Figure **3.7**). These were then heated to produce cracks that the priests might read and interpret. Not deciphered until the early twentieth century, "oracle bone script" provides a valuable record of Shang rulers, giving us vital information about their ceremonies, wars, and administrative history. The script also discloses intriguing details about weather, disease, and other routine topics relating to ancient Chinese life.

Eventually, the Chinese technique for writing script, known as **calligraphy**, became an artform in itself. Executed by means of a pliant brush filled with ink,

Figure 3.5 Ceremonial vessel with a cover, late Shang dynasty, China, ca. 1000 B.C.E. Bronze, height 20¹⁄₁₆ in. The surface of this ritual object is adorned with a complex pattern of dragons, birds, and geometric motifs arranged symmetrically. The object is a text that reflects its context: the ancient Chinese perception of the cosmos as both animated and regulated by a natural order.

Figure 3.6 Standing figure, late Shang dynasty, ca. 1300–1100 B.C.E., from Pit 2 at Sanxingdui, Guanghan, Sichuan province. Bronze, height 8 ft. 7 in. This barefooted figure was found among more than fifty bronze heads and twenty bronze masks. Holes in his earlobes suggest that he was adorned with earrings. His hands once grasped a cylindrical object, possibly an ivory tusk.

Figure 3.7 Inscribed oracle bone, China, ca. 1500–1000 B.C.E. 7 × 4½ in. Chinese characters were inscribed in columns and read from top to bottom.

Chronology

ca. 3500–2500 B.C.E.	Neolithic culture
ca. 2200–1766 B.C.E.	Xia dynasty
ca. 1766–1027 B.C.E.	Shang dynasty
ca. 1027–771 B.C.E.	Western Zhou dynasty

place in society. Within the natural hierarchy, those with greater intellectual abilities should govern, and those with lesser abilities should fulfill the physical needs of the state. Exactly how those with greater abilities were distinguished from those with lesser abilities is difficult to discern. Nevertheless, between the twelfth and eighth centuries B.C.E., when the Zhou kings took control of most of civilized China, the principle of the natural hierarchy already provided the basis for China's political and social order. Since the Zhou rulers delegated local authority to aristocrats of their choosing, it is probable that the assumptions of superiority and inferiority among people came after the fact of a division of labor among the members of society. Nevertheless, well before the second century B.C.E., the Chinese put into practice the world's first system whereby individuals were selected for government service on the basis of merit and education. Written examinations tested the competence and skill of those who sought government office. Such a system persisted for centuries and became the basis for an aristocracy of merit that has characterized Chinese culture well into modern times.

Repeated attacks by Central Asian tribes forced the Zhou dynasty into decline. In 771 B.C.E., the Zhou capital was moved eastward to Luoyang (see Map 3.2). While the Eastern Zhou dynasty would continue until 256 B.C.E., its rulers faced political turbulence and decades of warfare (see chapter 7).

Spirits, Gods, and the Natural Order

The agricultural communities of ancient China venerated an assortment of local spirits associated with the natural forces, and with rivers, mountains, and crops. Regulating the natural order of the universe was the creative principle known interchangeably as the Lord on High (Shang-di) and as Heaven (*Tian*). Chinese mythology describes cosmic unity as the marriage of Heaven (*Tian*) and Earth (*Kun*), the receptive principle. Although not anthropomorphic like the gods of Mesopotamia and Egypt, these celestial deities oversaw the workings of the universe, impartially guiding human destiny. But the most powerful personalized spirits of ancient China were those of deceased ancestors, the members of an extended familial community (Figure **3.8**). According to the Chinese, the spirits of their ancestors continued to exist in Heaven, where they assumed their role as mediators between Heaven and Earth. Since the ancestors exerted a direct influence upon

Chinese writing grew to some 4500 characters, many of which are still used today. Indeed, Chinese characters represent the world's oldest continuous writing system. Combining pictographic and phonetic elements, Chinese characters became the basis for writing throughout East Asia.

The Western Zhou Dynasty (1027–771 B.C.E.)

The sacred right to rule was known in China as the Mandate of Heaven. Although the notion of divine-right kingship began in the earliest centuries of China's dynasties, the concept of a divine mandate was not fixed until early in the Zhou Era, when the rebel Zhou clan justified their assault on the Shang by claiming that Shang kings had failed to rule virtuously; hence, Heaven (*Tian*) had withdrawn its mandate. Charged with maintaining the will of Heaven on earth, the king's political authority required obedience to established moral law, which, in turn, reflected the natural order.

According to the Chinese, nature determined human intelligence and ability, as well as the individual's proper

Figure 3.8 Mask, Shang dynasty, ca. 1500–1600 B.C.E. Bronze, 10 × 9¼ in.

human affairs, their eternal welfare was of deep concern to ancient Chinese families. They buried their dead in richly furnished tombs, regularly made sacrifices to them, and brought offerings of food and wine to their graves. One of the earliest odes in China's classic *Book of Songs* (*Shi jing*) celebrates the veneration of ancestors of both sexes:

Rich is the year with much millet and rice;
And we have tall granaries
With hundreds and thousands and millions of sheaves.
We make wind and sweet spirits
And offer them to our ancestors, male and female;
Thus to fulfill all the rites
And bring down blessings in full.

The Chinese Classics

The perception of an inviolable natural order dominated all aspects of Chinese culture. Its earliest expression is found in China's oldest known text, the *Book of Changes* (*I jing*). This classic text, a collection of ancient cosmic principles, is a guide for interpreting the workings of the universe. It centers on the principle that order is achieved through the dynamic balance of opposites. Originating in the Shang Era, but not recorded until the sixth century B.C.E., the *Book of Changes* consists of cosmological diagrams by means of which diviners were able to predict the future and advise others on the inevitability of change. The aim of such divination was to bring into balance that which had fallen out of balance—a key concept in Chinese thought, and one that continues to dominate Chinese medicine.

Basic to the natural order is the condition of balance between the four seasons, the five elements (wood, fire, earth, metal, and water), and the five creative powers

Science and Technology

3500 B.C.E.	silk manufacture begins in China
2700 B.C.E.	first experiments in acupuncture and herbal medicine are made in China
2296 B.C.E.	first reported sighting of a comet occurs in China
1350 B.C.E.	decimal numerals are introduced in China
1000 B.C.E.	the Chinese introduce an early version of the abacus

(heat, cold, dryness, moisture, and wind). It is symbolized by way of abstract symbols, the square and the circle, often represented on Shang bronzes. It is evident in the holistic idea that universal energy, called *qi* (pronounced "chee"), pervades all things, including the human body, to which balance is essential. And it is graphically expressed in the unity of opposites known as *yin/yang*. This principle, which ancient Chinese emperors called "the foundation of the entire universe," interprets all nature as the dynamic product of two interacting cosmic forces, or modes of energy, commonly configured as twin interpenetrating shapes enclosed within a circle (Figure **3.9**). The interaction of *yang*, the male principle (associated with lightness, hardness, brightness, warmth, and the sun), and *yin*, the female principle (associated with darkness, softness, moisture, coolness, the earth, and the moon), describes the creative energy of the universe and the natural order itself. For the Chinese, this order is inherent in the balance between the complementary yet opposing forces of hot and cold, day and night, heaven and earth, male and female.

Moral order, calling for subjects to obey their rulers and local landlords, and social order, emphasizing the value of family and the proper performance of religious rites, followed the basic precepts of the natural order. These were enshrined in documents that (along with the *Book of Changes*) became China's classic texts: the *Book of History* (*Shu jing*), the *Book of Songs* (*Shi jing*), and the *Book of Rites* (*Li jing*) (see chapter 7). Compiled after 600 B.C.E., these literary treasures preserve fragments of China's ancient past. The *Book of History*, for instance, records speeches from the Xia, Shang, and Zhou eras, while many of the 300 odes in the *Book of Songs* capture the intimate family loyalties of the Zhou period.

Figure 3.9 The *yin* and the *yang* as interpenetrating shapes in a circle, a figure with no beginning and no end.

Daoism

The most mystical expression of the natural order as it relates to humankind is preserved in the ancient Chinese belief system known as Daoism. As much a philosophy as a religion, Daoism embraces a universal and natural principle—the Dao, or "Way." While the Dao is ineffable—indeed, it resists all intellectual analysis—it manifests itself in the harmony of things. It may be thought of as the unity underlying nature's multiplicity; and it is understood only by those who live in total simplicity and in harmony with nature. Daoists seek to cultivate tranquility, spontaneity, compassion, and spiritual insight. Like the Hindu, the Daoist practices meditation and breath control, along with dietary and other physical means of prolonging and enriching life.

Daoism existed in China as early as 1000 B.C.E., but its basic text, the *Dao de jing* (*The Way and its Power*), did not appear until the sixth century B.C.E. This modest "scripture" of some 5000 words is associated with the name Lao Zi ("the Old One"), who may or may not have ever actually existed. The following poem, one of the eighty-one chapters of the *Dao de jing*, conveys the Daoist idea of nature's unity. It uses a series of simple images to illustrate the complementary and harmonious function of positive and negative elements in ordinary things, as in nature. Like all Daoist teaching, it relies on subtle wit and paradox as springboards to enlightenment.

READING 3.2 From the *Dao de jing* (ca. 550 B.C.E.)

Thirty spokes will converge	1
In the hub of a wheel;	
But the use of the cart	
Will depend on the part	
Of the hub that is void.	5
With a wall all around	
A clay bowl is molded;	
But the use of the bowl	
Will depend on the part	
Of the bowl that is void.	10
Cut out windows and doors	
In the house as you build;	
But the use of the house	
Will depend on the space	
In the walls that is void.	15
So advantage is had	
From whatever is there;	
But usefulness rises	
From whatever is not.	

Q **What images in this poem convey the idea of the Dao as a unity of opposites?**

The Americas

It is likely that the first Americans arrived 30,000 to 20,000 years ago, as successive waves of Asian nomads migrated across a land bridge that once linked Siberia and Alaska at the Bering Strait. Recent evidence suggests the possibility of other migrations by way of Scandinavian ice sheets or via small boats that brought settlers to various parts of the Pacific coast. Some archeologists suggest that Ice Age Europeans may have arrived at North America's east coast by way of boats that hugged the edges of the great ice sheets stretching west from Greenland. While debate continues on the details of this subject, it is clear that over a long period of time a mosaic of migrant peoples came to settle in North, South, and Middle ("Meso") America: parts of present-day Mexico and Central America. By the fifteenth century, when Europeans first made contact with the Americas, some 1000 agricultural societies flourished, and a number of new "American" civilizations had left the world their unique cultural legacies.

Ancient Peru

Until recently, it was believed that the earliest civilizations in the Americas dated from the middle of the second millennium B.C.E. In the first decade of the twenty-first century, however, archeologists established a dating of 3500 to 2600 B.C.E. for two ancient Peruvian sites, Caral and Sechin Bajo. Located in the coastal region northwest of Lima, these sites (only two of many recently uncovered in the area) are as old as, or older than, the Egyptian pyramids.

Caral, a site with six pyramids, wide plazas, numerous residences, and a sunken amphitheater, probably supported a population that exceeded 3000 people (Figure **3.10**). The remains of cotton nets suggest that fishing complemented native agricultural production. Other artifacts, such as flutes made of bird bones and cornets (horns) made from deer and llama bones, suggest a music-loving culture.

At Chankillo, a third site north of Lima, archeologists have identified a group of thirteen stone towers as a 2300-year-old solar observatory. Part of a heavily fortified complex that includes a stone temple, these monumental towers—resembling prehistoric teeth—appear to have functioned in a manner similar to the megalithic alignments at Stonehenge (see Figures 0.13 and 0.14), and other Neolithic European sites.

On the plains of southwestern Peru, archeologists continue to study a number of huge **geoglyphs** in the shape of geometric figures, insects, animals, reptiles, and birds (Figure **3.13**). Created by the removal of surface stones to expose the yellow soil beneath, these enormous images are fully visible only from very far above. While their exact function remains the subject of speculation, it is possible that they served as skymaps or calendars designed, like Stonehenge (see Figure 0.13), to mark seasonal change and help ancient farmers determine favorable times for planting crops. The recent discovery of a 2½-mile-long labyrinth and small stone platforms at this site suggests that these earthworks played a role in religious rituals.

Clearly, current research in Peru and elsewhere in the Americas raises many questions concerning the origins and development of ancient societies in the Western hemisphere. Capable of erecting mammoth temple complexes, the inhabitants of Caral clearly reached a level of political and social complexity beyond that of any typical

Figure 3.10 Amphitheater, Caral, Peru, ca. 2627 B.C.E.

MAKING CONNECTIONS

The largest of Caral's pyramids, the size of four football fields, boasts a wide, steep stairway leading to a ceremonial atrium and fire pit (Figure **3.11**). This type of stepped pyramid, the spiritual focus of a larger ceremonial complex, prevailed for centuries in the civilizations of the Olmec, Maya, Aztec, and Inca cultures, the last of which flourished some 3000 years later in Peru. There are striking similarities between the ziggurats of Mesopotamia (Figure **3.12**) and the stepped pyramids of the Americas. Whether both served similar purposes, and whether there exists any historical link between the two, remain as matters of speculation. Doubtless, however, those who ascended the steep stair of these sacred mounds saw themselves as moving closer to the heavens.

Figure 3.11 The largest of the Caral pyramids, a site of religious rituals, near Lima, Peru, ca. 2627 B.C.E.

Figure 3.12 Reconstruction of the ziggurat at Ur, Mesopotamia (Iraq), ca. 2100 B.C.E.

Figure 3.13 Giant hummingbird, Nasca culture, southwest Peru, ca. 200 B.C.E.–200 C.E. Wingspan 900 ft. This geoglyph was created by scraping away the weathered surface of the desert and removing stones. The giant hummingbird is one of eighteen bird images pictured on the Peruvian plain.

Neolithic village. Yet, at Caral, no draft animals, no wheeled vehicles, no evidence of writing, and no metal tools or weapons have been found. Although gold was mined in Peru as early as 2000 B.C.E., copper and bronze did not come into use in the Americas until the ninth century C.E. While Peru may prove to be the birthplace of civilization in the Americas, its culture differs dramatically from that of the first civilizations in Mesopotamia, Africa, India, and China. Ongoing excavation at Caral and nearby sites will surely continue to shape the historical record.

The Olmecs

Around 1300 B.C.E., Meso-America produced one of its largest and most advanced native cultures, that of the Olmecs (literally "rubber people," the name given by the Aztecs to those living among trees that produced this substance). On the coast of the Gulf of Mexico, south of the modern-day Mexican city of Veracruz, the Olmecs established urban centers. Here, priestly rulers governed on behalf of the gods. This elite cadre oversaw the spiritual life of the community—a population consisting of farmers and artisans at the lower end of the social order, and a ruling nobility at the upper end.

The Olmecs raised temple-pyramids on clay platforms fitted with elaborate drainage systems. They created a calendrical system, developed portraiture and mirror-making, and practiced rituals involving human sacrifice. They honored their rulers by carving colossal stone heads, which they placed facing outward from their ceremonial precincts (Figure **3.14**). The production of such massive sculptures and the building of monumental civic precincts required the labor of thousands, as well as a high degree of civic organization. Olmec culture flourished until ca. 400 B.C.E., but its political, religious, and artistic traditions survived for centuries in the civilizations of the Mayans and the Aztecs (see chapter 18).

One of the intriguing mysteries of Olmec culture is the existence of hollow ceramic "baby-face" figurines (see Figure 3.1). These nude, sexless, chubby figures, with oversized heads and puffy, slit eyes, often wear helmets similar to those on the colossal stone heads (see Figure 3.14). Found in graves and in household refuse, they may represent ancient Olmec deities, or may have served as substitutes for victims of infant sacrifice.

Figure 3.14 Olmec head, from San Lorenzo, Veracruz, Mexico, ca. 1000 B.C.E. Basalt, height 5 ft. 10⅞ in. Colossal heads like this one, weighing between 12 and 24 tons, range in height from 5 to 12 feet.

Ancient India

- India's earliest known civilization, located in the lower Indus valley, experienced a flourishing Bronze Age (ca. 2700–1500 B.C.E.) that featured planned communities, advanced sewage systems, and a pictographic script.
- During the Vedic Era (ca. 1500–500 B.C.E.), India's caste system, established by Aryan invaders, divided its people into four distinct castes: priests and scholars; rulers and warriors; artisans and merchants; and unskilled workers. Outside the social order lay those with the most degrading occupations: the Untouchables.
- The Aryans introduced Sanskrit, India's classic language, its early epics (the *Mahabharata* and the *Ramayana*), and its oldest devotional texts, the *Vedas*. Hinduism, the most ancient of today's world religions, came from this era. Markedly different from earlier religions, pantheistic Hinduism identified the sacred as an objective, all-pervading cosmic Spirit (Brahman).
- The goal of the ancient Hindu was *nirvana*: the union of Brahman with its individual manifestation (Atman), and release from the Wheel of Rebirth, achieved through meditation and the stilling of the senses.
- The fundamental teachings of pantheistic Hinduism are expressed in one of India's most popular religious poems: the *Bhagavad-Gita*.

Ancient China

- Early Chinese civilizations emerged between the Yellow and Yangzi rivers. As early as 3500 B.C.E., China was producing pottery, bronze, and silk, the commodity that would bring wealth and fame to Chinese culture.
- The Shang dynasty (1766–1027 B.C.E.), a warrior tribe, initiated the first fully developed urban culture and the earliest calligraphic script. Shang rulers ruled by divine right and were buried in elaborate tombs filled with bronze and jade artifacts.
- The Zhou clan eventually defeated the Shang, claiming that Shang kings had failed to rule virtuously, thus violating their right to rule: the Mandate of Heaven. The Western Zhou dynasty (1027–771 B.C.E.) put into practice the world's first administrative system whereby individuals were selected for government service on the basis of merit and education.
- According to the Chinese, the spirits of deceased ancestors continued to exist in Heaven, where they acted as mediators between Heaven and Earth.
- The idea of "balance," expressed by the cosmological principle known as *yin/yang*, dominated ancient Chinese spirituality. The *Book of Changes* (*I jing*) consists of cosmological diagrams used for divination and the interpretation of the natural order.
- Daoism, the most eloquent expression of the natural order, taught the individual to embrace the "Way" (Dao), a path to spiritual awareness that emphasized simplicity, meditation, and strict dietary practice.

The Americas

- It is likely that the first Americans arrived at least 20,000 years ago, as groups of Asian nomads migrated across a land bridge that once linked Siberia and Alaska at the Bering Strait, or by way of Scandinavian ice bridges.
- Archeologists recently established a dating of 3500 to 2600 B.C.E. for two ancient Peruvian cultures, Caral and Sechin Bajo (located in the coastal region northwest of Lima), that erected mammoth temple complexes as old as, or older than, the Egyptian pyramids.
- Between 1300 and 400 B.C.E., on Mexico's Gulf coast, the Olmecs raised temple-pyramids, created a calendar system, erected massive sculptures, and established political, religious, and artistic traditions that survived in the later civilizations of the Americas.

Glossary

Atman the Hindu name for the Self; the personal part of Brahman

Brahman the Hindu name for the Absolute Spirit; an impersonal World Soul that pervades all things

calligraphy (Greek, "beautiful writing") stylized or elegant writing usually executed with pen or brush and ink

caste system a rigid social stratification in India based on differences in wealth, rank, or occupation

geoglyph a large design or motif inscribed or imposed on the ground or on natural elements in the landscape

karma (Sanskrit, "deed") the law that holds that one's deeds determine one's future life in the Wheel of Rebirth

nirvana (Sanskrit, "liberation" or "extinction") the blissful reabsorption of the Self into the Absolute Spirit (Brahman): release from the endless cycle of rebirth (see also Buddhism, chapters 8 and 9)

pantheism the belief that a divine spirit pervades all things in the universe

qi (Chinese, "substance" or "breath") the material substance or vital force of the universe

yoga (Sanskrit, "to yoke or join") a system of spiritual exercises aimed at joining the Self and the One through control of mind and body

Greece: Humanism and the Speculative Leap
ca. 3000–332 B.C.E.

"I say that Athens is the school of Hellas, and that the individual Athenian in his own person seems to have the power of adapting himself to the most varied forms of action with the utmost versatility and grace."
Thucydides

Figure 4.1 Attr. **THE EUPHILETOS PAINTER**, detail from Greek black-figured Panathenaic prize amphora showing footrace, from Vulci, ca. 530 B.C.E. Terracotta, height 24½ in.

"We are all Greeks," proclaimed the nineteenth-century British poet Percy Bysshe Shelley. He meant by this that modern individuals—profoundly influenced by the Hellenic ideals of reason, beauty, and the good life on earth—bear the indelible stamp of ancient Greece. To the Greeks, we owe the refinement of almost all the basic forms of literary expression (including drama, lyric poetry, and historical narrative), the fundamentals of philosophic and scientific inquiry, and the formulation of a set of aesthetic values in art and music that—having persisted for well over a thousand years—have come to be called "Classical."

Greek urban life originated at the western end of the Asian landmass, north and west of the civilizations of ancient Mesopotamia and Egypt. During the second millennium B.C.E., the first Greek city-states emerged on islands and peninsulas in the Aegean Sea, the coast of Asia Minor, at the southern tip of Italy, and in Sicily (Map **4.1**). This ancient civilization called itself "Hellas" and its people "Hellenes" (the name "Greece" came into use later, from the Latin *Graecus*).

Few civilizations have been so deeply concerned with the quality of human life as that of the ancient Greeks. And few have been so committed to exploring human intellect and action, as they affect the individual and the community. Because Hellenic culture reflects a concern with life as it is lived here on earth, the Greeks have been called the humanists of the ancient world. The robust optimism of ancient Greece is apparent even in its formative stages, which are set in the Bronze Age civilizations of the Aegean Sea.

Bronze Age Civilizations of the Aegean (ca. 3000–1200 B.C.E.)

The Bronze Age culture of Mycenae was not known to the world until the late nineteenth century, when an amateur German archeologist named Heinrich Schliemann uncovered the first artifacts of ancient Troy (see Map 4.1). Schliemann's excavations brought to light the civilization of an adventuresome tribal people, the Mycenaeans, who had established themselves on the Greek mainland around 1600 B.C.E. In the first decade of the twentieth century, the British archeologist Sir Arthur Evans uncovered an even earlier pre-Greek civilization on the island of Crete in the Aegean Sea. He called it "Minoan" after the legendary King Minos, celebrated in ancient Greek legend. This maritime civilization flourished between 2000 and 1400 B.C.E., when it seems to have been absorbed or destroyed by the Mycenaeans.

Map 4.1 Ancient Greece, ca. 1200–332 B.C.E. Located in the eastern Mediterranean Sea, ancient Greece consisted of a group of islands and peninsulas, including Crete, the Cyclades (the islands of the Aegean Sea), the coast of Asia Minor, Sicily, and the southern tip of Italy. The entire area was smaller than the state of Maine.

Figure 4.2 Palace of Minos, Knossos, Crete, ca. 1500 B.C.E.

Minoan Civilization (ca. 2000–1400 B.C.E.)

Centered on the Palace of Minos at Knossos on the island of Crete (Figure **4.2**), Minoan culture was prosperous and seafaring. The absence of protective walls around the palace complex suggests that the Minoans enjoyed a sense of security. The three-story palace at Knossos was a labyrinthine masonry structure with dozens of rooms and corridors built around a central courtyard. The interior walls of the palace bear magnificent frescoes illustrating natural and marine motifs (Figure **4.3**), ceremonial processions, and other aspects of Cretan life.

The most famous of the palace frescoes, the so-called bull-leaping fresco, shows two women and a man, the latter vigorously somersaulting over the back of a bull (Figure **4.4**). Probably associated with the cult of the bull—an ancient symbol of virility (see Figures 1.1 and 2.4)—the ritual game prefigures the modern bullfight, the "rules" of which were codified in Roman times by Julius Caesar. Since 1979, when modern archeologists uncovered evidence of human sacrifice in Minoan Crete, historians have speculated on the meaning of ancient bull-vaulting (a sport still practiced in Portugal), and its possible relationship to

Figure 4.3 The queen's quarters, Palace of Minos, Knossos, Crete, ca. 1450 B.C.E.

Figure 4.4 Bull-leaping fresco from the Palace of Minos, Knossos, Crete, ca. 1500 B.C.E. Height 32 in.

rituals of blood sacrifice. Nevertheless, the significance of the representation lies in the authority it bestows upon the players: human beings are pictured here not as pawns in a divine game, but, rather, as challengers in a contest of wits and physical agility.

The Minoans developed a hieroglyphic script by 2000 B.C.E. Neither it nor a second type of writing (called by Evans "Linear A") have been deciphered; however, a later version of the script ("Linear B") found on mainland Greece appears to be an early form of Greek. Deciphered in the 1950s, Linear B was a language used for bureaucratic and administrative purposes. Some 4600 tablets are inscribed with lists of people, produce, animals, and manufactured goods. The search for more extensive archives containing poetry and other texts continues.

Modern archeologists were not the first to prize Minoan culture; the Greeks immortalized the Minoans in myth and legend. The most famous of the legends describes a

MAKING CONNECTIONS

Many Minoan artifacts suggest the persistence of ancient fertility cults honoring gods traditionally associated with procreation. The small statue of a bare-breasted female brandishing snakes may represent a popular fertility goddess; or it may depict a priestess performing specific cult rites, such as those accompanying ancient Greek dances that featured live snakes (Figure **4.5**). Because the head of the figure and the snake in her left hand are modern fabrications, recent scholarship has questioned the authenticity of this reconstruction, as well as the authenticity of related "snake goddess figurines." Nevertheless, statuettes and pendants similar to this figure are very common to second-millennium B.C.E. cultures of the eastern Mediterranean. Fabricated in ivory, gold, and other precious materials, they depict goddesses wearing a serpentine coil, holding or flanked by snakes (Figure **4.6**). Such figures are identified as agricultural deities, associated with the regenerative powers of the snake, an ancient symbol of rebirth.

Figure 4.5 Priestess with snakes, Minoan, ca. 1600 B.C.E. Faience, height 13½ in.

Figure 4.6 Goddess of growth (Astarte?) with two serpents (pendant). Ugarit, Phoenicia, fifteenth century B.C.E. Gold, 2⅝ × 1⅛ in.

Minotaur—a monstrous half-man, half-bull born of the union of Minos' queen and a sacred white bull. According to the story, the clever Athenian hero Theseus, aided by the king's daughter Ariadne, threaded his way through the Minotaur's labyrinthine lair to kill the monster, thus freeing Athens from its ancient bondage to the Minoans. Around 1700 B.C.E., some three centuries before mainland Greece absorbed Crete, an earthquake brought devastation to Minoan civilization.

Mycenaean Civilization (ca. 1600–1200 B.C.E.)

By 1600 B.C.E., the Mycenaeans had established themselves in the Aegean. By contrast with the Minoans, the Mycenaeans were a militant and aggressive people: their warships challenged other traders for control of the eastern Mediterranean. On mainland Greece at Tiryns and Mycenae (see Map 4.1), the Mycenaeans constructed heavily fortified citadels and walls so massive that later generations thought they had been built by a mythical race of giants known as the Cyclops. These "cyclopean" walls were guarded by symbols of royal power: in the triangular arch above the entrance gate to the citadel, two 9-foot-high stone lions flank a column that rests on a Minoan-style altar (Figure **4.7**).

Master stonemasons, the Mycenaeans buried their rulers in beehive-shaped tombs. The royal graves, uncovered by Schliemann in 1876, are filled with weapons and jewelry fit for an Egyptian pharaoh. These items, and in particular the gold death mask that once covered the face of the deceased, Schliemann identified as belonging to Agamemnon (Figure **4.8**), the legendary king who led the ancient Greeks against the city of Troy. This tale is immortalized in the first of the Greek epic poems, the *Iliad*. Although later archeologists have proved Schliemann wrong—the tombs are earlier than he thought—the legends and the myths of the Greek world would flower in Mycenaean soil.

Around 1200 B.C.E., the Mycenaeans attacked Troy ("Ilion" in Greek), a commercial stronghold on the northwest coast of Asia Minor. The ten-year-long war between Mycenae and Troy would provide the historical context for both the *Iliad* and the *Odyssey*, the other great epic poem of the ancient Greeks.

The Heroic Age (ca. 1200–750 B.C.E.)

Soon after 1200 B.C.E., more powerful, iron-bearing tribes of Dorians, a Greek-speaking people from the north, destroyed Mycenaean civilization. During the long period of darkness that followed, storytellers kept alive the history of early Greece, the adventures of the Mycenaeans, and the tales of the Trojan War, passing them orally from generation to generation. It was not until at least the ninth century B.C.E. that these stories were transcribed; and it was yet another 300 years before they reached their present form. The *Iliad* and the *Odyssey* became the "national"

Figure 4.7 Lion Gate, citadel at Mycenae, ca. 1500–1300 B.C.E. Limestone, height of relief 9 ft. 6 in. Huge rock-cut blocks of stone were set in projecting layers to hold in place the triangular relief above the entranceway. Heraldic lions, symbols of power, flank the central column. Carved separately, the heads of the lions are missing.

Figure 4.8 Funerary mask, once believed to be that of Agamemnon, ca. 1500 B.C.E. Gold, height 12 in.

Figure 4.9 **EUPHRONIOS** and **EUXITHEOS**, *Death of Sarpedon*, ca. 515 B.C.E. Ceramic krater with red-figure decoration, height 18 in. The legendary warrior and Trojan ally, Sarpedon, was killed by Patroclus in the course of the war. He is shown on this **krater** (a vessel used for mixing wine and water) being carried from the battlefield by the winged figures of Hypnos (Sleep) and Thanatos (Death). Central to the lyrically balanced composition is the figure of Hermes, messenger of the gods, who guides the dead to the underworld.

The *Odyssey* recounts the long, adventure-packed sea journey undertaken by Odysseus, a resourceful hero of the Trojan War, in his effort to return to his home and family, and reassume his authority as king of Ithaca. Like the *Epic of Gilgamesh*, the *Iliad* and the *Odyssey* belong to the oral tradition of a heroic age, but whereas the *Epic of Gilgamesh* takes as its theme the pursuit of everlasting life, the Greek epics give voice to the quest for individual honor and glory.

Almost 16,000 lines long, the *Iliad is* a robust tale of war (Figure **4.10**), but its true subject is Achilles, the offspring of Peleus, king of Thessaly, and the sea goddess Thetis. (Later legends report that Thetis, having dipped her infant son in the River Styx, made him invulnerable except for the heel by which she held him.) Like Gilgamesh, Achilles is part-god and part-man, but the Greek superhero is a more psychologically complex character than Gilgamesh; the emotions he exhibits—anger, love, rage, and grief—are wholly human. The plot of the *Iliad* turns on Achilles' decision to take action that will bring glory to his warriors and to himself. The importance of heroic action in proving virtue, or excellence (the Greek

poems of ancient Greece, uniting Greek-speaking people by giving literary authority to their common heritage. Although much of what is known about the early history of the Greeks comes from these epic poems, little is known about the blind poet Homer, to whom they are traditionally attributed. Scholars are not sure when or where he lived, or, indeed, if he existed at all. It is unlikely that he composed the poems, although legend has it that he actually memorized the whole of each poem. The only fact of which we can be fairly certain is that Homer represents the culmination of a long and vigorous tradition in which oral recitation—possibly to instrumental accompaniment—was a popular kind of entertainment.

The *Iliad* takes place in the last days of the Trojan War. It is the story of the Achaean (ancient Greek) hero Achilles (or Achilleus), who, moved to anger by an affront to his honor, refuses to join the battle against Troy alongside his Achaean comrades. Wearing Achilles' armor, his dearest friend, Patroclus, goes forth to rout the Trojans, slaying many of their allies (Figure **4.9**). Only after Patroclus is killed by Hector, leader of the Trojan forces, does Achilles finally, and vengefully, go to war. In a dramatic battle, he confronts and kills Hector, stripping him of his armor and dragging his nude corpse before the walls of Troy. Following this great indignity to the body and the memory of the Trojan prince, Hector's father, King Priam, humbles himself before Achilles and begs for the return of his son. The epic closes with Hector's funeral.

Figure 4.10 By the "**BOTKIN CLASS**," *Contest of Two Warriors*, ca. 540–530 B.C.E. Attic black-figured amphora, ceramic, 11⁹⁄₁₆ × 9½ in. Two black-figured warriors are shown on this **amphora** (a Greek vessel used for storing wine or oil). Both wear traditional Greek helmets and greaves (leg armor worn below the knee). Both are protected by handheld shields; one soldier is armed with a short sword, the other with a spear.

word *arete* connotes both), is central to the *Iliad* and to the male-dominated culture of the Heroic Age (see Figure 4.10). To the ancient Greeks, moral value lay in proper action, even if the consequence of that action was death. Indeed, death in battle was a sure path to honor.

The language of the *Iliad*, no less than its theme, is charged with heroic vigor. It makes use of vivid similes (anger "blinds like smoke"), graphic **epithets** ("the bronze-armed Achaeans"), and lengthy **catalogs** of particulars. Its majestic poetry and its heroic personalities have inspired generations of Western writers, including Virgil and Milton (discussed in later chapters). The following excerpts from the *Iliad*, rendered in a 1990 translation by Robert Fagles, illustrate the qualities that have made the work a classic.

┌─ READING 4.1 From the *Iliad* (ca. 850 B.C.E.)

(Book 18, ll. 1–42, 82–150; Book 19, ll. 423–77; Book 24, ll. 471–707)

So the men fought on like a mass of whirling fire   1
as swift Antilochus raced the message toward Achilles.
Sheltered under his curving, beaked ships he found him,
foreboding, deep down, all that had come to pass.
Agonizing now he probed his own great heart:
"Why, why? Our long-haired Achaeans[1] routed again,
driven in terror off the plain to crowd the ships, but why?
Dear gods, don't bring to pass the grief that haunts my heart—
the prophecy that mother revealed to me one time . . .
she said the best of the Myrmidons[2]—while I lived—   10
would fall at Trojan hands and leave the light of day.
And now he's dead, I know it: Menoetius' gallant son,[3]
my headstrong friend! And I told Patroclus clearly,
'Once you have beaten off the lethal fire, quick,
come back to the ships—you must not battle Hector!'"
   As such fears went churning through his mind
the warlord Nestor's son drew near him now,
streaming warm tears, to give the dreaded message:
"Ah son of royal Peleus, what you must hear from me!
What painful news—would to god it had never happened!   20
Patroclus has fallen. They're fighting over his corpse.
He's stripped, naked—Hector with that flashing helmet,
Hector has your arms!"
                    So the captain reported.
A black cloud of grief came shrouding over Achilles.
Both hands clawing the ground for soot and filth,
he poured it over his head, fouled his handsome face
and black ashes settled onto his fresh clean war-shirt.
Overpowered in all his power, he sprawled in the dust.
Achilles lay there, fallen . . .
tearing his hair, defiling it with his own hands.   30

---

[1] The Mycenaeans, who inhabited the kingdom near Thessaly, and, more broadly, the Greek army that besieged Troy.

[2] The name by which the subject warriors of Peleus and Achilles are known in Homer. It derives from the Greek word for ants, the creatures out of which Zeus was said to have created the inhabitants of the island of Aegina, ruled by Peleus.

[3] Patroclus, Achilles' favorite companion and friend.

And the women he and Patroclus carried off as captives
caught the grief in their hearts and keened and wailed,
out of the tents they ran to ring the great Achilles,
all of them beat their breasts with clenched fists,
sank to the ground, each woman's knees gave way.

Antilochus kneeling near, weeping uncontrollably,
clutched Achilles' hands as he wept his proud heart out—
for fear he would slash his throat with an iron blade.
Achilles suddenly loosed a terrible, wrenching cry
and his noble mother heard him, seated near her father,   40
the Old Man of the Sea[4] in the salt green depths,
and she cried out in turn.
          . . . .

As he groaned from the depths his mother rose before him
and sobbing a sharp cry, cradled her son's head in her hands
and her words were all compassion, winging pity: "My child—
why in tears? What sorrow has touched your heart?
Tell me, please. Don't harbor it deep inside you.
Zeus has accomplished everything you wanted,
just as you raised your hands and prayed that day.
All the sons of Achaea are pinned against the ships   50
and all for want of you—they suffer shattering losses."

   And groaning deeply the matchless runner answered,
"O dear mother, true! All those burning desires
Olympian Zeus has brought to pass for me—
but what joy to me now? My dear comrade's dead—
Patroclus—the man I loved beyond all other comrades,
loved as my own life—I've lost him—Hector's killed him,
stripped the gigantic armor off his back, a marvel to behold—
my burnished gear! Radiant gifts the gods presented Peleus
that day they drove you into a mortal's marriage bed . . .   60
I wish you'd lingered deep with the deathless sea-nymphs,
lived at ease, and Peleus carried home a mortal bride.
But now, as it is, sorrows, unending sorrows must surge
within your heart as well—for your own son's death.
Never again will you embrace him striding home.
My spirits rebel—I've lost the will to live,
to take my stand in the world of men—unless,
before all else, Hector's battered down by my spear
and gasps away his life, the blood-price for Patroclus,
Menoetius' gallant son he's killed and stripped!"   70

   But Thetis answered, warning through her tears,
"You're doomed to a short life, my son, from all you say!
For hard on the heels of Hector's death your death
must come at once—"
                  "Then let me die at once"—
Achilles burst out, despairing—"since it was not my fate
to save my dearest comrade from his death! Look,
a world away from his fatherland he's perished,
lacking me, my fighting strength, to defend him.
But now, since I shall not return to my fatherland . . .
nor did I bring one ray of hope to my Patroclus,   80

---

[4] A sea god, the "Old Man" of the sea and father of some 50–100 daughters, including Thetis, mother of Achilles.

nor to the rest of all my steadfast comrades,
countless ranks struck down by mighty Hector—
No, no, here I sit by the ships . . .
a useless, dead weight on the good green earth—
I, no man my equal among the bronze-armed Achaeans,
not in battle, only in wars of words that others win.
If only strife could die from the lives of gods and men
and anger that drives the sanest man to flare in outrage—
bitter gall, sweeter than dripping streams of honey,
that swarms in people's chests and blinds like smoke—   90
just like the anger Agamemnon[5] king of men
has roused within me now . . .
                          Enough.
Let bygones be bygones. Done is done.
Despite my anguish I will beat it down,
the fury mounting inside me, down by force.
But now I'll go and meet that murderer head-on,
that Hector who destroyed the dearest life I know.
For my own death, I'll meet it freely—whenever Zeus
and the other deathless gods would like to bring it on!
Not even Heracles fled his death, for all his power,   100
favorite son as he was to father Zeus the King.
Fate crushed him, and Hera's savage anger.
And I too, if the same fate waits for me . . .
I'll lie in peace, once I've gone down to death.
But now, for the moment, let me seize great glory!—
and drive some woman of Troy or deep-breasted Dardan
to claw with both hands at her tender cheeks and wipe away
her burning tears as the sobs come choking from her throat—
they'll learn that I refrained from war a good long time!
Don't try to hold me back from the fighting, mother,   110
love me as you do. You can't persuade me now."

              . . . .

*[Hephaestus (Hephaistos), god of fire and of metalworking,
has forged a special set of arms for Achilles. In the following
lines from Book 19, Achilles prepares to lead the Achaeans
into battle.]*

Thick-and-fast as the snow comes swirling down from Zeus,
frozen sharp when the North Wind born in heaven blasts it on—
so massed, so dense the glistening burnished helmets shone,
streaming out of the ships, and shields with jutting bosses,
breastplates welded front and back and the long ashen spears.
The glory of armor lit the skies and the whole earth laughed,
rippling under the glitter of bronze, thunder resounding
under trampling feet of armies. And in their midst
the brilliant Achilles began to arm for battle . . .   120
A sound of grinding came from the fighter's teeth,
his eyes blazed forth in searing points of fire,
unbearable grief came surging through his heart
and now, bursting with rage against the men of Troy,
he donned Hephaestus' gifts—magnificent armor
the god of fire forged with all his labor.
First he wrapped his legs with well-made greaves,
fastened behind his heels with silver ankle-clasps,

next he strapped the breastplate round his chest
then over his shoulder Achilles slung his sword,   130
the fine bronze blade with its silver-studded hilt,
then hoisted the massive shield flashing far and wide
like a full round moon—and gleaming bright as the light
that reaches sailors out at sea, the flare of a watchfire
burning strong in a lonely sheepfold up some mountain slope
when the gale-winds hurl the crew that fights against them
far over the fish-swarming sea, far from loved ones—
so the gleam from Achilles' well-wrought blazoned shield
shot up and hit the skies. Then lifting his rugged helmet
he set it down on his brows, and the horsehair crest   140
shone like a star and the waving golden plumes shook
that Hephaestus drove in bristling thick along its ridge.
And brilliant Achilles tested himself in all his gear,
Achilles spun on his heels to see if it fit tightly,
see if his shining limbs ran free within it, yes,
and it felt like buoyant wings lifting the great captain.
And then, last, Achilles drew his father's spear
from its socket-stand—weighted, heavy, tough.
No other Achaean fighter could heft that shaft,
only Achilles had the skill to wield it well;   150
Pelian ash it was, a gift to his father Peleus
presented by Chiron[6] once, hewn on Pelion's crest
to be the death of heroes.
                          Now the war-team—
Alcimus and Automedon worked to yoke them quickly.
They clinched the supple breast-straps round their chests
and driving the bridle irons home between their jaws,
pulled the reins back taut to the bolted chariot.
Seizing a glinting whip, his fist on the handgrip,
Automedon leapt aboard behind the team and behind
him Achilles struck his stance, helmed for battle now,   160
glittering in his armor like the sun astride the skies,
his ringing, daunting voice commanding his father's horses:
"Roan Beauty and Charger, illustrious foals of Lightfoot!
Try hard, do better this time—bring your charioteer
back home alive to his waiting Argive comrades
once we're through with fighting. Don't leave Achilles
there on the battlefield as you left Patroclus—dead!"

              . . . .

*[After Achilles defeats Hector, Priam, Hector's father and king
of Troy, comes to the Achaean camp. In the following lines
from Book 24, Priam begs for the return of his son's body.]*

. . . the old king went straight up to the lodge
where Achilles dear to Zeus would always sit.
Priam found the warrior there inside . . .   170
many captains sitting some way off, but two,
veteran Automedon and the fine fighter Alcimus
were busy serving him. He had just finished dinner,
eating, drinking, and the table still stood near.
The majestic king of Troy slipped past the rest
and kneeling down beside Achilles, clasped his knees
and kissed his hands, those terrible, man-killing hands

---

[5] King of Mycenae, who led the Greek forces in the Trojan War.

[6] A centaur (half-man, half-horse), one of the creatures driven from
Mount Pelion by the Lapiths (see Figure 5.23).

that had slaughtered Priam's many sons in battle.
Awesome—as when the grip of madness seizes one
who murders a man in his own fatherland and flees   180
abroad to foreign shores, to a wealthy, noble host,
and a sense of marvel runs through all who see him—
so Achilles marveled, beholding majestic Priam.
His men marveled too, trading startled glances.
But Priam prayed his heart out to Achilles:
"Remember your own father, great godlike Achilles—
as old as I am, past the threshold of deadly old age!
No doubt the countrymen round about him plague him now,
with no one there to defend him, beat away disaster.
No one—but at least he hears you're still alive   190
and his old heart rejoices, hopes rising, day by day,
to see his beloved son come sailing home from Troy.
But I—dear god, my life so cursed by fate . . .
I fathered hero sons in the wide realm of Troy
and now not a single one is left, I tell you.
Fifty sons I had when the sons of Achaea came,
nineteen born to me from a single mother's womb
and the rest by other women in the palace. Many,
most of them violent Ares cut the knees from under.
But one, one was left me, to guard my walls, my people—   200
the one you killed the other day, defending his fatherland,
my Hector! It's all for him I've come to the ships now,
to win him back from you—I bring a priceless ransom.
Revere the gods, Achilles! Pity me in my own right,
remember your own father! I deserve more pity . . .
I have endured what no one on earth has ever done before—
I put to my lips the hands of the man who killed my son."

   Those words stirred within Achilles a deep desire
to grieve for his own father. Taking the old man's hand
he gently moved him back. And overpowered by memory   210
both men gave way to grief. Priam wept freely
for man-killing Hector, throbbing, crouching
before Achilles' feet as Achilles wept himself,
now for his father, now for Patroclus once again,
and their sobbing rose and fell throughout the house.
Then, when brilliant Achilles had his fill of tears
and the longing for it had left his mind and body,
he rose from his seat, raised the old man by the hand
and filled with pity now for his gray head and gray beard,
he spoke out winging words, flying straight to the heart: 220
"Poor man, how much you've borne—pain to break the spirit!
What daring brought you down to the ships, all alone,
to face the glance of the man who killed your sons,
so many fine brave boys? You have a heart of iron.
Come, please, sit down on this chair here . . .
Let us put our griefs to rest in our own hearts,
rake them up no more, raw as we are with mourning.
What good's to be won from tears that chill the spirit?
So the immortals spun our lives that we, we wretched men
live on to bear such torments—the gods live free of sorrows.   230
There are two great jars that stand on the floor of Zeus's halls
and hold his gifts, our miseries one, the other blessings.
When Zeus who loves the lightning mixes gifts for a man,
now he meets with misfortune, now good times in turn.
When Zeus dispenses gifts from the jar of sorrows only,

he makes a man an outcast—brutal, ravenous hunger
drives him down the face of the shining earth,
stalking far and wide, cursed by gods and men.
So with my father, Peleus. What glittering gifts
the gods rained down from the day that he was born!   240
He excelled all men in wealth and pride of place,
he lorded the Myrmidons, and mortal that he was,
they gave the man an immortal goddess for a wife.
Yes, but even on him the Father piled hardships,
no powerful race of princes born in his royal halls,
only a single son he fathered, doomed at birth,
cut off in the spring of life— and I, I give the man
care as he grows old since here I sit in Troy,
no far from my fatherland, a grief to you, a grief
to all your children. And you too, old man, we hear   250
you prospered once: as far as Lesbos, Macar's
kingdom, bounds to seaward, Phrygia east and
upland, the Hellespont vast and north— that entire
realm, they say, you lorded over once, you excelled
all men, old king, in sons and wealth. But then the
gods of heaven brought this agony on you—ceaseless
battles round your walls, your armies slaughtered.
You must bear up now. Enough of endless tears,
the pain that breaks the spirit.
Grief for your son will do no good at all.   260
You will never bring him back to life—
sooner you must suffer something worse."

   But the old and noble Priam protested strongly:
"Don't make me sit on a chair, Achilles, Prince,
not while Hector lies uncared-for in your camp!
Give him back to me, now, no more delay—
I must see my son with my own eyes.
Accept the ransom I bring you, a king's ransom!
Enjoy it, all of it—return to your own native land,
safe and sound . . . since now you've spared my life."   270
   A dark glance—and the headstrong runner answered,
"No more, old man, don't tempt my wrath, not now!
My own mind's made up to give you back your son.
A messenger brought me word from Zeus—my mother,
Thetis who bore me, the Old Man of the Sea's daughter.
And what's more, I can see through you, Priam—
no hiding the fact from me: one of the gods
has led you down to Achaea's fast ships.
No man alive, not even a rugged young fighter,
would dare to venture into our camp. Never—   280
how could he slip past the sentries unchallenged?
Or shoot back the bolt of my gates with so much ease?
So don't anger me now. Don't stir my raging heart still more.
Or under my own roof I may not spare your life, old man—
suppliant that you are—may break the laws of Zeus!"

   The old man was terrified. He obeyed the order.
But Achilles bounded out of doors like a lion—
not alone but flanked by his two aides-in-arms,
veteran Automedon and Alcimus, steady comrades,
Achilles' favorites next to the dead Patroclus.   290
They loosed from harness the horses and the mules,
they led the herald in, the old king's crier,

and sat him down on a bench. From the polished wagon
they lifted the priceless ransom brought for Hector's corpse
but they left behind two capes and a finely-woven shirt
to shroud the body well when Priam bore him home.
Then Achilles called the serving-women out:
"Bathe and anoint the body—bear it aside first.
Priam must not see his son." He feared that,
overwhelmed by the sight of Hector, wild with   300
grief, Priam might let his anger flare and Achilles
might fly into fresh rage himself, cut the old man
down and break the laws of Zeus. So when the
maids had bathed and anointed the body sleek with
olive oil and wrapped it round and round in a braided
battle-shirt and handsome battle-cape, then Achilles
lifted Hector up in his own arms and laid him down
on a bier, and comrades helped him raise the bier
and body onto the sturdy wagon . . . Then with a
groan he called his dear friend by name: "Feel no   310
anger at me, Patroclus, if you learn— even there
in the House of Death—I let his father have
Prince Hector back. He gave me worthy ransom
and you shall have your share from me, as always,
your fitting, lordly share."

So he vowed and brilliant Achilles strode
back to his shelter, sat down on the well-carved
chair that he had left, at the far wall of the room,
leaned toward Priam and firmly spoke the words
the king had come to hear: "Your son is now set free,
old man, as you requested. Hector lies in state.   320
With the first light of day you will see for yourself
as you convey him home. Now, at last, let us turn
our thoughts to supper."

Q **How would you describe the personality of Achilles?**

Q **How do Achilles and Gilgamesh compare as epic heroes?**

The Greek Gods

The ancient Greeks envisioned their gods as a family of immortals who intervened in the lives of human beings. Originating in the cultures of Crete and Mycenae, the Greek pantheon exalted Zeus, the powerful sky god, and his wife, Hera, as the ruling deities. Among the lesser gods were Poseidon, god of the sea; Apollo, god of light, medicine, and music (Figure **4.11**); Dionysus, god of wine and vegetation; Athena, goddess of wisdom and war; and Aphrodite, goddess of love, beauty, and procreation. Around these and other deities there emerged an elaborate mythology.

Many Greek myths look back to the common pool of legends and tales that traveled throughout the Mediterranean and the Near East. In the *Theogony* (*The Birth of the Gods*), a poem recounting the history and genealogy of the gods, Homer's contemporary Hesiod (fl. 700 B.C.E.) describes the origins of the universe in a manner reminiscent of *The Babylonian Creation:*

First of all, the Void came into being, next broad-bosomed Earth, the solid and eternal home of all, and Eros [Desire], the most beautiful of the immortal gods, who in every man and every god softens the sinews and overpowers the prudent purpose of the mind. Out of Void came Darkness and black Night, and out of Night came Light and Day, her children conceived after union in love with Darkness. Earth first produced starry Sky, equal in size with herself . . .

The Greeks also had their own version of the Isis/Osiris myth. When Hades, god of the underworld, abducts the beautiful Persephone, her mother, Demeter, rescues her; tricked by Hades, however, this goddess of vegetation is forced to return annually to the underworld, leaving the earth above barren and desolate. Cults based in myths of death and rebirth offered their devotees the hope of personal regeneration.

The Greeks traced their origins to events related to the fury of Zeus: angered by human evil, Zeus decided to destroy humankind by sending a flood. Deucalion, the Greek Noah, built a boat for himself and his wife and obeyed an oracle that commanded them to throw the "bones" of Mother Earth overboard. From these stones sprang up human beings, the first of whom was Hellen, the legendary ancestor of the Greeks, or "Hellenes."

Principal Greek Gods

Greek Name	Roman Name	Signifies
Aphrodite	Venus	love, beauty, procreation
Apollo	Phoebus	solar light, medicine, music
Ares	Mars	war, strife
Artemis	Diana	hunting, wildlife, the moon
Athena	Minerva	war, wisdom
Demeter	Ceres	agriculture, grain
Dionysus	Bacchus	wine, vegetation
Eros	Amor/Cupid	erotic love, desire
Hades	Pluto	underworld
Helios	Phoebus	sun
Hephaestus	Vulcan	fire, metallurgy
Hera	Juno	queen of the gods
Heracles	Hercules	strength, courage
Hermes	Mercury	male messenger of the gods
Hestia	Vesta	hearth, domestic life
Nike	Victoria	victory
Persephone	Proserpina	underworld
Poseidon	Neptune	sea
Selene	Diana	moon
Zeus	Jupiter	king of the gods, sky

Figure 4.11 East frieze of the Parthenon, Athens, ca. 437–432 B.C.E. Marble, height 3 ft. 6 in. Immortal and flawless, the Greek gods (Poseidon, Apollo, and Artemis) depicted on the Parthenon were idealized surrogates of the Greeks themselves.

Although immortal, the Greek gods were much like the human beings who worshiped them: they were amorous, adulterous, capricious, and quarrelsome. They lived not in some remote heaven, but (conveniently enough) atop a mountain in northern Greece—that is, among the Greeks themselves. From their home on Mount Olympus, the gods might take sides in human combat (as they regularly do in the *Iliad*), seduce mortal women, and meddle in the lives of those they felt were worthy of their attention. The Greek gods were not always benevolent or just. Unlike the Hebrew god, they set forth no clear principles of moral conduct and no guidelines for religious worship. Priests and priestesses tended the temples and shrines and oversaw rituals, including human and animal sacrifices performed to win the favor of the gods.

Popular Greek religion produced no sacred scripture and no doctrines—circumstances that may have contributed to the freedom of intellectual inquiry for which the Greeks became famous. Equally famous, at least in ancient times, was the oracle at Delphi, the shrine of Apollo and the site that marked for the Greeks the center of the universe and the "navel" of the earth. Here the priestess of Apollo sat on a tripod over a fissure in the rock, and, in a state of ecstasy (which recent archeologists attribute to hallucinogenic fumes from narcotic gases in two geologic faults below) uttered inscrutable replies to the questions of supplicants from near and far. The oracle at Delphi remained the supreme source of prophecy and mystical wisdom until the temple-shrine was destroyed in late Roman times.

The Greek City-State and the Persian Wars (ca. 750–480 B.C.E.)

Toward the end of the Homeric Age, the Greeks formed small rural colonies that gradually grew into urban communities, mainly through maritime trade. Geographic conditions—a rocky terrain interrupted by mountains, valleys, and narrow rivers—made overland travel and trade difficult. At the same time, Greek geography (see Map 4.1) encouraged the evolution of the independent city-state (in Greek, *polis*). Ancient Greece consisted of a constellation of some 200 city-states, a few as large as 400 square miles and others as tiny as 2 square miles. Many of these (Athens, for instance) were small enough that a person might walk around their walls in only a few hours. Although all the Greek city-states shared the same language, traditions, and religion, each *polis* governed itself, issued its own coinage, and provided its own military defenses. The autonomy of the Greek city-states—so unlike the monolithic Egyptian state—fostered fierce competition and commercial rivalry. However, like the squabbling members of a family who are suddenly menaced by aggressive neighbors, the Greek city-states, confronted by the rising power of Persia, united in self-defense.

By the sixth century B.C.E., the Persian Empire had conquered most of the territories between the western frontier of India and Asia Minor. Advancing westward, Persia annexed Ionia, the Greek region on the coast of Asia Minor (see Map 4.1), a move that clearly threatened mainland Greece. Thus, when in 499 B.C.E. the Ionian cities revolted against Persian rule, their Greek neighbors came to their aid. In retaliation, the Persians sent military expeditions to punish the rebel cities of the Greek mainland. In 490 B.C.E., on the plain of Marathon, 25 miles from Athens, a Greek force of 11,000 men met a Persian army with twice its numbers and defeated them, losing only 192 men. Persian casualties exceeded 6000. The Greek warrior who brought news of the victory at Marathon to Athens died upon completing the 26-mile run. (Hence the word "marathon" has come to designate a long-distance endurance contest.) But the Greeks soon realized that without a strong navy even the combined land forces of all the city-states could not hope to oust the Persians. They thus proceeded to build a fleet of warships, which, in 480 B.C.E., ultimately defeated the Persian armada at Salamis, one of the final battles of the Persian Wars.

Herodotus

Much of what we know about the Persian Wars comes to us from the world's first known historian, Herodotus (ca. 485–425 B.C.E.), the "father of history." Writing not as an eyewitness to the wars, but a half-century later, Herodotus nevertheless brought keen critical judgment to sources that included hearsay as well as record. His sprawling narrative is filled with fascinating anecdotes and colorful digressions, including a "travelogue" of his visits to Egypt and Asia—accounts that remain among our most detailed sources of information about ancient African and West Asian life. Here, for instance, is our earliest information on Scythian royal burials and on the use of hemp as a hallucinogen. The chapters on Africa, filled with numerous comparisons between Greek and Egyptian social practices and religious beliefs, show Herodotus as an early investigator of what would today be called "comparative culture."

By presenting various (and often contradictory) pieces of evidence and weighing them against one another before arriving at a conclusion, Herodotus laid the basis for the historical method. Following the Homeric epics by some 300 years, the nine-volume *History of the Persian Wars* is not only the West's first historical narrative, it is the first major literary work written in prose. Like the Homeric epics, and designed (as Herodotus claimed) "to preserve the memory of the past," the *History* shaped the Greek national identity.

Athens and the Greek Golden Age (ca. 480–430 B.C.E.)

Although all the city-states had contributed to expelling the Persians, it was Athens that claimed the crown of victory. Indeed, in the wake of the Persian Wars, Athens assumed political dominion among the city-states, as well as commercial supremacy in the Aegean Sea. The defeat of Persia inspired a mood of confidence and a spirit of vigorous chauvinism. This spirit ushered in an age of drama, philosophy, music, art, and architecture. In fact, the period between 480 and 430 B.C.E., known as the Greek Golden Age, was one of the most creative in the history of the

world. In Athens, it was as if the heroic idealism of the *Iliad* had bloomed into civic patriotism.

Athens, the most cosmopolitan of the city-states, was unique among the Greek communities, for the **democratic** government that came to prevail there was the exception rather than the rule in ancient Greece. In its early history, Athens—like most of the other Greek city-states—was an **oligarchy**, that is, a government controlled by an elite minority. But a series of enlightened rulers who governed Athens between roughly 600 and 500 B.C.E. introduced reforms that placed increasing authority in the hands of its citizens. The Athenian statesman, poet, and legislator Solon (ca. 638–558 B.C.E.) fixed the democratic course of Athenian history by abolishing the custom of debt slavery and encouraging members of the lower classes to serve in public office. By broadening the civic responsibilities of Athenians, Solon educated citizens of all classes in the activities of government. By 550 B.C.E., the Popular Assembly of Citizens (made up of all citizens) was operating alongside the Council of Five Hundred (made up of aristocrats who handled routine state business) and the Board of Ten Generals (an annually elected executive body). When, at last, in the year 508 B.C.E., the Popular Assembly acquired the right to make laws, Athens became the first direct democracy in world history.

The word "democracy" derives from Greek words describing a government in which the people (*demos*) hold power (*kratos*). In the democracy of ancient Athens, Athenian citizens exercised political power directly, thus—unlike in the United States, where power rests in the hands of representatives of the people—the citizens of Athens themselves held the authority to make the laws and approve state policy. Athenian democracy was, however, highly exclusive. Its citizenry included only landowning males over the age of eighteen. Of an estimated population of 250,000, this probably constituted some 40,000 people. Women, children, resident aliens, and slaves did not qualify as citizens. Athenian women could not inherit or own property and had few legal rights. (Slaves, as in earlier civilizations, arrived at their unfree condition as a result of warfare or debt, not race.) Clearly, in the mind of the Athenian, Hellenes were superior to non-Greeks (or outsiders, whom the Greeks called *barbaros*, from which comes the English word "barbarians"), Athenians were superior to non-Athenians, Athenian males were superior to Athenian females, and all classes of free men and women were superior to slaves.

Fundamental to Athenian democracy was a commitment to the legal equality of its participants: one citizen's vote weighed as heavily as the next. Equally important to Athenian (as to any) democracy was the hypothesis that individuals who had the right to vote would do so, and, moreover, were willing to take responsible action in the interest of the common good. (Such ideals are still highly valued in many parts of the modern world.) The small size of Athens probably contributed to the success of its unique form of government. Although probably no more than 5000 Athenians attended the Assembly that met four times a month to make laws in the open-air marketplace (the

Agora) located at the foot of the Acropolis, these men were the proponents of a brave new enterprise in governing.

Golden Age Athens stands in vivid contrast to those ancient civilizations whose rulers—the incarnate representatives of the gods—held absolute power while citizens held none. Athens also stands in contrast to its rival, Sparta, the largest *polis* on the Peloponnesus (see Map 4.1). In Sparta, an oligarchy of five officials, elected annually, held tight reins on a society whose male citizens (from the age of seven on) were trained as soldiers. All physical labor fell to a class of unfree workers called *helots*, the captives of Sparta's frequent local wars. Spartan soldiers were renowned for their bravery; their women, expected to live up to the ideals of a warrior culture, enjoyed a measure of freedom that was unknown in Athens. Yet, the history of Sparta would be one in which a strict social order left little room for creativity, in government or in the arts.

Pericles' Glorification of Athens

The leading proponent of Athenian democracy was the statesman Pericles (ca. 495–429 B.C.E.) (Figure **4.12**), who dominated the Board of Ten Generals for more than thirty years until his death. An aristocrat by birth, Pericles was a democrat at heart. In the interest of broadening the democratic system, he initiated some of Athens' most sweeping domestic reforms, such as payment for holding public office and a system of public audit in which the finances of outgoing magistrates were subject to critical scrutiny. In

Figure 4.12 Bust inscribed with the name of Pericles, from Tivoli. Roman copy after a bronze original of 450–425 B.C.E. Marble, height 23 in. The helmet resting on Pericles' head signifies his role as a military general in the campaigns of the Peloponnesian Wars.

Pericles' time, many public offices were filled by lottery—a procedure that invited all citizens to seek governmental office, and one so egalitarian as to be unthinkable today.

Pericles' foreign policy was even more ambitious than his domestic policies. In the wake of the Persian Wars, he encouraged the Greek city-states to form a defensive alliance against future invaders. At the outset, the league's collective funds were kept in a treasury on the sacred island of Delos (hence the name "Delian League"). But, in a bold display of chauvinism, Pericles moved the fund to Athens and expropriated its monies to rebuild the Athenian temples that had been burned by the Persians.

Pericles' high-handed actions, along with his imperialistic efforts to dominate the commercial policies of league members, led to antagonism and armed dispute between Athens and a federation of rival city-states led by Sparta. The ensuing Peloponnesian Wars (431–404 B.C.E.), which culminated in the defeat of Athens, brought an end to the Greek Golden Age. Our knowledge of the Peloponnesian Wars is based mainly on the account written by the great historian Thucydides (ca. 460–400 B.C.E.), himself a general in the combat. Thucydides went beyond merely recording the events of the war to provide insights into its causes and a firsthand assessment of its political and moral consequences. Thucydides' terse, graphic descriptions and his detached analyses of events distinguish his style from that of Herodotus.

The following speech by Pericles, excerpted from Thucydides' *History of the Peloponnesian War*, was presented on the occasion of a mass funeral held outside the walls of Athens to honor those who had died in the first battles of the war. Nowhere are the concepts of humanism and individualism more closely linked to civic patriotism than in this speech. Pericles reviews the "principles of action" by which Athens rose to power. He describes Athens as "the school of Hellas"; that is, it is the model and the teacher for all the other Greek communities. The greatness of Athens, according to Pericles, lies not merely in its military might and in the superiority of its political institutions, but in the quality of its citizens, their nobility of spirit, and their love of beauty and wisdom. Pericles' views, which were shared by most Athenians as primary articles of faith, reflect the spirit of civic pride that characterized Hellenic culture at its peak.

READING 4.2 From Thucydides' *Peloponnesian War* (ca. 410 B.C.E)

Pericles' Funeral Speech

"I will speak first of our ancestors, for it is right and   1
becoming that now, when we are lamenting the dead, a
tribute should be paid to their memory. There has never been a
time when they did not inhabit this land, which by their valor
they have handed down from generation to generation, and
we have received from them a free state. But if they were
worthy of praise, still more were our fathers, who added to
their inheritance, and after many a struggle transmitted to us
their sons this great empire. And we ourselves assembled

here today, who are still most of us in the vigor of life, have chiefly done the work of improvement, and have richly endowed our city with all things, so that she is sufficient for herself both in peace and war. Of the military exploits by which our various possessions were acquired, or of the energy with which we or our fathers drove back the tide of war, Hellenic or barbarian, I will not speak; for the tale would be long and is familiar to you. But before I praise the dead, I should like to point out by what principles of action we rose to power, and under what institutions and through what manner of life our empire became great. For I conceive that such thoughts are not unsuited to the occasion, and that this numerous assembly of citizens and strangers may profitably listen to them.

"Our form of government does not enter into rivalry with the institutions of others. We do not copy our neighbors, but are an example to them. It is true that we are called a democracy, for the administration is in the hands of the many and not of the few. But while the law secures equal justice to all alike in their private disputes, the claim of excellence is also recognized; and when a citizen is in any way distinguished, he is preferred to the public service, not as a matter of privilege, but as the reward of merit. Neither is poverty a bar, but a man may benefit his country whatever be the obscurity of his condition. There is no exclusiveness in our public life, and in our private intercourse we are not suspicious of one another, nor angry with our neighbor if he does what he likes; we do not put on sour looks at him which, though harmless, are not pleasant. While we are thus unconstrained in our private intercourse, a spirit of reverence pervades our public acts; we are prevented from doing wrong by respect for authority and for the laws, having an especial regard to those which are ordained for the protection of the injured as well as to those unwritten laws which bring upon the transgressor of them the reprobation of the general sentiment.

"And we have not forgotten to provide for our weary spirits many relaxations from toil; we have regular games[1] and sacrifices throughout the year; at home the style of our life is refined; and the delight which we daily feel in all these things helps to banish melancholy. Because of the greatness of our city the fruits of the whole earth flow in upon us; so that we enjoy the goods of other countries as freely as of our own.

"Then, again, our military training is in many respects superior to that of our adversaries. Our city is thrown open to the world, and we never expel a foreigner or prevent him from seeing or learning anything of which the secret if revealed to an enemy might profit him. We rely not upon management or trickery, but upon our own hearts and hands. And in the matter of education, whereas they from early youth are always undergoing laborious exercises which are to make them brave, we live at ease, and yet are equally ready to face the perils which they face. And here is the proof. The Lacedaemonians[2] come into Attica not by themselves, but with their whole confederacy following; we go alone into a neighbor's country; and although our opponents are fighting for their homes and

we on a foreign soil, we have seldom any difficulty in overcoming them. Our enemies have never yet felt our united strength; the care of a navy divides our attention, and on land we are obliged to send our own citizens everywhere. But they, if they meet and defeat a part of our army, are as proud as if they had routed us all, and when defeated they pretend to have been vanquished by us all.

"If then we prefer to meet danger with a light heart but without laborious training, and with a courage which is gained by habit and not enforced by law, are we not greatly the gainers? Since we do not anticipate the pain, although, when the hour comes, we can be as brave as those who never allow themselves to rest; and thus too our city is equally admirable in peace and in war.

"For we are lovers of the beautiful, yet with economy, and we cultivate the mind without loss of manliness. Wealth we employ, not for talk and ostentation, but when there is a real use for it. To avow poverty with us is no disgrace; the true disgrace is in doing nothing to avoid it. An Athenian citizen does not neglect the state because he takes care of his own household; and even those of us who are engaged in business have a very fair idea of politics. We alone regard a man who takes no interest in public affairs, not as a harmless, but as a useless character; and if few of us are originators, we are all sound judges of a policy. The great impediment to action is, in our opinion, not discussion, but the want of that knowledge which is gained by discussion preparatory to action. For we have a peculiar power of thinking before we act and of acting too, whereas other men are courageous from ignorance but hesitate upon reflection. And they are surely to be esteemed the bravest spirits who, having the clearest sense both of the pains and pleasures of life, do not on that account shrink from danger. In doing good, again, we are unlike others; we make our friends by conferring, not by receiving favors. . . . We alone do good to our neighbors not upon a calculation of interest, but in the confidence of freedom and in a frank and fearless spirit.

"To sum up: I say that Athens is the school of Hellas, and that the individual Athenian in his own person seems to have the power of adapting himself to the most varied forms of action with the utmost versatility and grace. This is no passing and idle word, but truth and fact; and the assertion is verified by the position to which these qualities have raised the state. For in the hour of trial Athens alone among her contemporaries is superior to the report of her. No enemy who comes against her is indignant at the reverses which he sustains at the hands of such a city; no subject complains that his masters are unworthy of him. And we shall assuredly not be without witnesses; there are mighty monuments of our power which will make us the wonder of this and of succeeding ages; we shall not need the praises of Homer or of any other panegyrist whose poetry may please for the moment, although his representation of the facts will not bear the light of day. For we have compelled every land and every sea to open a path for our valor, and have everywhere planted eternal memorials of our friendship and of our enmity. Such is the city for whose sake these men nobly fought and died; they could not bear the thought that she might be taken from them; and every one of us who survive should gladly toil on her behalf.

---

[1] Athletic games were part of many Greek festivals, the most famous of which was the Panhellenic Festival (see below).

[2] Citizens of the city-state of Sparta, ideologically opposed to Athens.

Q In what way does Pericles find Athens unique?

Q What does he mean by saying "Athens is the school of Hellas"?

The Olympic Games

Pericles makes proud to the "regular games" that provide Athenians with "relaxations from toil." But, in fact, the most famous of the "games" were athletic contests in which all the city-states of Greece participated. These games were the chief feature of the Panhellenic ("all-Greek") Festival, instituted in 776 B.C.E. in honor of the Greek gods. Located in Olympia, one of the great religious centers of Greece, the festival took place at midsummer every four years, even during wartime: a sacred truce guaranteed safe conduct to all visitors. So significant were the games that they became the basis for the reckoning of time. While Mesopotamia and Egypt calculated time according to the rule of dynasties and kings, the ancient Greeks marked time in "Olympiads," four-year periods beginning with the first games, in 776 B.C.E. The central event of the games was a 200-yard sprint (see Figure **4.1**) called the *stadion* (hence our word "stadium"). But there were also many other contests: a footrace of one and a half miles, the discus throw (Figure **4.13**), the long jump, wrestling, boxing, and other games that probably looked back to Minoan tradition (see Figure 4.4). Greek athletes competed in the nude—from the Greek word *gymnos* ("naked") we get "gymnasium." Winners received amphoras filled with olive oil, garlands of wild olive or laurel leaves, and the enthusiastic acclaim of Greek painters and poets (see Reading 5.3), but no financial reward.

Figure 4.13 MYRON, *Discobolus* (*Discus Thrower*), reconstructed Roman marble copy of a bronze Greek original of ca. 450 B.C.E. Height 5 ft. 1 in.

Although women were not permitted to compete in the Olympics, they could hold games of their own. Prowess rather than cunning was valued in all games: in wrestling, hair-pulling and finger-bending were permitted, but biting and finger-breaking were forbidden. A match terminated when either wrestler gave up, lost consciousness, or fell dead. True "sport" was that which gave athletes an opportunity to rival the divinity of the gods. Nevertheless, the Olympics were a national event that, typically, promoted both individual excellence and communal pride.

The Individual and the Community

Greek Drama

While the Olympic Games were held only once in four years, theatrical performances in the city of Athens occurred twice annually. Like the games, Greek drama was a form of play that addressed the relationship between the individual, the community, and the gods. The ancient Greeks were the first masters in the art of drama. The literary genre that tells a story through the imitation of action, drama grew out of a complex of rituals associated with the worship of Dionysus, god of wine, vegetation, and seasonal regeneration. In early Homeric times, religious rites performed in honor of Dionysus featured a dialogue between two choruses or between a leader (originally perhaps the shaman or priest) and a chorus (the worshipers or ritual participants). With the advent of the poet Thespis (fl. 534 B.C.E.), actor and chorus (the performers) seem to have become separate from those who witnessed the action (the audience). At some point, dramatic action assumed two principal forms: *tragedy* and *comedy*. Although the origins of each are still the subject of speculation among scholars, tragedy probably evolved from fertility rituals surrounding the death and decay of the crops, while comedy seems to have developed out of village revels celebrating seasonal rebirth. It is possible, as well, that such performances had something to do with the healing cults of ancient Greece: the great theater at Epidaurus (Figure **4.14**) was dedicated to Asclepius, the god of medicine. Like the more ancient

Figure 4.14 POLYCLEITUS THE YOUNGER, theater at Epidaurus, Greece, ca. 350 B.C.E. Greek theaters like this one were typically great in size (13,000 capacity). Nevertheless, actors and chorus could be heard even from the top row.

theater of Dionysus in Athens, it stood adjacent to a chief sanctuary for the worship of the god of healing.

The two annual festivals dedicated to Dionysus were the occasion for the performances of tragedies and comedies, and on each occasion (lasting several days) the author of the best play in its category received a prize. By the fifth century B.C.E., Greece had become a mecca

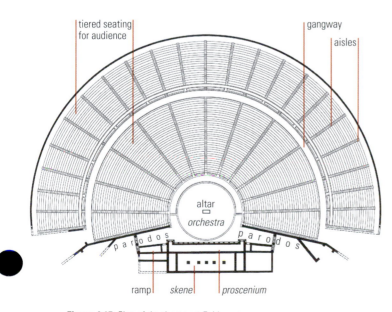

Figure 4.15 Plan of the theater at Epidaurus.

for theater, and while hundreds of plays were performed during the century in which Athenian theater flourished, only forty-four have survived.* They are the products of but four playwrights: Aeschylus (ca. 525–456 B.C.E.), Sophocles (496–406 B.C.E.), Euripides (480–406 B.C.E.), and Aristophanes (ca. 450–ca. 388 B.C.E.). Their plays were staged in the open-air theaters built into the hillsides at sacred sites throughout Greece. These acoustically superb structures, which seated between 13,000 and 27,000 people, featured an *orchestra* (the circular "dancing space" in front of the stage), a *skene* (an area that functioned as a stage set or dressing room), and an *altar* dedicated to the god Dionysus (Figure **4.15**). The *proscenium*, a raised stage in front of the *skene*, came into use somewhat later, in the Hellenistic era (see chapter 5). Music, dance, and song were essential to dramatic performance; scenery and props were few; and actors (all of whom were male) wore elaborate costumes, along with masks that served to amplify their voices.

The tragedies of Aeschylus, Sophocles, and Euripides deal with human conflicts as revealed in Greek history, myth, and legend. Since such stories would have been generally familiar to the average Greek theater-goer, it fell to the playwright to develop the story in an interesting manner. Dramatic action progressed from a specific moment

---

* All the Greek plays in English translation may be found at the website http://classics.mit.edu.

of friction between the individual and fate, the gods, or the community. The events of the play unfolded by way of dialogue spoken by individual characters, but also through the commentary of the chorus. Aeschylus, the author of the oldest surviving Western tragedy, introduced a second actor and gave the chorus a principal role in the drama. He brought deep religious feeling to his tragedies, the most famous of which is the series of three plays, or trilogy, known as the *Oresteia* (the plays of Orestes). These plays deal with the history of the family of Agamemnon, who led the Greeks to Troy, and whose murder at the hands of his wife upon his return from Troy is avenged by their son, Orestes.

While Aeschylus advanced the story of the play by way of sonorous language, Sophocles, the second of the great tragedians, developed his plots through the actions of the characters. He modified the ceremonial formality of earlier Greek tragedies by individualizing the characters and introducing moments of great psychological intimacy. Euripides, the last of the great tragedians, brought even greater realism to his characters. Plays such as *Medea* and *Electra* offer striking psychological portraits that explore the human soul in its experience of grief.

Tragedy, which gave formal expression to the most awful kinds of human experience—disaster and death—invited the spectator to participate vicariously in the dramatic action, thus undergoing a kind of emotional liberation. Comedy, on the other hand, drew its ability to provoke laughter from incongruity and the unexpected. Originating in association with fertility rites, and revels honoring Dionysus, comedy involved satire and parody of sexual union and erotic play of the kind found to this day in seasonal festivals and carnivals such as Mardi Gras. Obscene jokes, grotesque masks, fantastic costumes, and provocative dance and song were common to ancient comedy, as they are in various forms of modern slapstick and burlesque.

In the history of ancient Greek drama, the only comic plays to survive are those of Aristophanes. His inventive wit, sharply directed against Athenian politics and current affairs, is best revealed in the comedy *Lysistrata*, the oldest of his eleven surviving works. In this play, written in the wake of the bitter military conflict between Athens and Sparta, the playwright has the leading character—the wife of an Athenian soldier—launch a "strike" that will deprive all husbands of sexual satisfaction until they agree to refrain from war. As timely today as it was in ancient Athens, *Lysistrata* is a hilarious attack on the idealized, heroic image of armed combat.

The Case of *Antigone*

The drama that is most relevant to the theme of this chapter is Sophocles' *Antigone*, the third of a group of plays that includes *Oedipus the King* and *Oedipus at Colonus*. The story of *Antigone* proceeds from the last phase of the history of Thebes, a history with which most Athenians would have been familiar, since it recalled the ancient ascendancy of Athens over Thebes: following the death of Oedipus, king of Thebes, his sons Polynices and Eteocles kill each other in a dispute over the throne, thus leaving the crown to Creon, the brother-in-law of Oedipus and the only surviving male member of the ill-fated royal family. Upon becoming king, Creon forbids the burial of Polynices, contending that Eteocles had been the rightful ruler of Thebes. Driven by familial duty and the wish to fulfill the divine laws requiring burial of the dead, Oedipus' daughter Antigone violates Creon's decree and buries her brother Polynices. These circumstances provoke further violence and tragic death.

Antigone is a play that deals with many issues: it explores the conflict between the rights of the individual and the laws of the state; between dedication to family and loyalty to community; between personal and political obligations; between female willpower and male authority; and, finally, between human and divine law. It reflects Sophocles' effort to reconcile human passions, the will of the gods, and the sovereignty of the *polis*.

READING 4.3 From Sophocles' *Antigone* (ca. 440 B.C.E.)

Characters

Antigone, daughter of Oedipus and Iocasta

Ismene, her sister

Creon, King of Thebes, brother of Iocasta

Haemon, his son

A guard

Messenger

Eurydice, wife to Creon

Chorus of Theban elders

Guards, Attendants, etc.

Enter, from the palace, Antigone and Ismene

  Antigone: Ismene, my own sister, dear Ismene, how many   **1**
miseries our father caused! And is there one of them that
does not fall on us while yet we live? Unhappiness,
calamity, disgrace, dishonor—which of these have you
and I not known? And now again: there is the order which
they say brave Creon has proclaimed to all the city. You
understand? Or do you not yet know what outrage threatens
one of those we love?
  Ismene: Of them, Antigone, I have not heard good news or
bad—nothing, since we two sisters were robbed of our two   **10**
brothers on one day when each destroyed the other. During
the night the enemy has fled: so much I know, but nothing
more, either for grief or joy.
  Antigone: I knew it; therefore I have brought you here,
outside the doors, to tell you secretly.
  Ismene: What is it? Some dark shadow is upon you.
  Antigone: Our brother's burial.—Creon has ordained
honor for one, dishonor for the other. Eteocles, they say,
has been entombed with every solemn rite and ceremony
to do him honor in the world below; but as for Polyneices,   **20**

Creon has ordered that none shall bury him or mourn for him; he must be left to lie unwept, unburied, for hungry birds of prey to swoop and feast on his poor body. So he has decreed, our noble Creon, to all the citizens: to you, to me. To me! And he is coming to make it public here, that no one may be left in ignorance; nor does he hold it of little moment: he who disobeys in any detail shall be put to death by public stoning in the streets of Thebes. So it is now for you to show if you are worthy, or unworthy, of your birth.   30

    Ismene: O my poor sister! If it has come to this what can I do, either to help or hinder?

    Antigone: Will you join hands with me and share my task?

    Ismene: What dangerous enterprise have you in mind?

    Antigone: Will you join me in taking up the body?

    Ismene: What? Would you bury him, against the law?

    Antigone: No one shall say *I* failed him! I will bury my brother—and yours too, if you will not.

    Ismene: You reckless girl! When Creon has forbidden?

    Antigone: He has no right to keep me from my own!   40

    Ismene: Think of our father, dear Antigone, and how we saw him die, hated and scorned, when his own hands had blinded his own eyes because of sins which he himself disclosed; and how his mother-wife, two names in one, knotted a rope, and so destroyed herself. And, last of all, upon a single day our brothers fought each other to the death and shed upon the ground the blood that joined them. Now you and I are left, alone; and think: if we defy the King's prerogative and break the law, our death will be more shameful even than   50 theirs. Remember too that we are women, not made to fight with men. Since they who rule us now are stronger far than we, in this and worse than this we must obey them. Therefore, beseeching pardon from the dead, since what I do is done on hard compulsion, I yield to those who have authority; for useless meddling has no sense at all.

    Antigone: I will not urge you. Even if you should wish to give your help I would not take it now. Your choice is made. But I shall bury him. And if I have to die for this pure crime, I am content, for I shall rest beside him;   60 his love will answer mine. I have to please the dead far longer than I need to please the living; with them, I have to dwell for ever. But you, if so you choose, you may dishonor the sacred laws that Heaven holds in honor.

    Ismene: I do them no dishonor, but to act against the city's will I am too weak.

    Antigone: Make that your pretext! I will go and heap the earth upon the brother whom I love.

    Ismene: You reckless girl! I tremble for your life.

    Antigone: Look to yourself and do not fear for me.   70

    Ismene: At least let no one hear of it, but keep your purpose secret, and so too will I.

    Antigone: Go and denounce me! I shall hate you more if you keep silent and do not proclaim it.

    Ismene: Your heart is hot upon a wintry work!

    Antigone: I know I please whom most I ought to please.

    Ismene: But can you do it? It is impossible!

    Antigone: When I can do no more, then I will stop.

    Ismene: But why attempt a hopeless task at all?

    Antigone: O stop, or I shall hate you! He will hate you too,   80 for ever, justly. Let me be, me and my folly! I will face the danger that so dismays you, for it cannot be so dreadful as to die a coward's death.

    Ismene: Then go and do it, if you must. It is blind folly—but those who love you love you dearly.

.   .   .   .

    Creon: My lords: for what concerns the state, the gods who tossed it on the angry surge of strife have righted it again; and therefore you by royal edict I have summoned here, chosen from all our number. I know well how you revered the throne of Laius; and then, when Oedipus   90 maintained our state, and when he perished, round his sons you rallied, still firm and steadfast in your loyalty. Since they have fallen by a double doom upon a single day, two brothers each killing the other with polluted sword, I now possess the throne and royal power by right of nearest kinship with the dead. There is no art that teaches us to know the temper, mind, or spirit of any man until he has been proved by government and lawgiving. A man who rules a state and will not ever steer the wisest course, but is afraid, and says not what   100 he thinks, that man is worthless; and if any holds a friend of more account than his own city, I scorn him; for if I should see destruction threatening the safety of my citizens, I would not hold my peace, nor would I count that man my friend who was my country's foe, Zeus be my witness. For be sure of this: it is the city that protects us all; she bears us through the storm; only when she rides safe and sound can we make loyal friends. This I believe, and thus will I maintain our city's greatness.—Now, conformably, of Oedipus' two sons   110 I have proclaimed this edict: he who in his country's cause fought gloriously and so laid down his life, shall be entombed and graced with every rite that men can pay to those who die with honor; but for his brother, him called Polyneices, who came from exile to lay waste his land, to burn the temples of his native gods, to drink his kindred blood, and to enslave the rest, I have proclaimed to Thebes that none shall give him funeral honors or lament him, but leave him there unburied, to be devoured by dogs and birds, mangled most hideously.   120 Such is my will; never shall I allow the villain to win more honor than the upright; but any who show love to this our city in life and death alike shall win my praise.

    Chorus: Such is your will, my lord; so you requite our city's champion and our city's foe. You, being sovereign, make what laws you will both for the dead and those of us who live.

    Creon: See then that you defend the law now made.

    Chorus: No, lay that burden on some younger men.

    Creon: I have appointed guards to watch the body.   130

    Chorus: What further charge, then, do you lay on us?

    Creon: Not to connive at those that disobey me.

    Chorus: None are so foolish as to long for death.

Creon: Death is indeed the price, but love of gain has often lured a man to his destruction.

Enter a guard

Guard: My lord: I cannot say that I am come all out of breath with running. More than once I stopped and thought and turned round in my path and started to go back. My mind had much to say to me. One time it said "You fool! Why do you go to certain punishment?" Another time "What? Standing still, you wretch? You'll smart for it, if Creon comes to hear from someone else." And so I went along debating with myself, not swift nor sure. This way, a short road soon becomes a long one. At last this was the verdict: I must come and tell you. It may be worse than nothing; still, I'll tell you. I can suffer nothing more than what is in my fate. There is my comfort! 140

Creon: And what is this that makes you so despondent?

Guard: First for myself: I did not see it done, I do not know who did it. Plainly then, I cannot rightly come to any harm. 150

Creon: You are a cautious fellow, building up this barricade. You bring unpleasant news?

Guard: I do, and peril makes a man pause long.

Creon: O, won't you tell your story and be gone?

Guard: Then, here it is. The body: someone has just buried it, and gone away. He sprinkled dry dust on it, with all the sacred rites.

Creon: What? Buried it? What man has so defied me?

Guard. How can I tell? There was no mark of pickaxe, no sign of digging; the earth was hard and dry and undisturbed; no wagon had been there; he who had done it left no trace at all. So, when the first day-watchman showed it to us, we were appalled. We could not see the body; it was not buried but was thinly covered with dust, as if by someone who had sought to avoid a curse. Although we looked, we saw no sign that any dog or bird had come and torn the body. Angry accusations flew up between us; each man blamed another, and in the end it would have come to blows, for there was none to stop it. Each single man seemed guilty, yet proclaimed his ignorance and could not be convicted. We were all ready to take hot iron in our hands, to walk through fire, to swear by all the gods we had not done it, nor had secret knowledge of any man who did it or contrived it. We could not find a clue. Then one man spoke: it made us hang our heads in terror, yet no one could answer him, nor could we see much profit for ourselves if we should do it. He said "We must report this thing to Creon; we dare not hide it"; and his word prevailed. I am the unlucky man who drew the prize when we cast lots, and therefore I am come unwilling and, for certain, most unwelcome: nobody loves the bringer of bad news. 160 170 180

Chorus: My lord, the thought has risen in my mind: do we not see in this the hand of the gods?

Creon: Silence! or you will anger me. You are an old man: must you be a fool as well? Intolerable, that you suppose the gods should have a single thought for this dead body. What? should they honor him with burial as one who served them well, when he had come to burn their pillared temples, to destroy their treasuries, to devastate their land and overturn its laws? Or have you noticed the gods prefer the vile? No, from the first there was a muttering against my edict, wagging of heads in secret, restiveness and discontent with my authority. I know that some of these perverted others and bribed them to this act. Of all vile things current on earth, none is so vile as money. For money opens wide the city-gates to ravishers, it drives the citizens to exile, it perverts the honest mind to shamefulness, it teaches men to practice all forms of wickedness and impiety. These criminals who sold themselves for money have bought with it their certain punishment; for, as I reverence the throne of Zeus, I tell you plainly, and confirm it with my oath: unless you find, and bring before me, the very author of this burial-rite mere death shall not suffice; you shall be hanged alive, until you have disclosed the crime, that for the future you may ply your trade more cleverly, and learn not every pocket is safely to be picked. Ill-gotten gains more often lead to ruin than to safety. 190 200

Guard: May I reply? Or must I turn and go? 210

Creon: Now, as before, your very voice offends me.

Guard: Is it your ears that feel it, or your mind?

Creon: Why must you probe the seat of our displeasure?

Guard: The rebel hurts your mind; I but your ears.

Creon: No more of this! You are a babbling fool!

Guard: If so, I cannot be the one who did it.

Creon: Yes, but you did—selling your life for money!

Guard: It's bad, to judge at random, and judge wrong!

Creon: You judge my judgment as you will—but bring the man who did it, or you shall proclaim what punishment is earned by crooked dealings. 220

Guard: Gods grant he may be found! But whether he be found or not—for this must lie with chance—you will not see me coming *here* again. Alive beyond my hope and expectation, I thank the gods who have delivered me.

Creon goes into his house

Chorus: Wonders are many, yet of all things is Man the most wonderful. He can sail on the stormy sea though the tempest rage, and the loud waves roar around, as he makes his path amid the towering surge. Earth inexhaustible, ageless, he wearies, as backwards and forwards, from season to season, his ox-team drives along the ploughshare. He can entrap the cheerful birds, setting a snare, and all the wild beasts of the earth he has learned to catch, and fish that teem in the deep sea, with nets knotted of stout cords; of such inventiveness is man. Through his inventions he becomes lord even of the beasts of the mountain: the long-haired horse he subdues to the yoke on his neck, and the hill-bred bull, of strength untiring. And speech he has learned, and thought so swift, and the temper of mind to dwell within cities, and not to lie bare amid the keen, biting frosts or cower beneath pelting rain; full of 230 240 resource against all that comes to him is Man. Against Death alone he is left with no defence. But painful sickness he can cure by his own skill. Surpassing belief, the device and cunning that Man has attained, and it bringeth him now to evil, now to good. If he observe Law, and tread the righteous path the gods ordained, honored is he; dishonored, the man whose reckless heart 250 shall make him join hands with sin: may I not think like him, nor may such an impious man dwell in my house.

The guard reappears leading Antigone

Chorus: What evil spirit is abroad? I know her well: Antigone. But how can I believe it? Why, O you unlucky daughter of an unlucky father, what is this? Can it be you, so mad and so defiant, so disobedient to a King's decree?

Guard: Here is the one who did the deed, this girl; we caught her burying him.—But where is Creon?

Chorus: He comes, just as you need him, from the palace.

Creon comes from the house

Creon: How? What occasion makes my coming timely? 260

Guard: Sir, against nothing should a man take oath, for second thoughts belie him. Under your threats that lashed me like a hailstorm, I'd have said I would not quickly have come here again; but joy that comes beyond our dearest hope surpasses all in magnitude. So I return, though I had sworn I never would, bringing this girl detected in the act of honoring the body. This time no lot was cast; the windfall is my very own. And so, my lord, do as you please: take her yourself, examine her, cross-question her. I claim the right of free and final quittance. 270

Creon: Why do you bring this girl? Where was she taken?

Guard: In burying the body. That is all.

Creon: You know what you are saying? Do you mean it?

Guard: I saw her giving burial to the corpse you had forbidden. Is that plain and clear?

Creon: How did you see and take her so red-handed?

Guard: It was like this. When we had reached the place, those dreadful threats of yours upon our heads, we swept aside each grain of dust that hid the clammy body, leaving it quite bare, and sat down on a hill, to the 280 windward side that so we might avoid the smell of it. We kept sharp look-out; each man roundly cursed his neighbor, if he should neglect his duty. So the time passed, until the blazing sun reached his mid-course and burned us with his heat. Then, suddenly, a whirlwind came from heaven and raised a storm of dust, which blotted out the earth and sky; the air was filled with sand and leaves ripped from the trees. We closed our eyes and bore this visitation as we could. At last it ended; then we saw the girl. She raised a bitter cry, as will a bird returning to its nest and finding it 290 despoiled, a cradle empty of its young. So, when she saw the body bare, she raised a cry of anguish mixed with imprecations laid upon those who did it; then at once brought handfuls of dry dust, and raised aloft a shapely vase of bronze, and three times poured the funeral libation for the dead. We rushed upon her swiftly, seized our prey, and charged her both with this offence and that. She faced us calmly; she did not disown the double crime. How glad I was!—and yet how sorry too; it is a painful thing to bring a friend to ruin. Still, for me, my own escape comes 300 before everything.

Creon: You there, who keep your eyes fixed on the ground, do you admit this, or do you deny it?

Antigone: No, I do not deny it. I admit it.

Creon [*to Guard*]: Then you may go; go where you like. You have been fully cleared of that grave accusation.

Exit Guard

You: tell me briefly—I want no long speech: did you not know that this had been forbidden?

Antigone: Of course I knew. There was a proclamation.

Creon: And so you dared to disobey the law? 310

Antigone: It was not Zeus who published this decree, nor have the Powers who rule among the dead imposed such laws as this upon mankind; nor could I think that a decree of yours—a man—could override the laws of Heaven unwritten and unchanging. Not of today or yesterday is their authority; they are eternal; no man saw their birth. Was I to stand before the gods' tribunal for disobeying *them*, because I feared a man? I knew that I should have to die, even without your edict; if I die before my time, why then, I count it gain; to one who lives as I do, ringed 320 about with countless miseries, why, death is welcome. For me to meet this doom is little grief; but when my mother's son lay dead, had I neglected him and left him there unburied, that would have caused me grief; this causes none. And if you think it folly, then perhaps I am accused of folly by the fool.

Chorus: The daughter shows her father's temper—fierce, defiant; she will not yield to any storm.

Creon: But it is those that are most obstinate suffer the greatest fall; the hardest iron, most fiercely tempered 330 in the fire, that is most often snapped and splintered. I have seen the wildest horses tamed, and only by the tiny bit. There is no room for pride in one who is a slave! This girl already had fully learned the art of insolence when she transgressed the laws that I established; and now to that she adds a second outrage— to boast of what she did, and laugh at us. Now she would be the man, not I, if she defeated me and did not pay for it. But though she be my niece, or closer still than all our family, she shall not escape the direst 340 penalty; no, nor shall her sister: I judge her guilty too; she played her part in burying the body. Summon her. Just now I saw her raving and distracted within the palace. So it often is: those who plan crime in secret are betrayed despite themselves; they show it in their faces. But this is worst of all: to be convicted and then to glorify the crime as virtue.

Antigone: Would you do more than simply take and kill me?

Creon: I will have nothing more, and nothing less.

Antigone: Then why delay? To me no word of yours is 350

pleasing—gods forbid it should be so!—and everything in me displeases you. Yet what could I have done to win renown more glorious than giving burial to my own brother? These men too would say it, except that terror cows them into silence. A king has many a privilege: the greatest, that he can say and do all that he will.

Creon: You slander the race of Cadmus;[1] You are the only one in Thebes to think it!

Antigone: These think as I do—but they dare not speak.

Creon: Have you no shame, not to conform with others? 360

Antigone: To reverence a brother is no shame.

Creon: Was he no brother, he who died for Thebes?

Antigone: One mother and one father gave them birth.

Creon: Honoring the traitor, you dishonor *him*.

Antigone: He will not bear this testimony, in death.

Creon: Yes! if the traitor fare the same as he.

Antigone: It was a brother, not a slave who died!

Creon: He died attacking Thebes; the other saved us.

Antigone: Even so, the god of Death demands these rites.

Creon: The good demand more honor than the wicked. 370

Antigone: Who knows? In death they may be reconciled.

Creon: Death does not make an enemy a friend!

Antigone: Even so, I give both love, not share their hatred.

Creon: Down then to Hell! Love there, if love you must. While I am living, no woman shall have rule.

Ismene is led from the King's house by two attendants. She tries to share responsibility for Antigone's deed, but Antigone refuses. The Chorus laments the fate of Antigone. Haemon, Creon's son, comes before his father.

Creon: Soon we shall know, better than seers can tell us. My son: you have not come in rage against your father because your bride must die? Or are you still my loyal son, whatever I may do?

Haemon: Father, I am your son; may your wise judgment 380
rule me, and may I always follow it. No marriage shall be thought a greater prize for me to win than your good government.

Creon: So may you ever be resolved, my son, in all things to be guided by your father. It is for this men pray that they may have obedient children, that they may requite their father's enemy with enmity and honor whom their father loves to honor. One who begets unprofitable children makes trouble for himself, and gives his foes nothing but laughter. Therefore do not let your pleasure 390
in a woman overcome your judgment, knowing this, that if you have an evil wife to share your house, you'll find cold comfort in your bed. What other wound can cut so deep as treachery at home? So, think this girl your enemy; spit on her, and let her find her husband down in Hell! She is the only one that I have found in all the city disobedient. I will not make myself a liar. I have caught her; I will kill her. Let her sing her hymns to Sacred Kinship! If I breed rebellion in the house, then it is certain there'll be no lack of rebels out of doors. No man can rule a city uprightly 400
who is not just in ruling his own household. Never will I

---

[1] The ancestor of the noble families of Thebes.

approve of one who breaks and violates the law, or would dictate to those who rule. Lawful authority must be obeyed in all things, great or small, just and unjust alike; and such a man would win my confidence both in command and as a subject; standing at my side in the storm of battle he would hold his ground, not leave me unprotected. But there is no greater curse than disobedience. This brings destruction on a city, this drives men from hearth and home, this brings about a sudden panic in the battle-front. Where all goes well, 410
obedience is the cause. So we must vindicate the law; we must not be defeated by a woman. Better far be overthrown, if need be, by a man than to be called the victim of a woman.

Chorus: Unless the years have stolen away our wits, all you say is said most prudently.

Haemon: Father, it is the gods who give us wisdom; no gift of theirs more precious. I cannot say that you are wrong, nor would I ever learn that impudence, although perhaps another might fairly say it. But it falls to me, being your son, to note what others say, or do, or censure in you, for your glance 420
intimidates the common citizen; he will not say, before your face, what might displease you; I can listen freely, how the city mourns this girl. "No other woman", so they are saying, "so undeservedly has been condemned for such a glorious deed. When her own brother had been slain in battle she would not let his body lie unburied to be devoured by dogs or birds of prey. Is not this worthy of a crown of gold?"—such is the muttering that spreads everywhere. Father, no greater treasure can I have than your 430
prosperity; no son can find a greater prize than his own father's fame, no father than his son's. Therefore let not this single thought possess you: only what you say is right, and nothing else. The man who thinks that he alone is wise, that he is best in speech or counsel, such a man brought to the proof is found but emptiness. There's no disgrace, even if one is wise, in learning more, and knowing when to yield. See how the trees that grow beside a torrent preserve their branches, if they bend; 440
the others, those that resist, are torn out, root and branch. So too the captain of a ship; let him refuse to shorten sail, despite the storm— he'll end his voyage bottom uppermost. No, let your anger cool, and be persuaded. If one who is still young can speak with sense, then I would say that he does best who has most understanding; second best, the man who profits from the wisdom of another.

Chorus: My lord, he has not spoken foolishly; you each can learn some wisdom from the other. 450

Creon: What? Men of our age go to school again and take a lesson from a very boy?

Haemon: If it is worth the taking. I am young, but think what should be done, not of my age.

Creon: What should be done! To honor disobedience!

Haemon: I would not have you honor criminals.

Creon: And is this girl then not a criminal?

Haemon: The city with a single voice denies it.

Creon: Must I give orders then by their permission?

Haemon: If youth is folly, this is childishness. 460

Creon: Am I to rule for them, not for myself?

Haemon: That is not government, but tyranny.

Creon: The king is lord and master of his city.

Haemon: Then you had better rule a desert island!

Creon: This man, it seems, is the ally of the woman.

Haemon: If you're the woman, yes! I fight for you.

Creon: Villain! Do you oppose your father's will?

Haemon: Only because you are opposing Justice.

Creon: When I regard my own prerogative?

Haemon: Opposing the gods', you disregard your own.   470

Creon: Scoundrel, so to surrender to a woman!

Haemon: But not to anything that brings me shame.

Creon: Your every word is in defence of her.

Haemon: And me, and you—and of the gods below.

Creon: You shall not marry her this side the grave!

Haemon. So, she must die—and will not die alone.

Creon: What? Threaten me? Are you so insolent?

Haemon: It is no threat, if I reply to folly.

Creon: The fool would teach me sense! You'll pay for it.

Haemon: I'd call you mad, if you were not my father.   480

Creon: I'll hear no chatter from a woman's plaything.

Haemon: Would you have all the talk, and hear no answer?

Creon: So? I swear to the gods, you shall not bandy words with me and not repent it! Bring her out, that loathsome creature! I will have her killed at once, before her bridegroom's very eyes.

Haemon: How can you think it? I will not see that, nor shall you ever see my face again. Those friends of yours who can must tolerate your raging madness; I will not endure it.   490

Haemon rushes away.

.   .   .   .

Antigone engages in an impassioned lament over her destiny. Creon will not relent, and the guards lead Antigone to the tomb. The blind prophet Teiresias warns Creon that his actions have brought "sickness" to the state. Creon responds rudely to the Seer's claim that "it is the stubborn man who is the fool." The Chorus sings a hymn in praise of Dionysus. Then, a Messenger appears from the direction of the plain.

.   .   .   .

Messenger: You noblemen of Thebes, how insecure is human fortune! Chance will overthrow the great, and raise the lowly; nothing's firm, either for confidence or for despair; no one can prophesy what lies in store. An hour ago, how much I envied Creon! He had saved Thebes, we had accorded him the sovereign power; he ruled our land supported by a noble prince, his son. Now all is lost, and he who forfeits joy forfeits his life; he is a breathing corpse. Heap treasures in your palace, if you will, and wear the pomp of royalty; but if you have no happiness,   500
I would not give a straw for all of it, compared with joy.

Chorus: What is this weight of heavy news you bring?

Messenger: Death!—and the blood-guilt rests upon the living.

Chorus: Death? Who is dead? And who has killed him? Tell me.

Messenger: Haemon is dead, and by no stranger's hand.

Chorus: But by his father's? Or was it his own?

Messenger: His own—inflamed with anger at his father.

Chorus: Yours was no idle prophecy, Teiresias!   510

Messenger: That is my news. What next, remains with you.

Chorus: But look! There is his wife, Eurydice; she is coming from the palace. Has she heard about her son, or is she here by chance?

Eurydice comes from the house.

Eurydice: You citizens of Thebes, I overheard when I was standing at the gates, for I had come to make an offering at the shrine of Pallas, and my hand was on the bar that holds the gate, to draw it; then there fell upon my ears a voice that spoke of death. My terror took away my strength; I fell into my servants' arms and   520
swooned away. But tell it me once more; I can endure to listen; I am no stranger to bad news.

Messenger: Dear lady, I was there, and I will tell the truth; I will not keep it back from you. Why should I gloss it over? You would hear from someone else, and I should seem a liar. The truth is always best.
I went with Creon up to the hill where Polyneices' body still lay, unpitied, torn by animals. We gave it holy washing, and we prayed to Hecate and Pluto[2]   530
that they would restrain their anger and be merciful. And then we cut some branches, and we burned what little had been left, and built a mound over his ashes of his native soil. Then, to the cavern, to the home of death, the bridal-chamber with its bed of stone. One of us heard a cry of lamentation from that unhallowed place; he went to Creon and told him. On the wind, as he came near, cries of despair were borne. He groaned aloud in anguish: "O, and are my fears come true?   540
Of all the journeys I have made, am I to find this one the most calamitous? It is my son's voice greets me. Hurry, men; run to the place, and when you reach the tomb creep in between the gaping stones and see if it be Haemon there, or if the gods are cheating me." Upon this desperate order we ran and looked. Within the furthest chamber we saw her hanging, dead; strips from her dress had served her for a rope. Haemon we saw embracing her dead body and lamenting his loss, his father's deed, and her   550
destruction. When Creon saw him he cried out in anguish, went in, and called to him: "My son! my son! O why? What have you done? What brought you here? What is this madness? O come out, my son, come, I implore you!" Haemon glared at him with anger in

---

[2] Hecate is the goddess of the crossroads and transitions—such as that between life and death. Pluto is another name for Hades, the Greek god of the underworld, the shadowy realm where the souls of the dead were thought to rest.

his eyes, spat in his face, said nothing, drew his double-hiked sword, but missed his aim as Creon leapt aside. Then in remorse he leaned upon the blade and drove it half its length into his body. While yet the life was in him he embraced the girl [560] with failing arms, and breathing hard poured out his life-blood on to her white face. So side by side they lie, and both are dead. Not in this world but in the world below he wins his bride, and shows to all mankind that folly is the worst of human evils.

Eurydice goes into the house.

Chorus: What can we think of this? The Queen is gone without one word of good or evil omen.
Messenger: What can it mean? But yet we may sustain the hope that she would not display her grief in public, but will rouse the sad lament for Haemon's death among [570] her serving-women inside the palace. She has true discretion, and she would never do what is unseemly.
Chorus: I cannot say, but wild lament would be less ominous than this unnatural silence.
Messenger: It is unnatural; there may be danger. I'll follow her; it may be she is hiding some secret purpose in her passionate heart.

The Messenger enters the house. As he goes, Creon comes into the open place before the house with attendants carrying the shrouded body of Haemon on a bier.

Chorus: Look, Creon draws near, and the burden he bears gives witness to his misdeeds; the cause lies only in his blind error. [580]
Creon: Alas! The wrongs I have done by ill-counselling! Cruel and fraught with death. You behold, men of Thebes, the slayer, the slain; a father, a son. My own stubborn ways have borne bitter fruit. My son! Dead, my son! So soon torn from me, so young, so young! The fault only mine, not yours, O my son.
Chorus: Too late, too late you see the path of wisdom.
Creon: Alas! A bitter lesson I have learned! The god coming with all his weight has borne down on me, and smitten me with all his cruelty; my joy overturned, [590] trampled beneath his feet. What suffering besets the whole race of men!

The Messenger comes from the house.

Messenger: My master, when you came you brought a burden of sorrow with you; now, within your house, a second store of misery confronts you.
Creon: Another sorrow come to crown my sorrow?
Messenger: The Queen, true mother of her son, is dead; in grief she drove a blade into her heart.
Creon: Alas! Thou grim hand of death, greedy and unappeased, why so implacable? Voice of doom, you who [600] bring such dire news of grief, O, can it be true? What have you said, my son? O, you have slain the slain! Tell me, can it be true? Is death crowning death?

My wife! my wife! My son dead, and now my wife taken too!

The doors of the King's house are opened, and the corpse of Eurydice is disclosed.

Chorus: But raise your eyes: there is her lifeless body.
Creon: Alas! Here is a sorrow that redoubles sorrow. Where will it end? What else can Fate hold in store? While yet I clasp my dead son in my arms before me there lies another struck by death. Alas cruel doom! the mother's and the son's. [610]
Messenger: She took a sharp-edged knife, stood by the altar, and made lament for Megareus who was killed of old, and next for Haemon. Then at last, invoking evil upon you, the slayer of both her sons, she closed her eyes in death.
Creon: A curse, a thing of terror! O, is there none will unsheathe a sword to end all my woes with one deadly thrust? My grief crushes me.
Messenger: She cursed you for the guilt of Haemon's death and of the other son who died before.
Creon: What did she do? How did she end her life? [620]
Messenger: She heard my bitter story; then she put a dagger to her heart and drove it home.
Creon: The guilt falls on me alone; none but I have slain her; no other shares in the sin. 'Twas I dealt the blow. This is the truth, my friends. Away, take me away, far from the sight of men! My life now is death. Lead me away from here.
Chorus: That would be well, if anything is well. Briefest is best when such disaster comes.
Creon: O come, best of all the days I can see, [630] the last day of all, the day that brings death. O come quickly! Come, thou night with no dawn!
Chorus: That's for the future; here and now are duties that fall on those to whom they are allotted.
Creon: I prayed for death; I wish for nothing else.
Chorus: Then pray no more; from suffering that has been decreed no man will ever find escape.
Creon: Lead me away, a rash, a misguided man, whose blindness has killed a wife and a son. O where can I look? What strength can I find? [640] On me has fallen a doom greater than I can bear.

Creon is led into his house as the Chorus speaks.

Chorus: Of happiness, far the greatest part is wisdom, and reverence towards the gods. Proud words of the arrogant man, in the end, meet punishment, great as his pride was great, till at last he is schooled in wisdom.

Q **Who is the tragic figure in this play: Antigone or Creon?**

Q **How does the play illustrate "heroic idealism" and the conflict between personal and communal obligations?**

The tragic action in *Antigone* springs from the irreconcilability of Antigone's personal idealism and Creon's hardheaded political realism. Creon means well by the state; he is committed to the exercise of justice under the law. As a king newly come to power, he perceives his duty in terms of his authority: "whoever the city shall appoint to rule," says Creon, "that man must be obeyed, in little things and in great things, in just things and unjust; for the man who is a good subject is the one who would be a good ruler . . ." But Creon ignores the ancient imperatives of divine law and familial duty. His blind devotion to the state and his unwillingness to compromise trap him into making a decision whose consequences are disastrous.

In Greek tragedy, the weakness or "tragic flaw" of the **protagonist** (the leading character) brings that character into conflict with fate or with the **antagonist** (one who opposes the protagonist), and ultimately to his or her fall. Creon's excessive pride (in Greek, *hubris*) results in the loss of those who are dearest to him. But Antigone is also a victim of self-righteous inflexibility. In an age that confined women to the domestic household and expected them to conform to male opinion, Antigone was unique. In ancient Greece, a girl in her early teens might marry a man considerably older than she. Along with the other female members of the household, she oversaw the daily chores associated with child-rearing, food preparation, and the production of clothing—spinning, weaving, and sewing. She could not inherit or own property and could not choose to divorce her husband (although he could divorce her); hence she was subordinate to her husband, as she had been to her father. While there were exceptions to this pattern (usually among courtesans and prostitutes), it seems clear that by challenging male authority, Antigone threatened the status quo: "*She* is the man," Creon angrily objects, "if she can carry this off unpunished." Antigone's sister, Ismene, argues, "We must remember we were born women, not meant to strive with men." But Antigone persists: her heroism derives from her unswerving dedication to the ideals of divine justice and to the duty of the individual to honor family, even if it challenges the laws of the state.

Sophocles perceived the difficulties involved in reconciling public good and private conscience. In *Antigone*, he offers a moving plea for sound judgment and rational action, and for harmony between the individual and the community.

Aristotle on Tragedy

In modern parlance, the word "tragedy" is often used to describe a terrible act of fate that befalls an unwitting individual. With regard to drama, however, the word (and the form it describes) has a very different meaning. As a literary genre, tragedy deals not so much with catastrophic events as with *how* these events work to affect individuals in shaping their character and in determining their fate. The protagonist becomes a tragic hero not because of what befalls him, but rather as a result of the manner in which he confronts his destiny. In the *Poetics*, the world's first treatise on literary criticism, the Greek philosopher Aristotle

(384–322 B.C.E.) describes tragedy as an imitation of an action involving incidents that arouse pity and fear. Tragic action, he argues, should involve an error in judgment made by an individual who is "better than the ordinary man" but with whom the audience may sympathize.

The *Poetics* further clarifies the importance of "proper construction": the play must have a balanced arrangement of parts, and the action of the story should be limited to the events of a single day. The plot should consist of a single action made up of several closely connected incidents (without irrelevant additions). If we apply Aristotle's aesthetic principles of tragedy to Sophocles' *Antigone*, we discover the so-called unities of action and time that characterize Classic Greek tragedy. (Seventeenth-century playwrights added "unity of place" to Neoclassical drama.) In *Antigone*, the action rests on a single incident: the rash decision of Creon. The events of the play occur within a single place, and they are acted out within a time span comparable to their occurrence in real life. Every episode in the play is relevant to the central action. Proportion and order apply to the writing of drama, suggests Aristotle, even as they must apply to the conduct and the fate of the tragic hero.

Finally, Aristotle addresses the function of tragedy as a genre. It must arouse in the spectator a mixture of fear and pity; it must effect a **catharsis**, that is, a cleansing or purification that provokes change in the spectator's emotional life. Tragedy, the theatrical rendering of human frailty and its consequences, was—in the Greek world as in our own—no mere entertainment, but a vehicle for self-knowledge.

READING 4.4 From Aristotle's *Poetics* (ca. 340 B.C.E.)

. . . let us now consider the proper construction of the Fable **1**
or Plot, as that is at once the first and the most important
thing in Tragedy. We have laid it down that a tragedy is an
imitation of an action that is complete in itself, as a whole
of some magnitude; for a whole may be of no magnitude to
speak of. Now a whole is that which has beginning, middle,
and end. A beginning is that which is not itself necessarily
after anything else, and which has naturally something else
after it; an end is that which is naturally after something itself,
either as its necessary or usual consequent, and with nothing **10**
else after it; and a middle, that which is by nature after one
thing and has also another after it. A well-constructed Plot,
therefore, cannot either begin or end at any point one likes;
beginning and end in it must be of the forms just described.
Again: to be beautiful, a living creature, and every whole
made up of parts, must not only present a certain order in
its arrangement of parts, but also be of certain definite
magnitude. Beauty is a matter of size and order, and therefore
impossible either (1) in a very minute creature, since our
perception becomes indistinct as it approaches instantaneity; **20**
or (2) in a creature of vast size—one, say, 1000 miles long—
as in that case, instead of the object being seen all at once,
the unity and wholeness of it is lost to the beholder. Just in the
same way, then, as a beautiful whole made up of parts, or a
beautiful living creature, must be of some size, but a size to be

taken in by the eye, so a story or Plot must be of some length, but of a length to be taken in by the eye, so a story or Plot must be of some length, but of a length to be taken in by the memory. . . . The truth is that, just as in the other imitative arts one imitation is always of one thing, so in poetry the story, as an imitation of action, must represent one action, a complete whole, with its several incidents so closely connected that the transposal or withdrawal of any one of them will disjoin and dislocate the whole. For that which makes no perceptible difference by its presence or absence is no real part of the whole. . . . The perfect Plot, accordingly, must have a single, and not (as some tell us) a double issue; the change in the hero's fortunes must be not from misery to happiness, but on the contrary from happiness to misery; and the cause of it must lie not in any depravity, but in some great error on his part; . . . As Tragedy is an imitation of personages better than the ordinary man, we in our way should follow the example of good portrait-painters, who reproduce the distinctive features of a man, and at the same time, without losing the likeness, make him handsomer than he is. . . .

30

40

Q **Why does Aristotle require the length of a play to be equivalent to the course of its plot in real life?**

Q **How does a "great error" figure in the plot of a tragedy?**

Greek Philosophy: The Speculative Leap

During the sixth century B.C.E., a small group of Greek thinkers introduced methods of intellectual inquiry that combined careful observation, systematic analysis, and the exercise of pure reason. These individuals, whom we call philosophers (literally, "lovers of wisdom"), laid the foundations for Western science and philosophy. While they lived at a time in which most people viewed earthquakes, windstorms, and floods as expressions of divine anger, they theorized that such disasters might have natural, not supernatural, causes. Challenging all prevailing myths, the Greek philosophers made the speculative leap from supernatural to natural explanations of the unknown.

Naturalist Philosophy: The Pre-Socratics

The earliest of the Greek philosopher-scientists lived just prior to the time of Socrates in the city of Miletus on the Ionian coast of Asia Minor (see Map 4.1). Although their senses reported a world of constant change, they reasoned that there must be a single unifying substance that formed the basic "stuff" of nature. They asked, "What is everything made of?," "How do things come into existence?," and "What permanent substance lies behind the world of appearance?" Thales (ca. 625–ca. 547 B.C.E.), history's first philosopher, held that water was the fundamental substance and source from which all things proceeded. Water's potential for change (from solid to liquid to gas) and its pervasiveness on earth convinced him that water formed the primary matter of the universe. His followers challenged this view: "Air," said one, "Fire," countered another,

and still others identified the basic substance as a mixture of the primordial elements. The concept that a single unifying substance underlay reality drew opposition from some of the pre-Socratics. The universe, argued Heraclitus of Ephesus (ca. 540–ca. 480 B.C.E.), has no permanence, but, rather, is in constant process of flux. Heraclitus defended the idea that change itself was the basis of reality. "You cannot step twice into the same river," he wrote, "for fresh waters are ever flowing in upon you." Yet, Heraclitus believed that an underlying Form or Guiding Force (in Greek, *logos*) permeated nature, an idea that resembles Hindu pantheism and anticipates the Christian concept (found in the Gospel of John) of a Great Intelligence governing the beginning of time. For Heraclitus the Force was impersonal, universal, and eternal.

Around 500 B.C.E., Leucippus of Miletus theorized that physical reality consisted of minute, invisible particles that moved ceaselessly in the void. These he called *atoms*, the Greek word meaning "indivisible." Democritus (ca. 460–370 B.C.E.), a follower of Leucippus and the best known of the naturalist philosophers, developed the atomic theory of matter. For Democritus, the mind consisted of the same indivisible physical substances as everything else in nature. According to this materialist view, atoms moved constantly and eternally according to chance in infinite time and space. The atomic theory survived into Roman times, and, although forgotten for 2000 years thereafter, it was validated by physicists of the early twentieth century.

Pythagoras

Yet another pre-Socratic thinker, Pythagoras (ca. 580–ca. 500 B.C.E.), advanced an idea that departed from both the material and nonmaterial views of the universe. Pythagoras believed that proportion, discovered through number, was the true basis of reality. According to him, all universal relationships may be expressed through numbers, the truths of which are eternal and unchanging. The formula in plane geometry that equates the square of

Science and Technology

600 B.C.E.	Thales of Miletus produces an accurate theory of the solar eclipse; he also advances the study of deductive geometry[†]
540 B.C.E.	Anaximander claims that life evolved from beginnings in the sea and that man evolved from a more primitive species
530 B.C.E.	Pythagoras argues for a spherical earth around which five planets revolve; he also develops the "Pythagorean Theorem"
500 B.C.E.	Leucippus theorizes that all matter is composed of "atoms"
480 B.C.E.	Anaxagoras postulates that the sun is a large, glowing rock; he explains solar eclipses

†All dates in this chapter are approximate

the hypotenuse in right-angle triangles to the sum of the square of the other two sides—a theorem traditionally associated with Pythagoras—is an example of such an unchanging and eternal truth, as is the simplest of mathematical equations: $2 + 2 = 4$. Pythagoras was the founding father of pure mathematics. He was also the first to demonstrate the relationship between musical harmonics and numbers. His view that number gives order and harmony to the universe is basic to the principles of balance and proportion that dominate Classical art and music (see chapter 5).

In contrast with the Mesopotamians and Egyptians, who deified the sun, the rivers, and other natural elements, the pre-Socratics stripped nature of supernatural associations. They made accurate predictions of solar and lunar eclipses, plotted astronomical charts, and hypothesized on the processes of regeneration in plants and animals. Yet, in the areas of geometry, astronomy, and mathematics, it is likely that they inherited a large body of practical and theoretical data from the astrologists and palace engineers of Babylon, who knew how to solve linear and quadratic equations, and from the pyramid builders and calendar keepers of Egypt. It is also likely that the philosophic and religious theories originating in China and India influenced the speculative systems of Heraclitus, Pythagoras, and other pre-Socratics. Ideas, along with goods like silk, ivory, and cotton, moved back and forth along the overland trade routes that linked East Asia to the Mediterranean. For example, the Pythagorean proscription against eating animal flesh and certain plants suggests Greek familiarity with the Hindu belief in reincarnation and the transmigration of souls (see chapter 3).

Hippocrates

The Chinese association between illness and an imbalance of vital body energy seems to have made its way westward into the purview of Hippocrates. Hippocrates (ca. 460–377 B.C.E.), the most famous of the Greek physicians and so-called father of medicine, investigated the influence of diet and environment on general health and advanced the idea that an imbalance among bodily "humors"—blood, phlegm, black bile, and yellow bile—was the cause of

Science and Technology

470 B.C.E.	Greek physicians practice dissection in the study of human anatomy
430 B.C.E.	Democritus argues that atoms move freely in space and are eternal
400 B.C.E.	Hippocrates' treatises on medicine include a study of epidemics, a description of phobias, and an examination of the effects of the environment on health
330 B.C.E.	Agnodike, a female physician, successfully challenges the law that prohibits women from practicing medicine in Athens

disease. He insisted on the necessary relationship of cause and effect in matters of physical illness, and he raised questions concerning the influence of the mind on the body. He may also be deemed the "father of medical ethics": to this day, graduating physicians are encouraged to practice medicine according to the precepts of the Hippocratic Oath (probably not written by Hippocrates himself), which binds them to heal the sick and abstain from unprofessional medical practices.

The separation of the natural from the supernatural was as essential to the birth of medical science as it was to speculative philosophy. And although no agreement as to the nature of reality was ever reached among the pre-Socratics, these intellectuals laid the groundwork and the methodology for the rational investigation of the universe. Their efforts represent the beginnings of Western science and philosophy as formal disciplines.

Humanist Philosophy

The Sophists

The naturalist philosophers were concerned with describing physical reality in terms of the unity that lay behind the chaos of human perceptions. The philosophers who followed them pursued a different course: they turned their attention from the world of nature to the realm of the mind, from physical matters to moral concerns, and from the gathering of information to the cultivation of wisdom. Significantly, these thinkers fathered the field of inquiry known as metaphysics (literally, "beyond physics"), that branch of philosophy concerned with abstract thought. They asked not simply "*What* do we know (about nature)?" but "*How* do we know what we know?" The transition from the examination of matter to the exploration of mind established the humanistic direction of Greek philosophy for at least two centuries.

The first humanist philosophers were a group of traveling scholar-teachers called Sophists. Masters of formal debate, the Sophists were concerned with defining the limits of human knowledge. The Thracian Sophist Protagoras (ca. 485–410 B.C.E.) believed that knowledge could not exceed human opinion, a position summed up in his memorable dictum: "Man is the measure of all things." His contemporary Gorgias (ca. 483–ca. 376 B.C.E.) tried to prove that reality is incomprehensible and that even if one could comprehend it, one could not describe the real to others. Such skepticism was common to the Sophists, who argued that truth and justice were relative: what might be considered just and true for one individual or situation might not be just and true for another.

Socrates and the Quest for Virtue

Athens' foremost philosopher, Socrates (ca. 470–399 B.C.E.), vigorously opposed the views of the Sophists. Insisting on the absolute nature of truth and justice, he described the ethical life as belonging to a larger set of universal truths and an unchanging moral order. For Socrates, virtue was not discovered by means of clever

Figure 4.16 Portrait bust of Socrates, supposedly created by **LYSIPPOS**. Roman marble copy of an original bronze, ca. 350 B.C.E., height 13 in. (approx.)

but misleading argumentation—a kind of reasoning that would come to be called (after the Sophists) *sophistry*, nor was it relative to individual circumstances. Rather, virtue was a condition of the *psyche**, the seat of both the moral and intellectual faculties of the individual. Hence, understanding the true meaning of virtue was preliminary to acting virtuously: to know good is to do good.

The question of right conduct was central to Socrates' life and teachings. A stonemason by profession, Socrates preferred to roam the streets of Athens and engage his fellow citizens in conversation and debate (Figure **4.16**). Insisting that the unexamined life was not worth living, he challenged his peers on matters of public and private virtue, constantly posing the question, "What is the greatest good?" In this pursuit, Socrates employed a rigorous question-and-answer technique known as the **dialectical method**. Unlike the Sophists, he refused to charge fees for teaching: he argued that wealth did not produce excellence; rather, wealth derived *from* excellence. Socrates described himself as a large horsefly, alighting upon and pestering the well-bred but rather sluggish horse—that is, Athens. So Socrates "alighted" on the citizens of Athens, arousing, persuading, and reproaching them and—most importantly—demanding that they give rational justification for their actions.

Socrates established philosophy as a lived experience, rather than a set of doctrines. His style of cross-examination, the question-and-answer method, proceeded from his first principle of inquiry, "Know thyself," while the

progress of his analysis moved from specific examples to general principles, and from particular to universal truths, a type of reasoning known as *inductive*. The inductive method demands a process of abstraction: a shift of focus from the individual thing (the city) to all things (cities) and from the individual action (just or unjust) to the idea of justice. Central to Socratic inquiry was discourse (Figure **4.17**). The notion that talk itself humanizes the individual is typically Greek and even more typically Socratic. Indeed, the art of conversation—the dialectical exchange of ideas—united the citizens of the *polis*.

As gadfly, Socrates won as many enemies as he won friends. The great masses of Greek citizens found comfort in the traditional Greek gods and goddesses. They had little use for Socrates' religious skepticism and stringent methods of self-examination. Outspoken in his commitment to free inquiry, Socrates fell into disfavor with the reactionary regime that governed Athens after its defeat in the Peloponnesian Wars. Although he had fought bravely in the wars, he vigorously opposed the new regime and the moral chaos of postwar Athens. In the year 399 B.C.E., when he was over seventy years old, he was brought to trial for subversive behavior, impiety, and atheism. The Athenian jury found him guilty by a narrow margin of votes and sentenced him to death by drinking hemlock, a poisonous herb.

In his lifetime, Socrates wrote no books or letters: what we know of him comes mainly from his students' writings.

Figure 4.17 DOURIS, interior of a red-figured *kylix* (a Greek drinking cup), ca. 480 B.C.E. Terracotta, height 4⅜ in., diameter 11¾ in. The scene recreates a moment of conversation between a teacher and a student; scholars interpret the painting to depict an older man propositioning a younger one. The artist, Douris, is said to have ornamented some 10,000 pieces of pottery in the course of his career.

---

* "Psyche" is often translated as "soul," "spirit," or "mind," as distinguished from "body" or "matter."

The dialogue called *Crito* (written by Plato) narrates the last events of Socrates' life: Crito, Socrates' friend and pupil, urges him to escape from prison, but the old philosopher refuses. He explains that to run away would be to subvert the laws by which he has lived. His escape would represent an implicit criticism of the democratic system and the city-state that he had defended throughout his life. For Socrates, the loyalty of the citizen to the *polis*, like that of the child to its parents, is a primary obligation. To violate the will of the community to which he belongs would constitute dishonor. Like Antigone, Socrates prefers death to dishonor. In the excerpt from *Crito*, Socrates explains why right action is crucial to the destiny of both the individual and the community. These words reaffirm the Hellenic view that immortality is achieved through human deeds, which outlast human lives.

READING 4.5 From Plato's *Crito* (ca. 390 B.C.E.)

Crito: . . . O my good Socrates, I beg you for the last time   1
to listen to me and save yourself. For to me your death will be
more than a single disaster: not only shall I lose a friend the
like of whom I shall never find again, but many persons who
do not know you and me well will think that I might have
saved you if I had been willing to spend money, but that
I neglected to do so. And what reputation could be more
disgraceful than the reputation of caring more for money
than for one's friends? The public will never believe that we were
anxious to save you, but that you yourself refused to escape.   10

Socrates: But, my dear Crito, why should we care so much
about public opinion? Reasonable men, of whose opinion it is
worth our while to think, will believe that we acted as we
really did.

Crito: But you see, Socrates, that it is necessary to care
about public opinion, too. This very thing that has happened to
you proves that the multitude can do a man not the least, but
almost the greatest harm, if he is falsely accused to them.

Socrates: I wish that the multitude were able to do a man
the greatest harm, Crito, for then they would be able to do   20
him the greatest good, too. That would have been fine. But, as
it is, they can do neither. They cannot make a man either wise
or foolish: they act wholly at random. Consider it in this way.
Suppose the laws and the commonwealth were to come and
appear to me as I was preparing to run away (if that is the
right phrase to describe my escape) and were to ask, "Tell us,
Socrates, what have you in your mind to do? What do you
mean by trying to escape but to destroy us, the laws, and the
whole state, so far as you are able? Do you think that a state
can exist and not be overthrown, in which the decisions of   30
law are of no force, and are disregarded and undermined by
private individuals?" How shall we answer questions like that,
Crito? Much might be said, especially by an orator, in defense
of the law which makes judicial decisions supreme. Shall
I reply, "But the state has injured me by judging my case
unjustly." Shall we say that?

Crito: Certainly we will, Socrates.

Socrates: And suppose the laws were to reply, "Was that
our agreement? Or was it that you would abide by whatever

judgments the state should pronounce?" And if we were   40
surprised by their words, perhaps they would say, "Socrates,
don't be surprised by our words, but answer us; you yourself
are accustomed to ask questions and to answer them. What
complaint have you against us and the state, that you are
trying to destroy us? Are we not, first of all, your parents?
Through us your father took your mother and brought you into
the world. Tell us, have you any fault to find with those of us
that are the laws of marriage?" "I have none," I should reply.
"Or have you any fault to find with those of us that regulate
the raising of the child and the education which you, like   50
others, received? Did we not do well in telling your father to
educate you in music and athletics?" "You did," I should say.
"Well, then, since you were brought into the world and raised
and educated by us, how, in the first place, can you deny that
you are our child and our slave, as your fathers were before
you? And if this be so, do you think that your rights are on a
level with ours? Do you think that you have a right to retaliate
if we should try to do anything to you? You had not the same
rights that your father had, or that your master would have
had if you had been a slave. You had no right to retaliate if   60
they ill-treated you, or to answer them if they scolded you, or
to strike them back if they struck you, or to repay them evil
with evil in any way. And do you think that you may retaliate in
the case of your country and its laws? If we try to destroy you,
because we think it just, will you in return do all that you can
to destroy us, the laws, and your country, and say that in so
doing you are acting justly—you, the man who really thinks
so much of excellence? Or are you too wise to see that your
country is worthier, more to be revered, more sacred, and
held in higher honor both by the gods and by all men of   70
understanding, than your father and your mother and all your
ancestors; and that you ought to reverence it, and to submit to
it, and to approach it more humbly when it is angry with you
than you would approach your father; and either to do
whatever it tells you to do or to persuade it to excuse you;
and to obey in silence if it orders you to endure flogging
or imprisonment, or if it sends you to battle to be wounded
or die? That is just. You must not give way, nor retreat,
nor desert your station. In war, and in the court of justice,
and everywhere, you must do whatever your state and your   80
country tell you to do, or you must persuade them that their
commands are unjust. But it is impious to use violence against
your father or your mother; and much more impious to use
violence against your country." What answer shall we make,
Crito? Shall we say that the laws speak the truth, or not?

Crito: I think that they do.

Socrates: "Then consider, Socrates," perhaps they would
say, "if we are right in saying that by attempting to escape
you are attempting an injustice. We brought you into the
world, we raised you, we educated you, we gave you and   90
every other citizen a share of all the good things we could. Yet
we proclaim that if any man of the Athenians is dissatisfied
with us, he may take his goods and go away wherever he
pleases; we give that privilege to every man who chooses to
avail himself of it, so soon as he has reached manhood, and
sees us, the laws, and the administration of our state. No one
of us stands in his way or forbids him to take his goods and go
wherever he likes, whether it be to an Athenian colony, or to

any foreign country, if he is dissatisfied with us and with the
state. But we say that every man of you who remains here, 100
seeing how we administer justice, and how we govern the
state in other matters, has agreed, by the very fact of
remaining here, to do whatsoever we tell him. And, we say, he
who disobeys us acts unjustly on three counts: he disobeys us
who are his parents, and he disobeys us who reared him, and
he disobeys us after he has agreed to obey us, without
persuading us that we are wrong. Yet we did not tell him
sternly to do whatever we told him. We offered him an
alternative; we gave him his choice either to obey us or to
convince us that we were wrong; but he does neither. "These 110
are the charges, Socrates, to which we say that you will
expose yourself if you do what you intend; and you are more
exposed to these charges than other Athenians." And if I were
to ask, "Why?" they might retort with justice that I have bound
myself by the agreement with them more than other
Athenians. They would say, "Socrates, we have very strong
evidence that you were satisfied with us and with the state.
You would not have been content to stay at home in it more
than other Athenians unless you had been satisfied with it
more than they. You never went away from Athens to the 120
festivals, nor elsewhere except on military service; you never
made other journeys like other men; you had no desire to see
other states or other laws; you were contented with us and
our state; so strongly did you prefer us, and agree to be
governed by us. And what is more, you had children in this
city, you found it so satisfactory. Besides, if you had wished,
you might at your trial have offered to go into exile. At that
time you could have done with the state's consent what you
are trying now to do without it. But then you gloried in being
willing to die. You said that you preferred death to exile. And 130
now you do not honor those words: you do not respect us, the
laws, for you are trying to destroy us; and you are acting just
as a miserable slave would act, trying to run away, and
breaking the contracts and agreement which you made to live
as our citizen. First, therefore, answer this question. Are we
right, or are we wrong, in saying that you have agreed not
in mere words, but in your actions, to live under our
government?" What are we to say, Crito? Must we not admit
that it is true?

   Crito: We must, Socrates.... 140

─ **Q** **What reasons does Socrates give for refusing to
    escape from prison?**

─ **Q** **How does this reading illustrate the relationship
    between the individual and the community?**

Plato and the Theory of Forms

Socrates' teachings were an inspiration to his pupil Plato
(ca. 428–ca. 347 B.C.E.). Born in Athens during the
Peloponnesian Wars, Plato reaped the benefits of Golden
Age culture along with the insecurities of the postwar era.
In 387 B.C.E., more than a decade after the death of his
master, he founded the world's first school of philosophy,
the Academy. Plato wrote some two dozen treatises, most
of which were cast in the dialogue or dialectical format
that Socrates had made famous. Some of the dialogues may

be precise transcriptions of actual conversations, whereas
others are clearly fictional, but the major philosophical
arguments in almost all Plato's treatises are put into the
mouth of Socrates. Since Socrates himself wrote nothing,
it is almost impossible to distinguish between the ideas of
Plato and those of Socrates.

Plato's most famous treatise, the *Republic*, asks two
central questions: "What is the meaning of justice?" and
"What is the nature of a just society?" In trying to answer
these questions, Plato introduces a theory of knowledge
that is both visionary and dogmatic. It asserts the existence
of a two-level reality, one consisting of constantly changing
particulars available to our senses, the other consisting
of unchanging eternal truths understood by way of the
intellect. According to Plato, the higher reality of eternal
truths, which he calls Forms, is distinct from the imperfect
and transient objects of sensory experience, which are
mere copies of Forms. Plato's Theory of Forms proposes
that all sensory objects are imitations of the Forms, which,
like the simplest mathematical equations, are imperishable
and forever true. For example, the circle and its three-
dimensional counterpart, the sphere, exist independent of
any *particular* circle and sphere. They have always existed
and will always exist. But the beach ball I toss in the air, an
imperfect copy of the sphere, is transitory. Indeed, if all
the beach balls in the world were destroyed, the Universal
Form—Sphere—would still exist. Similarly, suggests Plato,
Justice, Love, and Beauty (along with other Forms) stand
as unchanging and eternal models for the many individual
and particular instances of each in the sensory world.

According to Plato, Forms descend from an ultimate
Form, the Form of the Good. Plato never located or
defined the Ultimate Good, except by analogy with the
sun. Like the sun, the Form of the Good illuminates all
that is intelligible and makes possible the mind's perception of Forms as objects of thought. The Ultimate Good,
knowledge of which is the goal of dialectical inquiry, is the
most difficult to reach.

In the *Republic*, Plato uses a literary device known as
allegory to illustrate the dilemma facing the psyche in its
ascent to knowledge of the imperishable and unchanging Forms. By way of allegory—the device by which the
literal meaning of the text implies a figurative or "hidden"

Figure 4.18 "Allegory of the Cave," from *The Great Dialogues of Plato*.

meaning—Plato describes a group of ordinary mortals chained within an underground chamber (the psyche imprisoned within the human body). Their woeful position permits them to see only the shadows on the walls of the cave (the imperfect and perishable imitations of the Forms that occupy the world of the senses), which the prisoners, in their ignorance, believe to be real (Figure **4.18**). Only when one of the prisoners (the philosopher-hero) ascends to the domain of light (true knowledge, or knowledge of the Forms) does it become clear that what the cave-dwellers perceive as truth is nothing more than shadows of Reality. This intriguing parable is presented as a dialogue between Socrates and Plato's older brother, Glaucon.

READING 4.6 From the "Allegory of the Cave" from Plato's *Republic* (ca. 375 B.C.E.)

Next, said [Socrates], here is a parable to illustrate the 1
degrees in which our nature may be enlightened or
unenlightened. Imagine the condition of men living in a sort of
cavernous chamber underground, with an entrance open to the
light and a long passage all down the cave. Here they have
been from childhood, chained by the leg and also by the neck,
so that they cannot move and can see only what is in front of
them, because the chains will not let them turn their heads.
At some distance higher up is the light of a fire burning behind
them; and between the prisoners and the fire is a track[1] with 10
a parapet built along it, like the screen at a puppet-show, which
hides the performers while they show their puppets over the top.
    I see, said he.
    Now behind this parapet imagine persons carrying along various
artificial objects, including figures of men and animals in wood or
stone or other materials, which project above the parapet.
Naturally, some of these persons will be talking, others silent.[2]
    It is a strange picture, he said, and a strange sort of 20
prisoners.
    Like ourselves, I replied; for in the first place prisoners so
confined would have seen nothing of themselves or of one
another, except the shadows thrown by the firelight on the
wall of the Cave facing them, would they?
    Not if all their lives they had been prevented from moving
their heads.
    And they would have seen as little of the objects
carried past.
    Of course. 30
    Now, if they could talk to one another, would they not

---

[1] The track crosses the passage into the Cave at right angles and is above the parapet built along it.

[2] A modern Plato would compare his Cave to an underground cinema, where the audience watch the play of shadows thrown by the film passing before a light at their backs. The film itself is only an image of "real" things and events in the world outside the cinema. For the film Plato has to substitute the clumsier apparatus of a procession of artificial objects carried on their heads by persons who are merely part of the machinery, providing for the movement of the objects and the sound whose echo the prisoners hear. The parapet prevents these persons' shadows from being cast on the wall of the Cave.

suppose that their words referred only to those passing
shadows which they saw?
    Necessarily.
    And suppose their prison had an echo from the wall facing
them? When one of the people crossing behind them spoke,
they could only suppose that the sound came from the shadow
passing before their eyes.
    No doubt.
    In every way, then, such prisoners would recognize as 40
reality nothing but the shadows of those artificial objects.
    Inevitably.
    Now consider what would happen if their release from the
chains and the healing of their unwisdom should come about
in this way. Suppose one of them were set free and forced
suddenly to stand up, turn his head, and walk with eyes lifted
to the light; all these movements would be painful, and he
would be too dazzled to make out the objects whose shadows
he had been used to see. What do you think he would say,
if someone told him that what he had formerly seen was 50
meaningless illusion, but now, being somewhat nearer to
reality and turned toward more real objects, he was getting a
truer view? Suppose further that he were shown the various
objects being carried by and were made to say, in reply to
questions, what each of them was. Would he not be perplexed
and believe the objects now shown him to be not so real as
what he formerly saw?
    Yes, not nearly so real.
    And if he were forced to look at the firelight itself, would
not his eyes ache, so that he would try to escape and turn 60
back to the things which he could see distinctly, convinced
that they really were clearer than these other objects now
being shown to him?
    Yes.
    And suppose someone were to drag him away forcibly up
the steep and rugged ascent and not let him go until he had
hauled him out into the sunlight, would he not suffer pain and
vexation at such treatment, and, when he had come out into
the light, find his eyes so full of its radiance that he could not
see a single one of the things that he was now told were 70
real?
    Certainly he would not see them all at once.
    He would need, then, to grow accustomed before he could
see things in that upper world. At first it would be easiest to
make out shadows, and then the images of men and things
reflected in water, and later on the things themselves. After
that, it would be easier to watch the heavenly bodies and the
sky itself by night, looking at the light of the moon and stars
rather than the Sun and the Sun's light in the day-time.
    Yes, surely. 80
    Last of all, he would be able to look at the Sun and
contemplate its nature, not as it appears when reflected
in water or any alien medium, but as it is in itself in its own
domain.
    No doubt.
    And now he would begin to draw the conclusion that it is
the Sun that produces the seasons and the course of the year
and controls everything in the visible world, and moreover is in
a way the cause of all that he and his companions used to see.
    Clearly he would come at last to that conclusion. 90

Then if he called to mind his fellow prisoners and what passed for wisdom in his former dwelling-place, he would surely think himself happy in the change and be sorry for them. They may have had a practice of honoring and commending one another, with prizes for the man who had the keenest eye for the passing shadows and the best memory for the order in which they followed or accompanied one another, so that he could make a good guess as to which was going to come next. Would our released prisoner be likely to covet those prizes or to envy the men exalted to honor and power in the Cave? Would he not feel like Homer's Achilles, that he would far sooner "be on earth as a hired servant in the house of a landless man"[3] or endure anything rather than go back to his old beliefs and live in the old way?

Yes, he would prefer any fate to such a life.

Now imagine what would happen if he went down again to take his former seat in the Cave. Coming suddenly out of the sunlight, his eyes would be filled with darkness. He might be required once more to deliver his opinion on those shadows, in competition with the prisoners who had never been released, while his eyesight was still dim and unsteady; and it might take some time to become used to the darkness. They would laugh at him and say that he had gone up only to come back with his sight ruined; it was worth no one's while even to attempt the ascent. If they could lay hands on the man who was trying to set them free and lead them up, they would kill him.[4]

Yes, they would.

Every feature in this parable, my dear Glaucon, is meant to fit our earlier analysis. The prison dwelling corresponds to the region revealed to us through the sense of sight, and the firelight within it to the power of the Sun. The ascent to see the things in the upper world you may take as standing for the upward journey of the soul into the region of the intelligible; then you will be in possession of what I surmise, since that is what you wish to be told. Heaven knows whether it is true; but this, at any rate, is how it appears to me. In the world of knowledge, the last thing to be perceived and only with great difficulty is the essential Form of Goodness. Once it is perceived, the conclusion must follow that, for all things, this is the cause of whatever is right and good; in the visible world it gives birth to light and to the lord of light, while it is itself sovereign in the intelligible world and the parent of intelligence and truth. Without having had a vision of this Form no one can act with wisdom, either in his own life or in matters of state.

So far as I can understand, I share your belief.

Then you may also agree that it is no wonder if those who have reached this height are reluctant to manage the affairs of men. Their souls long to spend all their time in that upper world—naturally enough, if here once more our parable holds true. Nor, again, is it at all strange that one who comes from the contemplation of divine things to the miseries of human life should appear awkward and ridiculous when, with eyes still dazed and not yet accustomed to the darkness, he is compelled, in a law court or elsewhere, to dispute about the shadows of justice or the images that cast those shadows, and to wrangle over the notions of what is right in the minds of men who have never beheld Justice itself.

It is not at all strange.

No; a sensible man will remember that the eyes may be confused in two ways—by a change from light to darkness or from darkness to light; and he will recognize that the same thing happens to the soul. When he sees it troubled and unable to discern anything clearly, instead of laughing thoughtlessly, he will ask whether, coming from a brighter existence, its unaccustomed vision is obscured by the darkness, in which case he will think its condition enviable and its life a happy one; or whether, emerging from the depths of ignorance, it is dazzled by excess of light. If so, he will rather feel sorry for it; or, if he were inclined to laugh, that would be less ridiculous than to laugh at the soul which has come down from the light.

That is a fair statement.

If this is true, then, we must conclude that education is not what it is said to be by some, who profess to put knowledge into a soul which does not possess it, as if they could put sight into blind eyes. On the contrary, our own account signifies that the soul of every man does possess the power of learning the truth and the organ to see it with; and that, just as one might have to turn the whole body round in order that the eye should see light instead of darkness, so the entire soul must be turned away from this changing world, until its eye can bear to contemplate reality and that supreme splendor which we have called the Good. Hence there may well be an art whose aim would be to effect this very thing, the conversion of the soul, in the readiest way; not to put the power of sight into the soul's eye, which already has it, but to ensure that, instead of looking in the wrong direction, it is turned the way it ought to be.

Yes, it may well be so.

It looks, then, as though wisdom were different from those ordinary virtues, as they are called, which are not far removed from bodily qualities, in that they can be produced by habituation and exercise in a soul which has not possessed them from the first. Wisdom, it seems, is certainly the virtue of some diviner faculty, which never loses its power, though its use for good or harm depends on the direction toward which it is turned. You must have noticed in dishonest men with a reputation for sagacity the shrewd glance of a narrow intelligence piercing the objects to which it is directed. There is nothing wrong with their power of vision, but it has been forced into the service of evil, so that the keener its sight, the more harm it works.

Quite true.

And yet if the growth of a nature like this had been pruned from earliest childhood, cleared of those clinging overgrowths which come of gluttony and all luxurious pleasure and, like leaden weights charged with affinity to this mortal world, hang upon the soul, bending its vision downward; if, freed from these, the soul were turned round toward true reality, then this same power in these very men would see the truth as keenly as the objects it is turned to now.

---

[3] This verse, spoken by the ghost of Achilles, suggests that the Cave is comparable with Hades, the Greek underworld.

[4] An allusion to the fate of Socrates.

Yes, very likely.

Is it not also likely, or indeed certain after what has been said, that a state can never be properly governed either by the uneducated who know nothing of truth or by men who are allowed to spend all their days in the pursuit of culture? The ignorant have no single mark before their eyes at which they must aim in all the conduct of their own lives and of affairs of state; and the others will not engage in action if they can help it, dreaming that, while still alive, they have been translated to the Island of the Blest.

Quite true.

It is for us, then, as founders of a commonwealth, to bring compulsion to bear on the noblest natures. They must be made to climb the ascent to the vision of Goodness, which we called the highest object of knowledge; and, when they have looked upon it long enough, they must not be allowed, as they now are, to remain on the heights, refusing to come down again to the prisoners or to take any part in their labors and rewards, however much or little these may be worth.

Shall we not be doing them an injustice, if we force on them a worse life than they might have?

You have forgotten again, my friend, that the law is not concerned to make any one class specially happy, but to ensure the welfare of the commonwealth as a whole. By persuasion or constraint it will unite the citizens in harmony, making them share whatever benefits each class can contribute to the common good; and its purpose in forming men of that spirit was not that each should be left to go his own way, but that they should be instrumental in binding the community into one.

True, I had forgotten.

You will see, then, Glaucon, that there will be no real injustice in compelling our philosophers to watch over and care for the other citizens. We can fairly tell them that their compeers in other states may quite reasonably refuse to collaborate: there they have sprung up, like a self-sown plant, in despite of their country's institutions; no one has fostered their growth, and they cannot be expected to show gratitude for a care they have never received. "But," we shall say, "it is not so with you. We have brought you into existence for your country's sake as well as for your own, to be like leaders and king-bees in a hive; you have been better and more thoroughly educated than those others and hence you are more capable of playing your part both as men of thought and as men of action. You must go down, then, each in his turn, to live with the rest and let your eyes grow accustomed to the darkness. You will then see a thousand times better than those who live there always; you will recognize every image for what it is and know what it represents, because you have seen justice, beauty, and goodness in their reality; and so you and we shall find life in our commonwealth no mere dream, as it is in most existing states, where men live fighting one another about shadows and quarreling for power, as if that were a great prize; whereas in truth government can be at its best and free from dissension only where the destined rulers are least desirous of holding office."

Quite true.

Then will our pupils refuse to listen and to take their turns at sharing in the work of the community, though they may live

together for most of their time in a purer air?

No; it is a fair demand, and they are fair-minded men. No doubt, unlike any ruler of the present day, they will think of holding power as an unavoidable necessity.

Yes, my friend; for the truth is that you can have a well-governed society only if you can discover for your future rulers a better way of life than being in office; then only will power be in the hands of men who are rich, not in gold, but in the wealth that brings happiness, a good and wise life. All goes wrong when, starved for lack of anything good in their own lives, men turn to public affairs hoping to snatch from thence the happiness they hunger for. They set about fighting for power, and this internecine conflict ruins them and their country. The life of true philosophy is the only one that looks down upon offices of state; and access to power must be confined to men who are not in love with it; otherwise rivals will start fighting. So whom else can you compel to undertake the guardianship of the commonwealth, if not those who, besides understanding best the principles of government, enjoy a nobler life than the politician's and look for rewards of a different kind?

There is indeed no other choice. . . .

Q **What does each allegorical figure (the Cave, the Sun, and so on) represent?**

Q **How does this education of the psyche contribute (according to Socrates) to the life of a "well-governed society"?**

The "Allegory of the Cave" illustrates some key theories in the teachings of Plato. The first of these is **idealism**, the theory that holds that reality lies in the realm of unchanging Forms, rather than in sensory objects. Platonic idealism implies a dualistic (spirit-and-matter or mind-and-body) model of the universe: the psyche (mind) belongs to the world of the eternal Forms, while the *soma* (body) belongs to the sensory or material world. Imprisoned in the body, the mind forgets its once-perfect knowledge of the Forms. It is, nevertheless, capable of recovering its prenatal intelligence. The business of philosophy is to educate the psyche, to draw it out of its material prison so that it can regain perfect awareness.

Plato's concept of an unchanging force behind the flux of our perceptions looks back to the theories of Heraclitus, while his description of the Forms resembles Pythagorean assertions of the unchanging reality of number. It is not without significance that Plato's Theory of Forms has been hailed in modern physics: the celebrated twentieth-century German physicist Werner Heisenberg argued that the smallest units of matter are not physical objects in the ordinary sense; rather, he asserted, they are "forms," or ideas that can be expressed unambiguously only in mathematical language.

In constructing the Theory of Forms, Plato may also have been influenced by Asian religious thought. The spiritual "spark" with which humans are born, according to Plato, and which must be kindled and cultivated, resembles the Hindu Atman (see chapter 3). And Plato's distinction between the realm of the senses and the ultimate, all-embracing Form recalls the Hindu belief that the illusory world of matter stands apart from Ultimate Being or Brahman. In contrast with Hinduism, however, Plato's teachings do not advocate enlightenment as escape from the material world. Rather, Plato perceives the mind's ascent to knowledge as a prerequisite of individual well-being and the attainment of the good life here on earth. Such enlightenment is essential to achieving a just state and a healthy society.

Plato's *Republic*: The Ideal State

Plato's *Republic* establishes a set of social and moral requirements for everyday life. While this utopian community permits no private property and little family life, it defends a practical system of education by which every citizen might arrive at knowledge of the Good. Education, fundamental to the good society, is available equally to men and women. If women are to be employed in the same duties as men, argues Plato, they must receive the same instruction, which includes music, gymnastics, and military training. In Book 5 of the *Republic*, Socrates explains:

> none of the occupations which comprehend the
> ordering of the state belong to woman as woman, nor
> yet to man as man: but natural gifts are to be found
> here and there in both sexes alike, and so far as her
> nature is concerned, the woman is admissible to all
> pursuits as well as the man, though in all of them the
> woman is weaker than the man.

While all citizens are educated equally, the ability of each determines that person's place within society. Thus the duties of all citizens—laborers, soldiers, or governors—will be consistent with their mental and physical abilities.

Plato had little use for democracy of the kind practiced in Athens. Governing, in his view, should fall to those who are the most intellectually able. That is, those who have most fully recovered a knowledge of the Forms are obliged to act as "king-bees" in the communal hive. (Plato might have been surprised to discover that the ruling bee in a beehive is female.) The life of contemplation carries with it heavy responsibilities, for in the hands of the philosopher-kings lies "the welfare of the commonwealth as a whole." Such views are remarkably compatible with ancient China's premise that a natural hierarchy determines who is fit to govern (see chapter 3).

Aristotle and the Life of Reason

Among Plato's students at the Academy was a young Macedonian named Aristotle, whose contributions to philosophy ultimately rivaled those of his teacher. After a period of travel in the eastern Mediterranean and a brief career as tutor to the young prince of Macedonia (the future Alexander the Great), Aristotle returned to Athens and founded a school known as the Lyceum. Aristotle's habit of walking up and down as he lectured in the *peripatos* ("covered walkway") of the school gave him the nickname the "peripatetic philosopher." His teachings, which exist only in the form of lecture notes compiled by his students,

cover a wider and more practical range of subjects than those of Plato.

Aristotle did not accept Plato's Theory of Forms. For him, the real was not a reflection of ideal Forms, but existed in the objects of the material world. He equated form (or *essence*) with the true nature of a thing, and held that its full possession was achieved by the proper performance of its function. Questioning Plato's theory of an eternal psyche, he theorized that the portion of the soul identified with reason (and with the impersonal force he called the Unmoved Mover) might be immortal.

Aristotle left a vast number of works on some 400 subjects, including biology, physics, politics, poetry, drama, logic, and ethics. To each of his inquiries he brought the habit of systematic classification, identifying each thing according to its essence—its unique and unchanging nature. He also brought to his inquiries the exercise of keen observation. The son of a physician, Aristotle gathered specimens of plant and animal life, and classified them according to their physical similarities and differences. Over 500 different animals, some of which Aristotle himself dissected, are mentioned in his zoological treatises, known as the *Historia Animalium*. Although he did little in the way of modern scientific experimentation, his practice of basing conclusions on very careful observation advanced the **empirical method**—a method of inquiry dependent on direct experience. He brought to his analysis of political life, literature, and human conduct the same principles he employed in classifying plants and animals: objectivity, clarity, and consistency. Before writing the *Politics*, he examined the constitutions of more than 150 Greek city-states. And in the *Poetics* he defined the various genres of literary expression (see chapter 5).

In the fields of biology, astronomy, and physics, Aristotle's conclusions (including many that were incorrect) remained unchallenged for centuries. For instance, Aristotle theorized that in sexual union, the male was the "generator" and the female the "receptacle," while procreation involved the imposition of life-giving form (the male) on chaotic matter (the female). In short, Aristotle's views on female biology and sexuality led centuries of scholars to regard woman as an imperfect and incomplete version of man.

Aristotle's application of scientific principles to the reasoning process was the basis for the science of logic. Aristotelian logic requires the division of an argument into individual terms, followed—in Socratic fashion—by

---

THE SYLLOGISM

All men are mortal.

a:b

Socrates is a man.

c:a

Therefore, Socrates is mortal.

∴ c = b

an examination of the meaning of those terms. Aristotle formulated the **syllogism**, a deductive scheme that presents two premises from which a conclusion may be drawn. As a procedure for reasoned thought without reference to specific content, the syllogism is a system of notation that is similar to mathematics.

Aristotle's *Ethics*

Not the least of Aristotle's contributions was that which he made to **ethics**, that branch of philosophy that sets forth the principles of human conduct. Proceeding from an examination of human values, Aristotle hypothesizes that happiness or "the good life" (the Greek word *eudaimonia* means both) is the only human value that might be considered a final goal or end (*telos*) in itself, rather than a means to any other end. Is not happiness the one goal to which all human beings aspire? If so, then how does one achieve it? The answer, says Aristotle, lies in recognizing one's defining essence, and functioning to fulfill it. The function of the eye is to see; the function of the racehorse is to run fast; the function of a knife is to cut, and so on. How well a thing performs is synonymous with its excellence or virtue (in Greek, the word *arete* denotes both): the excellence of the eye, then, lies in seeing well; the excellence of a racehorse lies in how fast it runs; the excellence of a knife depends on how well it cuts, and so on. The unique function of the human being, concludes Aristotle, is the ability to reason; hence, the excellence of any human creature lies in the exercise of reason.

In the *Ethics*, edited by Aristotle's son Nicomachus, Aristotle examines the Theory of the Good Life and the Nature of Happiness. He explains that action in accordance with reason is necessary for the acquisition of excellence, or virtue. Ideal conduct, suggests Aristotle, lies in the Golden Mean—the middle ground between any two extremes of behavior. Between cowardice and recklessness, for instance, one should seek the middle ground: courage. Between boastfulness and timidity, one should cultivate modesty. The Doctrine of the Mean rationalized the Classical search for moderation and balance. In contrast with the divinely ordained moral texts of other ancient cultures, Aristotle's *Ethics* required individuals to reason their way to ethical conduct.

READING 4.7 From Aristotle's *Nicomachean Ethics* (ca. 340 B.C.E.)

The Supreme Good

If it is true that in the sphere of action there is an end which   1
we wish for its own sake, and for the sake of which we wish
for everything else, and that we do not desire all things for the
sake of something else (for, if that is so, the process will go on
ad infinitum, and our desire will be idle and futile), it is clear
that this will be the good or the supreme good. Does it not
follow then that the knowledge of this supreme good is of
great importance for the conduct of life, and that, if we know
it, we shall be like archers who have a mark at which to aim,
we shall have a better chance of attaining what we want?

But, if this is the case, we must endeavor to comprehend,   10
at least in outline, its nature, and the science or faculty to
which it belongs. . . .

It seems not unreasonable that people should derive their
conception of the good or of happiness from men's lives.
Thus ordinary or vulgar people conceive it to be pleasure,
and accordingly approve a life of enjoyment. For there are
practically three prominent lives, the sensual, the political,
and, thirdly, the speculative. Now the mass of men present an
absolutely slavish appearance, as choosing the life of brute
beasts, but they meet with consideration because so many   20
persons in authority share the tastes of Sardanapalus.[1]
Cultivated and practical people, on the other hand, identify
happiness with honor, as honor is the general end of political
life. But this appears too superficial for our present purpose;
for honor seems to depend more upon the people who pay it
than upon the person to whom it is paid, and we have an
intuitive feeling that the good is something which is proper to
a man himself and cannot easily be taken away from him. It
seems too that the reason why men seek honor is that they
may be confident of their own goodness. Accordingly they   30
seek it at the hands of the wise and of those who know them
well, and they seek it on the ground of virtue; hence it is clear
that in their judgment at any rate virtue is superior to honor. . . .

We speak of that which is sought after for its own sake as
more final than that which is sought after as a means to
something else; we speak of that which is never desired as a
means to something else as more final than the things which
are desired both in themselves and as means to something
else; and we speak of a thing as absolutely final, if it is
always desired in itself and never as a means to something   40
else.

It seems that happiness preeminently answers to this
description, as we always desire happiness for its own sake
and never as a means to something else, whereas we desire
honor, pleasure, intellect, and every virtue, partly for their own
sakes (for we should desire them independently of what might
result from them) but partly also as being means to happiness,
because we suppose they will prove the instruments of
happiness. Happiness, on the other hand, nobody desires for
the sake of these things, nor indeed as a means to anything   50
else at all. . . .

Perhaps, however, it seems a truth which is generally
admitted, that happiness is the supreme good; what is wanted
is to define its nature a little more clearly. The best way of
arriving at such a definition will probably be to ascertain the
function of Man. For, as with a flute-player, a statuary, or any
artisan, or in fact anybody who has a definite function and
action, his goodness, or excellence, seems to lie in his
function, so it would seem to be with Man, if indeed he has a
definite function. Can it be said then that, while a carpenter   60
and a cobbler have definite functions and actions, Man,
unlike them, is naturally functionless? The reasonable view is
that, as the eye, the hand, the foot, and similarly each . . . part
of the body has a definite function, so Man may be regarded
as having a definite function apart from all these. What then,
can this function be? It is not life; for life is apparently

---

[1] The legendary king of Assyria, known for his sensuality.

something which man shares with the plants; and it is something peculiar to him that we are looking for. We must exclude therefore the life of nutrition and increase. There is next what may be called the life of sensation. But this, too, is apparently shared by Man with horses, cattle, and all other animals. There remains what I may call the practical life of the rational part of *Man's being*. But the rational part is twofold; it is rational partly in the sense of being obedient to reason, and partly in the sense of possessing reason and intelligence. The practical life too may be conceived of in two ways, viz., *either as a moral state, or as a moral activity*: but we must understand by it the life of activity, as this seems to be the truer form of the conception.

The function of Man then is an activity of soul in accordance with reason, or not independently of reason. . . .

The Golden Mean

Our present study is not, like other studies, purely speculative in its intention; for the object of our inquiry is not to know the nature of virtue but to become ourselves virtuous, as that is the sole benefit which it conveys. It is necessary therefore to consider the right way of performing actions, for it is actions as we have said that determine the character of the resulting moral states. . . .

The first point to be observed then is that in such matters as we are considering[,] deficiency and excess are equally fatal. It is so, as we observe, in regard to health and strength; for we must judge of what we cannot see by the evidence of what we do see. Excess or deficiency of gymnastic exercise is fatal to strength. Similarly an excess or deficiency of meat and drink is fatal to health, whereas a suitable amount produces, augments, and sustains it. It is the same then with temperance, courage, and the other virtues. A person who avoids and is afraid of everything and faces nothing becomes a coward; a person who is not afraid of anything but is ready to face everything becomes foolhardy. Similarly he who enjoys every pleasure and never abstains from any pleasure is licentious; he who eschews all pleasures like a boor is an insensible sort of person. For temperance and courage are destroyed by excess and deficiency but preserved by the mean [middle] state. . . .

The nature of virtue has been now generically described. But it is not enough to state merely that virtue is a moral state, we must also describe the character of that moral state. It must be laid down then that every virtue or excellence has the effect of producing a good condition of that of which it is a virtue or excellence, and of enabling it to perform its function well. Thus the excellence of the eye makes the eye good and its function good, as it is by the excellence of the eye that we see well. Similarly, the excellence of the horse makes a horse excellent and good at racing, at carrying its rider and at facing the enemy. If then this is universally true, the virtue or excellence of man will be such a moral state as makes a man good and able to perform his proper function well. We have already explained how this will be the case, but another way of making it clear will be to study the nature or character of this virtue.

Now in everything, whether it be continuous or discrete, it is possible to take a greater, a smaller, or an equal amount, and this either absolutely or in relation to ourselves, the equal being a mean between excess and deficiency. By the mean in respect of the thing itself, or the absolute mean, I understand that which is equally distinct from both extremes; and this is one and the same thing for everybody. By the mean considered relatively to ourselves I understand that which is neither too much nor too little; but this is not one thing, nor is it the same for everybody. Thus if 10 be too much and 2 too little we take 6 as a mean in respect of the thing itself; for 6 is as much greater than 2 as it is less than 10, and this is a mean in arithmetical proportion. But the mean considered relatively to ourselves must not be ascertained in this way. It does not follow that if 10 pounds of *meat* be too much and 2 too little for a man to eat, a trainer will order him 6 pounds, as this may itself be too much or too little for the person who is to take it; it will be too little [for instance] for Milo,[2] but too much for a beginner in gymnastics. It will be the same with running and wrestling; *the right amount will vary with the individual*. This being so, everybody who understands his business avoids alike excess and deficiency; he seeks and chooses the mean, not the absolute mean, but the mean considered relatively to ourselves.

Every science then performs its function well, if it regards the mean and refers the works which it produces to the mean. This is the reason why it is usually said of successful works that it is impossible to take anything from them or to add anything to them, which implies that excess or deficiency is fatal to excellence but that the mean state ensures it. Good artists too, as we say, have an eye to the mean in their works. But virtue, like Nature herself, is more accurate and better than any art; virtue therefore will aim at the mean;—I speak of moral virtue, as it is moral virtue which is concerned with emotions and actions, and it is these which admit of excess and deficiency and the mean. Thus it is possible to go too far, or not to go far enough, in respect of fear, courage, desire, anger, pity, and pleasure and pain generally, and the excess and the deficiency are alike wrong; but to experience these emotions at the right times and on the right occasions and toward the right persons and for the right causes and in the right manner is the mean or the supreme good, which is characteristic of virtue. Similarly there may be excess, deficiency, or the mean, in regard to actions. But virtue is concerned with emotions and actions, and here excess is an error and deficiency a fault, whereas the mean is successful and laudable, and success and merit are both characteristics of virtue.

Virtue then is a state of deliberate moral purpose consisting in a mean that is relative to ourselves, the mean being determined by reason, or as a prudent man would determine it. . . .

Q **What, according to Aristotle, is the supreme good?**

Q **How does one arrive at the Golden Mean?**

---

[2] A famous athlete from the Greek city-state of Crotona in southern Italy. As a teenager, he began lifting a calf each day, until, as both his strength and the calf grew, he could lift a fully grown bullock.

Aristotle and the State

While the Golden Mean gave every individual a method for determining right action, Aristotle was uncertain that citizens would put it to efficient use in governing themselves. Like Plato, he questioned the viability of the democratic state. Political privilege, argued Aristotle, was the logical consequence of the fact that some human beings were naturally superior to others: from the hour of their birth some were marked out for subjection and others for rule. Aristotle also insisted that governments must function in the interest of the state, not in the interest of any single individual or group. He criticized democracy because, at least in theory, it put power in the hands of great masses of poor people who might rule in their own interests. He also pointed out that Athenian demagogues were capable of persuading the Assembly to pass less-than-worthy laws. In his *Politics*, the first treatise on political theory produced in the West, Aristotle concluded that the best type of government was a constitutional one ruled by the middle class. Aristotle defined the human being as a *polis*-person (the term from which we derive the word "political"). Humans are, in other words, political creatures, who can reach their full potential only within the political framework of the state. Only beasts and gods, he noted, have no need for the state—he gracefully excluded women from such considerations. Aristotle resolved the relationship between the individual and the state as follows:

> [The] state is by nature clearly prior to the family and to the individual, since the whole is of necessity prior to the part. . . . The proof that the state is a creation of nature and prior to the individual is that the individual, when isolated, is not self-sufficing; and

therefore he is like a part in relation to the whole. But he who is unable to live in society, or who has no need because he is sufficient for himself, must be either a beast or a god: he is no part of a state. A social instinct is implanted in all men by nature, and yet he who first founded the state was the greatest of benefactors.

For man, when perfected, is the best of animals, but, when separated from law and justice, he is the worst of all; since armed injustice is the more dangerous, and he is equipped at birth with arms, meant to be used by intelligence and virtue, he is the most unholy and the most savage of animals, and the most full of lust and gluttony. But justice is the bond of men in states, for the administration of justice, which is the determination of what is just, is the principle of order in political society.

Science and Technology

390 B.C.E.	Plato coins the term "elements" to describe four primary substances: earth, air, fire, and water (earlier introduced by Empedocles)
350 B.C.E.	Aristotle posits a spherical earth based on observations of a lunar eclipse
340 B.C.E.	Eudemus of Rhodes writes the *History of Mathematics*
330 B.C.E.	Aristotle's *Historia Animalium* classifies animals and records details of animal life; other of his writings advance the study of medicine, biology, and physics

LOOKING BACK

Bronze Age Civilizations of the Aegean (ca. 3000–1200 B.C.E.)

- The Aegean civilizations of Crete and Mycenae laid the foundations for much of Greek life and legend. While the Minoans were peace-loving, the militant and aggressive Mycenaeans challenged other traders for control of the eastern Mediterranean.

The Heroic Age (ca. 1200–750 B.C.E.)

- The Homeric epics immortalize the Mycenaean attack on Troy in Asia Minor ca. 1200 B.C.E. and its legendary heroes. Transmitted orally

and recorded ca. 800 B.C.E., they became the "national" poems of Greece.

- The *Iliad* follows Achilles and his vengeful fight in the Trojan War as he attempts to reconcile his sense of personal honor and his obligations to his fellow warriors.
- The *Odyssey*, the second great epic of the Heroic Age, recounts the adventures of the Greek commander Odysseus during his long sea journey back to his native Ithaca.
- The Greek pantheon was seen as a family of gods who intervened in the lives of human beings.

The Greek City-State and the Persian Wars (ca. 750–480 B.C.E.)

- Greek geography encouraged the evolution of the *polis*; each of the 200 independent city-states established its own economy, government, and military defenses.
- When the Persian Empire attacked the Greek mainland during the sixth century B.C.E., the city-states formed an alliance and built a strong naval force to defeat the Persians.
- Herodotus, the "father of history," recorded an account of the Persian Wars that remains the Western world's first major work in prose.

Athens and the Greek Golden Age (ca. 480–430 B.C.E.)

- Following the Persian Wars, ancient Greece experienced a Golden Age in cultural productivity, with the city-state of Athens assuming political dominion as well as commercial supremacy in the Aegean Sea.
- When the Popular Assembly of Citizens acquired the right to make laws, in 508 B.C.E., Athens became the first direct democracy in world history.
- Beginning in 776 B.C.E., the Greeks enjoyed athletic contests in the form of the Olympic Games, in which all Greek city-states competed.

The Individual and the Community

- The Greeks were the first masters of the art of drama, presenting the Athenian community with regular theatrical performances and leaving the world its earliest tragedies and comedies.
- Such famous Greek trilogies as the *Oresteia* and *Oedipus* explore the moral dilemma that brings personal choice and action into conflict with the well-being of the community.
- Sophocles' tragedy *Antigone*, in which Oedipus' daughter violates the king's decree and buries her brother's dead body, examines the irreconcilability of personal and political obligations, and the consequences of excessive pride.

Greek Philosophy: The Speculative Leap

- During the sixth century B.C.E., Greek philosophers laid the foundations for Western scientific and philosophic inquiry; they argued for natural causes, using observation and systematic analysis to reach valid conclusions.
- The naturalist philosophers tried to determine the material basis of the universe: Democritus advanced the atomic theory of matter; Pythagoras held that proportion based on number constituted the underlying cosmic order; Hippocrates, the "father of medicine," separated science from superstition by seeking natural causes for disease.

Humanist Philosophy

- The Sophists and the humanist philosophers Socrates, Plato, and Aristotle moved beyond the naturalists to probe the nature of human knowledge, the question of right conduct, and the advance of wisdom.
- The Sophists argued that truth and justice were relative, while their critic Socrates pursued absolute standards for moral conduct.
- Plato's Theory of Forms laid the basis for philosophical idealism and for the separation of mind and matter. In the *Republic*, Plato explained how virtue might be cultivated for the mutual benefit of the individual and the community.
- Aristotle investigated a variety of subjects, ranging from logic and zoology to the art of poetry and the science of stagecraft. In his *Ethics*, Aristotle asserted that the good life was identical to the life of reason, a life guided by the Golden Mean.

Glossary

allegory a literary device in which objects, persons, or actions are equated with secondary, figurative meanings that underlie their literal meaning

amphora a two-handled vessel used for oil or wine (see Figures 4.1, 4.10, and 5.5)

antagonist the character that directly opposes the protagonist in drama or fiction

catalog a list of people, things, or attributes, characteristic of biblical and Homeric literature

catharsis (Greek, "purification" or "cleansing") in drama, an emotional experience that revitalizes the spectator

democracy a government in which supreme power is vested in the people

dialectical method a question-and-answer style of inquiry made famous by Socrates

empirical method a method of inquiry dependent on direct experience or observation

epithet a characterizing word or phrase; in Homeric verse, a compound adjective used to identify a person or thing

ethics that branch of philosophy that sets forth the principles of human conduct

hubris excessive pride; arrogance

idealism (Platonic) the theory that holds that things in the material world are manifestations of an independent realm of unchanging, immaterial ideas of forms (see also Kantian idealism, chapter 25)

krater A vessel used for mixing wine and water

oligarchy a government in which power lies in the hands of an elite minority

protagonist the leading character in a play or story

syllogism a deductive scheme of formal argument, consisting of two premises from which a conclusion may be drawn

The Classical Style
ca. 700–30 B.C.E.

"Men are day-bound. What is a man? What is he not? Man is a shadow's dream. But when divine advantage comes, men gain a radiance and a richer life."
Pindar

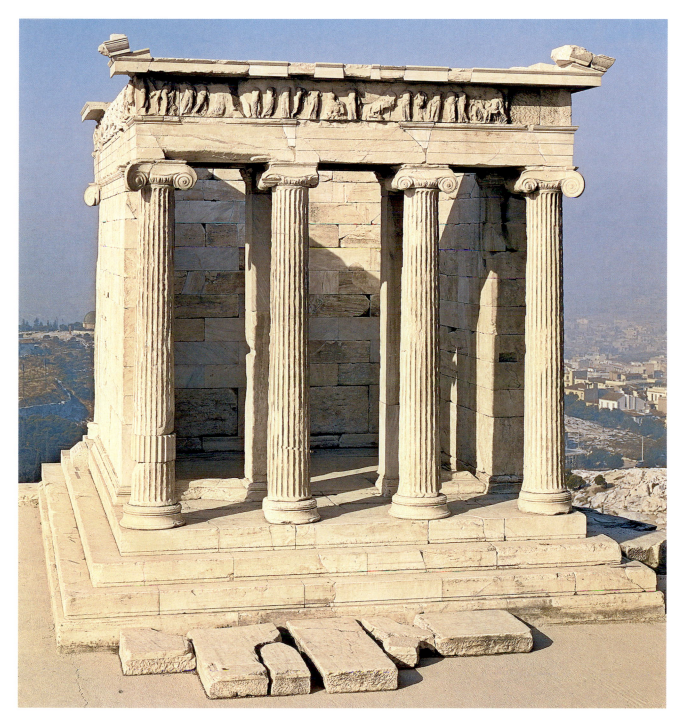

Figure 5.1 KALLICRATES, Temple of Athena Nike, Acropolis, Athens, ca. 427–424 B.C.E. Pentelic marble, 17 ft. 9 in. × 26 ft. 10 in.

The words "classic" and "classical" are commonly used to mean "first-rate" and "enduring." They also describe a style of creative expression marked by clarity, simplicity, balance, and harmonious proportion—features associated with moderation, rationalism, and dignity. This style dominated the arts of ancient Greece. It was brought to its height during the period that followed the Persian Wars (ca. 480–400 B.C.E.). In the visual arts, as well as in literature, philosophy, and music, the Greek "classics" provided a standard of beauty and excellence that was preserved and imitated for centuries. During the fourth century B.C.E., Alexander the Great carried Greek language and culture into North Africa and Central Asia, thus "Hellenizing" a vast part of the civilized world. Thereafter, the Romans absorbed Greek culture and transmitted its

legacy to the West.* Most of the free-standing sculptures of the Greek masters survive only in Roman replicas, and what remains is a fraction of what once existed. The balance fell to the ravages of time and vandals, who pulverized marble statues to make mortar and melted down bronze pieces to mint coins and cast cannons.

Despite these losses, the Classical conception of beauty has had a profound influence on Western cultural expression. Its mark is most visible in the numerous Neoclassical ("new Classical") revivals that have flourished over the centuries, beginning with the Renaissance in Italy (see chapters 16–17).

---

* The Roman contribution to the Classical style is discussed in chapter 6.

The Classical Style

The quest for harmonious proportion was the driving force behind the evolution of the Classical style, even as it was the impetus for the rise of Greek philosophy. In chapter 4, we saw that the naturalist philosophers worked to identify the fundamental order underlying the chaos of human perception. Pythagoras, for example, tried to show that the order of the universe could be understood by observing proportion (both geometric and numerical) in nature: he produced a taut string that, when plucked, sounded a specific pitch; by pinching that string in the middle and plucking either half he generated a sound exactly consonant with (and one **octave** higher than) the first pitch. Pythagoras claimed that relationships between musical sounds obeyed a natural symmetry that might be expressed numerically and geometrically. If music was governed by proportion, was not the universe as a whole subject to similar laws? And, if indeed nature itself obeyed laws of harmony and proportion, then should not artists work to imitate them?

Among Greek artists and architects, such ideas generated the search for a canon, or set of rules, for determining physical proportion. To establish a canon, the artist fixed on a *module*, or standard of measurement, that governed the relationships between all parts of the work of art and the whole. The module was not absolute, but varied according to the subject matter. In the human body, for instance, the distance from the chin to the top of the forehead, representing one-tenth of the whole body height, constituted a module by which body measurements might be calculated. Unlike the Egyptian canon (see Figure 2.19), the Greek canon was flexible: it did not employ a grid on which the human form was mapped, with fixed positions for parts of the body. Nevertheless, the Greek canon made active use of that principle of proportion known as *symmetry*, that is, correspondence of

opposite parts in size, shape, or position, as is evident in the human body.

Although little survives in the way of Greek literary evidence, Roman sources preserve information that helps us to understand the canon that, after three centuries of experimentation, artists of the Greek Golden Age put into practice. Among these sources, the best is the *Ten Books on Architecture* written by the Roman architect and engineer Vitruvius Pollio (?–26 B.C.E.). Vitruvius recorded many of the aesthetic principles and structural techniques used by the ancient Greeks. In defining the Classical canon, he advised that the construction of a building and the relationship between its parts must imitate the proportions of the human body. Without proportion, that is, the correspondence between the various parts of the whole, there can be no design, argued Vitruvius. And without design, there can be no art. The eminent Greek Golden Age sculptor Polycleitus, himself the author of a manual on proportion (no longer in existence), is believed to have employed the canon Vitruvius describes (Figure **5.2**). But it was the Vitruvian model itself that, thanks to the efforts of the Renaissance artist–scientist Leonardo da Vinci (see chapter 17), became a symbol for the centrality of the ideally proportioned human being in an ideally proportioned universe (Figure **5.3**).

READING 5.1 From Vitruvius' *Principles of Symmetry* (ca. 46–30 B.C.E.)

On Symmetry: In Temples and in the Human Body

1 The Design of a temple depends on symmetry, the principles of which must be most carefully observed by the architect. They are due to proportion. . . . Proportion is a correspondence among the measures of the members of an entire work, and of the whole to a certain part selected as standard. From this result the principles of symmetry. Without symmetry and proportion there can be no principles

1

Figure 5.2 POLYCLEITUS, *Doryphorus* (*Spear-Bearer*), Roman copy after a bronze Greek original of ca. 450–440 B.C.E. Marble, height 6 ft. 11½ in. The figure, who once held a spear in his left hand, strides forward in a manner that unites motion and repose, energy and poise, confidence and grace—the qualities of the ideal warrior-athlete.

Figure 5.3 LEONARDO DA VINCI, *Proportional Study of a Man in the Manner of Vitruvius*, ca. 1487. Pen and ink, 13½ × 9⅝ in.

in the design of any temple; that is, if there is no precise relation between its members, as in the case of those of a well-shaped man. **10**

2 For the human body is so designed by nature that the face, from the chin to the top of the forehead and lowest roots of the hair, is a tenth part of the whole height; the open hand from the wrist to the tip of the middle finger is just the same; the head from the chin to the crown is an eighth, and with the neck and shoulder from the top of the breast to the lowest roots of the hair is a sixth; from the middle of the breast to the summit of the crown is a fourth. If we take the height of the face itself, the distance from the bottom of the chin to the underside of the nostrils is one third of it; the nose from the underside of the **20** nostrils to a line between the eyebrows is the same; from there to the lowest roots of the hair is also a third, comprising the forehead. The length of the foot is one sixth of the height of the body; of the forearm, one fourth; and the breadth of the breast is also one fourth. The other members, too, have their own symmetrical proportions, and it was by employing them that famous painters and sculptors of antiquity attained to great and endless renown.

3 Similarly, in the members of a temple there ought to be the greatest harmony in the symmetrical relations of the different **30**

parts to the general magnitude of the whole. Then again, in the human body the central point is naturally the navel. For if a man be placed flat on his back, with hands and feet extended, and a pair of compasses centered at his navel, the fingers and toes of his two hands and feet will touch the circumference of a circle described therefrom. And just as the human body yields a circular outline, so too a square figure may be found from it [see Figure 5.3]. For if we measure the distance from the soles of the feet to the top of the head, and then apply that measure to the outstretched arms, the breadth will be found to be the same as the height, as in the case of plane surfaces which are perfectly square.

40

4 Therefore, since nature has designed the human body so that its members are duly proportioned to the frame as a whole, it appears that the ancients had good reason for their rule, that in perfect buildings the different members must be in exact symmetrical relations to the whole general scheme. Hence, while transmitting to us the proper arrangements for buildings of all kinds, they are particularly careful to do so in the case of temples of the gods, buildings in which merits and faults usually last forever. . . .

50

> **Q** **Should the proportions of the human body govern architectural design, as Vitruvius suggests?**

Humanism, Realism, and Idealism

While proportion and order are guiding principles of the Classical style, other features informed Greek Classicism from earliest times. One of the most apparent is *humanism*. Greek art is said to be humanistic not only because it observes fundamental laws derived from the human physique, but also because it focuses so consistently on the actions of human beings. Greek art is fundamentally *realistic*, that is, faithful to nature; but it refines nature in a process of *idealization*, that is, the effort to achieve a perfection that surpasses nature. Humanism, Realism, and Idealism are hallmarks of Greek art.

Because almost all Greek frescoes have disappeared, decorated vases are our main source of information about Greek painting. During the first 300 years of Greek art—the *Geometric period* (ca. 1200–700 B.C.E.)—artists painted their ceramic wares with angular figures and complex geometric patterns arranged to enhance the shape of the vessel. Scenes from a warrior's funeral dominate the upper register of a krater; the funeral procession, with horse-drawn chariots, occupies the lower register (Figure **5.4**). By the *Archaic period* (ca. 700–480 B.C.E.), scenes from mythology, literature, and everyday life came to inhabit the central zone of the vase (Figure **5.5**; see also Figures 4.1 and 4.10). Water jars, wine jugs, storage vessels, drinking cups, and bowls all record the keen enjoyment of everyday activities among the Greeks: working, dancing, feasting, fighting, and gaming. In these compositions, little if any physical setting is provided for the action. Indeed, in their decorative simplicity, the flat black figures often resemble the abstract shapes that ornament the rim, handle, and foot of the vessel (see Figure 5.5). The principles of clarity and order so apparent in the Geometric style (see

Figure 5.4) remain dominant in the decoration of later black-figured vases, where a startling clarity of design is produced by the interplay of dark and light areas of figure and ground.

During the *Classical period* (480–323 B.C.E.), artists replaced the black-figured style with one in which the human body was left the color of the clay and the ground was painted black (Figure **5.6**). They refined their efforts to position figures and objects to complement the shape of the vessel (see also Figures 4.17 and 5.5). However, with the newly developed red-figured style, artists might delineate physical details on the buff-colored surface, thereby making the human form appear more lifelike. Although still flattened and aligned side by side, figures are posed

Figure 5.4 Funerary krater with "Geometric" decoration, ca. 750 B.C.E. Terracotta, height 3 ft. 4½ in. The Greeks used monumental vases like this one as grave markers. The deceased is laid out on the bier, surrounded by his family and a group of mourners. The foot soldiers in the procession below carry full-body ("hourglass") shields and lances.

naturally. *Realism*, that is, fidelity to nature, has overtaken the decorative aspect of the Geometric and Archaic styles. At the same time, artists of the Classical period moved toward aesthetic *idealism*. Socrates is noted for having described the idealizing process: he advised the painter Parrhasius that he must reach beyond the flawed world of appearances by selecting and combining the most beautiful details of many different models. To achieve ideal form, the artist must simplify the subject matter, free it of incidental detail, and impose the accepted canon of proportion. Accordingly, the art object will surpass the imperfect and transient objects of sensory experience. Like Plato's Ideal Forms, the artist's imitations of reality are lifelike in appearance, but they aim to improve upon or perfect sensory reality. Among the Greeks, as among the Egyptians, conception played a large part in the art-making process; with the Greeks, however, the created object was no longer a static sacred sign, but a dynamic, rationalized replica of the physical world.

Figure 5.6 EPICTETUS, cup (detail), ca. 510 B.C.E. Terracotta, diameter 13 in.

Figure 5.5 EXEKIAS, black-figured amphora with Achilles and Ajax playing dice, ca. 530 B.C.E. Height 24 in.

The Evolution of the Classical Style

Greek Sculpture: The Archaic Period (ca. 700–480 B.C.E.)

Nowhere is the Greek affection for the natural beauty of the human body so evident as in Hellenic sculpture, where the male nude form assumed major importance as a subject. Free-standing Greek sculptures fulfilled the same purpose as Mesopotamian and Egyptian votive statues: they paid perpetual homage to the gods. They also served as cult statues, funerary monuments, and memorials designed to honor the victors of the athletic games. Since athletes both trained and competed in the nude, the unclothed body was completely appropriate to visual representation. Ultimately, however, the dominance of the nude in Greek art reflects the Hellenic regard for the human body as nature's perfect creation. (The fig leaves that cover the genitals of some Greek sculptures are additions dating from the Christian era.)

In sculpture, as in painting, the quest for realism was balanced by the effort to idealize form. Achieving the delicate balance between real and ideal was a slow process, one that had its beginnings early in Greek history. During the Archaic phase of Greek sculpture, free-standing representations of the male youth (***kouros***) retain the rigid verticality of tree trunks from which earlier Greek sculptures were carved.

Produced some fifty years after the Attica *kouros* (Figure **5.7**), the *Calf-Bearer* is more gently and more realistically

Greek culture owed much to the ancient Egyptians. That debt is evident in representations of the Greek life-sized male nude. In the Archaic phase of Greek art, the *kouros* is pictured in a frontal pose, with head and body erect; the figure is composed symmetrically around a central axis, and the anatomy of the torso is delineated with geometric precision (Figure **5.7**). As with ancient Egyptian figures (Figure **5.8**), the left leg of the *kouros* is shown in advance, while his arms are locked at the sides.

The pose reflects the inflexibility of the medium, but it also lends a sense of dignity and authority to the figure. This life-sized *kouros*, one of the earliest carved in Attica, marked the grave of a young Athenian aristocrat.

Figure 5.8 Statue of Mycerinus (Queen Kha-merer-nebty II cropped out to his left; see Figure 2.3 for full pair statue). Height 4 ft.

Figure 5.7 DIPYLON MASTER, *New York Kouros*, from Attica, ca. 600 B.C.E. Marble, height 6 ft. 4 in.

smile" that, in contrast with the awestruck countenances of Mesopotamian votive statues (see Figure 1.9), reflects the buoyant optimism of the early Greeks.

Greek Sculpture: The Classical Period (480–323 B.C.E.)

By the early fifth century B.C.E., a major transformation occurred in Hellenic art. With the *Kritios Boy* (Figure **5.11**), the Greek sculptor had arrived at the natural positioning of the human body that would characterize the Classical style. The sensuously modeled torso turns on the axis of the spine, and the weight of the body shifts from equal distribution on both legs to greater weight on the left leg—a kind of balanced opposition that is at once natural and graceful. (This counterpositioning would be called ***contrapposto*** by

Figure 5.9 *Calf-Bearer*, ca. 575–550 B.C.E. Marble, height 5 ft. 6 in.

modeled—note especially the abdominal muscles and the sensitively carved bull calf (Figure **5.9**). The hollow eyes of the shepherd once held inlays of semiprecious stones (mother-of-pearl, gray agate, and lapis lazuli) that would have given the smiling face a strikingly realistic appearance. Such lifelike effects were enhanced by the brightly colored paint (now almost gone) that enlivened the lips, hair, and other parts of the figure. A quarter of a century later, the robust likeness of a warrior named Kroisos (found marking his grave) shows close anatomical attention to knee and calf muscles. Like his Archaic predecessors, he strides aggressively forward, but his forearms now turn in toward his body, and his chest, arms, and legs swell with powerful energy (Figure **5.10**). He also bears the "Archaic blissful

Figure 5.10 Kroisos from Anavyssos, ca. 525 B.C.E. Marble with traces of paint, height 6 ft. 4½ in. Kroisos was a young warrior who died heroically in battle some time before 530 B.C.E. Inscribed on the base of the statue is the inscription, "Stay and mourn at the tomb of dead Kroisos, whom raging Ares destroyed one day as he fought in the foremost ranks."

Figure 5.11 *Kritios Boy*, ca. 480 B.C.E. Marble, height 46¼ in.

Figure 5.12 Zeus (or Poseidon), ca. 460 B.C.E. Bronze, height 6 ft. 10 in. The Greeks did not invent the lost-wax method of bronze casting (see Figure 0.19), but they were the first to employ this technique for large artworks, such as this one. This sophisticated technique allowed artists to depict more vigorous physical action and to include greater detail than was possible in the more restrictive medium of marble.

Italian Renaissance artists.) The muscles of the *Kritios Boy* are no longer geometrically schematized, but protrude subtly; the figure is no longer smiling, but instead solemn and contemplative. The new poised stance, along with the naturalistic treatment of human anatomy and proportion, are features of the High Classical style that flourished between ca. 480 and 400 B.C.E. At midcentury, Polycleitus brought that style to perfection with the *Doryphorus* (*Spear-Bearer*; see Figure 5.2). Known today only by way of Roman copies, the *Doryphorus* is widely regarded as the embodiment of the canon of ideal human proportions (see Reading 5.1).

The Classical Ideal: Male and Female

There is little to distinguish man from god in the bronze statue of Zeus (or Poseidon) hurling a weapon, the work of an unknown sculptor (Figure 5.12). This nude, which conveys the majesty and physical vitality of a mighty Greek deity, might just as well represent a victor of the Olympic Games. Dynamically posed—the artist has deliberately exaggerated the length of the arms—the god fixes the decisive moment just before the action, when every muscle in the body is tensed, ready to achieve the mark. The sculptor has also idealized the physique in the direction of geometric clarity. Hence the muscles of the stomach are indicated as symmetrical trapezoids, and the strands of the

god's hair and beard assume a distinctive pattern of parallel wavy lines.

Greek and Roman sculptors often made marble copies of popular bronze-cast figures. The *Discobolus* (*Discus Thrower*) (see Figure 4.13), originally executed in bronze by Myron around 450 B.C.E., but surviving only in various Roman marble copies, is one example. Like the majestic bronze in Figure 5.12, it captures the instant before the action, the ideal moment when intellect guides performance. The male nudes of the High Classical Age fulfill Aristotle's idea of excellence as the exercise of human will dominated by reason.

The evolution of the female figure (*kore*) underwent a somewhat different course from that of the male. Early on, *korai* were fully clothed; they did not appear in the nude until the fourth century B.C.E. Female statues of the Archaic period were ornamental, columnar, and (like their male counterparts) smiling (Figure 5.13). Not until the Late Classical Age (400–323 B.C.E.) did Greek sculptors arrive at the sensuous female nude figures that so inspired Hellenistic, Roman, and (centuries later) Renaissance artists. The *Aphrodite of Knidos* (Figure 5.14) by Praxiteles is the first such figure. It established a model for the ideal female nude: tall and poised, with small breasts and broad hips. Regarded by the Romans as the finest statue in the world, Praxiteles' goddess of love exhibits a subtle counterposition of shoulders and hips, smooth body curves, and a face that bears a dreamy, melting gaze. She is distinguished by the famous Praxitelean technique of carving that coaxed a translucent shimmer from the fine white marble.

Figure 5.13 *Kore* from Chios (?), ca. 520 B.C.E. Marble with traces of paint, height 22 in. (approx., lower part missing).

Figure 5.14 PRAXITELES, *Aphrodite of Knidos*, Roman copy of marble Greek original of ca. 350 B.C.E. Marble, height 6 ft. 8 in. Commissioned by the citizens of the city of Knidos, this image of their patron goddess would become a Classical icon of love and beauty. Imitated in some sixty versions, the celebrated nude is shown holding her robe, having just emerged from her bath, or (according to legend) from the sea foam.

Our brief study of Greek statuary from the Archaic through the Late Classical Age concludes with some important general observations concerning the Classical ideal: its history is one of increasing realism, freed of incidental detail. Human imperfections (wrinkles, warts, blemishes) are purged in favor of a radiant flawlessness. The ideal figure is neither very old nor very young, neither very thin nor very fat. He or she is eternally youthful, healthy, serene, dignified, and liberated from all accidents of nature. This synthesis of Humanism, Realism, and Idealism in the representation of the free-standing figure was one of the great achievements of Greek art. It defined the standard of beauty in Western art for centuries.

The Parthenon

Figure 5.15 **ICTINUS** and **KALLICRATES**, west end of the Parthenon, Athens, 448–432 B.C.E. Pentelic marble, height of columns 34 ft.

The Parthenon represents the apex of a long history of post-and-lintel temple building among the Greeks. The plan of the temple, a rectangle delimited on all four sides by a colonnaded walkway, reflects the typically Classical reverence for clarity, balance, and harmonious proportion (Figure **5.15**). Free-standing columns (each 34 feet tall) make up an exterior colonnade, while two further rows of columns on the east and west ends of the temple provide inner **porticos** (Figure **5.16**). The interior of the Parthenon is divided into two rooms: a central hall (or *cella*), which held the 40-foot-high cult statue of Athena; and a smaller room used as a treasury. It was here that the much-disputed Delian League funds were stored. Entirely elevated on a raised platform, the Parthenon invited the individual to move around it, as if it were a monumental shrine. Indeed, scholars have suggested that the Parthenon was both a shrine to Athena and a victory monument.

Figure 5.16 Plan of the Parthenon, Athens.

portico

cella

statue of Athena

Doric colonnade

treasury

portico

steps   frieze

0   100 ft.

N

1

1.618

Figure 5.17 Line drawing of the Parthenon elevation with Golden Ratio indicated. Two quantities are in Golden Ratio when their ratio is the same as the ratio of their sum to the maximum. The fundamentals of the Golden Section were formulated by Euclid in the late fourth century B.C.E. (see page 132) and were later enshrined in the Vitruvian canon (see Reading 5.1).

Greek Architecture: The Parthenon

The great monuments of Classical architecture were designed to serve the living, not—as in Egypt—the dead. In contrast with the superhuman scale of the Egyptian pyramid, the Greek temple, as Vitruvius observed, was proportioned according to the human body. Greek theaters (see Figure 4.14) celebrated life here on earth rather than the life in the hereafter, and Greek temples served as shrines for the gods and depositories for civic and religious treasures. Both theaters and temples functioned as public meeting places. Much like the Mesopotamian ziggurat (see Figure 1.8), the Greek temple was a communal symbol of reverence for the gods. However, while the ziggurat enforced the separation of priesthood and populace, the Greek temple united religious and secular domains.

The outstanding architectural achievement of Golden Age Athens is the Parthenon (see LOOKING INTO, Figures **5.15**, **5.16**, and **5.17**), a temple dedicated to Athena, the goddess of war, patron of the arts and crafts, and the personification of wisdom. The name "Parthenon" derives from the Greek *parthenos* ("maiden" or "virgin"), popular epithets for Athena. Built in glittering Pentelic marble upon the ruins of an earlier temple burned during the Persian Wars, and housing a colossal statue of Athena (which no longer exists), the Parthenon overlooks Athens from the highest point on the Acropolis (Figure **5.18**). Athens' preeminent temple was commissioned by Pericles, designed by the architects Ictinus and Kallicrates, and embellished by the sculptor Phidias (fl. ca. 490–430 B.C.E.). Phidias directed and supervised the construction of the temple over a period of more than ten years, from 448 to 432 B.C.E. In the tradition of Egyptian builders,

Greek architects used no mortar. Rather, they employed bronze clamps and dowels to fasten the individually cut marble segments.

The Parthenon makes use of the Doric **order**, one of three programs of architectural design developed by the ancient Greeks (Figure **5.19**). Each of the orders—Doric, Ionic, and (in Hellenistic times) Corinthian—prescribes a fundamental set of structural and decorative parts that stand in fixed relation to one another. Each order differs in details and in the relative proportions of the parts. The Doric order, which originated on the Greek mainland, is simple and severe. In the Parthenon it reached its most refined expression. The Ionic order, originating in Asia Minor and the Aegean Islands, is more delicate and ornamental. Its slender columns terminate in capitals with paired volutes or scrolls. The Ionic order is employed in some of the small temples on the Acropolis (see Figure **5.1**). The Corinthian, the most ornate of the orders, is characterized by capitals consisting of acanthus leaves. It is often found on victory monuments, in **tholos** (circular) sanctuaries and shrines, and in various Hellenistic and Roman structures (see Figure 6.14).

While symmetry and order governed the structural elements of the Parthenon, a similar set of laws determined its proportions. The precise canon of proportion adopted by Phidias for the construction of the Parthenon is still the subject of debate. Nevertheless, most architectural historians agree that a module governed the entire project. It is likely that this module was both geometric and numerical, adhering to a specific ratio: the famous "Golden Section" (see Figure 5.17). The system of proportion known as the "Golden Section" or "Golden Ratio" is expressed

Figure 5.18 Model of the Classical Acropolis at Athens.

Figure 5.19 The Greek orders: (a) Doric; (b) Ionic; and (c) Corinthian.

numerically by the ratio 1.618:1, or approximately 8:5; it is represented by the Greek letter φ (phi), which derives from the name of the Parthenon's designer, Phidias. This ratio, which governs the proportions of the ground plan of the Parthenon and the relationship between its structural parts, represents an aesthetic ideal found in nature and in the human anatomy.

An analysis of the Parthenon's construction is further complicated by the fact that there are virtually no straight lines in the entire building. Its Doric columns, for instance, swell near the center to counter the optical effect of

Figure 5.20 Sculptural and architectural detail of the Parthenon. **Frieze**, a decorative band along the top of a wall; metopes, segmented spaces on a frieze; pediment, a gable.

thinning that occurs when the normal eye views an uninterrupted set of parallel lines. All columns tilt slightly inward. Corner columns are thicker than the others to compensate for the attenuating effect produced by the bright light of the sky against which the columns are viewed, and also to ensure their ability to bear the weight of the terminal segments of the superstructure. The top step of the platform on which the columns rest is not parallel to the ground, but rises four and a quarter inches at the center, allowing rainwater to run off the convex surface even as it corrects the optical impression of sagging along the extended length of the platform. Consistently, the architects of the Parthenon corrected negative optical illusions produced by strict conformity to geometric regularity. Avoiding rigid systems of proportion, they took as their primary consideration the aesthetic and functional integrity of the building. Today, the Parthenon stands as a noble ruin, the victim of an accidental gunpowder explosion in the seventeenth century, followed by centuries of vandalism, air pollution, and unrelenting tourist traffic.

The Sculpture of the Parthenon

Between 448 and 432 B.C.E., Phidias and the members of his workshop executed the sculptures that would appear in three main locations on the Parthenon: in the **pediments** of the roof **gables**, on the **metopes** or square panels between the beam ends under the roof, and in the area along the outer wall of the *cella* (Figure **5.20**). Brightly painted, as were the decorative portions of the building, the Parthenon sculptures relieved the stark angularity of the post-and-lintel structure. In subject matter, the temple sculptures paid homage to the patron deity of Athens: the east pediment narrates the birth of Athena with gods and goddesses in attendance (Figures **5.21** and **5.22**). The west pediment shows the contest between Poseidon

The Battle Over Antiquities

Only one-half of the Parthenon's original sculptures survive, and half of these are displayed at the British Museum in London. The rest are in the recently opened Acropolis Museum in Athens.

In 1687, when the Ottoman Turks ruled Greece (see chapter 21), an enemy firebomb ignited the Ottoman gunpowder supply stored in the Parthenon, destroying much of the building's interior. In the early 1800s, England's ambassador to the Ottoman Empire, Thomas Bruce, the seventh earl of Elgin, rescued the sculptures from rubble and ruin, and shipped them to England. A few years later, the trustees of the British Museum purchased the marbles with money given by Parliament. Since achieving independence in 1832, the Greeks have demanded the return of the sculptures. Britain, however, claims legitimate ownership. The issue remains in dispute today.

Similar debates are currently raging over the question of "cultural patrimony." Do antiquities (and other artworks) belong to the country in which they were produced, or do they belong to those individuals and institutions who have bought them for private collections or for public display? The issue is complicated by the fact that many works of art, both ancient and modern, were looted from ancient graves or taken forcibly from their owners during times of war. Some museum curators and art dealers have faced trial for buying and selling objects that were illegally excavated or stolen from ancient tombs. In 2008, the Metropolitan Museum in New York City was forced to return the magnificent Euphronios krater (see Figure 4.9) it had purchased in the early 1970s. While the museum insisted the artifact had a reliable provenance, evidence gathered by the Italian police proved that the piece had been stolen from a tomb in Cerveteri, an Etruscan site north of Rome. How similar cases are resolved will have a major effect on the global art market, and on the availability of visual landmarks for public display in the world's great art collections.

Figure 5.21 Three Goddesses: Hestia, Dione, Aphrodite, from the east pediment of the Parthenon, Athens, ca. 437–432 B.C.E. Marble, over life-sized.

Figure 5.22 A reconstruction of the three goddesses shown above.

of two contestants, one human and the other bestial. Appropriate to a temple honoring the goddess of wisdom, the sculptural program of the Parthenon celebrates the victory of intellect over unbridled passion, hence barbarism.

Completing Phidias' program of architectural decoration for the Parthenon is the continuous frieze that winds around the outer wall of the *cella* where that wall meets the roofline. The 524-foot-long sculptured band is thought by most scholars to depict the Panathenaic Festival, a celebration held every four years in honor of the goddess Athena. (Other interpretations, however, exist, the most recent of which views the frieze as a mythic account of virgin sacrifice by the daughters of Erectheus, legendary king of Athens.) Hundreds of figures—a cavalcade of horsemen (Figure **5.24**), water-bearers,

and Athena for domination of Athens. The ninety-two metopes that occupy the frieze (see Figure 5.20) illustrate the legendary combat between the Greeks (the bearers of civilization) and Giants, Amazons, and Centaurs (the forces of barbarism). Figure **5.23**, for instance, shows one of the Lapiths (an ancient Greek tribe) defeating a centaur (a fabulous hybrid of horse and man) after a group of drunken centaurs tried to abduct the Lapiths' women. Carved in high relief, each metope is a masterful depiction

musicians, and votaries—are shown filing in calm procession toward an assembled group of gods and goddesses (see Figure 4.11). The figures move with graceful rhythms, in tempos that could well be translated into music. Once brightly painted and ornamented with metal details, these noble figures must have appeared impressively lifelike. To increase this effect and satisfy a viewpoint from below, Phidias graded the relief, cutting the marble more deeply at the top than at the bottom. Housed today in the British

Figure 5.24 Group of young horsemen, from the north frieze of the Parthenon, Athens, 447–438 B.C.E. Marble, height 3 ft. 7 in. The horsemen ride bareback. Their bridles and reins, cast originally in metal, are now missing, as are the bright colors with which the frieze was painted.

Museum in London, where it is hung at approximately eye level, the Parthenon frieze loses much of its illusionistic subtlety. Nevertheless, this masterpiece of the Greek Golden Age reveals the harmonious reconciliation of Humanism, Realism, and Idealism that is the hallmark of the Classical style.

The Gold of Greece

The famous statue of Athena that stood in the *cella* of the Parthenon disappeared many centuries ago. However, there are images of the goddess in Hellenic art. One of the most spectacular appears in the form of a gold pendant disk that shows the head of Athena wearing a helmet bearing a sphinx, deer, and griffin heads, and an elaborate triple crest (Figure **5.25**). From Athena's shoulders snakes spring forth, and by her head stands an owl (the symbol of wisdom)—both motifs recalling the powers of the Minoan priestess (see Figure 4.5). Rosettes of gold filigree and enameled buds ornament the complex of looped chains that hang from the disk.

The Greeks gained international acclaim for their goldworking techniques, many of which had been inherited from Persia and from the nomadic Scythians of northern Asia. Gold-rich mining areas of northern Greece provided craftspeople with materials for the manufacture of jewelry. Particularly popular were pendants, earrings, and headpieces in the form of miniature sculptures, some of which (like the pendant of Athena) reproduced familiar images of the gods. Much like today, gold jewelry was a mark of wealth that also bore sentimental and religious value. In Greece and especially in the cities of Asia Minor, men as well as women adorned themselves with stylish earrings and bracelets.

The Classical Style in Poetry

In Classical Greece, as in other parts of the ancient world, distinctions between individual forms of artistic expression were neither clear-cut nor definitive. A combination of the arts prevailed in most forms of religious ritual and in public and private entertainment. In *Antigone*, for instance, choric pantomime and dance complemented dramatic poetry (see Reading 4.3). The intimate relationship between music and poetry is revealed in the fact that many of the words we use to describe lyric forms, such as "**ode**" and "**hymn**," are also musical terms. The word lyric, meaning "accompanied by the lyre," describes verse that was meant to be sung, not read silently. As in ancient Egypt, this genre of poetry gave voice to deep emotions.

Hellenic culture produced an impressive group of lyric poets, the greatest of whom was Sappho (ca. 610–ca. 580 B.C.E.). The details of her personal life remain a mystery. Born into an aristocratic family on the island of Lesbos, she seems to have married and mothered a daughter. On Lesbos, she instructed a group of women, dedicated to the cult of Aphrodite, in the production of lyric poetry. She herself produced some nine books of poems, of which only a fraction remain. Her highly self-conscious lyrics, many of which come to us only as fragments, are filled

Figure 5.25 Gold pendant disk with the head of Athena (one of a pair), from Kul Oba, ca. 400–350 B.C.E. Height 31⁹⁄₂₀ in., diameter of disk 1½ in.

with passion and tenderness. They offer only a glimpse of a body of poetry that inspired Sappho's contemporaries to regard her as "the female Homer."

Ancient and modern poets alike admired Sappho for her economy of expression and her inventive combinations of sense and sound—features that are extremely difficult to convey in translation. The first of these features, however, is apparent in the following poem:

> Although they are
> only breath, words
> which I command
> are immortal.

Here, in the space of four short lines, Sappho captures the spirit of confident optimism that marks her poetry and her age: while words are "only breath," they are the tools by which the poet claims her immortality.

In the first of the four poems reproduced below, Sappho expresses her affection for one of the women of the Lesbian community. Romantic bonds between female members of a given circle were commonplace in Greek society, as were homoerotic attachments between men—usually between an older man and a youth (see Figure 4.17). And while Hellenic literature and art offers ample evidence of bisexual and homosexual relationships, Sappho's poems reveal a passionate intensity often missing from other erotic works of art.

The last of the selections below is a pensive but brief meditation on death: it reflects the intense love of life and the generally negative view of death that pervaded the Hellenic world.

READING 5.2 The Poems of Sappho (ca. 590 B.C.E.)

He is more than a hero	1
He is a god in my eyes	
the man who is allowed	
to sit beside you—he	
who listens intimately	5
to the sweet murmur of	
your voice, the enticing	
laughter that makes my own	
heart beat fast. If I meet	
you suddenly, I can't	10
speak—my tongue is broken;	
a thin flame runs under	
my skin; seeing nothing,	
hearing only my own ears	
drumming, I drip with sweat;	15
trembling shakes my body	
and I turn paler than	
dry grass. At such times	
death isn't far from me	

◆

With his venom	1
Irresistible	
and bittersweet	
that loosener	
of limbs, Love	5
reptile-like	
strikes me down	

◆

I took my lyre and said:	1
Come now, my heavenly	
tortoise shell; become	
a speaking instrument	

◆

We know this much	1
Death is an evil;	
we have the gods'	

word for it; they too
would die if death   5
were a good thing

Q   What themes are treated in these four poems?

Q   How do the poems illustrate "economy of expression"?

While lyric poetry conveyed deeply personal feelings, certain types of lyrics, namely odes, served as public eulogies or songs of praise. Odes honoring Greek athletes bear strong similarities to songs of divine praise, such as the Egyptian "Hymn to the Aten" (see chapter 2) and the Hebrew psalms (see chapter 1). But the sentiments conveyed in the odes of the noted Greek poet Pindar (ca. 522–438 B.C.E.) are firmly planted in the secular world. They celebrate the achievements of the athletes who competed at the games held at the great sanctuaries of Olympia, Delphi, Nemea, and elsewhere (see Figure 4.1). Perpetuating the heroic idealism of the *Iliad*, Pindar's odes make the claim that prowess, not chance, leads to victory, which in turn renders the victor immortal. The first lines of his *Nemean Ode VI* honoring Alcimidas of Aegina (winner in the boys' division of wrestling) make the case that gods and men share a common origin. The closest human beings can come to achieving godlike immortality, however, lies in the exercise of "greatness of mind/Or of body." The ode thus narrows the gap between hero-athletes and their divine prototypes.

In his *Pythian Ode VIII* (dedicated to yet another victorious wrestler), Pindar develops a more modest balance of opposites: he sets the glories of youth against the adversities of aging and mortality itself. Although mortal limitations separate human beings from the ageless and undying gods, "manly action" secures the "richer life."

READING 5.3 From Pindar's Odes (ca. 465–445 B.C.E.)

From *Nemean Ode VI*

Single is the race, single	1
Of men and of gods;	
From a single mother we both draw breath.	
But a difference of power in everything	
Keeps us apart;	5
For the one is as nothing, but the brazen sky	
Stays a fixed habitation for ever.	
Yet we can in greatness of mind	
Or of body be like the Immortals,	
Though we know not to what goal	10
By day or in the nights	
Fate has written that we shall run.	

From *Pythian Ode VIII*

In the Pythian games	1

you pinned four wrestlers
unrelentingly, and sent
them home in losers' gloom;
no pleasant laughter cheered them as they reached   5
their mothers' sides; shunning ridicule,
they took to alleys, licking losers' wounds.
And he, who in his youth
secures a fine advantage
gathers hope and flies   10
on wings of manly action,
disdaining cost. Men's happiness is early-
ripened fruit that falls to earth
from shakings of adversity.
Men are day-bound. What is a man? What is   15
he *not*? Man is a shadow's dream. But when divine
advantage comes, men gain a radiance and a richer life.

Q How does Pindar answer his own question
(line 15), "What is a man?"

Q How does his answer compare to other
responses to this question in Readings 1.2, 1.4e,
and 4.3, lines 233–49?

The Classical Style in Music and Dance

The English word *music* derives from *muse*, the Greek word describing any of the nine mythological daughters of Zeus and the goddess of memory. According to Greek mythology, the muses presided over the arts and the sciences. Pythagoras observed that music was governed by mathematical ratios and therefore constituted both a science and an art. As with other arts, music played a major role in Greek life. Both vocal and instrumental music were commonplace, and contests between musicians, like those between playwrights, were a regular part of public life. Nevertheless, we know almost as little about how Greek music sounded as we do in the cases of Sumerian or Egyptian music.

The ancient Greeks did not invent a system of notation with which to record instrumental or vocal sounds. Apart from written and visual descriptions of musical performances, there exist only a few fourth-century B.C.E. treatises on music theory and some primitively notated musical works. The only complete piece of ancient Greek music that has survived is an ancient song found chiseled on a first-century B.C.E. gravestone. It reads: "So long as you live, be radiant, and do not grieve at all. Life's span is short and time exacts the final reckoning." Vase paintings reveal that the principal musical instruments of ancient Greece were the lyre, the **kithara**—both belonging to the harp family and differing only in shape, size, and number of strings (Figure **5.26**)—and the **aulos**, a flute or reed pipe (see Figure 5.6). Along with percussion devices often used to accompany dancing, these string and wind instruments were probably inherited from Egypt.

♪ See Music Listening Selections at end of chapter.

The Greeks devised a system of **modes**, or types of **scale** characterized by fixed patterns of pitch and tempo within the octave. (The sound of the ancient Greek Dorian mode is approximated by playing the eight white keys of the piano beginning with the white key two notes above middle C.) Modified variously in Christian times, the modes were preserved in Gregorian chant and Byzantine church hymnology (see chapter 9). Although the modes themselves may have been inspired by the music of ancient India, the diatonic scale (familiar to Westerners as the series of notes C, D, E, F, G, A, B, C) originated in Greece. Greek music lacked harmony as we know it. It was thus **monophonic**, that is, confined to a single unaccompanied line of melody. The strong association between poetry and music suggests that the human voice had a significant influence in both melody and rhythm.

Figure 5.26 THE BERLIN PAINTER, red-figured amphora, ca. 490 B.C.E. Terracotta, height of vase 16⅜ in. Head thrown back, a young man sings to the accompaniment of a kithara, a type of lyre used in public performance and in the recitation of epic poetry. Pictured on the reverse of this amphora is a figure holding a wand—probably the judge of a music competition.

From earliest times, music was believed to hold magical powers and therefore exercise great spiritual influence. Greek and Roman mythology describes gods and heroes who used music to heal or destroy. Following Pythagoras, who equated musical ratios with the unchanging cosmic order, many believed that music might put one "in tune with" the universe. The planets, which Pythagoras described as a series of spheres moving at varying speeds in concentric orbits around the earth, were said to produce a special harmony, the so-called *music of the spheres*. The Greeks believed, moreover, that music had a moral influence. This argument, often referred to as the "Doctrine of Ethos," held that some modes strengthened the will, whereas others undermined it and thus damaged the development of moral character. In the *Republic*, Plato encourages the use of the Dorian mode, which settles the temper and inspires courage, but he condemns the Lydian mode, which arouses sensuality. Because of music's potential for affecting character and mood, both Plato and Aristotle recommended that the type of music used in the education of young children be regulated by law. Such music should reflect the Classical features of balance, harmony, and dignity.

Dance was prized for its moral value, as well as for its ability to give pleasure and induce good health (see Figure 5.6). For Plato the uneducated man was a "danceless" man. Both Plato and Aristotle advised that children be instructed at an early age in music and dancing. However, both men distinguished noble dances from ignoble ones. Dionysian and comic dances were considered unfit for Athenian citizens and therefore inappropriate to the educational curriculum. Nevertheless, such dances are often depicted on vases and in sculptured reliefs (Figure **5.27**). The wildest types of dance, those associated with celebrations honoring Dionysus, the god of vegetation and wine, were performed by cult followers known as *maenads*, whose intoxicated revelries were favorite Hellenic subjects.

Figure 5.27 A *maenad* leaning on a *thyrsos*, Roman copy of Greek original, ca. 420–410 B.C.E. Marble relief, height 56¼ in. The mythical followers of Dionysus, known as *maenads* (or *bacchantes*), were said to roam the forests singing and dancing with ecstatic abandon. This barefoot *maenad* holds a *thyrsos*, a fennel stalk ornamented with berries and ivy leaves, symbolic of vegetation and fertility. The movement of the dance is suggested by the swaying motion of her diaphanous draperies.

The Diffusion of the Classical Style: The Hellenistic Age (323–30 B.C.E.)

The fourth century B.C.E. was a turbulent era marked by rivalry and warfare among the Greek city-states. Ironically, however, the failure of the Greek city-states to live in peace would lead to the spread of Hellenic culture throughout the civilized world. Manipulating the shifting confederacies and internecine strife to his advantage, Philip of Macedonia eventually defeated the Greeks in 338 B.C.E. When he was assassinated two years later, his twenty-year-old son, Alexander (356–323 B.C.E.), assumed the Macedonian throne (Figure **5.28**). A student of Aristotle, Alexander brought to his role as ruler the same far-reaching ambition and imagination that his teacher had exercised in the intellectual realm. Alexander was a military genius: within twelve years, he created an empire that stretched from Greece to the borders of modern India (Map **5.1**). To all parts of his empire, but especially to the cities he founded—many of which he named after himself—Alexander carried Greek language and culture. Greek art and literature made a major impact on civilizations as far east as India, where it influenced Buddhist art and Sanskrit literature (see chapters 9 and 14).

Alexander carved out his empire with the help of an army of 35,000 Greeks and Macedonians equipped with weapons that were superior to any in the ancient world. Siege machines such as catapults and battering rams were used to destroy the walls of the best-defended cities of Asia Minor, Egypt, Syria, and Persia. Finally, in northwest India, facing the prospect of confronting the formidable army of the king of Ganges and his force of 5000 elephants, Alexander's troops refused to go any further. Shortly thereafter, the thirty-two-year-old general died (probably of malaria), and his empire split into three segments: Egypt was governed by the Ptolemy dynasty; Persia came under the leadership of the Seleucid rulers; and Macedonia-Greece was governed by the family of Antigonus the One-Eyed (see Map 5.1, inset).

The era that followed, called Hellenistic ("Greek-like"), lasted from 323 to 30 B.C.E. The defining features of the Hellenistic Age were cosmopolitanism, urbanism, and the blending of Greek, African, and Asian cultures. Trade routes linked Arabia, East Africa, and Central Asia, bringing great wealth to the cities of Alexandria, Antioch, Pergamon, and Rhodes. Alexandria, which replaced Athens as a cultural center, boasted a population of more than one million people and a library of half a million books (the collection was destroyed by fire when Julius Caesar besieged the city in 47 B.C.E.). The Great Library, part of the cultural complex known as the Temple of the Muses (or "Museum"), was an ancient "think tank" that housed both scholars and books. At the rival library of Pergamon (with some 200,000 books), scribes prepared sheepskin to produce "pergamene paper," that is, parchment, the medium that would be used for centuries of manuscript production prior to the dissemination of paper. Textual criticism and the editing of Classical manuscripts produced the scholarly

Figure 5.28 Head of Alexander, from Pergamon, Hellenistic portrait, ca. 200 B.C.E. Marble, height 16 in.

Map 5.1 The Hellenistic World. The cities of Pergamon, Antioch, and Alexandria were vital urban centers of Alexander's empire, which broke into three successor states (located in the regions of Greece, Egypt, and Persia) after Alexander's death.

editions of Homer's epics and other classics that would be passed on to generations of Western readers.

The Hellenistic Age made important advances in geography, astronomy, and mathematics. Euclid, who taught mathematics in Alexandria during the late fourth century B.C.E., produced a textbook of existing geometric learning that systematized the theorems of plane and solid geometry (see Figure 5.17). His contemporary, the astronomer Aristarchus of Samos, proposed that the earth and all the planets revolved around the sun, a theory abandoned by his followers and not confirmed until the seventeenth century.

Archimedes of Syracuse, who flourished a century later, calculated the value of *pi* (the ratio of the circumference of a circle to its diameter). An engineer as well as a mathematician, he invented the compound pulley, a windlass for moving heavy weights, and many other mechanical devices. "Give me a place to stand," he is said to have boasted, "and I shall move the earth." Legend describes Archimedes as the typical absent-minded scientist, who often forgot to eat; upon realizing that the water he displaced in his bathtub explained the law of specific gravity, he is said to have jumped out of the bathtub and run naked through the streets of Syracuse, shouting "*Eureka*" ("I have found it!").

Hellenistic Schools of Thought

The Hellenistic world was considerably different from the world of the Greek city-states. In the latter, citizens identified with their community, which was itself the state; but in Alexander's vast empire, communal loyalties were unsteady and—especially in sprawling urban centers—impersonal. The intellectuals of the Hellenistic Age did not formulate rational methods of investigation in the style of Plato and Aristotle; rather they espoused philosophic schools of thought that guided everyday existence: Skepticism, Cynicism, Epicureanism, and Stoicism.

The Skeptics—much like the Sophists of Socrates' time—denied the possibility of knowing anything with certainty: they argued for the suspension of all intellectual judgment. The Cynics held that spiritual satisfaction was only possible if one renounced societal values, conventions, and material wealth. The Epicureans, followers of

the Greek thinker Epicurus (341–270 B.C.E.), taught that happiness depended on avoiding all forms of physical excess; they valued plain living and the perfect union of body and mind. Epicurus held that the gods played no part in human life, and that death was nothing more than the rearrangement of atoms of which the body and all of nature consisted. Finally, the Stoics found tranquility of mind in a doctrine of detachment that allowed them to accept even the worst of life's circumstances. The aim of the Stoic was to bring the individual will into complete harmony with the will of nature, which they believed was governed by an impersonal intelligence. Stoicism, which became increasingly influential among Roman intellectuals (see chapter 6), also advanced the notion of universal equality. All four of these schools of thought placed the personal needs and emotions of the individual over and above the good of the community at large; in this, they constituted a practical and radical departure from the Hellenic quest for universal truth.

Hellenistic Art

The shift from city-state to empire that accompanied the advent of the Hellenistic Era was reflected in larger, more monumental forms of architecture and in the construction of utilitarian structures, such as lighthouses, theaters, and libraries. Circular sanctuaries and colossal Corinthian temples with triumphant decorative friezes were particularly popular in the fourth century B.C.E. and thereafter. At Pergamon (see Map 5.1) stood the largest sculptural complex in the ancient world: the Altar of Zeus (Figure 5.29). Erected around 180 B.C.E. to celebrate the victory of the minor kingdom of Pergamon over the invading tribal Gauls, achieved some fifty years earlier, the altar stands atop a 20-foot-high platform enclosed by an Ionic

Figure 5.29 The Altar of Zeus (reconstructed), Pergamon, ca. 175 B.C.E. Marble. Dedicated to Zeus and Athena, the Great Altar once stood on a hillside above the city. It has been reconstructed by the Pergamon Museum in Berlin. The theatrical stairway ascends some 30 feet to the shrine at the top.

colonnade. A massive stairway reaches upward to the shrine. Around the base of the platform runs a 300-foot-long sculptured frieze depicting the mythological battle between the Olympic gods and the race of giants known as Titans. Its subject matter, alluding to Pergamon's victory over the Gauls (hence, the victory of civilization over barbarism), recalls the program of the Parthenon metopes. However, both the altar and the frieze are far more theatrical in style than anything created in Classical Greece. The drama of the structure itself, which more resembles a stage than a temple, is made emphatic in the frieze, where colossal high-relief figures writhe in rhythmic patterns, engaging one another in fierce combat. The goddess Athena, some 7 feet tall, grasps by the hair a serpent-tailed male, the son of the Earth Mother who rises from the ground on

the lower right (Figure **5.30**). The deeply cut figures produce strong light and dark contrasts; indeed, some seem to break free of the architectural frame. In the Altar of Zeus, Classical restraint has given way to violent passion.

Hellenistic artists brought a similar kind of dramatic energy to mosaics, a medium that employs small bits of colored stone, glass, or marble (see Figure 1.6). Using mosaics as a permanent waterproof medium for walls and floors, they often copied earlier paintings that ornamented homes and palaces. Violent action dominates the turbulent narrative rendering of Alexander's confrontation with the king of Persia at the Battle of Issos (Figure **5.31**). Realistic details, radical foreshortening (note the foreground horse), and careful shading bring the scene vividly and illusionistically to life.

Figure 5.30 Athena battling with Acyoneus, from the frieze of the Altar of Zeus, Pergamon, ca. 180 B.C.E. Marble, height 7 ft. 6 in.

Figure 5.31 *Alexander the Great Confronts Darius III at the Battle of Issos*, detail of a mosaic floor decoration from Pompeii, Italy. First century C.E. Roman copy after a Hellenistic painting of ca. 310 B.C.E. Alexander appears heroically at left, with no helmet, windblown hair, and bare neck.

In free-standing Hellenistic sculpture, the new emphasis on personal emotion gave rise to portraits that were more lifelike and less idealized than those of the Hellenic era. A marble portrait of the ruler Alexander (see Figure 5.28) manifests the new effort to capture fleeting mood and momentary expression.

Hellenistic art is also notable for its celebration of the female nude figure, which, in the tradition of Praxiteles, became an iconic symbol of erotic love (see Figure 5.14). Equally sensuous, however, is the Hellenistic treatment of the male nude, the most famous example of which is the statue known as the *Apollo Belvedere* (Figure **5.32**). This Roman copy of a Hellenistic statue was destined to exercise a major influence in Western art from the moment it was recovered in Rome in 1503. A comparison of the *Apollo* with its Hellenic counterpart, the *Spear-Bearer* (see Figure 5.2), reveals the transition from the contained movement of the High Classical style to the more animated, feminized expressionism of the Hellenistic Era.

Moving toward greater naturalism, Hellenistic sculptors broadened the range of subjects to include the young, the elderly, and even deformed people. They refined the long tradition of technical virtuosity in Greek sculpture by introducing new carving techniques that yielded complex patterns of light and dark, dramatic displays of vigorous movement, and a wide range of expressive details. These features are evident in the larger-than-life **Nike** (the Greek personification of victory) erected at Rhodes to celebrate a naval triumph over Syria (Figure **5.33**). The deeply cut drapery of the *Nike of Samothrace* clings sensuously to the body as the figure strides, wings extended, into the wind like some gigantic ship's figurehead.

The work that best sums up the Hellenistic aesthetic is *Laocoön and His Sons* (Figure **5.34**). This monumental sculpture recreates the dramatic moment, famous in Greek legend, when Laocoön (Trojan priest of Apollo)

and his two sons succumb to the strangling attack of sea serpents (sent by gods friendly to the Achaeans) to punish him for his effort to warn the Trojans of the Greek ruse: a wooden horse filled with Achaean soldiers who would destroy Troy and bring an end to the Trojan War.

Figure 5.32 *Apollo Belvedere.* Roman marble copy of a Greek original, late fourth century B.C.E. Height 7ft. 4in.

The writing limbs, strained muscles, and anguished expressions of the doomed family contribute to a sense of turbulence and agitation that departs from the dignified restraint of Hellenic art. Indeed, the *Laocoön* is the landmark of an age in which Classical Idealism had already become part of history.

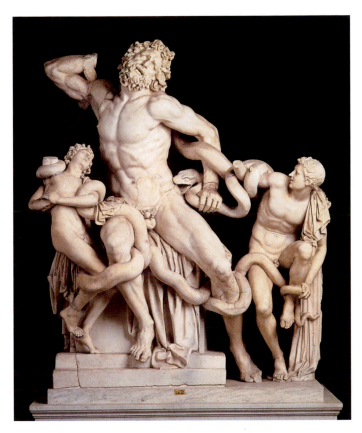

Figure 5.34 AGESANDER, POLYDORUS, and **ATHENODORUS OF RHODES,** *Laocoön and His Sons*, second to first century B.C.E. or a Roman copy of first century C.E. Marble, height 7 ft. 10½ in. Unearthed in 1506, the sculpture had an enormous influence on Michelangelo and other High Renaissance sculptors (see chapter 17). The piece is not carved out of a single block of marble, as was claimed by the Roman writer Pliny the Elder.

Figure 5.33 PYTHOCRITOS OF RHODES, *Nike of Samothrace,* ca. 190 B.C.E. Marble, height 8 ft.

LOOKING BACK

The Classical Style

- Classical style reflects the Hellenic quest for rational laws of proportion, order, clarity, and balance.
- The Classical style is characterized by Humanism, a this-worldly belief in the dignity and inherent worth of human beings; by Realism, or fidelity to nature; and by Idealism, that is, the commitment to an underlying standard of perfection.
- The human body and human experience, as evidenced in Greek vase-paintings and in multiple sculptures of the Classical nude, are central to the art of Classical Greece.

The Evolution of the Classical Style

- A study of Greek statuary from the Archaic through the Late Classical Age reflects increasing refinements in Realism and Idealism: all imperfections have been purged in favor of radiant flawlessness. In the Classical nude figure, Hellenic sculptors achieved a balance between realistic and idealized form.
- The monument that best mirrors the Classical style is the Parthenon, the Greek temple built atop the Acropolis to honor Athens' patron goddess of wisdom and war. The Parthenon is notable for its application of the Doric order, the integration of geometric and technical refinements, and the intelligent use of architectural decoration.

The Classical Style in Poetry

- The lyric poetry of Sappho and Pindar makes the human being the measure of earthly experience.
- Sappho conveys deep personal feelings with elegant economy of expression.
- The odes of Pindar celebrate the athletes who competed at the games held in Olympia and elsewhere. Pindar's odes make the claim that ability, not chance, leads to victory, which in turn renders the victor immortal.

The Classical Style in Music and Dance

- In Greek music, where the clarity of the single line of melody prevails, modal patterns of pitch and tempo were held to influence the moral condition of the listener.
- Although music played a major role in Greek life, we know very little about Greek music apart from written and visual descriptions of musical performances, a few remaining treatises on music theory, and some primitively notated musical works.

The Diffusion of the Classical Style: The Hellenistic Age (323–30 B.C.E.)

- During the fourth century B.C.E., Alexander the Great spread Greek language and culture throughout a vast empire that extended from Macedonia to India.
- Metaphysics gave way to practical philosophies such as Skepticism, Cynicism, Epicureanism, and Stoicism; and scientific advances in astronomy, geography, and mathematics were made by Archimedes, Euclid, and others.
- Cosmopolitanism, urbanism, and the blending of Greek, African, and Asian cultures were defining features of the Hellenistic Age. Monumental forms of architecture and utilitarian structures, such as libraries and lighthouses, became landmarks of this era.
- While the Classical style spread to other parts of Asia, Hellenistic art moved toward detailed Realism and melodramatic expressiveness.

Music Listening Selection

- Anonymous, "Epitaph for Seikilos," Greek, ca. 50 C.E.

Glossary

aulos a wind instrument used in ancient Greece; it had a double reed (held inside the mouth) and a number of finger holes and was always played in pairs, that is, with the performer holding one in each hand; a leather band was often tied around the head to support the cheeks, thus enabling the player to blow harder (see Figure 5.6)

contrapposto (Italian, "counterpoised") a position assumed by the human body in which one part is turned in opposition to another part

frieze in architecture, a sculptured or ornamented band

gable the triangular section of a wall at the end of a pitched roof

hymn a lyric poem offering divine praise or glorification

kithara a large version of the lyre (having seven to eleven strings) and the principal instrument of ancient Greek music

kouros (Greek, "youth"; plural kouroi) a youthful male figure, usually depicted nude in ancient Greek sculpture; the female counterpart is the kore (Greek, "maiden"; plural korai)

metope the square panel between the beam ends under the roof of a structure (see Figure 5.17)

mode a type of musical scale characterized by a fixed pattern of pitch and tempo within the octave; because the Greeks associated each of the modes with a different emotional state, it is likely that the mode involved something more than a particular musical scale—perhaps a set of rhythms and melodic turns associated with each scale pattern

monophony (Greek, "one voice") a musical texture consisting of a single, unaccompanied line of melody

Nike the Greek goddess of victory

octave the series of eight tones forming any major or minor scale

ode a lyric poem expressing exalted emotion in honor of a person or a special occasion

order in Classical architecture, the parts of a building that stand in fixed and constant relation to one another; the three Classical orders are the Doric, the Ionic, and the Corinthian (see Figure 5.19)

pediment the triangular space forming the gable of a two-pitched roof in Classical architecture; any similar triangular form found over a portico, door, or window

portico a porch with a roof supported by columns

scale (Latin, scala, "ladder") a series of tones arranged in ascending or descending consecutive order; the diatonic scale, characteristic of Western music, consists of the eight tones (or series of notes C, D, E, F, G, A, B, C) of the twelve-tone octave; the chromatic scale consists of all twelve tones (represented by the twelve piano keys, seven white and five black) of the octave, each a semitone apart

tholos a circular structure, generally in Classical Greek style and probably derived from early tombs

Rome: The Rise to Empire

ca. 1000 B.C.E.–476 C.E.

". . . remember, Roman,
To rule the people under law, to establish
The way of peace, to battle down the haughty,
To spare the meek. Our fine arts, these forever."
Virgil

Figure 6.1 Detail from Trajan's Victory Column, Rome, 113 C.E. Marble. The 625-foot-long continuous frieze that documents the two Balkan campaigns of the Roman emperor Trajan resembles a documentary war film. The pictorial narrative, in which Trajan appears fifty-nine times, features realistic depictions of the military activities for which the Romans were famous, but it also includes scenes of comradery and suffering (see Figure 6.20).

"In the second century of the Christian Era, the empire of Rome comprehended the fairest part of the earth, and the most civilized portion of mankind. The frontiers of that extensive monarchy were guarded by ancient renown and disciplined valor. The gentle, but powerful, influence of laws and manners had gradually cemented the union of the provinces." So wrote the eighteenth-century historian Edward Gibbon, who voiced universal and abiding respect for the longest-lasting and most complex empire in Western history.

The rise and fall of the Roman Empire is too long a story to be told in these pages. Rather, this chapter explores Rome's imperial presence in Classical antiquity and its enduring contributions in architecture, the visual arts, literature, and law. Along with these achievements, the Romans would transmit to the West the legacy of Classical Greece and the fundamentals of a young religious faith called Christianity.

The Roman Rise to Empire

Rome's Early History

Rome's origins are to be found among tribes of Iron Age folk called Latins, who invaded the Italian peninsula just after the beginning of the first millennium B.C.E. By the mid-eighth century B.C.E., these people had founded the city of Rome in the lower valley of the Tiber River, a spot strategically located for control of the Italian peninsula and for convenient access to the Mediterranean Sea (Map 6.1). While central Italy became the domain of the Latins, the rest of the peninsula received a continuous infusion of eastern Mediterranean people—Etruscans, Greeks, and Phoenicians—who brought with them cultures richer and more complex than that of the Latins. The Etruscans, whose origins are unknown, established themselves in northwest Italy. A sophisticated, Hellenized people with commercial contacts throughout the Mediterranean, they

were experts in the arts of metallurgy, town building, and city planning. The Greeks, who colonized the tip of the Italian peninsula and Sicily, were masters of philosophy and the arts. The Phoenicians, who settled on the northern coast of Africa, brought westward their alphabet and their commercial and maritime skills. From all these people, but especially from the first two groups, the Latins borrowed elements that would enhance their own history.

From the Etruscans, the Romans absorbed the fundamentals of urban planning, chariot racing, the toga, bronze- and gold-crafting, and the most ingenious structural principle of Mesopotamian architecture—the arch. Roman numerals were based on an Etruscan system that was borrowed in turn from the Greeks. And from Etruscan tradition came one of Rome's founding myths by which the twin sons of Mars, Romulus and Remus—abandoned on the Tiber River but suckled by a she-wolf—established the city of Rome in 753 B.C.E. The Etruscans provided their

Map 6.1 The Roman Empire in 180 C.E.

Figure 6.2 Sarcophagus from Cerveteri, ca. 520 B.C.E. Painted terracotta, length 6 ft. 7 in. The hands of the couple are positioned in a manner that suggests they are enjoying lively conversation.

dead with tombs designed to resemble the lavish dwelling places of the deceased. On the lids of the **sarcophagi** (stone coffins) that held the remains, Etruscan artists carved portraits of the dead, depicting husbands and wives relaxing and socializing on their dining couch, as if still enjoying a family banquet (Figure **6.2**).

From the Greeks, the Romans borrowed a pantheon of gods and goddesses, linguistic and literary principles, and the aesthetics of the Classical style. A passion for Greek art made the Romans collectors and imitators of Hellenic sculpture; Roman copies of Greek art would fill palaces and public places. As the Latins absorbed Etruscan and Greek culture, so they drew these and other peoples into what would become the most powerful world-state in ancient history.

The Roman Republic (509–133 B.C.E.)

For three centuries, Etruscan kings ruled the Latin population, but in 509 B.C.E. the Latins overthrew the Etruscans. Over the next 200 years, monarchy slowly gave way to a government "of the people" (*res publica*). The agricultural population of ancient Rome consisted of a powerful class of large landowners, the *patricians*, and a more populous class of farmers and small landowners called *plebeians*. The plebeians constituted the membership of a Popular Assembly. Although this body conferred civil and military authority (the **imperium**) upon two elected magistrates (called *consuls*), its lower-class members had little voice in government. The wealthy patricians—life members of the Roman Senate—controlled the lawmaking process. But step by step, the plebeians gained increasing political influence. Using as leverage their service as soldiers in the Roman army and their power to veto laws initiated by the Senate, the plebeians—through their leaders, the *tribunes*—made themselves heard. Eventually, they won the freedom to intermarry with the patricians, the right

to hold executive office, and, finally, in 287 B.C.E., the privilege of making laws. The stern and independent population of Roman farmers had arrived at a *res publica* by peaceful means. But no sooner had Rome become a Republic than it adopted an expansionist course that would erode these democratic achievements.

Obedience to the Roman state and service in its powerful army were essential to the life of the early Republic. Both contributed to the rise of Roman imperialism, which proceeded by means of long wars of conquest similar to those that had marked the history of earlier empires. After expelling the last of the Etruscan kings, Rome extended its power over all parts of the Italian peninsula. By the middle of the third century B.C.E., having united all of Italy by force or negotiation, Rome stood poised to rule the Mediterranean.

A long-standing distrust of the Phoenicians and rivalry with the city of Carthage, Phoenicia's commercial stronghold in northeastern Africa, led Rome into the Punic (Latin for "Phoenician") Wars—a 150-year period of intermittent violence that ended with the destruction of Carthage in 146 B.C.E. With the defeat of that city, Rome assumed naval and commercial leadership in the western Mediterranean, the sea they would come to call *mare nostrum* ("our sea"). But the ambitions of army generals and the impetus of a century of warfare fueled the fire of Roman imperialism. Rome seized every opportunity for conquest, and by the end of the first century B.C.E., the Empire included most of North Africa, the Iberian peninsula, Greece, Egypt, much of Southwest Asia, and the territories constituting present-day Europe as far as the Rhine River (see Map 6.1).

Despite the difficulties presented by the task of governing such far-flung territories, the Romans proved to be efficient administrators. They demanded from their foreign provinces taxes, soldiers to serve in the Roman army, tribute, and slaves. Roman governors, appointed by the Senate from among the higher ranks of the military, ruled within the conquered provinces. Usually, local customs and even local governments were permitted to continue unmodified, for the Romans considered tolerance of provincial customs politically practical. The Romans brought the Latin language and Roman law to the provinces. They built paved roads, freshwater aqueducts, and bridges, and eventually granted the people of their conquered territories Roman citizenship.

Rome's highly disciplined army was the backbone of the Empire. During the Republic, the army consisted of citizens who served two-year terms, but by the first century C.E., the military had become a profession to which all free men might devote twenty-five years (or more) of their lives. Since serving for this length of time allowed a non-Roman to gain Roman citizenship for himself and his children, military service acted as a means of Romanizing foreigners. The Roman army was the object of fear and admiration among those familiar with Rome's rise to power. Josephus (ca. 37–100 C.E.), a Jewish historian who witnessed the Roman destruction of Jerusalem in 70 C.E., described the superiority of the Roman military machine, which he estimated to include more than 300,000 armed men. According to Josephus, Roman soldiers performed as though they "had been born with weapons in their hands." The efficiency of the army, he reported, was the consequence of superior organization and discipline. The following description of a Roman military camp reflects the admiration and awe with which non-Romans viewed Roman might. It also describes the nature of that "perfect discipline" and dedication to duty that characterized the Roman ethos and Roman culture in general.

READING 6.1 Josephus' *Description of the Roman Army* (ca. 70 C.E.)

. . . one cannot but admire the forethought shown in this particular by the Romans, in making their servant class useful to them not only for the ministrations of ordinary life but also for war. If one goes on to study the organization of their army as a whole, it will be seen that this vast empire of theirs has come to them as the prize of valor, and not as a gift of fortune.

For their nation does not wait for the outbreak of war to give men their first lesson on arms; they do not sit with folded hands in peacetime only to put them in motion in the hour of need. On the contrary, as though they had been born with weapons in hand, they never have a truce from training, never wait for emergencies to arise. Moreover, their peace maneuvers are no less strenuous than veritable warfare; each soldier daily throws all his energy into his drill, as though he were in action. Hence that perfect ease with which they sustain the shock of battle: no confusion breaks their customary formation, no panic paralyzes, no fatigue exhausts them; and as their opponents cannot match these qualities, victory is the invariable and certain consequence. Indeed, it would not be wrong to describe their maneuvers as bloodless combats and combats as sanguinary maneuvers.

The Romans never lay themselves open to a surprise attack; for, whatever hostile territory they may invade, they engage in no battle until they have fortified their camp. This camp is not erected at random or unevenly; they do not all work at once or in disorderly parties; if the ground is uneven, it is first leveled; a site for the camp is then measured out in the form of a square. For this purpose the army is accompanied by a multitude of workmen and of tools for building.

The interior of the camp is divided into rows of tents. The exterior circuit presents the appearance of a wall and is furnished with towers at regular intervals; and on the spaces between the towers are placed "quick-firers," catapults, "stone-throwers," and every variety of artillery engines, all ready for use. In this surrounding wall are set four gates, one on each side, spacious enough for beasts of burden to enter without difficulty and wide enough for sallies of troops in emergencies. The camp is intersected by streets symmetrically

laid out; in the middle are the tents of the officers, and precisely in the center the headquarters of the commander-in-chief, resembling a small temple. Thus, as it were, an improvised city springs up, with its marketplace, its artisan quarter, its seats of judgment, where captains and colonels adjudicate upon any differences which may arise. . . .

Once entrenched, the soldiers take up their quarters in their tents by companies, quietly and in good order. All their fatigue duties are performed with the same discipline, the same regard for security; the procuring of wood, food-supplies, and water, as required—each party has its allotted task. . . . The same precision is maintained on the battlefield: the troops wheel smartly round in the requisite direction, and, whether advancing to the attack or retreating, all move as a unit at the word of command.

When the camp is to be broken up, the trumpet sounds a first call; at that none remain idle: instantly, at this signal, they strike the tents and make all ready for departure. The trumpets sound a second call to prepare for the march: at once they pile their baggage on the mules and other beasts of burden and stand ready to start, like runners breasting the cord on the race-course. They then set fire to the encampment, both because they can easily construct another [on the spot], and to prevent the enemy from ever making use of it. . . .

Then they advance, all marching in silence and in good order, each man keeping his place in the ranks, as if in face of the enemy. . . . By their military exercises the Romans instill into their soldiers fortitude not only of body but also of soul; fear, too, plays its part in their training. For they have laws which punish with death not merely desertion of the ranks, but even a slight neglect of duty; and their generals are held in even greater awe than the laws. For the high honors with which they reward the brave prevent the offenders whom they punish from regarding themselves as treated cruelly.

This perfect discipline makes the army an ornament of peacetime and in war welds the whole into a single body; so compact are their ranks, so alert their movements in wheeling to right or left, so quick their ears for orders, their eyes for signals, their hands to act upon them. Prompt as they consequently ever are in action, none are slower than they in succumbing to suffering, and never have they been known in any predicament to be beaten by numbers, by ruse, by difficulties of ground, or even by fortune; for they have more assurance of victory than of fortune. Where counsel thus precedes active operations, where the leaders' plan of campaign is followed up by so efficient an army, no wonder that the Empire has extended its boundaries on the east to the Euphrates, on the west to the ocean,[1] on the south to the most fertile tracts of Libya, on the north to the Ister[2] and the Rhine. One might say without exaggeration that, great as are their possessions, the people that won them are greater still. . . .

Q **What, according to Josephus, are the admirable features of the Roman army?**

---

[1] The Atlantic.
[2] The Roman name for the Danube River.

The Collapse of the Republic (133–30 B.C.E.)

By the beginning of the first millennium C.E., Rome had become the watchdog of the ancient world. Roman imperialism, however, worked to effect changes within the Republic itself. By its authority to handle all military matters, the Senate became increasingly powerful, as did a new class of men, wealthy Roman entrepreneurs (known as *equestrians*), who filled the jobs of provincial administration. The army, by its domination of Rome's overseas provinces, also became more powerful. Precious metals, booty, and slaves from foreign conquests brought enormous wealth to army generals and influential patricians; corruption became widespread. Captives of war were shipped back to Rome and auctioned off to the highest bidders, usually patrician landowners, whose farms soon became large-scale plantations (*latifundia*) worked by slaves. The increased agricultural productivity of the *latifundia* gave economic advantage to large landowners who easily undersold the lesser landowners and drove them out of business. Increasingly, the small farmers were forced to sell their farms to neighboring patricians in return for the right to remain on the land. Or, they simply moved to the city to join, by the end of the first century B.C.E., a growing unemployed population. The disappearance of the small farmer signaled the decline of the Republic.

While Rome's rich citizens grew richer and its poor citizens poorer, the patricians fiercely resisted efforts to redistribute wealth more equally. But reform measures failed and political rivalries increased. Ultimately, Rome fell victim to the ambitions of army generals, who, having conquered in the name of Rome, now turned to conquering Rome itself. The first century B.C.E. was an age of military dictators, whose competing claims to power fueled a spate of civil wars. As bloody confrontations replaced reasoned compromises, the Republic crumbled.

In 46 B.C.E., an extraordinary army commander named Gaius Julius Caesar (Figure **6.3**) triumphantly entered the city of Rome and established a dictatorship. Caesar, who had spent nine years conquering Gaul (present-day France and Belgium), was as shrewd in politics as he was brilliant in war. These campaigns are described in his prose *Commentaries on the Gallic War*. His brief but successful campaigns in Syria, Asia Minor, and Egypt—where his union with the Egyptian queen Cleopatra (69–30 B.C.E.) produced a son—inspired his famous boast: *veni, vidi, vici* ("I came, I saw, I conquered"). A superb organizer, Caesar took strong measures to restabilize Rome: he codified the

Figure 6.3 Bust of Julius Caesar, first century B.C.E. Green schist, height 16⅛ in.

laws, regulated taxation, reduced debts, sent large numbers of the unemployed proletariat to overseas colonies, and inaugurated public works projects. He laid out Rome's first urban center: the Forum, a public meeting place that combined the functions of government, law, commerce, and religion, which would be enlarged and embellished by his imperial followers. Caesar granted citizenship to non-Italians and reformed the Western calendar to comprise 365 days and twelve months (one of which—July—he named after himself). Threatened by Caesar's populist reforms and his contempt for republican institutions, a group of his senatorial opponents, led by Marcus Junius Brutus, assassinated him in 44 B.C.E. Despite his inglorious death, the name *Caesar* would be used as an honorific title by all his imperial successors well into the second century C.E., as well as by many modern-day dictators.

The Roman Empire (30 B.C.E.–180 C.E.)

Following the assassination of Julius Caesar, a struggle for power ensued between Caesar's first lieutenant, Mark Anthony (ca. 80–30 B.C.E.), and his grandnephew (and adopted son) Octavian (63 B.C.E.–14 C.E.). The contest between the two was resolved at Actium in 31 B.C.E., when Octavian's navy routed the combined forces of Mark Anthony and Queen Cleopatra. The alliance between Anthony and Cleopatra, like that between Cleopatra and Julius Caesar, advanced the political ambitions of Egypt's most seductive queen, who sought not only to unite the eastern and western portions of Rome's great empire, but also to govern a vast Roman world-state. That destiny, however, would fall to Octavian. In 43 B.C.E., Octavian usurped the consulship and gained the approval of the Senate to rule for life. Although he called himself "first citizen" (*princeps*), his title of Emperor betrayed the reality that he was first and foremost Rome's army general (*imperator*). The Senate, however, bestowed on him the title *Augustus* ("the Revered One"). Augustus shared legislative power with the Senate, but retained the right to veto legislation. Thus, to all intents and purposes, the Republic was defunct. The future of Rome lay once again in the hands of a military dictator. It is in this guise that Augustus appears in Roman sculpture (Figure **6.4**).

In this free-standing, larger-than-life statue from Primaporta, Octavian raises his arm in a gesture of leadership and imperial authority. He wears a breastplate celebrating his victory over the Parthians in 20 B.C.E. At his feet appear Cupid and a dolphin, reminders of his alleged divine descent from Venus—the mother of Aeneas, Rome's legendary founder. Octavian's stance and physical proportions are modeled on the *Doryphorus* by Polycleitus (see Figure 5.2).

active commercial contact with all parts of the civilized world, including India and China. Augustus tried to arrest the tide of moral decay that had swept into Rome: in an effort to restore family values and the begetting of legitimate children, he passed laws (which ultimately failed in their purpose) to curb adultery and to prevent bachelors from receiving inheritances.

The *Pax Romana* was also a time of artistic and literary productivity. An enthusiastic patron of the arts, Augustus commissioned literature, sculpture, and architecture. He boasted that he had come to power when Rome was a city of brick and would leave it a city of marble. In most cases, this meant a veneer of marble that was, by standard Roman building practices, laid over the brick surface. In a city blighted by crime, noise, poor hygiene, and a frequent scarcity of food and water, Augustus initiated many new public works (including three new aqueducts and

Figure 6.4 Augustus of Primaporta, early first century C.E., after a bronze of ca. 20 B.C.E. Marble, height 6 ft. 8 in.

His handsome face and tall, muscular physique serve to complete the heroic image. In reality, however, the emperor was only 5 feet 4 inches tall—the average height of the Roman male.

Augustus' reign ushered in an era of peace and stability, a *Pax Romana*; from 30 B.C.E. to 180 C.E., the Roman peace prevailed throughout the Empire, and Rome enjoyed

Principal Roman Emperors

The Julio-Claudian Dynasty

27 B.C.E.–14 C.E.	Augustus
14–37	Tiberius
37–41	Gaius Caligula
41–54	Claudius
54–68	Nero

The Flavian Dynasty

68–79	Vespasian
79–81	Titus
81–96	Domitian

The "Good Emperors"

96–98	Nerva
97–117	Trajan
117–138	Hadrian
138–161	Antoninus Pius
161–180	Marcus Aurelius

Beginning of Decline

180–192	Commodus

The Severan Dynasty

193–211	Septimius Severus
211–217	Caracalla
222–235	Alexander Severus
235–284	Anarchy
284–305	Diocletian
306–337	Constantine I

some 500 fountains) and such civic services as a police force and a fire department. The reign of Octavian also witnessed the birth of a new religion, Christianity, which, in later centuries, would spread throughout the Empire (see chapters 8 and 9).

Augustus put an end to the civil wars of the preceding century, but he revived neither the political nor the social equilibrium of the early Republic. Following his death, Rome continued to be ruled by military officials. Since there was no machinery for succession to the imperial throne, Rome's rulers held office until they either died or were assassinated. Of the twenty-six emperors who governed Rome during the fifty-year period between 335 and 385 C.E., only one died a natural death. Government by and for the people had been the hallmark of Rome's early history, but the enterprise of imperialism ultimately overtook these lofty republican ideals.

Roman Law

Against this backdrop of conquest and dominion, it is no surprise that Rome's contributions to the humanistic tradition were practical rather than theoretical. The sheer size of the Roman Empire inspired engineering programs, such as bridge and road building, that united all regions under Roman rule. Law—a less tangible means of unification—was equally important in this regard. The development of a system of law was one of Rome's most original and influential achievements.

Roman law (the Latin *jus* means both "law" and "justice") evolved out of the practical need to rule a world-state, rather than—as in ancient Greece—as the product of a dialectic between the citizen and the *polis*. Inspired by the laws of Solon, the Romans published their first civil code, the Twelve Tables of Law, in 450 B.C.E. They placed these laws on view in the Forum. The Twelve Tables of Law provided Rome's basic legal code for almost a thousand years. To this body of law were added the acts of the Assembly and the Senate, and public decrees of the emperors. For some 500 years, *praetors* (magistrates who administered justice) and *jurisconsults* (experts in the law) interpreted the laws, bringing commonsense resolutions to private disputes. Their interpretations constituted a body of "case law." In giving consideration to individual needs, these magistrates cultivated the concept of equity, which puts the spirit of the law above the letter of the law. The decisions of Roman jurists became precedents that established comprehensive guidelines for future judgments. Thus, Roman law was not fixed, but was an evolving body of opinions on the nature and dispensation of justice.

Early in Roman history, the law of the land (*jus civile*) applied only to Roman citizens, but as Roman citizenship was extended to the provinces, so too was the law. Law that embraced a wider range of peoples and customs, the law of the people (*jus gentium*), assumed an international quality that acknowledged compromises between conflicting customs and traditions. The law of the people was, in effect, a law based on universal principles, that is, the law of nature (*jus naturale*). The full body of Roman law came to incorporate the decisions of the jurists, the acts passed by Roman legislative assemblies, and the edicts of Roman emperors. In the sixth century C.E., 200 years after the division of the Empire into eastern and western portions and a hundred years after the collapse of Rome, the Byzantine (East Roman) emperor Justinian would codify this huge body of law, thereafter known as the *Corpus Juris Civilis*. The Roman system of law influenced the development of codified law in all European countries with the exception of England.

The Roman Contribution to Literature

Roman Philosophic Thought

Roman contributions to law were numerous, but such was not the case with philosophy. More a practical than a speculative people, the Romans produced no systems of philosophic thought comparable to those of Plato and Aristotle. However, they preserved the writings of Hellenic and Hellenistic thinkers. Educated Romans admired Aristotle and absorbed the works of the Epicureans and the Stoics. The Latin poet Lucretius (ca. 95–ca. 55 B.C.E.) popularized the materialist theories of Democritus and Leucippus, which describe the world in purely physical terms, denying the existence of the gods and other supernatural beings. Since all of reality, including the human soul, consists of atoms, Lucretius argues in his only work, *On the Nature of Things*, there is no reason to fear death: "We shall not feel because we shall not be."

In the vast, impersonal world of the Empire, many Romans cultivated the attitude of rational detachment popular among the Stoics (see chapter 5). Like their third-century B.C.E. forebears, Roman Stoics believed that an impersonal force (Providence or Divine Reason) governed the world, and that happiness lay in one's ability to accept the will of the universe. Stoics rejected any emotional attachments that might enslave them. The ideal spiritual condition and the one most conducive to contentment, according to the Stoic point of view, depends on self-control and the subjugation of the emotions to reason.

Science and Technology

312 B.C.E.	Consul Appius Claudius orders construction of the "Appian Way," the first in a strategic network of Roman roads
101 B.C.E.	the Romans use water power for milling grain
46 B.C.E.	Caesar inaugurates the "Julian Calendar," on which the modern calendar is based
77 C.E.	Pliny the Elder completes a 37-volume encyclopedia called *Natural History*, which summarized information about astronomy, geography, and zoology
79 C.E.	Pliny the Younger writes a detailed account of the eruption of Mount Vesuvius

The commonsense tenets of Stoicism encouraged the Roman sense of duty. At the same time, the Stoic belief in the equality of all people had a humanizing effect on Roman jurisprudence and anticipated the all-embracing direction of Early Christian thought (see chapter 8). Stoicism was especially popular among such intellectuals as the noted playwright and essayist Lucius Annaeus Seneca (ca. 4 B.C.E.–65 C.E.) and the emperor Marcus Aurelius (121–180 C.E.), both of whom wrote classic treatises on the subject. Seneca's *On Tranquility of Mind*, an excerpt from which follows, argues that one may achieve peace of mind by avoiding burdensome responsibilities, gloomy companions, and excessive wealth. Stoicism offered a reasoned retreat from psychic pain and moral despair, as well as a practical set of solutions to the daily strife between the self and society.

READING 6.2 From Seneca's *On Tranquility of Mind* (ca. 40 C.E.)

... our question, then, is how the mind can maintain a consistent and advantageous course, be kind to itself and take pleasure in its attributes, never interrupt this satisfaction but abide in its serenity, without excitement or depression. This amounts to tranquility. We shall inquire how it may be attained... [1]

A correct estimate of self is prerequisite, for we are generally inclined to overrate our capacities. One man is tripped by confidence in his eloquence, another makes greater demands upon his estate than it can stand, another burdens a [10] frail body with an exhausting office. Some are too bashful for politics, which requires aggressiveness; some are too headstrong for court; some do not control their temper and break into unguarded language at the slightest provocation; some cannot restrain their wit or resist making risky jokes. For all such people retirement is better than a career; an assertive and intolerant temperament should avoid incitements to outspokenness that will prove harmful.

Next we must appraise the career and compare our strength with the task we shall attempt. The worker must be stronger [20] than his project; loads larger than the bearer must necessarily crush him. Certain careers, moreover, are not so demanding in themselves as they are prolific in begetting a mass of other activities. Enterprises which give rise to new and multifarious activities should be avoided; you must not commit yourself to a task from which there is no free egress. Put your hand to one you can finish or at least hope to finish; leave alone those that expand as you work at them and do not stop where you intend they should.

In our choice of men we should be particularly careful to [30] see whether they are worth spending part of our life on and whether they will appreciate our loss of time; some people think we are in their debt if we do them a service. Athenadorus said he would not even go to dine with a man who would not feel indebted for his coming. Much less would he dine with people, as I suppose you understand, who discharge indebtedness for services rendered by giving a dinner and count the courses as favors, as if their lavishness

was a mark of honor to others. Take away witnesses and spectators and they will take no pleasure in secret [40] gormandizing.

But nothing can equal the pleasures of faithful and congenial friendship. How good it is to have willing hearts as safe repositories for your every secret, whose privity[1] you fear less than your own, whose conversation allays your anxiety, whose counsel promotes your plans, whose cheerfulness dissipates your gloom, whose very appearance gives you joy! But we must choose friends who are, so far as possible, free from passions. Vices are contagious; they light upon whoever is nearest and infect by contact. During a plague we must be [50] careful not to sit near people caught in the throes and burning with fever, because we would be courting danger and drawing poison in with our breath; just so in choosing friends we must pay attention to character and take those least tainted. To mingle the healthy with the sick is the beginning of disease. But I would not prescribe that you become attached to or attract no one who is not a sage. Where would you find him? We have been searching for him for centuries. Call the least bad man the best. You could not have a more opulent choice, if you were looking for good men, than among the Platos and [60] Xenophons[2] and the famous Socratic brood, or if you had at your disposal the age of Cato,[3] which produced many characters worthy to be his contemporaries (just as it produced many unprecedentedly bad, who engineered monstrous crimes. Both kinds were necessary to make Cato's quality understood: he needed bad men against whom he could make his strength effective and good men to appreciate his effectiveness). But now there is a great dearth of good men, and your choice cannot be fastidious. But gloomy people who deplore everything and find reason to complain you must [70] take pains to avoid. With all his loyalty and goodwill, a grumbling and touchy companion militates against tranquility.

We pass now to property, the greatest source of affliction to humanity. If you balance all our other troubles—deaths, diseases, fears, longings, subjection to labor and pain—with the miseries in which our money involves us, the latter will far outweigh the former. Reflect, then, how much less a grief it is not to have money than to lose it, and then you will realize that poverty has less to torment us with in the degree that it has less to lose. If you suppose that rich men take their losses [80] with greater equanimity you are mistaken; a wound hurts a big man as much as it does a little. Bion[4] put it smartly: a bald man is as bothered when his hair is plucked as a man with a full head. The same applies to rich and poor, you may be sure; in either case the money is glued on and cannot be torn away without a twinge, so that both suffer alike. It is less distressing, as I have said, and easier not to acquire money than to lose it, and you will therefore notice that people upon whom Fortune never has smiled are more cheerful than those she has deserted. ... [90]

---

[1] Private or secret knowledge.
[2] Greek historian and biographer who lived ca. 428–354 B.C.E.
[3] Marcus Porcius Cato (234–149 B.C.E.), known as "the Censor," a Roman champion of austerity and simplicity.
[4] A Greek poet who lived around 100 B.C.E.

All life is bondage. Man must therefore habituate himself to his condition, complain of it as little as possible, and grasp whatever good lies within his reach. No situation is so harsh that a dispassionate mind cannot find some consolation in it. If a man lays even a very small area out skillfully it will provide ample space for many uses, and even a foothold can be made livable by deft arrangement. Apply good sense to your problems; the hard can be softened, the narrow widened, and the heavy made lighter by the skillful bearer. . . .

Q **How, according to Seneca, does one achieve "tranquility of mind"?**

Q **What, in his view, is humanity's greatest source of affliction?**

Latin Prose Literature

Roman literature reveals a masterful use of Latin prose for the purposes of entertainment, instruction, and record keeping. Applying knowledge to practical ends, the Romans found prose the ideal vehicle for compiling and transmitting information. Rome gave the West its first geographies and encyclopedias, as well as some of its finest biographies, histories, and manuals of instruction. In the writing of history, in particular, the Romans demonstrated their talent for the collection and analysis of factual evidence. Although Roman historians tended to glorify Rome and its leadership, their attention to accurate detail often surpassed that of the Greek historians. One of Rome's greatest historians, Titus Livius ("Livy," ca. 59 B.C.E.–17 C.E.), wrote a history of Rome from the eighth century B.C.E. to his own day. Although only a small portion of Livy's original 142 books survive, this monumental work—commissioned by Octavian himself—constitutes our most reliable account of political and social life in the days of the Roman Republic.

The Romans were masters, as well, of **oratory**, that is, the art of public speaking, and in the writing of **epistles** (letters). In both of these genres, the statesman Marcus Tullius Cicero (106–43 B.C.E.) excelled. A contemporary of Julius Caesar, Cicero produced more than 900 letters—sometimes writing three a day to the same person—and more than 100 speeches and essays. Clarity and eloquence are the hallmarks of Cicero's prose style, which Renaissance humanists hailed as the model for literary excellence (see chapter 16). Cicero was familiar with the theoretical works of Aristotle and the Stoics, but his letters reflect a profound concern for the practical realities of his own day. In his lifetime, Cicero served Rome as consul, statesman, and orator; his carefully reasoned speeches helped to shape public opinion. While he praised Julius Caesar's literary style, he openly opposed his patron's dictatorship. Nevertheless, Caesar congenially confessed to Cicero, "It is nobler to enlarge the boundaries of human intelligence than those of the Roman Empire." During the tumultuous years following Caesar's assassination, Cicero too was murdered, and his head and hands put on public display at the Forum. As we see in the following excerpt from his essay *On Duty*, Cicero considered public service the noblest of human activities—one that demanded the

exercise of personal courage equal to that required in military combat.

READING 6.3 From Cicero's *On Duty* (ca. 44 B.C.E.)

. . . that moral goodness which we look for in a lofty, high-minded spirit is secured, of course, by moral, not by physical, strength. And yet the body must be trained and so disciplined that it can obey the dictates of judgment and reason in attending to business and in enduring toil. But that moral goodness which is our theme depends wholly upon the thought and attention given to it by the mind. And, in this way, the men who in a civil capacity direct the affairs of the nation render no less important service than they who conduct its wars: by their statesmanship oftentimes wars are either [10] averted or terminated; sometimes also they are declared. Upon Marcus Cato's[1] counsel, for example, the Third Punic War was undertaken, and in its conduct his influence was dominant, even after he was dead. And so diplomacy in the friendly settlement of controversies is more desirable than courage in settling them on the battlefield; but we must be careful not to take that course merely for the sake of avoiding war rather than for the sake of public expediency. War, however, should be undertaken in such a way as to make it evident that it has no other object than to secure peace. [20]

But it takes a brave and resolute spirit not to be disconcerted in times of difficulty or ruffled and thrown off one's feet, as the saying is, but to keep one's presence of mind and one's self-possession and not to swerve from the path of reason.

Now all this requires great personal courage; but it calls also for great intellectual ability by reflection to anticipate the future, to discover some time in advance what may happen whether for good or for ill, and what must be done in any possible event, and never to be reduced to having to say [30] "I had not thought of that."

These are the activities that mark a spirit strong, high, and self-reliant in its prudence and wisdom. But to mix rashly in the fray and to fight hand to hand with the enemy is but a barbarous and brutish kind of business. Yet when the stress of circumstances demands it, we must gird on the sword and prefer death to slavery and disgrace.

As to destroying and plundering cities, let me say that great care should be taken that nothing be done in reckless cruelty or wantonness. And it is a great man's duty in troublous times [40] to single out the guilty for punishment, to spare the many, and in every turn of fortune to hold to a true and honorable course. For whereas there are many, as I have said before, who place the achievements of war above those of peace, so one may find many to whom adventurous, hot-headed counsels seem more brilliant and more impressive than calm and well-considered measures.

We must, of course, never be guilty of seeming cowardly and craven in our avoidance of danger; but we must also beware of exposing ourselves to danger needlessly. Nothing [50]

[1] The Roman senator Cato repeatedly demanded the total destruction of Carthage.

can be more foolhardy than that. Accordingly, in encountering danger we should do as doctors do in their practice: in light cases of illness they give mild treatment; in cases of dangerous sickness they are compelled to apply hazardous and even desperate remedies. It is, therefore, only a madman who, in a calm, would pray for a storm; a wise man's way is, when the storm does come, to withstand it with all the means at his command, and especially when the advantages to be expected in case of a successful issue are greater than the hazards of the struggle. 60

The dangers attending great affairs of state fall sometimes upon those who undertake them, sometimes upon the state. In carrying out such enterprises, some run the risk of losing their lives, others their reputation and the goodwill of their fellow-citizens. It is our duty, then, to be more ready to endanger our own than the public welfare and to hazard honor and glory more readily than other advantages. . . .

Q **According to Cicero, under what circumstances is war justified?**

Q **What are the main duties of a statesman?**

As Cicero suggests, Roman education emphasized civic duty. It aimed at training the young for active roles in civic life. For careers in law and political administration, the art of public speaking was essential. Indeed, in the provinces, where people of many languages mingled, oratory was the ultimate form of political influence. Since the art of public speaking was the distinctive mark of the educated Roman, the practical skills of grammar and rhetoric held an important place in Roman education. One of the greatest spokesmen for the significance of oratory in public affairs was the Roman historian and politician P. Cornelius Tacitus (ca. 56–120 C.E.). Tacitus' *Dialogue on Oratory* describes the role of public speaking in ancient Roman life. It bemoans the passing of a time when "eloquence not only led to great rewards, but was also a sheer necessity."

READING 6.4 From Tacitus' *Dialogue on Oratory*

(ca. 100–105 C.E.)

. . . great oratory is like a flame: it needs fuel to feed it, 1
movement to fan it, and it brightens as it burns.

At Rome too the eloquence of our forefathers owed its development to [special] conditions. For although the orators of today have also succeeded in obtaining all the influence that it would be proper to allow them under settled, peaceable, and prosperous political conditions, yet their predecessors in those days of unrest and unrestraint thought they could accomplish more when, in the general ferment and without the strong hand of a single ruler, a speaker's political 10 wisdom was measured by his power of carrying conviction to the unstable populace. This was the source of the constant succession of measures put forward by champions of the people's rights, of the harangues of state officials who almost spent the night on the hustings,[1] of the impeachments of powerful criminals and hereditary feuds between whole

families, of schisms among the aristocracy and never-ending struggles between the senate and the commons.[2] All this tore the commonwealth in pieces, but it provided a sphere for the oratory of those days and heaped on it what one saw were 20 vast rewards. The more influence a man could wield by his powers of speech, the more readily did he attain to high office, the further did he, when in office, outstrip his colleagues in the race for precedence, the more did he gain favor with the great, authority with the senate, and name and fame with the common people. These were the men who had whole nations of foreigners under their protection, several at a time; the men to whom state officials presented their humble duty on the eve of their departure to take up the government of a province, and to whom they paid their respects on their 30 return; the men who, without any effort on their own part, seemed to have praetorships and consulates at their beck and call; the men who even when out of office were in power, seeing that by their advice and authority they could bend both the senate and the people to their will. With them, moreover, it was a conviction that without eloquence it was impossible for anyone either to attain to a position of distinction and prominence in the community, or to maintain it; and no wonder they cherished this conviction, when they were called on to appear in public even when they would rather not, when it 40 was not enough to move a brief resolution in the senate, unless one made good one's opinion in an able speech, when persons who had in some way or other incurred odium, or else were definitely charged with some offence, had to put in an appearance in person, when, moreover, evidence in criminal trials had to be given not indirectly or by affidavit, but personally and by word of mouth. So it was that eloquence not only led to great rewards, but was also a sheer necessity; and just as it was considered great and glorious to have the reputation of being a good speaker, so, on the other hand, it 50 was accounted discreditable to be inarticulate and incapable of utterance. . . .

Q **What role, according to Tacitus, did oratory play in Roman life? Is this true of oratory today?**

Roman Epic Poetry

While the Romans excelled in didactic prose, they also produced some of the world's finest verse. Under the patronage of Octavian, Rome enjoyed a golden age of Latin literature whose most notable representative was Virgil (Publius Vergilius Maro, 70–19 B.C.E.). Rome's foremost poet-publicist, Virgil wrote the semilegendary epic that immortalized Rome's destiny as world ruler. The *Aeneid* was not the product of an oral tradition, as were the Homeric epics; rather, it is a literary epic, undertaken as a work that might rival the epics of Homer. The hero of Virgil's poem is Rome's mythical founder, the Trojan-born Aeneas. As epic hero, Aeneas undertakes a long journey filled with adventures that test his prowess. The first six books of the *Aeneid* recount the hero's voyage from Troy to Italy and his love affair with the beautiful Carthaginian

---

[1] The speaker's platform.
[2] The Popular Assembly.

princess Dido. The second six books describe the Trojan conquest of Latium and the establishment of the Roman state. No summary of the *Aeneid* can represent adequately the monumental impact of a work that would become the foundation for education in the Latin language. Yet, the following two excerpts capture the spirit of Virgil's vision. In the first, Aeneas, pressed to meet his destiny, prepares to take leave of the passionate Dido. Here, his Stoic sense of duty overcomes his desire for personal fulfillment. The second passage, selected from the lengthy monologue spoken by the ghost of Aeneas' father, Anchises, sums up the meaning and purpose of Rome's historic mission.

— **READING 6.5** From Virgil's *Aeneid*
  (Books Four and Six) (ca. 20 B.C.E.)

[Mercury, the divine herald, urges Aeneas to leave Carthage and proceed to Italy.]

Mercury wastes no time:—"What are you doing,   1
Forgetful of your kingdom and your fortunes,
Building for Carthage? Woman-crazy fellow,
The ruler of the Gods, the great compeller
Of heaven and earth, has sent me from Olympus   5
With no more word than this: what are you doing,
With what ambition wasting time in Libya?
If your own fame and fortune count as nothing,
Think of Ascanius[1] at least, whose kingdom
In Italy, whose Roman land, are waiting   10
As promise justly due." He spoke, and vanished
Into thin air. Appalled, amazed, Aeneas
Is stricken dumb; his hair stands up in terror,
His voice sticks in his throat. He is more than eager
To flee that pleasant land, awed by the warning   15
Of the divine command. But how to do it?
How get around that passionate queen?[2] What opening
Try first? His mind runs out in all directions,
Shifting and veering. Finally, he has it,
Or thinks he has: he calls his comrades to him,   20
The leaders, bids them quietly prepare
The fleet for voyage, meanwhile saying nothing
About the new activity; since Dido
Is unaware, has no idea that passion
As strong as theirs is on the verge of breaking,   25
He will see what he can do, find the right moment
To let her know, all in good time. Rejoicing,
The captains move to carry out the orders.
     Who can deceive a woman in love? The queen
Anticipates each move, is fearful even   30
While everything is safe, foresees this cunning,
And the same troublemaking goddess, Rumor,
Tells her the fleet is being armed, made ready
For voyaging. She rages through the city
Like a woman mad, or drunk, the way the Maenads[3]   35

Go howling through the night-time on Cithaeron[4]
When Bacchus' cymbals summon with their clashing.
She waits no explanation from Aeneas;
She is the first to speak: "And so, betrayer,
You hoped to hide your wickedness, go sneaking   40
Out of my land without a word? Our love
Means nothing to you, our exchange of vows,
And even the death of Dido could not hold you.
The season is dead of winter, and you labor
Over the fleet; the northern gales are nothing—   45
You must be cruel, must you not? Why, even,
If ancient Troy remained, and you were seeking
Not unknown homes and lands, but Troy again,
Would you be venturing Troyward in this weather?
I am the one you flee from: true? I beg you   50
By my own tears, and your right hand—(I have nothing
Else left my wretchedness)—by the beginnings
Of marriage, wedlock, what we had, if ever
I served you well, if anything of mine
Was ever sweet to you, I beg you, pity   55
A falling house; if there is room for pleading
As late as this, I plead, put off that purpose.
You are the reason I am hated; Libyans,
Numidians, Tyrians, hate me; and my honor
Is lost, and the fame I had, that almost brought me   60
High as the stars, is gone. To whom, O guest—
I must not call you husband any longer—
To whom do you leave me? I am a dying woman;
Why do I linger on? Until Pygmalion,
My brother, brings destruction to this city?   65
Until the prince Iarbas leads me captive?
At least if there had been some hope of children
Before your flight, a little Aeneas playing
Around my courts, to bring you back, in feature
At least, I would seem less taken and deserted."   70
     There was nothing he could say. Jove[5] bade him keep
Affection from his eyes, and grief in his heart
With never a sign. At last, he managed something:—
"Never, O Queen, will I deny you merit
Whatever you have strength to claim; I will not   75
Regret remembering Dido, while I have
Breath in my body, or consciousness of spirit.
I have a point or two to make. I did not,
Believe me, hope to hide my flight by cunning;
I did not, ever, claim to be a husband,   80
Made no such vows. If I had fate's permission
To live my life my way, to settle my troubles
At my own will, I would be watching over
The city of Troy, and caring for my people,
Those whom the Greeks had spared, and Priam's palace   85
Would still be standing; for the vanquished people
I would have built the town again. But now
It is Italy I must seek, great Italy,
Apollo orders, and his oracles
Call me to Italy. There is my love,   90
There is my country. If the towers of Carthage,

---

[1] Aeneas' son.
[2] Dido, Queen of Carthage.
[3] "Mad women," the votaries of Bacchus (Dionysus).

[4] A mountain range between Attica and Boetia.
[5] Jupiter, the sky god.

The Libyan citadels, can please a woman
Who came from Tyre,[6] why must you grudge the Trojans
Ausonian land?[7] It is proper for us also
To seek a foreign kingdom. I am warned   95
Of this in dreams: when the earth is veiled in shadow
And the fiery stars are burning, I see my father,
Anchises, or his ghost, and I am frightened;
I am troubled for the wrong I do my son,
Cheating him out of his kingdom in the west,   100
And lands that fate assigns him. And a herald,
Jove's messenger—I call them both to witness—
Has brought me, through the rush of air, his orders;
I saw the god myself, in the full daylight,
Enter these walls, I heard the words he brought me.   105
Cease to inflame us both with your complainings;
I follow Italy not because I want to."

[In the Underworld described in Book Six, Aeneas encounters the
soul of his father, Anchises, who foretells the destiny of Rome.]

"Others, no doubt, will better mold the bronze
To the semblance of soft breathing, draw from marble,
The living countenance; and others please   110
With greater eloquence, or learn to measure
Better than we, the pathways of the heavens,
The risings of the stars: remember, Roman,
To rule the people under law, to establish
The way of peace, to battle down the haughty,   115
To spare the meek. Our fine arts, these forever."

Q Why does Aeneas abandon Dido?

**Q How do Aeneas and Achilles (Reading 4.1)
    compare as epic heroes?**

Roman Lyric Poetry

While Virgil is best known for the *Aeneid*, he also wrote
pastoral poems, or **eclogues**, that glorify the natural landscape and its rustic inhabitants. Virgil's *Eclogues* found
inspiration in the pastoral sketches of Theocritus, a third-
century B.C.E. Sicilian poet. Many Classicists besides Virgil
looked to Hellenic prototypes. The poetry of Catullus
(ca. 84–54 B.C.E.), for instance, reflects familiarity with the
art of Sappho, whose lyrics he admired. The greatest of the
Latin lyric poets, Catullus came to Rome from Verona. A
young man of some wealth and charm, he wrote primarily
on the subjects that consumed his short but intense life:
friendship, love, and sex. His passionate affair with Clodia,
the adulterous wife of a Roman consul, inspired some of his
finest poems, three of which appear below. These trace the
trajectory from the poet's first fevered amorous passions
to his despair and bitterness at the collapse of the affair.
The fourth poem betrays the raw invective and caustic

---

[6] A maritime city of ancient Phoenicia, ruled by Dido's father.
[7] From Ausones, the ancient name for the inhabitants of middle and
   southern Italy.

wit that Catullus brought to many of his verses, including
those with themes of jealousy and possession related to his
bisexual liaisons. Candid and deeply personal, these poems
strike us with the immediacy of a modern, secular voice.

READING 6.6 The Poems of Catullus (ca. 60 B.C.E.)

Come, Lesbia,[1] let us live and love,   1
nor give a damn what sour old men say.
The sun that sets may rise again
but when our light has sunk into the earth,
it is gone forever.   5
  Give me a thousand kisses,
then a hundred, another thousand,
another hundred
  and in one breath
still kiss another thousand,   10
another hundred.
  O then with lips and bodies joined
many deep thousands;
  confuse
their number,   15
  so that poor fools and cuckolds (envious
even now) shall never
learn our wealth and curse us
with their
evil eyes.   20

◆

He is changed to a god he who looks on her,   1
godlike he shines when he's seated beside her,
immortal joy to gaze and hear the fall of
  her sweet laughter.

All of my senses are lost and confounded;   5
Lesbia rises before me and trembling
I sink into earth and swift dissolution
  seizes my body.

Limbs are pierced with fire and the heavy tongue fails,
ears resound with noise of distant storms shaking   10
this earth, eyes gaze on stars that fall forever
  into deep midnight.

This languid madness destroys you Catullus,
long day and night shall be desolate, broken,
as long ago ancient kings and rich cities   15
  fell into ruin.

◆

Lesbia, forever spitting fire at me, is never silent, And now   1
if Lesbia fails to love me, I shall die. Why
do I know in truth her passion burns for me? Because I am
  like her,

---

[1] The name Catullus gave to Clodia, a reference to Sappho of Lesbos.

because I curse her endlessly. And still, O hear me gods,   5
I love her.

———◆———

Furius, Aurelius, I'll work your own perversions   1
upon you and your persons, since you say my poems
prove that I'm effeminate, deep in homosexual vice.
A genuine poet must be chaste, industrious,
though his verse may give us   5
rich, voluptuous passion to please the
taste of those who read him and not only
delicate boys, but bearded men whose limbs are
stiff and out of practice. And you because my verses
contain many (thousands of) kisses, look at me   10
as though I were a girl. Come at me, and I'll be ready
to defile you and seduce you.

Q How do the poems of Catullus compare with those of Sappho?

The poetry of Catullus notwithstanding, passion and personal feeling were not typical of Latin literature, which inclined more usually toward instruction and satire. One of Rome's most notable poets, Publius Ovidius Naso, or Ovid (43 B.C.E.–17 C.E.), earned centuries of fame for his narrative poem the *Metamorphoses*; this vast collection of stories about Greek and Roman gods develops the theme of supernatural transformation. Ovid himself pursued a career of poetry and love. Married three times, he seems to have been a master in the art of seduction. His witty guide on the subject, *The Art of Love*, brought him into disfavor with Augustus, who (finding the work morally threatening) sent Ovid into exile. Although written with tongue in cheek, *The Art of Love* swelled an already large canon of misogynistic, or antifemale, Classical literature. In this humorous "handbook," Ovid offers vivid glimpses into everyday life in Rome, but he clearly holds that the greatest human crimes issue from women's lust, which, according to the poet, is "keener, fiercer, and more wanton" than men's.

The Poems of Horace

Roman poets were at their most typical when they were moralizing. Octavian's poet laureate, Quintus Haeredes Flaccus, better known as Horace (65–8 B.C.E.), took a critical view of life. Although lacking the grandeur of Virgil and the virtuosity of Ovid, Horace composed verse that pointed up the contradictions between practical realities and philosophic ideals. Having lived through the devastating civil wars of the first century B.C.E., Horace brought a commonsense insight to the subject of war, as we see in the first of the following poems. The second poem exemplifies the Roman taste for **satire**, a literary genre that uses humor to denounce human vice and folly. Satire—Rome's unique contribution to world literature—is a kind of moralizing in which human imperfection is not simply criticized, but rather mocked through biting wit and comic exaggeration. "To Be Quite Frank" is a caustic description of a

middle-aged lady with teenage pretensions, a characterization as unvarnished and true to life as most Roman portraits. Finally, in the third poem below, Horace discloses his Stoic disbelief in human perfection: he advises us to "seize the day" (*carpe diem*) and "learn to accept whatever is to be."

READING 6.7 The Poems of Horace (ca. 30–15 B.C.E.)

Civil War

Why do ye rush, oh wicked folk,   1
    To a fresh war?
Again the cries, the sword, the smoke—
    What for?

Has not sufficient precious blood   5
    Been fiercely shed?
Must ye spill more until ye flood
    The dead?

Not even armed in rivalry
    Your hate's employed;   10
But 'gainst yourselves until ye be
    Destroyed!

Even when beasts slay beasts, they kill
    Some other kind.
Can it be madness makes ye still   15
    So blind?

Make answer! Is your conscience numb?
    Each ashy face
Admits, with silent lips, the dumb
    Disgrace.   20

Murder of brothers! Of all crime,
    Vilest and worst!
Pause—lest ye be, through all of time,
    Accursed.

To Be Quite Frank

Your conduct, naughty Chloris, is   1
    Not just exactly Horace's
Ideal of a lady
    At the shady
Time of life;   5
You mustn't throw your soul away
On foolishness, like Pholoë—
    Her days are folly-laden—
    She's a maiden,
                    You're a wife.   10

Your daughter, with propriety,
May look for male society,
    Do one thing and another
    In which mother
                    Shouldn't mix;   15

But revels Bacchanalian
Are—or should be—quite alien
   To you a married person,
   Something worse'n
          Forty-six!   20

Yes, Chloris, you cut up too much,
You love the dance and cup too much,
   Your years are quickly flitting—
   To your knitting
          Right about!   25
Forget the incidental things
That keep you from parental things—
   The World, the Flesh, the Devil,
   On the level,
          Cut 'em out!   30

Carpe Diem

Pry not in forbidden lore,   1
   Ask no more, Leuconoë,
How many years—to you?—to me?—
The gods will send us
Before they end us;   5
Nor, questing, fix your hopes
On Babylonian horoscopes.
Learn to accept whatever is to be:
Whether Jove grant us many winters,
Or make of this the last, which splinters   10
Now on opposing cliffs the Tuscan sea.

Be wise; decant your wine; condense
Large aims to fit life's cramped circumference.
We talk, time flies—you've said it!
Make hay today,   15
Tomorrow rates no credit.

Q **How does each of these poems reflect Horace's "critical view of life"?**

The Satires of Juvenal

While Horace's satirical lyrics are, for the most part, genial, those of Rome's most famous satirist, Juvenal (Decimus Junius Juvenalis, ca. 60–130 C.E.), are among the most devastating ever written. Juvenal came to Rome from the provinces. His subsequent career as a magistrate and his experience of poverty and financial failure contributed to his negative perception of Roman society, which he describes in his sixteen bitter *Satires* as swollen with greed and corruption. Juvenal's attack on the city of Rome paints a picture of a noisy, dirty, and crowded urban community inhabited by selfish, violent, and self-indulgent people.

READING 6.8a From Juvenal's "Against the City of Rome" (ca. 110–127 C.E.)

"Rome, good-bye! Let the rest stay in the town if they want to,   1
Fellows like A, B, and C, who make black white at their pleasure,

Finding it easy to grab contracts for rivers and harbors,
Putting up temples, or cleaning out sewers, or hauling off corpses,
Or, if it comes to that, auctioning slaves in the market.   5
Once they used to be hornblowers, working the carneys;
Every wide place in the road knew their puffed-out cheeks and their
   squealing.
Now they give shows of their own. Thumbs up! Thumbs down![1] And
   the killers
Spare or slay, and then go back to concessions for private privies.
Nothing they won't take on. Why not?—since the kindness of Fortune 10
(Fortune is out for laughs) has exalted them out of the gutter.

. . . .

"If you're poor, you're a joke, on each and every occasion.
What a laugh, if your cloak is dirty or torn, if your toga
Seems a little bit soiled, if your shoe has a crack in the leather,
Or if more than one patch attests to more than one mending!   15
Poverty's greatest curse, much worse than the fact of it, is that
It makes men objects of mirth, ridiculed, humbled, embarrassed.
'Out of the front-row seats!' they cry when you're out of money,
Yield your place to the sons of some pimp, the spawn of some
   cathouse,
Some slick auctioneer's brat, or the louts some trainer has fathered 20
Or the well-groomed boys whose sire is a gladiator.

. . . .

"Here in town the sick die from insomnia mostly.
Undigested food, on a stomach burning with ulcers,
Brings on listlessness, but who can sleep in a flophouse?
Who but the rich can afford sleep and a garden apartment?   25
That's the source of infection. The wheels creak by on the narrow
Streets of the wards, the drivers squabble and brawl when they're
   stopped,
More than enough to frustrate the drowsiest son of a sea cow.
When his business calls, the crowd makes way, as the rich man,
Carried high in his car, rides over them, reading or writing,   30
Even taking a snooze, perhaps, for the motion's composing.
Still, he gets where he wants before we do; for all of our hurry
Traffic gets in our way, in front, around and behind us.
Somebody gives me a shove with an elbow, or two-by-four
   scantling.[2]
One clunks my head with a beam, another cracks down with
   a beer keg.   35
Mud is thick on my shins, I am trampled by somebody's big feet.
Now what?—a soldier grinds his hobnails into my toes."

Q **What urban ills does Juvenal describe in this poem? Are they exclusive to ancient Rome?**

If Juvenal found much to criticize among his peers, he was equally hostile toward foreigners and women. His sixth *Satire*, "Against Women," is one of the most bitter anti-female diatribes in the history of Western literature. Here, the poet laments the disappearance of the chaste Latin woman whose virtues, he submits, have been corrupted by

---

[1] To turn the thumb down was the signal to kill a wounded gladiator; to turn it up signaled that he should be spared.
[2] A piece of lumber.

life, and the consorts of Rome's rulers often shaped matters of succession and politics by way of their influence on their husbands and sons. Roman records confirm that in addition to the traditional occupations of women in food and textile production and in prostitution, they also held positions as musicians, painters, priestesses, midwives, and gladiators. Nevertheless, in 200 C.E., the emperor Septimius Severus banned female combat, finding it an affront to military dignity.

READING 6.8b From Juvenal's "Against Women" (ca. 110–127 C.E.)

Where, you ask, do they come from, such monsters as these? In the old days   1
Latin women were chaste by dint of their lowly fortunes.
Toil and short hours for sleep kept cottages free from contagion,
Hands were hard from working the wood, and husbands were watching,
Standing to arms at the Colline Gate, and the shadow of Hannibal's looming.[1]   5
Now we suffer the evils of long peace. Luxury hatches
Terrors worse than the wars, avenging a world beaten down.
Every crime is here, and every lust, as they have been
Since the day, long since, when Roman poverty perished.
Over our seven hills,[2] from that day on, they came pouring.   10
The rabble and rout of the East, Sybaris, Rhodes, Miletus,
Yes, and Tarentum[3] too, garlanded, drunken, shameless.
Dirty money it was that first imported among us
Foreign vice and our times broke down with overindulgence.
Riches are flabby, soft. And what does Venus care for   15
When she is drunk? She can't tell one end of a thing from another,
Gulping big oysters down at midnight, making the unguents
Foam in the unmixed wine, and drinking out of a conchhorn
While the walls spin round, and the table starts in dancing,
And the glow of the lamps is blurred by double their number.   20

. . . .

There's nothing a woman won't do, nothing she thinks is disgraceful
With the green gems at her neck, or pearls distending her ear lobes.
Nothing is worse to endure than your Mrs. Richbitch, whose visage
Is padded and plastered with dough, in the most ridiculous manner.
Furthermore, she reeks of unguents, so God help her husband   25
With his wretched face stunk up with these, smeared by her lipstick.
To her lovers she comes with her skin washed clean. But at home
Why does she need to look pretty? Nard[4] is assumed for the lover,
For the lover she buys all the Arabian perfumes.
It takes her some time to strip down to her face, removing the layers 30
One by one, till at last she is recognizable, almost,
Then she uses a lotion, she-asses' milk; she'd need herds

---

[1] In 213 B.C.E., the Carthaginian general Hannibal, Rome's most formidable enemy, was camped only a few miles outside Rome, poised to attack (see Livy, xxvi:10).
[2] The hills surrounding the city of Rome.
[3] Greek cities associated with luxury and vice.
[4] Spikenard, a fragrant ointment.

Figure 6.5 Flavian women, ca. 89 C.E. Marble, life-sized. Elegant hairstyles of this period often involved attaching curls to the front of the head, while the hair in back might be braided and coiled into a bun.

luxury. Indeed, upper-class women were notorious for the luxuries that Rome provided: exquisite jewelry, fine perfumes, and elegant wigs (Figure **6.5**). Although Juvenal's bias against womankind strikes a personal note, it is likely that he was reflecting the public outcry against the licentiousness that was widespread in his own day. Increasingly during the second century, men openly enjoyed concubines, mistresses, and prostitutes. Infidelity among married women was on the rise, and divorce was common, as were second and third marriages for both sexes.

The women of imperial Rome did not have many more civil rights than did their Golden Age Athenian sisters. They could neither vote nor hold public office. However, they did not occupy separate household quarters from males, they could own property, and they were free to manage their own legal affairs. Roman girls were educated along with boys, and most middle-class women could read and write. Some female aristocrats were active in public

Of these creatures to keep her supplied on her northernmost journeys.
But when she's given herself the treatment in full, from the ground
   base
Through the last layer of mud pack, from the first wash to a poultice, 35
What lies under all this—a human face, or an ulcer?

> **Q** **What complaints does Juvenal launch against the women of imperial Rome?**

> **Q** **What does he mean by saying Rome suffers "the evils of long peace"?**

Roman Drama

Roman tragedies were roughly modeled on those of Greece. They were moral and didactic in intent, and their themes were drawn from Greek and Roman history. Theatrical performances in Rome did not share, however, the religious solemnity of those in Greece. Rather, they were a form of entertainment offered along with the public games, known as *ludi*, that marked the major civic festivals. Unlike the rituals and athletic contests of the Greeks, *ludi* featured displays of armed combat and other violent amusements. The nature of these public spectacles may explain why many of the tragedies written to compete with them were bloody and ghoulish in character. The lurid plays of the Stoic writer Seneca drew crowds in Roman times and were to inspire—some 1500 years later—such playwrights as William Shakespeare.

The Romans seem to have preferred comedies to tragedies, for most surviving Roman plays are in the comic genre. Comic writers employed simple plots and broad (often obscene) humor. The plays of Plautus (ca. 250–184 B.C.E.) and Terence (ca. 185–159 B.C.E.) are filled with stock characters, such as the good-hearted prostitute, the shrewish wife, and the clever servant. The characters engage in farcical schemes and broad slapstick action of the kind common to today's television situation comedies. In the comic theater of the Romans, as in Roman culture in general, everyday life took precedence over fantasy, and the real, if imperfect, world was the natural setting for down-to-earth human beings.

The Arts of the Roman Empire

Roman Architecture

Rome's architecture reflected the practical needs of a sprawling empire whose urban centers suffered from the congestion, noise, and filth described by Juvenal. To link the provinces that ranged from the Atlantic Ocean to the Euphrates River, Roman engineers built 50,000 miles of paved roads, many of which are still in use today. The need to house, govern, and entertain large numbers of citizens inspired the construction of tenements, meeting halls, baths, and amphitheaters. Eight- and nine-story tenements provided thousands with cheap (if often rat-infested) housing. Roman bridges and tunnels defied natural barriers, while some eighteen aqueducts brought fresh water to Rome's major cities. The aqueducts, some of which

Science and Technology

45 C.E.	the Romans invent the technique of glassblowing
90 C.E.	a system of aqueducts provides water for the city of Rome
122 C.E.	in Roman Britain, the emperor Hadrian begins construction of a wall to protect against invasion from the north
140 C.E.	the Alexandrian astronomer Ptolemy produces the *Almagest*, which posits a geocentric (earth-centered) universe (and becomes the basis for Western astronomy for centuries)
160 C.E.	Claudius Galen writes over 100 medical treatises (despite errors, they become the basis for Western medical practice for centuries)

delivered well over forty million gallons of water per day to a single site, were the public works that the Romans considered their most significant technological achievement.

Superb engineers, the Romans employed the structural advantages of the arch (the knowledge of which they inherited from the Etruscans) to enclose great volumes of uninterrupted space. The arch constituted a clear technical advance over the post-and-lintel construction used by the Greeks in buildings like the Parthenon (see Figure 5.15). The Romans adapted this structural principle inventively: they placed arches back to back to form a barrel **vault**, at right angles to each other to form a cross or groined vault, and around a central point to form a dome (Figure **6.6**). Roman building techniques reveal a combination of practicality and innovation: the Romans were the first to use concrete (an aggregate of sand, lime, brick-and-stone rubble, and water), a medium that made possible cheap large-scale construction. They laid their foundations with concrete, raised structures with brick, rubble, and stone, and finished exterior surfaces with veneers of marble, tile, bronze, or plaster.

Roman architecture and engineering were considered one and the same discipline. Vitruvius' *Ten Books on Architecture* (see chapter 5), the oldest and most influential work of its kind, includes instructions for hydraulic systems, city planning, and mechanical devices. For the Roman architect, the function of a building determined its formal design. The design of villas, theaters, and temples received the same close attention as that given to hospitals, fortresses, and—as Josephus reveals—military camps. One of Rome's most spectacular large-scale engineering projects is the 900-foot-long Pont du Gard, part of a 25-mile-long aqueduct that brought fresh water to the city of Nîmes in southern France (Figure **6.7**). Built of 6-ton stones and assembled without mortar, the structure reflects the practical function of arches at three levels, the bottom row supporting a bridge and the second row undergirding the top channel, through which water ran by gravity to its destination.

Figure 6.6 Arches and vaults. (**A**) round arch; (**B**) barrel or tunnel vault; (**C**) groin vault; (**D**) arch consisting of voussoirs, wedge-shaped blocks (a,b,c); (**E**) post-and-lintel; (**F**) inside of groin vault; (**G**) dome.

Figure 6.7 Pont du Gard, near Nîmes, France, ca. 20–10 B.C.E. Stone, height 180 ft., length ca. 900 ft.

Figure 6.8 Reconstruction of fourth-century C.E. Rome.

Circus Maximus

Colosseum

Figure 6.9 Colosseum, Rome (aerial view), 70–82 C.E. By its sheer size, this structure, once surfaced with gleaming marble, advertised the power of Rome and its will to serve the pleasures of its huge urban population.

Figure 6.10 Detail from a fourth-century C.E. mosaic portraying a gladiator fighting a wild beast. Gladiatorial contests were introduced in Rome in 264 B.C.E. Most gladiators were criminals, prisoners of war, or slaves. They were trained in special schools. While they often fought to the death, they might be pardoned (or even win their freedom) if they displayed outstanding valor.

The sheer magnitude of such Roman amphitheaters as the Circus Maximus, which seated 200,000 spectators (Figure **6.8**, foreground), and the Colosseum, which covered 6 acres and accommodated 50,000 (Figure **6.9**), is a reminder that during the first century C.E. Rome's population exceeded one million people. By this time, many Romans were the impoverished recipients of relief in the form of wheat and free entertainment, hence the phrase "bread and circuses." The Roman amphitheaters testify to the popular taste for entertainments that included chariot races, mock sea battles, gladiatorial contests, and a variety of brutal blood sports (Figure **6.10**). At the Colosseum, three levels of seating rose above the arena floor. Beneath the floor was a complex of rooms and tunnels from which athletes, gladiators, and wild animals emerged to entertain the cheering crowd. To provide shade from the sun, an awning at the roof level could be extended by means of a system of pulleys. On each level of the exterior, arches were framed by a series of decorative, or engaged, columns displaying the three Greek orders: Doric (at ground level), Ionic, and Corinthian.

The ingenious combination of arch and post-and-lintel structural elements would be widely imitated for centuries, and especially during the Italian Renaissance. More generally, the long-standing influence of this Roman amphitheater is apparent in the design of the modern sports arena.

Roman architectural genius may be best illustrated by the Pantheon, a temple whose structural majesty depends on the combination of Roman technical ingenuity and dramatic spatial design. Dedicated to the seven planetary deities, the Pantheon was built in the early second century C.E. Its monumental exterior—once covered with a veneer of white marble and bronze—features a portico with eight Corinthian columns originally elevated by a flight of stairs that now lie buried beneath the city street (Figure **6.11**). One of the few buildings from Classical antiquity to have remained almost intact, the Pantheon boasts a 19-foot-thick rotunda that is capped by a solid dome consisting of 5000 tons of concrete (see Figure 6.12). The interior of the dome, once painted blue and gold to resemble the vault of heaven, is pierced by a 30-foot-wide

Figure 6.11 Plan and section of the Pantheon.

rotunda

niche

portico   *oculus*

0   100 ft.

oculus, or "eye," that admits light and air (Figure **6.14**). The proportions of the Pantheon observe the Classical principles of symmetry and harmony as described by Vitruvius (see Reading 5.1): the height from the floor to the apex of the dome (143 feet) equals the diameter of the rotunda.

The Pantheon is distinctly Roman in spirit; however, other Roman buildings imitated Greek models. The temple in Nîmes, France, for instance, known as the Maison Carrée, stands like a miniature Greek shrine atop a high podium (Figure **6.15**). A stairway and a colonnaded portico accentuate the single entranceway and give the building a frontal "focus" usually lacking in Greek temples. The Corinthian order (see Figure 5.19) appears in the portico, and engaged columns adorn the exterior wall. The epitome of Classical refinement, the Maison Carrée inspired numerous European and American copies. Indeed, the Virginia State Capitol, designed by Thomas Jefferson, offers clear evidence of the use of Classical models to convey

MAKING CONNECTIONS

Figure 6.12 The Pantheon, Rome, ca. 118–125 C.E.

The Pantheon (Figure **6.12**) has inspired more works of architecture than any other monument in Greco-Roman history. It awed and delighted such eminent late eighteenth-century Neoclassicists as Thomas Jefferson, who used it as the model for many architectural designs, including that of his country estate at Monticello in Charlottesville, Virginia, and the Rotunda of the University of Virginia (Figure **6.13**). Jefferson was faithful to the original plan of the Roman temple, which included the stairway leading up to the portico.

Figure 6.13 THOMAS JEFFERSON, the Rotunda, University of Virginia, Charlottesville, Virginia, 1822–1826.

Figure 6.14 GIOVANNI PAOLO PANINI, *The Interior of the Pantheon*, ca. 1734–1735. Oil on canvas, 4 ft. 2½ in. × 3 ft. 3 in. In its sheer size and its uninterrupted interior space, the Pantheon exceeded any previous temple built in antiquity. The difference between its stolid exterior and its breathtaking cylindrical interior is captured in this eighteenth-century painting, which shows the dramatic effects of the *oculus* "spotlight."

Figure 6.15 Maison Carrée, Nîmes, France, ca. 16 B.C.E.

the dignity, stability, and authority that Neoclassicists associated with the world of Greece and Rome.

If temples such as the Pantheon and the Maison Carrée answered the spiritual needs of the Romans, the baths, such as those named for the emperor Caracalla, satisfied some of their temporal requirements. Elaborate structures fed by natural hot springs (Figure 6.16), the baths provided a welcome refuge from the noise and grime of the city streets. In addition to rooms in which pools of water were heated to varying degrees, such spas often included steam rooms, exercise rooms, art galleries, shops, cafés, reading rooms, and chambers for physical intimacy. Although most baths had separate women's quarters, many permitted mixed bathing. The popularity of the baths is reflected in the fact that by the third century C.E., there were more than 900 of them in the city of Rome.

Roman baths incorporated the **basilica**, a rectangular colonnaded hall commonly used for public assemblies. The basilica was the ideal structure for courts of law, meeting halls, and marketplaces. The huge meeting hall known

Figure 6.16 Great Bath, Roman bath complex, Bath, England, 54 C.E. Part of the finest group of Roman remains in England, this sumptuous pool is still fed by natural hot springs.

apse added by Constantine

barrel-vaulted bays

apse

groin-vaulted nave

original entrance

groin-vaulted porch

barrel-vaulted bays

0   100 ft.   entrance added by Constantine

Figure 6.17 (above) Plan of the Basilica of Maxentius and Constantine.

as the Basilica of Maxentius consisted of a 300-foot-long central nave, four side aisles, and a semicircular recess called an **apse** (Figure **6.17**). The Roman basilica might be roofed by wooden beams or—as in the case of the Basilica of Maxentius (Figures **6.18** and **6.19**)—by gigantic stone vaults. Completed by the emperor Constantine in the fourth century C.E., these enormous vaults rested on brick-faced concrete walls some 20 feet thick. In its floor plan and construction features, the Roman basilica became the model for the Early Christian church in the West.

Figure 6.18 (below) Basilica of Maxentius and Constantine, Rome, begun 306–310 C.E., completed by Constantine after 313 C.E. This basilica was the last and largest of all those commissioned by Rome's emperors. The original central hall (nave) rose to a height of 115 feet. Load-bearing walls 20 feet thick supported the weight of the ceiling. A colossal statue of Constantine (of which only the head remains) once sat in the apse.

Figure 6.19 The Basilica of Maxentius and Constantine.

Roman Sculpture

Like its imperialistic predecessors, Rome advertised its military achievements in monumental public works of art. These consisted mainly of triumphal arches and victory columns, which, like the obelisks of Egyptian pharaohs, commemorated the conquests of strong rulers. The 100-foot-tall marble column erected in 113 C.E. by Emperor Trajan to celebrate his victory over Dacia (present-day Romania) includes 2500 figures—a huge picture scroll carved in brilliant low relief (Figures **6.1** and **6.20**). Here, a documentary vitality is achieved by the piling up of figures in illusionistic space, and by a plethora of realistic details describing Roman military fortifications and weaponry.

The triumphal arch was the landmark image of Roman imperial victory. More rightly classed with sculpture than with architecture, where arches function mainly to enclose interior space, this distinctive structure—made of concrete and faced with marble—served as visual propaganda. Commemorative arches were first erected by Augustus to celebrate his military triumphs. They also functioned as monumental gateways. Some thirty-four, embellished with sculptures and laudatory inscriptions, were raised in Rome; and many more throughout the Empire bear witness to the power and the geographic reach of the Roman state. The Arch of Titus, marking the upper end of the Roman Forum, commemorates the final days of the Jewish Wars (66–70 C.E.) fought by the emperors Vespasian and Titus (Figure **6.21**). The marble-faced concrete vault of the arch

Figure 6.20 Trajan's Victory Column, Rome, 113 C.E. Marble, height (with base) 125 ft. This column is the sole surviving monument of Trajan's Forum, which once included judicial courts, temples, shops, and two library buildings, one for Greek texts and one for Latin texts. The column, a booklike scroll inspired by the (lost) *Commentaries* of Trajan, stood (approximately) between the Greek and Roman libraries.

Figure 6.21 Arch of Titus, Rome, ca. 81 C.E. Marble, height 50 ft., width 40 ft. (approx.). The Latin inscription on the superstructure declares that the Senate and the Roman people (SPQR) dedicate the arch to Titus, son of Vespasian.

Figure 6.22 *The Spoils of Jerusalem.* Relief from the Arch of Titus, Rome, ca. 81 C.E. Marble, height 7 ft. (approx.).

is elevated between two massive piers that bear engaged Corinthian columns and an **attic** or superstructure carrying a commemorative inscription. Narrative relief panels on the interior sides of the vault depict a typical Roman triumphal procession celebrating the destruction of Jerusalem and the pillage of the Temple of Solomon (Figure **6.22**). Crowned with laurel wreaths of victory, Roman soldiers march through a city gate carrying the menorah and other spoils of victory. Subtly carved in various depths from low to high relief, the scene evokes the illusion of deep space. Even in its damaged state, *The Spoils of Jerusalem* remains a vivid record of conquest and triumph. It is the product of an age that depended on realistic narrative relief—as we today depend on photography and film—to document (and immortalize) key historical events.

While triumphal arches served as visual propaganda for Rome's military exploits, monumental sculpture glorified Roman rulers. The statue of Augustus from Primaporta (see Figure 6.4) is one of the best examples of Roman heroic portraiture. It exemplifies the Classical synthesis of realistic detail (most evident in the treatment of the breastplate and toga) and idealized form (obvious in the handsome face and canonic proportions) that dominated official Roman art, including that found on Rome's mass-produced coins.

During the second century C.E., the tradition of heroic portraiture assumed an even more magisterial stamp in the image of the ruler on horseback: the **equestrian** statue (Figure **6.23**). The equestrian portrait of the Roman

Figure 6.23 Equestrian statue of Marcus Aurelius, ca. 173 C.E. Bronze, height 16 ft. 8 in. Piazza del Campidoglio, Rome. This gilded bronze sculpture by an unknown artist escaped destruction because it was thought to represent the emperor Constantine, the first ruler officially to adopt Christianity. In 1997, the original (pictured here) was moved to the Capitoline Museum in Rome. A copy, made from a mold created with computer-generated photographs, now stands in this Roman square.

Figure 6.24 Roman aristocrat holding portrait busts of his ancestors, late first century B.C.E. Marble, height 5 ft. 5 in.

emperor Marcus Aurelius depicts the general addressing his troops with the traditional gesture of imperial authority. The body of a conquered warrior once lay under the raised right hoof of the spirited charger, whose veins and muscles seem to burst from beneath his bronze skin.

While public portrayal of the ruler usually demanded a degree of flattering idealization, images intended for private use invited naturalistic detail. The Roman taste for Realism is perhaps best illustrated in three-dimensional portraits of Roman men and women, often members of the ruling class or wealthy patricians. In contrast to the idealized portraits of Golden Age Greece (see Figure 4.12), many Roman likenesses reflect obsessive fidelity to nature. So true to life seem some Roman portrait heads that scholars suspect they may have been executed from wax death masks. Roman portrait sculpture tends to reflect the personality and character of the sitter, a fact perhaps related to the ancient custom of honoring the "genius" or in-dwelling spirit of the dead ancestor. The lifelike portrait bust of Julius Caesar, carved in green schist with inset crystal eyes, captures the spirit of resolute determination (see Figure 6.3). It is the record of a particular person at a particular time in his life; as such it conveys a degree of psychological Realism absent from most Classical Greek portraits.

In that portrait sculpture served much as our photographs do today—as physical reminders of favorite relatives and friends—the emphasis on Realism is understandable. The balding patrician who carries two portrait busts of his ancestors (Figure **6.24**) reminds us that the Roman family placed extraordinary emphasis on its lineage, honoring the father of the family (*paterfamilias*) no less devotedly than did the ancient Chinese. Such intimate likenesses of the deceased would have been displayed and venerated at special altars and shrines within the Roman home. Roman women were similarly honored: the portrait of the square-jawed aristocratic female, whose wig or hairdo surely required the fastidious application of the curling iron, discloses the proud confidence of a Roman matron (see Figure 6.5). Whether cast in bronze, or carved in marble, slate, or terracotta, these

Figure 6.25 Atrium, House of the Vetii. Pompeii, Italy, first century C.E.

Figure 6.26 *Seated Woman Playing a Kithara*, Roman, Late Republic, ca. 40–30 B.C.E. Villa of P. Fannius Synistor at Boscoreale. The fresco, which decorated a reception hall, belongs to a set that probably celebrated a dynastic marriage. Both figures wear gold diadems and earrings. The red colors, derived from cinnabar and vermilion, were among the most expensive pigments used in Pompeian wall-painting.

psychologically penetrating studies are often as unflattering as they are honest. In their lack of idealization and their affection for literal detail, they reveal Roman sculpture as a record of commonplace reality.

Roman Painting and Mosaics

Pictorial Realism also dominates the frescoes and mosaics with which the Romans decorated their meeting halls, baths, and country villas (see Figures 5.31 and 6.10). Probably inspired by Greek murals, of which only a few examples survive, Roman artists painted scenes drawn from literature, mythology, and daily life. Among the finest examples of Roman frescoes are those found in and around Pompeii and Herculaneum, two southern Italian cities that attracted a population of wealthy Romans. But even in the outer reaches of the Empire, such as at Zeugma in modern Turkey (uncovered as recently as 1992), the Roman taste for visual representation is evident in magnificently decorated palatial villas. Pompeii and Herculaneum

remain the showcases of Roman suburban life: both cities were engulfed by a mountain of ash from the volcanic eruption of Mount Vesuvius in 79 C.E., but the lava from the disaster preserved many of the area's suburban homes. These residential villas, constructed around an **atrium** (a large central hall open to the sky), are valuable sources of information concerning the lifestyles of upper-class Romans (Figure **6.25**).

At a villa in Boscoreale, about a mile north of Pompeii, floors and walls display fine ornamental motifs and scenes illustrated in mosaic, a technique by which small pieces of stone or glass are embedded into wet cement surfaces or plaster surfaces (see Figure 6.10). The walls of some rooms are painted with frescoes designed to give viewers the impression that they are looking out upon gardens and distant buildings. Others show scenes of everyday life. A handsome Roman matron sits on an elegant wooden chair playing a kithara; her daughter stands behind (Figure **6.26**). Both look at us directly, as though we have interrupted a private moment. Light coming from the right illuminates the figures, which, shaded uniformly on the left, assume a true-to-life presence. Illusionism of this kind, known as *trompe l'oeil* ("fool the eye"), makes use of pictorial devices that render a sense of three-dimensional space on a two-dimensional surface. One such device, famously employed by Roman artists, was empirical perspective. Another was the manipulation of light and shade that seduces the eye into believing that it perceives real objects in deep space. In the extraordinary *Still Life with Eggs and Thrushes*, one of a series of frescoes celebrating food, from a villa at Pompeii, light seems to bounce off the metal pitcher, whose shiny surface contrasts with the densely textured towel and the ceramic plate holding ten lifelike eggs (Figure **6.27**). The objects cast shadows to the right, suggesting a light source coming from the left. Roman artists integrated illusionistic devices in ways that would not be seen again in Western art for a thousand years (see chapter 23). The invention of still life as an independent genre (or type) of art confirmed the Roman fondness for the tangible things of everyday life.

Yet another subject, the natural landscape, reflects Rome's attachment to the world of the senses. Although both the Egyptians and the Greeks used natural settings for human activities, it was the Romans who pioneered landscape as a subject in and of itself. First-century B.C.E. frescoes illustrating the adventures of the Greek hero Odysseus feature spacious landscapes filled with rocky plains, feathery trees, animals, and people (Figure **6.28**). Bathed in light and shade, the naturalistically modeled figures cast shadows to indicate their physical presence in atmospheric space.

Roman landscapes show a deep affection for the countryside and for the pleasures of nature. Arcadia, the mountainous region in the central Peloponnesus (inhabited by the peace-loving shepherds and nymphs of ancient Greek legend), provided the model for the Classical landscape. Described by Virgil as a pastoral paradise, it was celebrated in both Greek and Latin **pastoral** poetry as the setting for a life of innocence and simplicity. The glorification of bucolic freedom—the "Arcadian Myth"—reflected the Roman disenchantment with city life and became a recurring theme in the arts of the West, especially during periods of rising urbanization.

Roman Music

While Roman civilization left abundant visual and literary resources, the absence of surviving examples in music makes it almost impossible to evaluate the Roman contribution in this domain. Passages from the writings of Roman historians suggest that Roman music theory was adopted from that of the Greeks, as were most Roman instruments.

Figure 6.27 *Still Life with Eggs and Thrushes*, from the House (or Villa) of Julia Felix, Pompeii, before 79 C.E. Fresco, 35 × 48 in. In contrast to the fresco secco (dry fresco) technique used in ancient Egypt, Roman wall-paintings were executed on freshly laid plaster; pigments were applied to sections while they were still damp. This technique is known as "true fresco."

Figure 6.28 *Odysseus in the Land of the Lestrygonians*, part of the *Odyssey Landscapes*, second-style ("architectural") wall-paintings from a house in Rome, late first century B.C.E. Height 5 ft. (approx.). Illusionism is heightened by way of the shadows cast by the lively figures, and by the foreshortened figure of the sheep (left foreground) that views its own reflection in a pool of water.

In drama, musical interludes replaced the Greek choral odes—a change that suggests the growing distance between drama and its ancient ritual function. Music was, however, essential to most forms of public entertainment and also played an important role in military life; for the latter, the Romans developed brass instruments, such as trumpets and horns, and drums for military processions.

The Fall of Rome

Why and how the mighty Roman Empire came to collapse in the fifth century C.E. has intrigued scholars for centuries. A great many theories have been advanced, ranging from soil exhaustion and lead poisoning to the malaria epidemic of the third century, and the absence of a system

for legitimate succession to the throne. In reality, it is likely that no *one* problem was responsible. Rome's slow decline was probably the result of a combination of internal circumstances: the difficulties of governing so huge an empire, the decline of the slave trade, and the increasing gap between the rich and the poor—during the *Pax Romana*, one-third to one-half of Rome's urban population received some form of public welfare. The Empire's internal problems were made all the worse by repeated barbarian attacks on Rome's borders. The emperors Diocletian (245–316) and Constantine (ca. 274–337) tried, but failed, to arrest the decline. Finally, in 476, a Germanic army commander led a successful attack on Rome and deposed the reigning Roman emperor, Romulus Augustulus. The great Empire had fallen.

The Roman Rise to Empire

- From its Latin beginnings, Rome showed an extraordinary talent for adopting and adapting the best of other cultures: Etruscan and Greek.
- The Romans preserved and transmitted the culture of the Hellenic and Hellenistic world.
- Although the Roman Republic engaged all citizens in government, power rested largely with the wealthy and influential patrician class.
- As Rome built an empire and assumed mastery of the civilized world, the Republic fell increasingly into the hands of military dictators, the greatest of whom was Julius Caesar.
- Caesar's heir, Octavian, ushered in the *Pax Romana*, a time of peace and high cultural productivity.
- Rome's highly disciplined army was the backbone of the Empire.
- The sheer size of the Roman Empire inspired engineering programs, such as bridge and road building, that united all regions under Roman rule. The need to rule a world-state brought about a practical system of law.

The Roman Contribution to Literature

- The Romans produced no original philosophy, but cultivated Hellenistic schools of thought such as Stoicism.
- Roman literature manifests a practical bias for factual information. The Romans gave the world its first encyclopedias, as well as memorable biographies, essays, speeches, histories, and letters.
- The high moral tone and lucid prose of Cicero and Tacitus characterize Latin literature at its best.
- In poetry, Virgil paid homage to the Roman state in the monumental epic the *Aeneid*. Catullus left memorable love lyrics, while Horace and Juvenal both offered a critical view of Roman life in satiric verse.

The Arts of the Roman Empire

- Rome's architectural and engineering projects featured the inventive use of the arch and the techniques of concrete and brick construction. The Romans contributed domed and stone-vaulted types of construction that enclose vast areas of interior space.
- Rome's monumental building projects often served as visual imperial propaganda.
- The Romans imitated and borrowed Hellenic models, but their taste for realistic representation and naturalistic detail dominated relief sculptures, portrait busts, and fresco paintings.
- Roman music theory was adopted from the Greeks, as were most Roman instruments. However, the Romans developed brass instruments, such as trumpets, horns, and drums for military use.

The Fall of Rome

- For almost a thousand years, the Romans ruled a geographically and ethnically diverse realm. Their contribution is imprinted on the language, laws, and architecture of the West.
- The collapse of Rome was hastened by a combination of factors: the overreaching imperial ambitions of its rulers, political and economic problems, and the attacks of Germanic tribes on the borders of the Empire.

Glossary

apse a vaulted semicircular recess at one or both ends of a basilica

atrium the inner courtyard of a Roman house, usually colonnaded and open to the sky

attic the superstructure or low upper story above the main order of a façade

basilica a large colonnaded hall commonly used for public assemblies, law courts, baths, and marketplaces

eclogue a pastoral poem, usually involving shepherds in an idyllic rural setting

epistle a formal letter

equestrian mounted on horseback

imperium (Latin, "command," "empire") the civil and military authority exercised by the rulers of ancient Rome (and the root of the English words "imperialism" and "empire"); symbolized in ancient Rome by an eagle-headed scepter and the *fasces*, an ax bound in a bundle of rods

oratory the art of public speaking

pastoral pertaining to the country, to shepherds, and the simple rural life; also, any work of art presenting an idealized picture of country life

res publica (Latin, "of the people") a government in which power resides in citizens entitled to vote and is exercised by representatives responsible to them and to a body of law

sarcophagus (plural **sarcophagi**) a stone coffin

satire a literary genre that ridicules or pokes fun at human vices and follies

trompe l'oeil (French, "fool the eye") a form of illusionistic painting that tries to convince the viewer that the image is real and not painted

vault a roof or ceiling constructed on the arch principle (see Figure 6.6)

China: The Rise to Empire

ca. 770 B.C.E.–220 C.E.

*"He who learns but does not think is lost.
He who thinks but does not learn is in great danger."*
Confucius

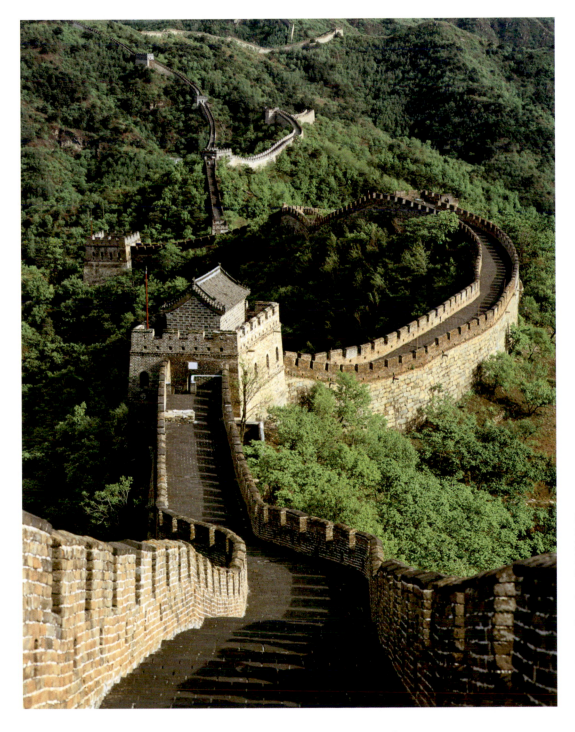

Figure 7.1 The Great Wall, near Beijing, China, begun 214 B.C.E. Length 1500 miles, height and width 25 ft. (approx.). Constructed of rubble and earth, and faced with stone, the Great Wall required a labor force of thousands. Watchtowers and military barracks were situated strategically along the wall, which reached its present extent (seen in this photograph) under Ming rulers in the seventeenth century.

In the thousand-year period (ca. 500 B.C.E. to 500 C.E.) during which Greco-Roman civilization flourished in the West, both China and India* brought forth cultures that were definitive and enduring, hence "classical." China and India each generated a body of learning and an artistic heritage that became the cultural bedrock of their respective countries, and served as models for the rest of East Asia. Their legacies, like those of ancient Greece and Rome, reached beyond their time and place to shape the larger humanistic tradition. The focus of this chapter is classical China. China's dynastic development and its rise to empire offer intriguing parallels with the histories of Greece and Rome. The philosophic traditions of both China and Greece were launched by the great thinkers of the fifth and sixth

centuries B.C.E. Equally interesting is the comparison between Han China and the Roman Empire. These two great empires, located at either end of the Eurasian landmass, brought political stability and cultural unity to vast stretches of territory. Both were profoundly secular in their approach to the world and to the conduct of human beings. Both inherited age-old forms and practices in religion, law, literature, and the arts; these they self-consciously preserved and transmitted to future generations. The classical legacies of China and Rome would come to shape the respective histories of East and West.

---

* India's classical history—the birth of Buddhism and the revival of Hindu culture—is surveyed in chapters 8, 9, and 14.

Confucius and the Classics

The Eastern Zhou Dynasty (ca. 771–256 B.C.E.)

After 771 B.C.E., the Zhou dynasty, which had ruled since 1027 B.C.E., slowly disintegrated. Zhou rulers, who had moved their capital eastward, faced perilous attacks by the nomadic Mongol and Turkic horsemen of Central Asia and increasing warfare between independent Chinese states. Nevertheless, trade and urban life continued to flourish, and China developed some of its most significant and lasting material and philosophic traditions. Chopsticks, cast iron, square-holed coins, and finely lacquered objects were all developed during the sixth century B.C.E. At the same time, and parallel with (but totally independent of) the rise of philosophic thought in Greece, China experienced a burst of intellectual creativity: its classical texts date from this period, and with them came the formulation of some of China's oldest moral and religious precepts.

As we saw in chapter 3, the ancient Chinese regarded the natural order as the basis for spiritual life, political stability (witness the Mandate of Heaven), and the social order. To know one's place within the order and to act accordingly were essential to the well-being of both the individual and the community. The Chinese describe this ethical imperative with the word *li*, which translates variously as "propriety," "ritual," and "arrangement." The original meaning of the word *li* is found in the act of ritual sacrifice, that is, the proper performance of traditional Chinese rites. But by the middle of the Zhou Era, *li* had come to refer to the pattern or principles governing appropriate behavior, or action in conformity with the rules of decorum and civility. Formative in the evolution of this concept were the teachings of the philosopher Kongfuzi (551–479 B.C.E.), better known as Confucius, a Latinization of his Chinese name.

Confucius was China's most notable thinker. According to tradition, he was also the compiler and editor of the "Five Chinese Classics" (see chapter 3 and box). A self-educated man, who served as a local administrator, Confucius pursued the career of a teacher and social reformer. Like his Greek counterpart, Socrates, he himself wrote nothing. He earned renown through the force of his teachings, which his disciples transcribed after his death. This collection of writings came to be known as the *Analects*. As eclectic in origin and dating as the Hebrew Bible, the *Analects* embody the words of Confucius on matters as diverse as music, marriage, and death. But they focus on questions of conduct: the proper behavior of the individual in the society at large. They articulate the ancient Chinese conviction that human beings must heed a moral order that is fixed in nature, not in divine pronouncement. Confucius confidently maintained that human character, not birth, determined the worth and status of the individual. He had little to say about gods and spirits; nor did he speculate on the nature of reality (in the manner of the Greek philosophers). Rather, he taught the importance of tradition, filial piety (respect for one's elders), and the exercise of *li*. In doing so, he formulated the first expression of the so-called Golden Rule: "What you do not wish for yourself, do not do to others."

The Five Chinese Classics*

1 *I jing* (*Book of Changes*)—a text for divination

2 *Shu jing* (*Book of History*)—government records: speeches, reports, and announcements by rulers and ministers of ancient China

3 *Shi jing* (*Book of Songs*)—an anthology of some 300 poems: folk songs, ceremonial and secular poems

4 *Li ji* (*Book of Rites*)—a collection of texts centering on rules of conduct for everyday life

5 *Lushi chunqiu* (*Spring and Autumn Annals*)—commentaries that chronicle events up to the fifth century B.C.E.

*A sixth classic, on music, is no longer in existence

The teachings of Confucius preserved social and political ideas as old as the Shang and Zhou dynasties. In that Confucius lived during the turbulent years just prior to the collapse of the Zhou and the era of the Warring States (ca. 403–221 B.C.E.), he worked to ensure the survival of traditional values. Basic to these ideals was the notion that the ruler was the "parent" of the people. The cultivation of character and the successful regulation of the family preceded the ruler's ability to govern. The good influence and high moral status of the ruler—a figure much like Plato's philosopher-king—was of greater political value than physical force or the threat of punishment. If a ruler was not himself virtuous, he could not expect to inspire virtue among his subjects. For Confucius, as for Plato, moral and political life were one. Moral harmony was the root of political harmony, and moral rectitude made government all but unnecessary. Such precepts were basic to humanist thought in China for well over 2000 years.

READING 7.1 From the *Analects* of Confucius

2.1 The Master said: "He who rules by virtue is like the polestar, which remains unmoving in its mansion while all the other stars revolve respectfully around it."

2.2 The Master said: "The three hundred *Poems* are summed up in one single phrase: 'Think no evil.' "

2.3 The Master said: "Lead them by political maneuvers, restrain them with punishments: the people will become cunning and shameless. Lead them by virtue, restrain them with ritual: they will develop a sense of shame and a sense of participation."

2.13 Zigong asked about the true gentleman. The Master said: "He preaches only what he practices."

2.14 The Master said: "The gentleman considers the whole rather than the parts. The small man considers the parts rather than the whole."

2.15 The Master said: "To study without thinking is futile. To think without studying is dangerous."

2.17 The Master said: "Zilu, I am going to teach you what knowledge is. To take what you know for what you know, and what you do not know for what you do not know, that is knowledge indeed."

2.20 Lord Ji Kang asked: "What should I do in order to make the people respectful, loyal, and zealous?" The Master said: "Approach them with dignity and they will be respectful. Be yourself a good son and a kind father, and they will be loyal. Raise the good and train the incompetent, and they will be zealous."

2.24 The Master said: "To worship gods that are not yours, that is toadyism. Not to act when justice commands, that is cowardice."

4.7 The Master said: "Your faults define you. From your very faults one can know your quality."

4.11 The Master said: "A gentleman seeks virtue; a small man seeks land. A gentleman seeks justice; a small man seeks favors."

4.14 The Master said: "Do not worry if you are without a position; worry lest you do not deserve a position. Do not worry if you are not famous; worry lest you do not deserve to be famous."

4.16 The Master said: "A gentleman considers what is just; a small man considers what is expedient."

4.17 The Master said: "When you see a worthy man, seek to emulate him. When you see an unworthy man, examine yourself."

4.19 The Master said: "While your parents are alive, do not travel afar. If you have to travel, you must leave an address."

4.21 The Master said: "Always keep in mind the age of your parents. Let this thought be both your joy and your worry."

4.24 The Master said: "A gentleman should be slow to speak and prompt to act."

12.16 The Master said: "A gentleman brings out the good that is in people, he does not bring out the bad. A vulgar man does the opposite."

12.21 Fan Chi was taking a walk with Confucius under the Rain Dance Terrace. He said: "May I ask how one can accumulate moral power, neutralize hostility, and recognize emotional incoherence?" The Master said: "Excellent question! Always put the effort before the reward: is this not the way to accumulate moral power? To attack evil in itself and not the evil that is in people: is this not the way to neutralize hostility? To endanger oneself and one's kin in a sudden fit of anger: is this not an instance of incoherence?"

15.6 Zizhang asked about conduct. The Master said: "Speak with loyalty and good faith, act with dedication and deference, and even among the barbarians your conduct will be irreproachable. If you speak without loyalty and good faith, if you act without dedication or deference, your conduct will be unacceptable, even in your own village. Wherever you stand, you should have this precept always in front of your eyes; have it carved upon the yoke of your chariot, and only then will you be able to move ahead." Zizhang wrote it on his sash.

15.8 The Master said: "When dealing with a man who is capable of understanding your teaching, if you do not teach him, you waste the man. When dealing with a man who is incapable of understanding your teaching, if you do teach him, you waste your teaching. A wise teacher wastes no man and wastes no teaching."

15.9 The Master said: "A righteous man, a man attached to humanity, does not seek life at the expense of his humanity; there are instances where he will give his life in order to fulfill his humanity."

15.12 The Master said: "A man with no concern for the future is bound to worry about the present."

15.13 The Master said: "The fact remains that I have never seen a man who loved virtue as much as sex."

15.15 The Master said: "Demand much from yourself, little from others, and you will prevent discontent."

15.18 The Master said: "A gentleman takes justice as his basis, enacts it in conformity with the ritual, expounds it with modesty, and through good faith, brings it to fruition. This is how a gentleman proceeds."

15.19 The Master said: "A gentleman resents his incompetence; he does not resent his obscurity."

15.20 The Master said: "A gentleman worries lest he might disappear from this world without having made a name for himself."

15.21 The Master said: "A gentleman makes demands on himself; a vulgar man makes demands on others."

15.24 Zigong asked: "Is there any single word that could guide one's entire life?" The Master said: "Should it not be *reciprocity*? What you do not wish for yourself, do not do to others."

Q What aspects of moral conduct occupy Confucius in the *Analects*?

Q What do the *Analects* reveal about ancient Chinese values?

Confucianism and Legalism

The two centuries following the death of Confucius marked an era of social upheaval inflicted by the armies of China's warring states. *Bing Fa* (*The Art of War*), the world's oldest treatise on military strategy, reflects the spirit of the age. Probably written between 500 and 400 B.C.E., and attributed to Sun Wu, this Chinese classic, which deals with the tactical as well as the psychological aspects of combat—including the use of spies—was prized by China's rulers and by later military strategists, including Napoleon and Winston Churchill.

The instability of the era of the Warring States generated competing schools of thought concerning human nature and, by extension, the ideal form of government. Such speculation took place among the class of China's scholars, who, much like Aristotle, took a practical approach to the investigation of morality. Mencius (372–289 B.C.E.), China's most significant voice after Confucius, expanded Confucian concepts of government as a civilizing force and the ruler as the moral model. Mencius held that human beings are born good; they fall into evil only by neglect or abuse. In defining human nature, Mencius insisted:

> The tendency of human nature to do good is like that of water to flow downward. There is no man who does not tend to do good; there is not water that does not flow downward. Now you may strike water and make it splash over your forehead, or you may even force it up the hills. But is this in the nature of water? It is of course due to the force of circumstances. Similarly, man may be brought to do evil, and that is because the same is done to his nature.

Based on this view of humankind, Mencius envisioned the state as an agent for cultivating the goodness of the individual.

An opposing body of thought challenged this point of view. In contrast to the Confucians, who generally perceived humankind as good, those who came to be called Legalists described the nature of humankind as inherently evil. From this negative premise, the Legalists concluded that the best state was one in which rulers held absolute authority to uphold (strict) laws and dole out punishment to violators. The leading Legalist, Han Fei Zi (?–233 B.C.E.), argued that the rationality of an adult was no more reliable than that of an infant. The innate selfishness of humankind justified strong central authority and harsh punishment. "Now take a young fellow who is a bad character," he writes:

> His parents may get angry at him, but he never makes any change. The villagers may reprove him, but he is not moved. His teachers and elders may admonish him, but he never reforms. The love of his parents, the efforts of the villagers, and the wisdom of his teachers and elders . . . are applied to him, and yet not even a hair on his chin is altered. It is only after the district magistrate sends out his soldiers and in the name of the law searches for wicked individuals that the young man becomes afraid and changes his ways and alters his deeds. So while the love of parents is not sufficient to discipline the children, the severe penalties of the district magistrate are. This is because men become naturally spoiled by love, but are submissive to authority.

The Legalism of Han Fei would become the fundamental philosophy of China's first empire.

The Chinese Rise to Empire

The Qin Dynasty (221–206 B.C.E.)

Even as the great Roman *imperium* came to dominate the Western world, a comparable empire arose on the eastern end of the vast Asian landmass. The first great period of unity in China came about under the Qin (pronounced "chin"), the dynasty from which the English word "China" derives. By the fifth century B.C.E., the different autonomous states into which the Zhou realm had dissolved were in open warfare, vying with one another for supremacy. In 221 B.C.E., King Zheng (ca. 259–210 B.C.E.) of the state of Qin finally succeeded in conquering all the other rival states, unifying their domains under his rule. He declared himself "First Emperor" (Shi Huang Di), and—like the first Roman emperor, Augustus—immediately set about eliminating the possibility of further conflict. Like the Shang and Zhou kings, the Qin emperors held absolute responsibility for maintaining order and harmony. However, the First Emperor took the additional step of replacing the old system of governing based on a landowning aristocracy with a new imperial government centered on his capital, Xianyang (near present-day Xi'an), and organized into a network of provinces and districts governed by nonhereditary officials. By way of these governors, the Qin enforced the laws, collected taxes, and drafted men to defend the newly annexed regions of their former rival states.

This large, salaried bureaucracy worked to centralize political power by various administrative devices. These included a census of China's population (the first of its kind in world history), the standardization of the written Chinese language, the creation of uniform coinage, as well as a system of weights and measures, and the division of China into administrative provinces that exist more or less intact to this day. In a practical move worthy of the Romans, the First Emperor standardized the width of all axles manufactured for Chinese wagons, so that the wagons would fit the existing ruts in Chinese roads (thus speeding travel and trade). Royal promotion of the silk industry attracted long-distance merchants and brought increasing wealth to China; the Romans called the Chinese the Seres ("Silk People"). While imperial policies fostered the private ownership of land by peasant farmers, the new system permitted the governors to tax those farmers, which they did mercilessly. Peasant protest was a constant threat to imperial power, but the most serious challenge to Qin safety came from the repeated invasions by the nomadic Central Asian peoples along China's northern borders. To discourage invasion, the Qin commissioned the construction of the then roughly 3000-mile-long Great Wall, which stretched from northeast to northwest China (see Map 3.2 and Figure 7.1). This spectacular feat of engineering may be compared with the defensive wall built by the Roman emperor Hadrian: Hadrian's Wall, only 73 miles long, would be raised in the early second century C.E. in an effort to deter barbarian attacks on Roman Britain's northernmost border. Like Hadrian's Wall, the Great Wall of China could not stop an army on foot; rather, it discouraged mounted men, wagons, and the like from making raids across the borders.

The building of the Great Wall required the labor of some 700,000 people. An equal number of workers is said to have labored for eleven years on the emperor's tomb. The entrance to that tomb, part of a 21-square-mile burial site near the Qin capital, provides an immortal record of the Qin military machine. It contains almost 8000 life-sized **terracotta** soldiers, most of which are armed with actual swords, spears, and crossbows (Figure **7.2**).

Standing at strict attention, the huge army of foot soldiers and cavalry guards the tomb itself, which has not yet been excavated. These figures may have served to replace the living sacrifices that went into the graves of the Shang kings (see chapter 3). The bodies of the ceramic warriors were mass-produced from molds, but the faces, no two of which are exactly alike, were individually carved and brightly painted (Figure **7.3**). In their lifelike intensity, these images resemble Roman portrait busts (see Figure 6.3). But while the latter honored the dead among the living, the Chinese figures were designed to serve the dead in the afterlife. Nevertheless, the subterranean legions of the First Emperor glorify an armed force that the Romans might have envied.

Legalist theory provided justification for the stringency of the law under the Qin, as well as for the civil and political oppressiveness of imperial authority. The Legalist First Emperor so feared public opposition and the free exercise of thought that he required all privately owned copies of the Confucian classics burned and all who opposed his government beheaded, along with their families. These policies, compounded by the oppressive taxes levied to pay for imperial projects, brought the Qin Empire to its end.

The Han Dynasty (206 B.C.E.–220 C.E.)

The Qin dynasty survived only fifteen years, but the succeeding Han Empire would last more than four centuries. Just as the Roman Empire marked the culmination of Classical civilization in the West, so the Han dynasty represented the high point and the classical phase of Chinese civilization. The intellectual and cultural achievements of the Han also made an indelible mark on the history of neighboring Korea, Vietnam, and Japan, whose cultures adopted Chinese methods of writing and the Confucian precepts of filial piety and propriety. The Chinese have long regarded the era of the Han as their classical age, and to this day refer to themselves as the "children of the Han." Han intellectual achievements ranged from the literary and artistic to the domains of **cartography**, medicine, mathematics, and astronomy. The invention of paper, block printing, the seismograph, the crossbow, the horse collar, and the wheelbarrow are but a few of the technological advances of the late Han era.

Han rulers tripled the size of the empire they inherited from the Qin. At its height, the Han Empire was roughly equivalent to that of Rome in power and prestige, but

Science and Technology

350 B.C.E.	Shin Shen completes a catalog of some 800 stars
300 B.C.E.	cast iron is produced in China
250 B.C.E.	the crossbow is invented in China
214 B.C.E.	the First Emperor orders construction to begin on the Great Wall (which will not take its final form until the seventeenth century)

Figure 7.2 Terracotta army of soldiers, horses, and chariots, tomb of the First Emperor of the Qin dynasty, 221–206 B.C.E. Some 1000 figures of the 8000 have been excavated. They were painted with earth pigments of green, black, white, and red. Recently, however, conservators identified the unique synthetic compound called "Chinese purple," used in painting the uniforms of some ceramic warriors. This rare pigment was a mark of royalty and wealth.

larger in actual population—a total of 57 million people, according to the census of 2 C.E. (Map **7.1**). Improvements in farming and advances in technology insured economic prosperity, which in turn stimulated vigorous long-distance trade. In exchange for Western linen, wool, glass, and metalware, the Chinese exported silk, ivory, gems, and spices. Spices were essentials in the ancient world, serving not only to flavor food, but also as drugs, perfumes, preservatives, and anesthetics. Trade proceeded by way of Asian intermediaries, who led camel caravans along the vast "Silk Road" that stretched from Asia Minor to the Pacific Ocean. Trade with the peoples of the Silk Road was brought to its height by the great Han emperor Wudi (140–86 B.C.E.). Impressed with the superior mobility of West Asian peoples, he launched military campaigns to capture the large and sturdy steeds the Chinese called "Celestial Horses" (Figure **7.4**). Bred thereafter by the Han, these horses became status symbols for rich merchants and administrators.

In accordance with Confucian thought, China traditionally scorned its merchants (who were perceived as profiting from the labor of others) and regarded its farmers as

Figure 7.3 Terracotta soldier, tomb of the First Emperor of the Qin dynasty, 221–86 B.C.E. Height 4 ft. Carrying bronze and iron weapons, kneeling and standing alongside terracotta horses and actual chariots, the army of the First Emperor of China guarded his tomb.

Map 7.1 Han and Roman Empires, ca. 180 C.E. The Roman Empire reached its height by 180 C.E. Two hundred years earlier, Han emperors had extended their authority throughout most of Central Asia and eastward into Korea.

honorable. Nevertheless, while Chinese merchants flourished, Chinese peasants failed to reap the benefits of Han prosperity. Conscripted for repeated wars, they fought the nomadic tribes along the bitterly cold northern frontier. They also served in the armies that conquered western Korea and northern Vietnam. Heavy taxes levied on Chinese farmers to support the Han machinery of state forced many to sell their lands. Wealthy landowners purchased these lands, on which (in a manner reminiscent of the late Roman Republic) bankrupt farmers became tenants or unfree peasants. By the early third century, violent peasant revolts accompanied by "barbarian" incursions led to the overthrow of the Han dynasty. Like the Roman Empire, the great Han Empire fell victim to internal and external pressures it could not withstand.

Science and Technology

150 B.C.E.	iron wheels are designed for shaping jade and reeling silk
110 B.C.E.	the Chinese devise the collar harness (for horses)
100 B.C.E.	the Chinese invent the crank (for turning wheels)
1 B.C.E.	cast iron is used in Chinese suspension bridges

Figure 7.4 Prancing horse, Eastern Han dynasty, second century C.E. Bronze, 13 × 10 in (approx.). The Chinese believed the larger and finer horses of Central Asia were descendants of celestial horses. They were reported to sweat blood, a condition that may have been caused by parasitic infections that caused swellings that burst and bled.

The Literary Contributions of Imperial China

Just as the Romans borrowed the best of the cultural achievements that preceded them, so Han rulers preserved the enduring works of their forebears. These they passed on to future generations as a body of classical learning and thought. Where the Qin rulers had preferred Legalist thought, the Han emperors restored Confucianism to its place at the heart of China's intellectual traditions, and with it came the restoration of Confucian texts and the Confucian scholar/official.

Chinese Prose Literature

The Chinese placed high value on record keeping: the writing of history was one of China's greatest achievements. According to tradition, Chinese court historians kept chronicles of events as far back as 1000 years before the Han Era. Unfortunately, many of these chronicles were lost in the wars and notorious "book-burnings" of the Qin Era. Beginning with the second century B.C.E., however, palace historians kept a continuous record of rulership. Ancient China's greatest historian, Sima Qian (145–90 B.C.E.), the rival of both Thucydides and Livy, produced the monumental *Shi ji* (*Records of the Grand Historian*), a narrative account of Chinese history from earliest times through the lifetime of the author. Sima Qian, himself the son of a palace historian-astronomer, served at the court of the emperor Wudi. After Sima's death, China's first woman historian, Ban Zhao (45–114 C.E.), continued his court chronicle. Ban also won fame for her handbook *Lessons for Women*, which outlined the obligations and duties of the wife to her husband.

The following excerpt from Sima Qian's chapter on "Wealth and Commerce" offers a detailed description of the Han economy, as well as its social and moral life. Whereas economic activity follows the natural order, morals, observes the author, "come as the effects of wealth." In Sima's view, wealth and virtue are interdependent. A flourishing economy will encourage the people to be virtuous, while poverty leads inevitably to moral decay. Stylistically, Sima Qian's *Records* display the economy and vigor of expression that characterize the finest Han prose.

READING 7.2 From Sima Qian's *Records of the Grand Historian* (ca. 100 B.C.E.)

I do not know about prehistoric times before Shennong,[1] but since [Emperor Yu and the Xia dynasty, after the] twenty-second century B.C.E. during the period discussed by the historical records, human nature has always struggled for good food, dress, amusements, and physical comfort, and has always tended to be proud of wealth and ostentation. No matter 1

how the philosophers may teach otherwise, the people cannot be changed. Therefore, the best of men leave it alone, and next in order come those who try to guide it, then those who moralize about it, and then those who try to make adjustments to it, and lastly come those who get into the scramble themselves. Briefly, Shanxi produces timber, grains, linen, ox hair, and jades. Shandong produces fish, salt, lacquer, silks, and musical instruments. Jiangnan [south of the Yangzi] produces cedar, *zi* [a hard wood for making wood blocks], ginger, cinnamon, gold and tin ores, cinnabar, rhinoceros horn, tortoise shell, pearls, and hides. Longmen produces stone for tablets. The north produces horses, cattle, sheep, furs, and horns. As for copper and iron, they are often found in mountains everywhere, spread out like pawns on a chessboard. These are what the people of China like and what provide the necessities for their living and for ceremonies for the dead. The farmers produce them, the wholesalers bring them from the country, the artisans work on them, and the merchants trade on them. All this takes place without the intervention of government or of the philosophers. Everybody exerts his best and uses his labor to get what he wants. Therefore prices seek their level, cheap goods going to where they are expensive and higher prices are brought down. People follow their respective professions and do it on their own initiative. It is like flowing water which seeks the lower level day and night without stop. All things are produced by the people themselves without being asked and transported to where they are wanted. Is it not true that these operations happen naturally in accord with their own principles? *The Book of Zhou*[2] says, "Without the farmers, food will not be produced; without the artisans, industry will not develop; without the merchants, the valuable goods will disappear; and without the wholesalers, there will be no capital and the natural resources of lakes and mountains will not be opened up." Our food and our dress come from these four classes, and wealth and poverty vary with the size of these sources. On a larger scale, it benefits a country, and on a smaller scale, it enriches a family. These are the inescapable laws of wealth and poverty. The clever ones have enough and to spare, while the stupid ones have not enough. . . . 10 20 30 40

Therefore, first the granaries must be full before the people can talk of culture. The people must have sufficient food and good dress before they can talk of honor. The good customs and social amenities come from wealth and disappear when the country is poor. Even as fish thrive in a deep lake and the beasts gravitate toward a deep jungle, so the morals of mankind come as effects of wealth. The rich acquire power and influence, while the poor are unhappy and have no place to turn to. This is even truer of the barbarians. Therefore it is said: "A wealthy man's son does not die in the marketplace," and it is not an empty saying. It is said: 50

> The world hustles
>   Where money beckons.
> The world jostles 60
>   Where profit thickens.

---

[1] A legendary cultural hero, inventor of agriculture and commerce, ca. 2737 B.C.E.

[2] The book of documents devoted to the Zhou dynasty (1111–221 B.C.E.)

Even kings and dukes and the wealthy gentry worry about poverty. Why wonder that the common people and the slaves do the same? . . .

[Here follows a long section on the economic products and conditions and the people's character and way of living of the different regions.]

Therefore you see the distinguished scholars who argue at courts and temples about policies and talk about honesty and self-sacrifice, and the mountain recluses who achieve a great reputation. Where do they go? They seek after the rich. The honest officials acquire wealth as time goes on, and the honest merchants become wealthier and wealthier. For wealth is something which man seeks instinctively without being taught. You see soldiers rush in front of battle and perform great exploits in a hail of arrows and rocks and against great dangers, because there is a great reward. You see young men steal and rob and commit violence and dig up tombs for treasures, and even risk the punishments by law, throwing all considerations of their own safety to the winds—all because of money. The courtesans of Zhao and Zheng dress up and play music and wear long sleeves and pointed dancing shoes. They flirt and wink, and do not mind being called to a great distance, irrespective of the age of the men—all are attracted by the rich. The sons of the rich dress up in caps and carry swords and go about with a fleet of carriages just to show off their wealth. The hunters and the fishermen go out at night, in snow and frost, roam in the wooded valleys haunted by wild beasts, because they want to catch game. Others gamble, have cockfights, and match dogs in order to win. Physicians and magicians practice their arts in expectation of compensation for their services. Bureaucrats play hide-and-seek with the law and even commit forgery and falsify seals at the risk of penal sentences because they have received bribes. And so all farmers, artisans, and merchants and cattle raisers try to reach the same goal. Everybody knows this, and one hardly ever hears of one who works and declines pay for it. . . .

Q What is Sima Qian's attitude toward wealth?

Q Based on this reading, how might one describe second-century B.C.E. Chinese society?

Sima Qian's narrative describes the men and women of the Han Era as practical and this-worldly—in fact, as remarkably similar to Romans. This sensibility, which unites a typically Chinese holism with sober realism, is also visible in the large body of Confucianist essays from the Han period. Of these, only one brief example may be cited, for its similarity to the rationalism of Seneca, Lucretius, and other Roman thinkers is striking. *A Discussion of Death* by Wang Chong (17–100 C.E.), offers a skeptical view of the supernaturalism that attracted the vast majority of Chinese people. Wang writes:

Before a man is born he has no consciousness, so when he dies and returns to this original unconscious state how could he still have consciousness? The reason a man is intelligent and understanding is that

he possesses the forces of the five virtues [humanity, righteousness, decorum, wisdom, and faith]. The reason he possesses these is that he has within him the five organs [heart, liver, stomach, lungs, and kidneys]. If these five organs are unimpaired, a man has understanding, but if they are diseased, then he becomes vague and confused and behaves like a fool or an idiot. When a man dies, the five organs rot away and the five virtues no longer have any place to reside. Both the seat and the faculty of understanding are destroyed. The body must await the vital force [*qi*] before it is complete, and the vital force must await the body before it can have consciousness. Nowhere is there a fire that burns all by itself. How then could there be a spirit with consciousness existing without a body?

Chinese Poetry

The writing of poetry has a long and rich history in China. While China's *Book of Songs* drew on an ancient oral tradition (see chapter 3), the poems of the Han Era originated as written works—a circumstance that may have been encouraged by the Chinese invention of paper. Chinese poetry is striking in its simplicity and its refinement. Humanism and common sense are fundamental to Han poetic expression, and Han verse seems to have played an indispensable part in everyday life. As with Greek and Roman lyrics, Chinese poetry took the form of hymns and ritual songs accompanied by the lute or other stringed instruments. Poems served as entertainments for various occasions, such as banquets, and as expressions of affection that were often exchanged as gifts. In contrast with the Greco-Roman world, however, the Chinese produced neither epics nor heroic poems. Their poetry does not so much glorify individual prowess or valorous achievement as it meditates on human experience. Han poetry, much of which takes the form of the "prose-poem," is personal and intimate rather than moralizing and eulogistic. Even in cases where the poem is the medium for social or political complaint, it is more a mirror of the poet's mood than a vehicle of instruction. Notable too is the large number of female poets among the Chinese. The four poems that follow (translated by Burton Watson) are drawn from the

Science and Technology

70 C.E.	China begins building the Grand Canal (eventually 600 miles long)
90 C.E.	the Chinese invent a winnowing device that separates grain from the chaff
100 C.E.	the first insecticide is produced from dried chrysanthemums in China
105 C.E.	cellulose-based paper is first produced in China
132 C.E.	Zhang Heng invents a seismometer that detects the direction of earthquakes

vast corpus of Han poetry. They have been selected not only for their lyric beauty, but also as expressions of some of the deepest concerns of Han poets, such as the practice of bestowing women upon neighboring tribes as "conciliatory" gifts and the conscription of laborers for public works projects. The perceptive reader should discover a number of interesting parallels, as well as contrasts, between these poems and those of the Greeks Sappho and Pindar, and the Romans Virgil, Horace, and Juvenal.

READING 7.3 A Selection of Han Poems

Song of Sorrow

My family has married me   1
   in this far corner of the world,
sent me to a strange land,
   to the king of the Wu-sun.
A yurt[1] is my chamber,   5
   felt is my walls,
flesh my only food,[2]
   kumiss[3] to drink.
My thoughts are all of my homeland,
my heart aches within.   10
Oh to be the yellow crane
   winging home again!

Liu Xijun, ca. 107 B.C.E.

Song: I Watered My Horse at the Long Wall Caves

I watered my horse at the Long Wall caves,   1
water so cold it hurt his bones;
I went and spoke to the Long Wall boss:
"We're soldiers from Tai-yuan—will you keep us here forever?"
"Public works go according to schedule—   5
swing your hammer, pitch your voice in with the rest!"
A man'd be better off to die in battle
than eat his heart out building the Long Wall!
The Long Wall—how it winds and winds,
winds and winds three thousand li;[4]   10
here on the border, so many strong boys;
in the houses back home, so many widows and wives.
I sent a letter to my wife:
"Better remarry than wait any longer—
serve your new mother-in-law with care   15
and sometimes remember the husband you once had."
In answer her letter came to the border:
"What nonsense do you write me now?
Now when you're in the thick of danger,
how could I rest by another man's side?"   20
(HE) If you bear a son, don't bring him up!

---

[1] A circular tent of felt and skins on a framework of poles, the common habitation of the nomads of Mongolia.
[2] Meat was a staple of the Mongol diet.
[3] The fermented milk of a horse, mule, or donkey.
[4] A *li* equals approximately one-third of a mile.

But a daughter—feed her good dried meat.
Only *you* can't see, here by the Long Wall,
the bones of the dead men heaped about!
(SHE) I bound up my hair and went to serve you;   25
   constant constant was the care of my heart.
Too well I know your borderland troubles;
and I—can I go on like this much longer?

Chen Lin (d. 217 C.E.)

Two Selections from *Nineteen Old Poems of the Han*

I turn the carriage, yoke and set off,   1
far, far, over the never-ending roads.
In the four directions, broad plain on plain;
east wind shakes the hundred grasses.
Among all I meet, nothing of the past;   5
what can save us from sudden old age?
Fullness and decay, each has its season;
success—I hate it, so late in coming!
Man is not made of metal or stone;
how can he hope to live for long?   10
Swiftly he follows in the wake of change.
A shining name—let that be the prize!

Anonymous, late second century C.E.

Man's years fall short of a hundred;   1
a thousand years of worry crowd his heart.
If the day is short and you hate the long night,
why not take the torch and go wandering?
Seek out happiness in season;   5
who can wait for the coming year?
Fools who cling too fondly to gold
earn no more than posterity's jeers.
Prince Qiao,[5] that immortal man—
small hope we have of matching him!   10

Anonymous, late second century C.E.

Q   **What personal sentiments are expressed in each of these poems?**

Q   **How do these poems compare with those of Sappho, Catullus, and Horace (Readings 5.2, 6.6, and 6.7)?**

The Visual Arts and Music

Because the Chinese built primarily in the impermanent medium of wood, nothing remains of the palaces and temple structures erected during the Han Era, and therefore no monumental architecture survives from China's classical period comparable to that of Rome. Such engineering projects as the Great Wall, however, testify to the high level of Qin and Han building skills.

    Some idea of Chinese architecture is provided by the polychromed, glazed earthenware models of traditional multistoried buildings—houses surmounted by

---

[5] According to Chinese legend, a prince who became an immortal spirit.

watchtowers—that are found in Chinese tombs. In the four-story replica fronted by a courtyard (Figure **7.5**), the middle two stories would have been occupied by the family. All levels of the building were roofed by projecting eaves that would become typical of East Asian architecture (see Figure 14.21).

China's royal tombs were replicas of the imperial palace, which was laid out according to a cosmological model: the central building was symmetrical and bisected by a north–south axis. Its foundation was square, symbolizing the earth (*Kun*), and its roof was round, symbolizing Heaven (*Tian*). The plan for tombs, palaces, and cities adhered to the ancient Chinese practice of **feng shui**, by which one seeks to adjust the physical environment in accordance with the five elements (see chapter 3), universal energy (*qi*), and balance (*yin/yang*). The invention of the magnetic compass (see Science and Technology box, page 178) made it possible to bring these "laws of heaven" into conjunction with the needs of the human being. Similar to the Hellenic quest for harmonious proportion, this cosmological practice was less an effort to idealize nature than a means of embracing the natural order. Han royal tombs (many of which still await excavation) held the bodies of rulers and their families, often encased in jade shrouds (Figure **7.6**) and surrounded by their servants. Stone entrances with carved designs combine scenes of everyday life and ritual ceremonies with a variety of protective symbols, all of which reflect the theme of immortality (Figure **7.7**).

Like their forebears, the Han excelled in bronze casting: bronze chariots, horses (see Figure 7.4), weapons, mirrors, and lamps (Figure **7.8**) are found in royal burial tombs. Han craftspeople also produced exquisite works in jade and gold, lacquered wood, and silk. But it is in the medium of terracotta—glazed for durability—that the Han left a record of daily life almost as detailed as that found in ancient Egyptian tombs. Scenes of threshing, baking, juggling, music-making, game-playing, and other everyday

Figure 7.5 Tomb model of a house, Eastern Han dynasty, first century C.E. Earthenware with unfired pigments, 52 × 33½ × 27 in. The surface of the exterior is ornamented with geometric designs; to the courtyard exterior, the artist has added trees occupied by birds.

Figure 7.6 Shroud, from the tomb of Liu Sheng at Lingshan, Mancheng, Hebei province, Han dynasty, 206 B.C.E.–24 C.E. Jade and gold wire, length 6 ft. 2 in. Found resting in a lacquered coffin in a cliffside tomb excavated in 1968, the deceased wore a shroud consisting of some 2000 jade wafers (sewn together with golden thread), thought to protect the body from decay and assist in achieving immortality.

Science and Technology

140 C.E. early Chinese compass devised with magnetic silver that always points north–south

190 C.E. Chinese mathematicians use powers of ten to express numbers

200 C.E. the double-yoke harness is invented in China

220 C.E. Chinese make ink from lampblack for early block printing

270 C.E. Chinese alchemists create gunpowder

302 C.E. the stirrup is depicted for the first time in Chinese art

Figure 7.8 Lamp held by kneeling servant-girl. Gilt bronze, height 19 in. From the tomb of Tou Wan (died ca. 113 B.C.E.), Man-ch'eng, Hopei, People's Republic of China. Western Han dynasty. The sleeve and arm of the kneeling servant cleverly become the chimney of this elegant lamp, which was found in the tomb of a Han princess.

Figure 7.7 Reliefs on tomb entrance, Eastern Han dynasty, 25–220 C.E. Stone, height 4ft. (approx.). The top register of the lintel depicts a lively procession of chariots and horses. Beneath are scenes of hunting, while on each side of the portal, figures with weapons and winged ancestral spirits protect the chamber. On the doors appear (top to bottom) phoenixes (symbols of resurrection), beast masks, and raging unicorns.

Figure 7.9 Bells from the tomb of the Marquis Yi of Zeng, Hubei province, fifth century B.C.E. Bronze, height of largest nearly 5 ft.

activities appear routinely in three-dimensional polychromed ceramic models recovered from Han funerary chambers. The Han nobility spent so much money on tomb furnishings that the emperors issued edicts to curb excess.

The technical and aesthetic achievements of the Han in the visual arts seem to have been matched in music. Han rulers established an Office of Music in charge of collecting China's folk music—it continued to operate until 1914. They continued the centuries-old practice of burying bronze bells in royal tombs, the most spectacular example of which comes from the late Zhou Era. A set of sixty-five bells, seven large **zithers**, two panpipes, three transverse flutes, three drums, and other musical instruments accompanied the fifth-century B.C.E. Marquis Yi of Zeng to his grave (Figure **7.9**). The instruments (along with the bodies of eight young women and a dog) occupied a subterranean room that replicated the great hall of a palace. Each bell can produce two notes (depending on where the bell is struck), and the name of each note is inscribed in gold on the bell. A set of bells was thus able to range over several octaves, each containing up to ten notes. Whether the bells were used in ceremonial, ritual, or secular events is unclear, but other evidence of other sorts, such as the bronze buckle with dancers holding cymbals (Figure **7.10**), suggests the Han enjoyed a variety of musical entertainments.

Figure 7.10 Buckle ornament with dancers, Western Han dynasty, 206 B.C.E.–8 C.E. Gilt bronze, 4¾ × 7¼ in.

Confucius and the Classics

- During the fifth century B.C.E., Confucius, China's leading thinker, articulated the fundamental rules of proper conduct and proper behavior, which, along with the "Five Chinese Classics," came to provide the basis for Chinese education and culture.
- The two centuries following the death of Confucius brought about an opposing body of thought called Legalism, which challenged Confucius' teachings by describing the nature of humankind as inherently evil.

The Chinese Rise to Empire

- The short-lived, militant Qin dynasty created China's first unified empire. Qin emperors embraced the harsh principles of Legalism, rather than the humanistic teachings of Confucius.
- The Han tripled the size of the empire, which rivaled that of Rome in size and power.
- Han rulers played a vital part in establishing China's classical culture. Over a period of 400 years, an educated bureaucracy revived the teachings of Confucius, while a healthy economy encouraged long-distance trade between East and West.
- Such inventions as the crossbow, the magnetic compass, gunpowder, and paper testify to the high level of Chinese technology.

The Literary Contributions of Imperial China

- Han China produced a body of literature that displays a this-worldly affection for nature and a passion for the good life.
- Ancient China's greatest historian, Sima Qian, wrote the monumental *Shi ji*, a narrative account of Chinese history from earliest times through the lifetime of the author.
- Chinese poetry is striking in its simplicity and its refinement. Humanism and common sense are fundamental to Han poetic expression.

The Visual Arts and Music

- Because the Chinese built primarily in wood, nothing remains of the palaces and temple structures of the Han Era; yet some idea of ancient Chinese architecture is provided by the Great Wall and by earthenware models of traditional buildings.
- China's royal tombs were laid out according to a cosmological model: the central building was symmetrical and bisected by a north–south axis. Its foundation was square, symbolizing the earth, and its roof was round, symbolizing Heaven.
- Grave goods in Han royal tombs reflect China's excellence in bronze casting, silk weaving, jade carving, and the arts of ceramics and lacquered wood. These items, along with spices and other goods, were traded on the Silk Road that stretched from East Asia to the Mediterranean.
- Ancient China's achievements in the visual arts were probably matched in music, as evidenced by the number and variety of musical instruments found in imperial tombs.

Glossary

cartography the art of making maps or charts

feng shui (Chinese, "wind-water") the practice of arranging the physical environment in accordance with the five elements, the balance of nature (*yin/yang*), and universal energy (*qi*)

li (Chinese, "propriety", "ritual," or "arrangement") originally, the proper performance of ritual, but eventually also the natural and moral order, thus, appropriate behavior in all aspects of life

terracotta (Italian, "baked earth") a clay medium that may be glazed or painted; also called "earthenware"

zither a five- or seven-stringed instrument positioned horizontally and usually plucked with a plectrum and the fingertips; the favorite instrument of ancient China

Picture Credits

Cover

© J. Paul Getty Trust. Wim Swaan Photograph Collection. The Getty Research Institute, Los Angeles (96.P.21)

Frontispiece and page x: © English Heritage (J870257)

Introduction

0.1 Photo by Dean R. Snow; **0.2** Sisse Brimberg/ National Geographic Creative; **0.3** © Goran Burenhult/Heritage-Images; **0.4** Naturhistorisches Museum, Wien; **0.5** Erich Lessing/akg-images; **0.6** Courtesy of the Oriental Institute of the University of Chicago; **0.7** Photo © RMN-Grand Palais (Musée du Louvre). Photo: Gérard Blot; **0.8** Image © The Metropolitan Museum of Art, New York/Art Resource, NY/Scala, Florence; **0.10** Ancient Art & Architecture Collection Ltd.; **0.11** Photo: Klaus Schmidt. Deutsches Archäologisches Institut; **0.12** Fernando G. Baptista/ National Geographic Creative; **0.13** © English Heritage (J940113); **0.14** © English Heritage (A910713 & A910714); **0.15** Adapted from Samuel Noah Kramer, The Sumerians, © 1957 by Scientific American, Inc.; **0.16** Ashmolean Museum, University of Oxford/Bridgeman Images; **0.17** © The Trustees of the British Museum, London; **0.18** Photo © RMN-Grand Palais (Musée du Louvre). Photo: Hervé Lewandowski; **0.20** Private Collection/Photo © Dirk Bakker/Bridgeman Images; **0.21** Prisma Bildagentur AG/Alamy

Chapter 1

1.1 Photo © RMN-Grand Palais (Musée du Louvre); **1.2** © The Trustees of the British Museum, London, **1.3** Courtesy of The University of Pennsylvania Museum of Archaeology & Anthropology, Philadelphia (Image #150082); **1.4** © The Trustees of the British Museum, London; **1.5** Photo Scala, Florence; **1.6** © The Trustees of the British Museum, London; **1.7** Photo © RMN-Grand Palais (Musée du Louvre). Photo: Franck Raux; **1.8** Silvio Fiore/SuperStock; **1.9** Courtesy of the Oriental Institute of the University of Chicago; **1.10** Erich Lessing/akg-images; **1.11** www.BibleLandPictures.com/Alamy; **1.12** Courtesy of the Oriental Institute of the University of Chicago; **1.14** Erich Lessing/akg-images; **1.15** © The Trustees of the British Museum, London; **1.16** Image © The Metropolitan Museum of Art, New York/Art Resource, NY/Scala, Florence

Chapter 2

2.1 De Agostini Picture Library/SuperStock; **2.2** Andrea Jemolo/akg-images; **2.3** Egyptian Museum, Cairo/Werner Forman Archive; **2.4** Photograph © 2015 Museum of Fine Arts, Boston. Harvard University - Boston Museum of Fine Arts Exhibition 11.1738; **2.5** © The Trustees of the British Museum, London; **2.6** © Paul M.R. Maeyaert; **2.7** Heritage Image Partnership Ltd./Alamy; **2.11** Photo © RMN-Grand Palais (Musée du Louvre). Photo: Franck Raux; **2.12** © J. Paul Getty Trust. Wim Swaan Photograph Collection. The Getty Research Institute, Los Angeles (96.P.21); **2.13** Image © The Metropolitan Museum of Art, New York/Art Resource, NY/Scala, Florence; **2.14** © Araldo de Luca; **2.15** Andrea Jemolo/akg-images; **2.16** BPK, Bildagentur für Kunst, Kultur und Geschichte, Berlin/Photo Scala, Florence; **2.17** Image © The Metropolitan Museum of Art, New York/Art Resource, NY/Scala, Florence; **2.18** © The Trustees of the British Museum, London; **2.21** Photo Jean Vertut; **2.22** National Museum, Athens. Photo: Stournaras. © Hellenic Ministry of Culture and Sports/Archaeological Receipts Fund; **2.23** Private Collection/Photo © Dirk Bakker/Bridgeman Images

Chapter 3

3.1 Image © The Metropolitan Museum of Art, New York/Art Resource, NY/Scala, Florence; **3.2** National Museum, New Delhi; **3.3** Robert Harding Productions; **3.4** The Nelson-Atkins Museum of Art, Kansas City, Missouri. Purchase: William Rockhill Nelson Trust, 33-81. Photo: John Lamberton; **3.5** Freer Gallery, Smithsonian Institution, Washington, D.C./Bridgeman Images; **3.6** Cultural Relics Press, Beijing; **3.7** Courtesy of C. V. Starr. East Asian Library, Columbia University; **3.8** Courtesy of the Institute of History and Philology, Academia Sinica; **3.10** George Steinmetz/ Corbis; **3.13** Stock Connection/SuperStock; **3.14** Anthropology Museum, Veracruz University, Jalapa/ Werner Forman Archive

Chapter 4

4.1 Image © The Metropolitan Museum of Art, New York/Art Resource, NY/Scala, Florence; **4.2** Gloria K. Fiero; **4.3** Ancient Art & Architecture Collection Ltd.; **4.4** © Craig & Marie Mauzy, Athens; **4.5** © Craig & Marie Mauzy, Athens; **4.6** Musée du Louvre, Paris/Giraudon/Bridgeman Images; **4.7** Photo Spectrum/Heritage Images/Scala, Florence; **4.8** © Craig & Marie Mauzy, Athens; **4.9** Courtesy of the Ministero Beni e Att. Culturali/Photo Scala, Florence; **4.10** Photograph © 2015 Museum of Fine Arts, Boston. Henry Lillie Pierce Fund 98.923; **4.11** G. Nimatallah/DeA Picture Library/The Art Archive; **4.12** JFB/The Art Archive; **4.13** © Vincenzo Pirozzi, Rome; **4.14** Marka/SuperStock; **4.16** A. Dagli Orti/ De Agostini Picture Library/Getty Images; **4.17** Image © The Metropolitan Museum of Art, New York/Art Resource, NY/Scala, Florence; **4.18** "line drawing of the cave, page 316", from THE GREAT DIALOGUES OF PLATO by Plato, translated by W.H.D. Rouse, translation copy © 1956, renewed © 1984 by J.C.G. Rouse. Used by permission of Dutton Signet, a division of Penguin Group (USA) LLC.

Chapter 5

5.1 Photo Scala, Florence; **5.2** © Fotografica Foglia, Naples; **5.3** Galleria dell'Accademia, Venice; **5.4** Image © The Metropolitan Museum of Art, New York/Art Resource, NY/Scala, Florence; **5.5** Photo Scala, Florence; **5.6** © The Trustees of the British Museum, London; **5.7** Image © The Metropolitan Museum of Art, New York/Art Resource, NY/Scala, Florence; **5.8** Photograph © 2015 Museum of Fine Arts, Boston. Harvard University - Boston Museum of Fine Arts Exhibition 11.1738; **5.9** Universal Images Group/SuperStock; **5.10** De Agostini Picture Library/ SuperStock; **5.11** © Craig & Marie Mauzy, Athens; **5.12** © Craig & Marie Mauzy, Athens; **5.13** © Craig & Marie Mauzy, Athens; **5.14** Photo Scala, Florence; **5.15** Paul Stepan/Photo Researchers, Inc./Science Photo Library; **5.16** The American School of Classical Studies at Athens; **5.18** The American School of Classical Studies at Athens; **5.20** Sayre, Henry M., The Humanities: Culture, Continuity and Change, Volume 1: Prehistory to 1600, 2nd edition, © 2012, p. 142. Reprinted by permission of Pearson Education, Inc., Upper Saddle River, NJ.; **5.21** © The Trustees of the British Museum, London; **5.22** Peter Connolly/ akg-images; **5.23** British Museum, London/Bridgeman Images; **5.24** Peter Barritt/SuperStock; **5.25** RIA Novosti/akg-images; **5.26** Image © The Metropolitan Museum of Art, New York/Art Resource, NY/Scala, Florence; **5.27** Image © The Metropolitan Museum of Art, New York/Art Resource, NY/Scala, Florence; **5.28** Universal Images Group/SuperStock; **5.29** BPK, Bildagentur für Kunst, Kultur und Geschichte, Berlin/ Photo Scala, Florence; **5.30** E. Lessing/De Agostini Picture Library/Getty Images; **5.31** Erich Lessing/ akg-images; **5.32** White Images/Scala, Florence; **5.33** Photo © RMN-Grand Palais (Musée du Louvre). Photo: Gérard Blot/Christian Jean; **5.34** Araldo de Luca/Corbis

Chapter 6

6.1 Courtesy of the Ministero Beni e Att. Culturali/ Photo Scala, Florence; **6.2** akg-images; **6.3** BPK, Bildagentur für Kunst, Kultur und Geschichte, Berlin/ Photo Scala, Florence; **6.4** Photo Scala, Florence; **6.5** Museo Capitolino, Rome/Collection Dagli Orti/The Art Archive; **6.7** © Paul M.R. Maeyaert; **6.8** Reconstruction by I. Gismondi. Image courtesy the Museum of Roman Civilization, Rome; **6.9** Alinari Archives/Corbis; **6.10** Galleria Borghese, Rome/Collection Dagli Orti/The Art Archive; **6.11** McGraw-Hill Education; **6.12** © Vincenzo Pirozzi, Rome; **6.13** Courtesy of The Library of Virginia; **6.14** Courtesy National Gallery of Art, Washington, D.C., Samuel H. Kress Collection (1939.1.24); **6.15** Bjanka Kadic/age fotostock/SuperStock; **6.16** Jerry Driendl/Photodisc/Getty Images; **6.18** Courtesy of the Ministero Beni e Att. Culturali/Photo Scala, Florence; **6.20** Courtesy of the Ministero Beni e Att. Culturali/ Photo Scala, Florence; **6.21** Courtesy of the Ministero Beni e Att. Culturali/Photo Scala, Florence; **6.22** Erich Lessing/akg-images; **6.23** Photo Scala, Florence; **6.24** Mondadori Portfolio/Electa/akg-images; **6.25** Photo © Tarker/Bridgeman Images; **6.26** Image © The Metropolitan Museum of Art, New York/Art Resource, NY/Scala, Florence; **6.27** © Fotografica Foglia, Naples; **6.28** Photo Scala, Florence

Chapter 7

7.1 Photo Spectrum/Heritage Images/Scala, Florence; **7.2** Jean-Pierre De Mann/Robert Harding World Imagery; **7.3** Zhang Shui Cheng/Bridgeman Images; **7.4** Cultural Relics Press, Beijing; **7.5** The Nelson-Atkins Museum of Art, Kansas City, Missouri. Purchase: William Rockhill Nelson Trust, 33–521. Photo: John Lamberton; **7.6** Cultural Relics Press, Beijing; **7.7** Cultural Relics Press, Beijing; **7.8** Cultural Relics Press, Beijing; **7.9** Cultural Relics Press, Beijing; **7.10** Cultural Relics Press, Beijing

Literary Credits

Introduction
READING:

0.1 (pp. 15–16): A.L. Basham, "The Song of Creation" translated from the Rig Veda, from *The Wonder That Was India*, copyright © A.L. Basham, 1985. Reproduced by permission of Pan Macmillan and Namita Catherine Basham; Dennis Tedlock, from *Popol Vuh*, copyright © 1985, 1996 Dennis Tedlock. Reprinted with the permission of Simon & Schuster Publishing Group and The Ward & Balkin Agency, Inc.

Chapter 1

1.1 (pp. 19–20): from *Poems of Heaven and Hell from Ancient Mesopotamia*, translated and introduced by N. K. Sandars (Penguin Classics, 1971), copyright © N. K. Sandars, 1971. Reproduced by permission of Penguin Books Ltd.

1.2 (pp. 23–24): from *The Epic of Gilgamesh*, translated with an introduction by N. K. Sandars (Penguin Classics, 1960, Third edition 1972), copyright © N. K. Sandars, 1960, 1964, 1972. Reproduced by permission of Penguin Books Ltd.

1.4a–e (pp. 31–39): Scripture quotations taken from the New American Standard Bible, copyright © 1960, 1962, 1963, 1968, 1971, 1972, 1973, 1975, 1977, 1995 by The Lockman Foundation. Used by permission. (www.Lockman.org).

Chapter 2

2.1 (p. 55): "The Hymn to the Aten" from *The Literature of Ancient Egypt*, 1973, ed William Kelley Simpson, Yale University Press. Reproduced by permission of the publisher;

2.2 (p. 58): Mariam Lichtheim, "My Sister Has Come" from *Ancient Egyptian Literature: Volume II: The New Kingdom*, copyright © 2006 by the Regents of the University of California. Published by the University of California Press.

Chapter 3

3.1 (pp. 66–67): *The Song of God: The Bhagavad-Gita*, translated by Swami Prabhavanda and Christopher Isherwood (Vedanta Press, 1951). Reprinted by permission of the publisher.

3.2 (p. 72): Lao Tzu, "Thirty spokes will converge (11)", from *The Way of Life*, translated by Raymond B. Blakney, translation copyright © 1955 by Raymond B. Blakney, renewed © 1983 by Charles Philip Blakney. Used by permission of Dutton Signet, a division of Penguin Group (USA) LLC; and Dorrie and Charles Blakney for the Estate of Raymond B. Blakney.

Chapter 4

4.1 (pp. 82–85): *The Iliad of Homer*, translated by Richmond Lattimore, University of Chicago Press, copyright © 2011, CCC Republication.

4.2 (pp. 88–90): Thucydides, from *The History of the Peloponnesian War*, translated by Rex Warner with an introduction and notes by M. I. Finley (Penguin Classics 1954, Revised edition 1972). Translation copyright © Rex Warner, 1954. Introduction and Appendices copyright © M. I. Finley, 1972. Reproduced by permission of Penguin Books Ltd and Curtis Brown Group Ltd, London on behalf of the Estate of Rex Warner.

4.3 (pp. 92–98): Sophocles, from "Antigone", from ANTIGONE, OEDIPUS THE KING, ELECTRA, edited by Edith Hall, translated by H. D. F Kitto (Oxford University Press, 2008) pp.3-6, 8-19, 23-27, 39-45. By permission of Oxford University Press.

4.4 (pp. 99–100): Aristotle, from "De Poetica" translated by Ingram Bywater from *Rhetoric & Poetics* from The Oxford Translation of Aristotle edited by W. D. Ross (Volume II, 1925). By permission of Oxford University Press.

4.5 (p. 103–104): Plato, *from EUTHYPHRO, APOLOGY, CRITO,* translated by F.J. Churc h, copyright ©1956. Printed and Electronically reproduced by permission of Pearson Education, Inc., Upper Saddle River, New Jersey.

4.6 (pp. 105–107): Plato, from *The Republic*, translated by F. M. Cornford (1975) from "Allegory of the Cave". By permission of Oxford University Press.

Chapter 5

5.1 (pp. 114–116): Vitruvius, from *Ten Books on Architecture*, translated by Morris Hicky Morgan, 1960. Reprinted by permission of Dover Publications, Inc.

5.2 (p. 128): *Sappho: A New Translation*, translated by Mary Barnard, copyright © 1986 by Mary Barnard. Published by the University of California Press. By permission of the publisher.

5.3 (pp. 128–129): *Pindar*, by C. M. Bowra (1964) from Nemean Ode VI & Pythian Ode VII. By permission of Oxford University Press.

Chapter 6

6.1 (p.140): *Josephus: Volume III, The Jewish War, Books III–IV*, Loeb Classical Library Volume 487, translated by H. St. J. Thackeray, pp.25, 27, 29, 31, 33, 35, 37, Cambridge, Mass.: Harvard University Press, 1927. Loeb Classical Library® is a registered trademark of the President and Fellows of Harvard College. Reprinted by permission of the publishers and the Trustees of the Loeb Classical Library.

6.2 (pp. 144–145): Seneca, from *The Stoic Philosophy of Seneca*, by Moses Hadas, translation copyright © 1958 by Moses Hadas. Used by permission of Doubleday, an imprint of the Knopf Doubleday Publishing Group, a division of Random House LLC. All rights reserved.

6.3 (pp. 145–146): *Cicero: Volume XXI, De Officiis*, Loeb Classical Library Volume 30, translated by Walter Miller, pp.81, 83, 85, Cambridge, Mass.: Harvard University Press, 1913. Loeb Classical Library® is a registered trademark of the President and Fellows of Harvard College. Reprinted by permission of the publishers and the Trustees of the Loeb Classical Library.

6.4 (p. 146): *Tacitus: Volume I, Dialogue On Oratory*, translated by William Peterson, revised by M. Winterbottom, Loeb Classical Library Volume 35, pp.329, 331, 333, Cambridge, Mass.: Harvard University Press, copyright © 1970 by the President and Fellows of Harvard College. Loeb Classical Library® is a registered trademark of the President and Fellows of Harvard College. Reprinted by permission of the publishers and the Trustees of the Loeb Classical Library.

6.5 (pp. 147–148): *The Aeneid of Virgil*, translated by Rolfe Humphries, 1951. Reproduced by permission of Archives & Special Collections, Amherst College Library.

6.6 (pp. 148–149): *Poems of Catullus*, translated by Horace Gregory (W. W. Norton, 1972) copyright © 1956, 1972 by the Estate of Horace Gregory. Used with permission from Alison Bond Associates.

6.8a,b (pp. 150–152): "Against the City of Rome" and "Against Women" from *The Satires of Juvenal*, translated by Rolfe Humphries, copyright © 1960, Indiana University Press. Reprinted with permission of Indiana University Press.

Chapter 7

7.1 (pp. 169–170): *The Analects of Confucius*, translated by Simon Leys, copyright © 1997 by Pierre Ryckmans. Used by permission of W. W. Norton & Company, Inc.

7.3 (p.176): Liu Xijun, "Song of Sorrow", "I Watered My Horse at the Long Wall Caves" and "Nineteen Old Poems of the Han" from *The Columbia Book of Chinese Poetry*, translated by Burton Watson, copyright © 1984, Columbia University Press. Reprinted with permission of the publisher.

Index